Hodder Gibson

Scottish Examination Materials

STANDARD GRADE

ENGLISH

The Student Guide

Second Edition

George Sutherland

Hodder Gibson
2A Christie Street, Paisley, PA1 1NB

Acknowledgements

Extracts from Question Papers and from a specimen certificate are reprinted by permission of the Scottish Qualifications Authority.

The passage printed in the Reading Question Paper is from the story *Application* by Michael Munro, which appeared in the anthology Streets of Gold, edited by Hamish Whyte and Moira Burgess, and appears by kind permission of the authors.

My thanks are due also to my wife, Lys Hansen, for patience and forbearance during the writing of this work.

I thank the Headteachers, the Principal Teachers of English and students of both Alva Academy and Hillhead High School for valuable help and for their willing permission to include the folio work of students as illustration in the Guide.

Thanks to the pupils of Castlehead High School, Paisley.

Orders: please contact Bookprint Ltd, 130 Milton Park, Abingdon, Oxon OX14 4SB. Telephone: (44) 01235 827720. Fax: (44) 01235 400454. Lines are open from 9.00–6.00, Monday to Saturday, with a 24 hour message answering service. You can also order through our website www.hodderheadline.co.uk.

British Library Cataloguing in Publication Data
A catalogue record for this title is available from the British Library

ISBN 0 340 813105

Published by Hodder Gibson, 2a Christie Street, Paisley PA1 1NB.
Tel: 0141 848 1609; Fax: 0141 889 6315; Email: hoddergibson@hodder.co.uk
First Published 2003
Impression number   10 9 8 7 6 5 4 3 2 1
Year   2009 2008 2007 2006 2005 2004 2003

Typeset by Phoenix Photosetting, Chatham, Kent
Printed in Great Britain for Hodder Gibson, 2a Christie Street, Paisley, PA1 1NB, Scotland, UK

PREFACE

This is a new edition of the very first Guide to Standard Grade English that was originally published in 1989. The Guide was written to give essential help, reliable and authoritative information and sound advice directly to students.

That was a long time ago, and some things have changed since the first edition. The course and the examination are no longer new to teachers, or at least not to experienced teachers.

Two very important things remain unchanged since the 1980s, however:

◆ the general arrangements and the detail of Standard Grade English have astonishingly remained completely unchanged since 1987 … before you were even born

◆ though the arrangements and requirements in Standard Grade English are now familiar to most teachers, the important thing is that, regardless of whether there had been changes or not, they don't actually matter to you, because the whole of Standard Grade English is still new to you. You still need the Guide. Every year, new S3 students like you start courses in English that are new to them. This time it's YOUR turn, and that is all that matters to YOU. That's why this Guide is written for YOU.

The Guide does not attempt to replace your teacher, but to work in conjunction with him or her to help YOU directly.

There is still a huge increase in the demands that will be made on you when you move on from Standard Grade English to **Higher Grade** English. At **Intermediate 1** and **Intermediate 2**, however, the standard required is equivalent to Standard Grade.

If you look only at what you have to produce (the types of writing, the form of the exams, etc.), what you actually have to do for Standard Grade is different from Intermediate 1 and Intermediate 2. However, the **skills** you must master in English and the **standards** you must reach are just the same.

For this reason, the information and advice contained in the Guide will be valuable for you later if you intend to tackle Intermediate 1 or Intermediate 2 when you enter your Higher (S5) year at school.

The Guide to English has been re-written this year to be completely up-to-date for you. Current information has been included to make sure that this guide is full of relevant information and advice to help you directly in the work and assessments during the course you have begun and for the examinations you will be sitting at the end of the course.

Let's move to the Introduction.
Read it now, because it outlines what Standard Grade English is all about, and how it works. Very often students are not given much information about what they are getting into. It's important to know what the next two years of your English studies are intended to achieve for you.

CONTENTS

INTRODUCTION

This Guide will help students like you to find your way through the course and examination system in English and to come through as survivors.

The Guide sets out to:

◆ give you direct advice
◆ provide you with clear, authoritative information
◆ build your confidence
◆ improve your knowledge
◆ strengthen your self-awareness.

The Guide is not a *course book* with practice exercises and question papers for you to attempt. It is a source of essential information about how the course and the exams work. It makes clear for you what your part in this is, and how to make sure that you achieve what is required for you to come out at the end with a certificate to show how well you can do. It will be very useful to you in helping you to work better with your teacher, who is your best guide.

The Guide sets out to explain to you what Standard Grade is all about, what makes it different from the kind of course and exams that your parents were used to, what you are expected to be able to do during the course and at the end of it, what the examiners expect and what they are looking for in your work. It will also make clear what your Standard Grade English certificate will tell others about your abilities and how suited you might be for further study and for whatever you choose to do after you leave school.

First of all, then, a little bit of background to Standard Grade that will help you to understand why all third and fourth year students are involved in it.

The concepts behind Standard Grade are:

1 All students should study a balanced curriculum.
2 All students should sit examinations and gain certificates to show what they can do.

Naturally, there's much more to it than that, but this Introduction is only meant to be a "little bit of background", and as you know, not everybody reads the part of any book that is headed "Introduction". Indeed, it wouldn't surprise me to know that you are reading this now long after you have read the rest of the Guide. That's why I have included reminders for you later on in the Guide to go back and read the Introduction and the Preface. Maybe you've already found them and have come back. Good.

Out of the two concepts noted above come two very important ideas:

1 Courses need to be constructed in schools by teachers following guidelines in a book called *Arrangements in English at Standard Grade*. (It will be called *Arrangements* all through the Guide).

2 Examinations need to be suitable for all students.

That's probably enough of the background of Standard Grade. I hope you are much more interested in what you have to do because of it.

> **Glossary***
> Words in the text that might need explanation are marked with an asterisk like this * and you will find brief definitions in the Glossary at the end of the Guide.

CHAPTER ONE

STANDARD GRADE ENGLISH: GENERAL INFORMATION

In those parts of the Guide that deal with the course (Chapters 3, 4 and 6) you will find out that, because of the two main features of Standard Grade that you read about at the end of the Introduction (go back and look at them now), you will be given the chance to show what you *can* do (when you choose), rather than be obliged to reveal what you *can't* do (when the examiner chooses).

There are many parts of the course where you can have a choice.

In the section of the Guide that deals with the examinations and assessment (Chapter 5 and then Chapters 4 and 6 again), you will find that the same opportunity is there for you to show what you can do when you are making the choices: you will not always be trying to do what the examiner demands, thus tending to uncover what you can't do. It's up to you — or *down* to you as people now seem to say — to put on your best performance and offer that to the examiner. For quite a lot of the examination and other assessments the examiner happens to be your teacher anyway.

If that all sounds a bit mysterious and contradictory, you'll see that it's all clear enough once you have understood more of what follows in these chapters in the Guide. Believe me.

The next chapter gives you an outline of Standard Grade English and near the beginning of the chapter you will find a diagram — a pie–chart from Maths — that sets out how your final grade is determined. Firstly, the coursework you do in class (in a Folio) and secondly, the examinations you will sit at the end of fourth year are combined to produce a set of grades and marks for all of your work. This will be reported on your certificate as the "Final Award".

Although the diagram has got more to do with the examinations and assessments for your work, it is in there at the beginning of the course section because it also shows how the whole system of Standard Grade, with its "elements", forms one complete package covering the two school years you will be doing the course in. It shows that the two things, the course and the examinations, are closely linked together and this is very important to realise if you are to do well at Standard Grade.

If you are to have any success at all in English at this level, you have to understand and accept that you can't sit like a zombie and do very little during the course, hoping that you'll do well enough in the exams at the end to make up for it.

It's also impossible to gain a certificate for your two years' work by simply doing the coursework and not bothering about the exams at the end. The two go together and you can't get an award in English by doing just one or the other.

It's probably dawning on you now that Standard Grade involves a lot more work and responsibility for your own work than was ever the case in the first and second year. The chapter on the Folio (Chapter 4) will make this very clear to you.

We had better turn to the promised outline description of how Standard Grade works and of what you will have to do over the next two years, because all this talk of courses, examinations, folios, grades and the rest of it could become quite puzzling and boring unless you can see it in perspective.

CHAPTER TWO

A GENERAL DESCRIPTION

Most students begin their Standard Grade English course at the beginning of S3. It is a course that lasts for (almost) two years, and at the end of that period, they will sit examinations and be awarded a certificate.

What is printed on your certificate will depend on what subjects you have taken, of course, and also on how well you have done in the course and in the exams. There's a specimen certificate at the end of the Guide so that you can see what yours might look like.

Under the entry for English there will be grades for Reading, Writing and Talking and also a Final Award for English as a whole. The final award is arrived at by combining the separate "profile" awards for the "elements" (Reading, Writing, Talking) as they are called. What isn't obvious on the certificate is how they are combined. Since there are more ways of killing a cat than by choking it with cream, it isn't safe to assume that the elements are all equal in weight when "aggregated" (added together). This is why the diagram is printed — to show you the weighting of these elements. It is doubly useful because it not only shows the weighting of the elements and how they combine to make the final award, but it also gives an outline of the activities you will undertake in the course, and shows how each is assessed, either by external exam or by internal assessment or by a cross between these methods.

It may look back–to–front to you to begin describing the system by using the assessment structure first, instead of the course that you'd think comes before it. This is true, but because of the particular way in which Standard Grade English is designed, using the assessment picture gives a good overall view of how the parts of the whole system — the course, the assessment and the exams — fits together.

Standard Grade English was changed in 1987 to make the assessment more straightforward for your teachers. One of the changes was that a separate exam in Listening was dropped. Now, although there are no separate exams in Listening for you to bother about, there is still a great deal of listening in the course you will follow in your school. It also contributes to some extent to the overall award you will get, because listening is required in the discussion part of Talking … and Talking (as you can see from Diagram A) is worth one third of the whole value of the award you get for English.

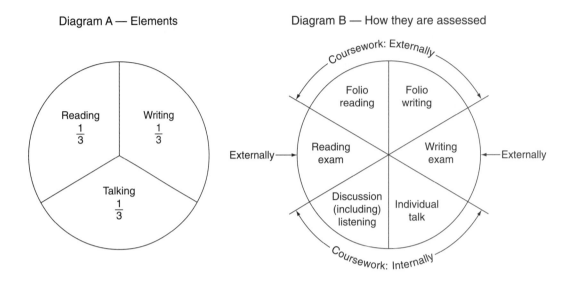

Diagram A — Elements

Reading
$\frac{1}{3}$

Writing
$\frac{1}{3}$

Talking
$\frac{1}{3}$

Diagram B — How they are assessed

Coursework: Externally

Folio reading

Folio writing

Externally → Reading exam

Writing exam ← Externally

Discussion (including) listening

Individual talk

Coursework: Internally

Diagram A simply shows the three elements and the value that each contributes to the overall award. Note that it's not all about Reading and Writing. Talking is worth the same as each of these. This is a very distinctive feature of Standard Grade English. You will find that there is much information, advice and commentary on Talking in Chapter 6.

Diagram B breaks the elements down into more detailed sub-elements and also shows how they are assessed.

If you read the information in the inner part of the pie-chart you will find the sub-elements named there.

If you look at the outer ring of information, you will see how each of the six sub-elements is assessed. You can see that there are:

◆ two kinds of Writing
◆ two kinds of Reading and
◆ two kinds of Talking.

There are three different forms of assessment in Standard Grade English.

◆ External — in a written exam set and assessed by SQA.
◆ Internal — set and assessed by your teacher during the course.
◆ Coursework that is externally assessed — a mix of the first two. (You do the work in class set by your teacher during the course and it is then sent to the SQA at Dalkeith and assessed there by examiners.)

What is obvious from the diagram is that quite a lot of the value of the grades comes directly from what you do in the classroom: all of the Talking, for example, comes from the grade awarded by your teacher over the two years of the course. **This is internal assessment**.

For Reading and Writing one half of the value of the grades comes from the exams you sit at the end of the course. **This is external assessment**.

The other half of the value of Reading and Writing comes from the grades awarded (this time by the SQA) for work done in the class which is graded at the SQA. This is external assessment too, really, but you can see that it's not quite the same as the exam, and not quite the same as coursework assessed internally. It's a hybrid form.

The package that is sent in to the SQA contains samples of your best work in Reading and Writing. This is your **Folio**, and it is largely your own responsibility to make sure that it contains the best work that you have done, and that the contents match the specification (what the examiners have asked for). Your teacher will help you with this, of course, but it is a good idea for you to know as much as you can about what is required. There is a whole chapter on the Folio further on in the Guide (Chapter 4). You can also find out all about the specification in the book mentioned already, the *Arrangements*. Your English teacher will have a copy. Some pages from it are reprinted later in the Guide, because they make clear exactly what you are expected to do in examinations, or explain how your work is assessed. Unfortunately, it's written for teachers, not for students, and it uses much specialised language that might not be too easy to grasp.

I have tried to help you by explaining terms as we go along, or by including certain words and phrases in the Glossary at the end of the guide. You should use the Glossary and learn what the words in it mean. More importantly, you should start using these words in your everyday work.

By now you will have gathered that during the course much of what you do will be assessed by your teacher. This does not mean that you will be sitting endless tests. Your teacher will be using what is called **continuous assessment**. There is a big difference between *continuous* assessment and what we could call *continual* assessment.

Look at these two sentences.

IT RAINED CONTINUOUSLY. IT RAINED CONTINUALLY.

They don't mean the same as each other.

Continuously indicates an unbroken sequence.

So, "It rained continuously for three days" means that it never stopped raining at all for three whole days.

Continually refers to things that happen repeatedly but not constantly.

So, "It rained continually for three days" means that it certainly rained a lot, but that there were interruptions.

A dictionary example will not tell you who got wetter in these examples, but it will give you a better idea of how your work will be assessed. At least, it might give you an idea, but then again it might give you entirely the wrong idea. The assessment of your work won't really go on uninterrupted for two years, as the description suggests. There's a possible mis-use of the word "continuous" here. It really means simply that assessment will take place at intervals throughout the course, rather than just at the end. Though the assessment will cover all your work during the two years of the course it does not mean that every word you utter during that time, or that every scrap of paper with writing that you produce will be graded. Teachers will carry out what is called **formative assessment**. This is a lot less painful than it sounds.

A lot less painful than it sounds

Basically, it means that when they "mark" your work, they will be using the chance to see how it could be improved and will then show you how to do that. The initial work won't necessarily be counted towards your grading. You will get used to one of the main ways of working in the Standard Grade English course — the improving or "re-drafting" of your work. This is not simply re-writing a neat copy of what you have written. There is an example of re-drafting later on in the Guide (page 24) which shows what can be done to improve almost anything. The sentences you are reading here have been re-drafted. I think they are better than the original version, but you can judge for yourself whether the re-drafting has worked. If it has, then the few sentences above will be clear and understandable. The illustration on page 24 shows what the paragraph above looked like when I first wrote it.

There is much more information on re-drafting at pages 22–23 and warnings about some aspects of it in the Folio chapter in the Guide, Chapter 4.

CHAPTER THREE

THE COURSE: ESSENTIAL INFORMATION

The pretty diagrams in the previous chapter don't make everything clear, of course. You'll need a few more words for that. Well, actually you'll need more than a few words.

Here is a list of some of the main features of the Standard Grade English course, followed by more information about each of them that you need to know.

The course

◆ Lasts for two years
◆ Covers four "modes" of language
◆ Is specially designed for you
◆ Is the same course for all students
◆ Is made up of "units"
◆ Includes both internal and external assessment
◆ Involves individual/group/whole class teaching
◆ Requires re-drafting and storage of your work
◆ Includes your class work in the assessment
◆ Is completed by external exams
◆ Leads to a certificate when completed.

Because each of these is now explained separately in more detail, this chapter's quite long. If you stick with it, however, you'll understand things much better when you move on to the chapters on the Folio and the exams. Because you might just be reading the Guide to find specific information on any particular aspect of the whole system, there are separate chapters on these, Chapters 4 and 5.

Course Length

You already know that the course begins at the start of third year and ends two years later with the exams at the end of fourth year. All the work you do in class and in the exams will count in one way or another towards the final award you achieve.

Four Modes of Language

People communicate with each other through language. Communication is a two-way process. We send messages and we receive them.

As has already been mentioned, the course will deal with four modes (kinds) of language: reading, writing, talking and listening. Two of these (writing and talking) are **expressive** modes of language. That simply means that they are the forms of language we use to **express** ourselves or tell (in speech or in written language) other people what we want to communicate to them — our message, if you like.

The other two forms or modes of language are the **receptive** modes. They allow us to **receive** (by reading or by listening) what other people want to communicate to us — their message, if you like.

You can think of the communication system that humans have as if it were a much more sophisticated form or combination of the various technologies we have available to us at the moment. None of these technologies is anything like as complex as the system we carry about with us in our brains. Radio, television, film, telephone, fax machine, tape recorder, computer, e-mail, the Internet, mobile telephones (with or without texting or camera facilities) are all very limited means of expressing and receiving information to or from other people, no matter how highly developed and amazing we might think they are. They are only media that help us to communicate with people who are not right there in front of us. If you're not convinced about this, think of all the things that you can't do using any one or all of these. Our language with its four modes is direct communication. The current wonder, the text message, is particularly sad in comparison with the real thing. Think of all that geeky language compared with speaking, for example. Think how primitive the fax-machine really is. Think of how frustrating it can be to use a mobile 'phone if you're in a place where the coverage is poor or non-existent, or the battery is low. Some of the technological communication systems only allow us to operate one of the modes, or to express but not receive, or vice versa.

The basic thing about these technological communication systems is that they all depend on our being able to read, write, talk and listen anyway, so they are really only secondary or indirect means of communicating. However, they are better than ancient communication systems, such as Morse code, or semaphore with flags or signal lamps or smoke signals or the telegraph you see in all those Hollywood Westerns. The only way to improve the communication system of human beings is the kind you see in all those science-fiction scenarios ... telepathy, for example. But that's all they are at the moment ... science fiction.

However, there is a little problem with how to assess the receptive modes (reading and writing). We can find out if the teaching has worked only by assessing them through the expressive modes. This is getting complicated, I agree.

Read the next sentence very slowly and carefully:

> **I can find out if you have been listening or reading with understanding** (receptive modes) **only by asking you to tell me or write down** (expressive modes) **what you have received.**

In the earliest days of Standard Grade development there were many unfunny and now politically incorrect jokes about how the assessment of listening could be done. Though there were experiments with individual tape recorders, language labs and CCTV, one suggestion that was not adopted was to attach sensors or electrodes directly to the brain of each student and measure the listening activity using a spectroscope.

The same goes for reading, naturally.

Language does not operate in the separate compartments that we call its four modes. Though the four modes seem to be assessed separately, your course will not deal with them separately. You don't need to be reminded that when you are working in class you will perhaps read something — a story or a poem or a set of instructions, for example. If you are going on to write something connected with it, you will very probably talk about it in groups with your classmates, or in pairs or with your teacher alone. All of this will have involved all four modes of language — reading, talking, listening, writing — in the one activity.

A system not adopted

Each of these four modes of language will be dealt with later on in the Guide, in this chapter and in the chapters on the Folio (Chapter 4), the Examinations (Chapter 5) and on Talking (Chapter 6).

You'll probably be glad to know that there's no exam in Listening, as you can see from the diagrams in Chapter 2. So forget about the electrodes.

Course Design

It would be difficult to say anything about the course in Standard Grade English without mentioning the *Arrangements*. These are very important because they explain the design of Standard Grade English to all teachers of English. The basic design of Standard Grade requires courses to take account of what students need. That means that the course you are following has been designed and made by the teachers in your school for you and the students in your school.

There are some parts of the course which might have been supplied to your school, but it is not all made up somewhere centrally and then sent to your school in Bettyhill or Eyemouth or Glasgow or wherever. It might have local material built in to it. Whatever it contains, you can be assured that it was made by teachers who know your needs probably better than anyone else does, including yourself.

The Unitary Course

In all subjects at Standard Grade the examinations and the awards on the certificate are offered at **different levels**. Most subjects have three levels: **Foundation**, **General** and **Credit**. This applies to English, too.

Some subjects offer courses which are different at each level, but this is not the case in English. Please notice that I am making a very clear distinction between **examinations** (assessment) and **courses**.

In English, the course, designed by your teachers, will be what is called unitary.

That means that it does not have totally different activities and learning opportunities or different content at different levels, but that all students do the same kind of things in the course. What you take out of it, and the work you produce, will of course be different from what other students in the same year-group or even in the same class might learn or produce from the same course. Although everyone has a different level of ability, everyone is given the same opportunity. So, although everyone does the same course, it is possible for you and your classmates to gain different levels of award from each other at the end of the course.

Later on in the Guide, when we come to describe the examination system (Chapter 5) you will see that quite a lot of the examination is the same for all students. Only the Reading exam is set on different levels. The award you gain on your certificate depends mainly on your performance in the classroom, not only on sitting a different level in the examination.

This system is possible in English because the subject is not what we call linear — meaning that what you learn one day does not depend on what you learned the day before or the week before, as it tends to do in some other subjects where there is great deal of dependence on knowledge of the content or facts. English isn't entirely concerned with facts. The method of teaching and learning that is used in English depends more on the improvement and extension of the quality of what you have learned. Examples are not easy in this area, but let's try to provide one that will help you to understand this rather difficult idea. The example will be quite crude, and your teachers of Geography probably won't like it and will think it unfair.

Take for example one of the things you might learn in the Geography department:

The northernmost point of the mainland of Scotland is at Dunnet Head (not John o' Groats).

Quite obviously that is a fact, and no amount of discussion or argument or opinion is going to alter the truth of that fact. Therefore, in a sense, there is not a lot more to be said about it. The truth of it can be tested by measurement and direct observation, and it's not possible to come up with a different correct version of the question, "Which is the most northerly point of the mainland of Scotland?". You can produce a different answer but it would be wrong. You can produce a different correct answer only if you change the question by asking, say, "What is the most northerly *inhabited* point of the mainland of Scotland?".

Remember that this is a very crude comparison between the ways in which learning in English operates and in some other subjects (not only Geography). Let's take something that you might deal with in your English course:

For one of his poems, the Irish poet, Seamus Heaney, uses the title, *Mid-Term Break*.

If someone asks, "What do you think the title means?" there could be a number of different correct answers. Somebody might say that it refers to the event of the poem: a boy is sent for from his (boarding) school and goes home. It's mid-term, and he has a mid-term break from school. That's true. It would be unwise to say, however, that the title definitely means that. It cannot be a fact in the same way that the statement about Dunnet Head is a fact. There are other possible reasons for the title, and the interesting thing about these reasons is that it is perfectly acceptable in English for the reason to be based on opinions — not only your opinion, or my opinion, or your teacher's opinion, or the poet's opinion, or the opinion of other people in your class. The opinion of the reader — and that includes you and me and all the other people in your class — can be completely valid, provided it can be supported by some evidence from what you have read in the poem, or from something you have read or heard about the poem even in a completely different situation.

In this case, the boy went home at mid-term, certainly, but he went home to attend

13

the funeral of his younger brother, who had been killed in an accident (probably). The four-year old brother's life had been broken off in the mid-term of his childhood, or before its natural end. It was cut short. In old Victorian cemeteries you can see gravestones in the form of a stone or marble column that has been deliberately broken off. It's a poetic image used to signify a life cut short, broken off. Is this what Heaney meant? Well, it's as good a reason as the other.

It is possible to go on at length discussing the quality of language and so on, but this was meant to be an example of the way in which English studies tend to be different from many other subjects. In this way the course can be unitary (one course for all pupils).

In one case the information is clear and fixed and once you have learned it, you may go on to learn other things that depend upon it: in the other case, the learning is not closed. What you have learned is not very different from what you already knew. What tends to be happening is that the quality of your understanding is being strengthened by repeatedly returning to instances of very similar use of language. What changes is not just the quantity of your knowledge and understanding, not only how many things you know, but how well you know many things. This leads to courses in English being designed for students of all abilities, taking part in the same kind of activities.

Many of these activities are designed to teach you how to learn. Later on we will look at Folio reading work. It's actually writing about what you have been reading. You will see that you are reading, and writing about it, so that you can learn how to read literature, and how to write or talk about any of the literature you will come across later in your life. It's not just so that you can memorise what you have just read and then reproduce what you have heard about it. Many of the poems, plays, stories and novels you read in class are meant as **models** in your learning, and you use these models to apply your general understanding and learning to other works that you come across later for yourself. You are learning how to learn, in a way.

Because teaching and learning work in this unitary way, they allow for certain ways of organising it. In your school, the classes may be arranged in a mixed-ability system, or grouped in ways that allow some of the classes to work in ways that suit the needs of the students in them. Some arrangements may have the purpose of aiming more at the Credit and General levels of the examinations than at the General and Foundation levels. There may be other combinations: that is entirely up to the individual school to decide.

No matter which way the classes are organised, all the students will be following a course that is basically the same for all of them. It is quite important for you to know this. Whatever class group you are in, you still have the opportunity to do your best class work in the course, and then later, because of your performance in the examinations at the end of fourth year, to gain an award **at any level**. You will see how this works when you read a later section of the Guide on "The External

Examinations". It's Chapter 5. It is particularly important to read the section on Reading, where the arrangements are just slightly different from this general rule.

The Units of the Course

It's easy to tell you that the course is made up of units, but that doesn't help much, does it? They could be kitchen units, Special Units (as at Barlinnie Prison), units of electricity, army units, seating units or whatever. Like "Centre", the word *unit* is over-used these days.

So, "Unit" is one of those weaselly words when it comes to fixing its meaning. It's like asking,

"How long is a piece of string?" to which the answer is, "Half its length doubled", of course.

We still don't know what we wanted to know, even though we've had an answer that is just as sensible as the question was.

In the *Arrangements* there is a definition or description of what a unit is. Although the business of units in the course is mostly a matter for your teachers, it **is** necessary for you to know how the course is constructed, how it works and most of all why it is constructed in this way.

It works like this: you learn about the language by using it — in reading, writing, speaking and listening — and the unit is a way of grouping activities (things for you to do) in language to allow you to use the language naturally, to do real things as opposed to artificial exercises. The units form a kind of framework or "**context**" as it's called, which brings together various things for you and the class and your teacher to do that all involve using language in situations where it really works. This makes sure that you develop not only your language skills, but also your own self-awareness and personality. It also allows your teacher to deal naturally and sensibly with what you do and to learn from the activities contained in the unit, because he or she is involved too.

So, a unit is a way of organising the study and use of language into manageable sets. One of the best sources for the study of language is in the study of literature. It shows how language is used by those very skilled and creative in using it, and offers the chance to have what the *Arrangements* call *vicarious experience**. There will be many units based on works of literature, then. A single unit may be based on, for example, a novel or story, out of which will grow a variety of things to be done which encourage you to use the language skills of the different "modes". It might require:

◆ reading the novel or story

- reading other writings connected with it in some way
- giving an individual talk on a character in the story
- discussing incidents or characters or ideas in the story
- writing a story of your own that is inspired by the original or connected with it
- listening to others in the discussion of it
- watching a film or video or DVD dramatisation of the story … and so on.

A unit like this might last for several weeks and contain many activities for you to undertake. During that time you will be using language in many different ways. The important thing, though, is that you will be **learning by doing**: you will notice that fewer of your lessons in English will consist of the whole class being talked to by your teacher.

Not all units will be like that. Some may be quite short, perhaps covering only a few English periods or even just one, and dealing with something quite specific — for example, the particular skills required in writing a summary, or how to construct a questionnaire, or how to use certain reference books in the school or public library or on the Internet. Or even, it has been suggested, on how to use the apostrophe. One on how **NOT** to use the apostrophe would definitely be useful. Have a look at these examples of its use … and think … what if the writers had had a wee apostrophe unit at school?

Paisleys newest Italian cuisine at it's best …

The cottage is a traditional shepherd's house, its pleasantly detached within it's own walled garden …

Farm fresh vegetables! Tomatoe's, lettuce, potatoe's, leek's, carrot's. Also Orchard Fresh Fruit's!

By the way, if you don't see anything unusual in these examples, the wee apostrophe unit would help you too.

Whatever the unit is based upon, it will be designed to suit your needs: it will involve you in a variety of language activities: it will bring you into experiences, real and imagined, and ideas that are intended to develop your learning and thinking: it will allow your teacher to help, inform and improve your work in English, and it will leave you with something to show for your efforts. It will also be enjoyable and meaningful.

Most units will contain written or printed materials: many will have drawings, photographs, maps, diagrams, extracts and short texts (maybe poems and short stories, etc.) as well as information about what you are to do and for what purpose.

There will almost always be choices for you to make within the unit. There will also be assignments of work of various kinds, of course.

You may be asked to read other articles or stories, or to carry out research into some subject arising from the unit's materials, or to discuss with your group, interview people, write in many different forms, for example, letters, new endings, opinions, personal experiences, newspaper or magazine articles. You may have to listen to radio or TV, or record audio/video tapes, or watch video or DVD, visit places or find out things from elsewhere. The possibilities are as wide as your teacher's imagination and limited only by what is possible in the situation in your own school.

What you might not find are artificial situations. Most teachers know the story of the primary schoolgirls out on a field trip.

Sharon suddenly says,

"Look, Jade! There's a wee green frog."

Jade takes one look at it and says,

"Quick, look away. Don't let on you've seen it or we'll have to do some creative writing about it turning into a prince or something."

I have mentioned a few times already that these units will be designed and made up by your teachers in the English Department. Some of the units you will meet in the course will not be like that. Some will have been supplied to your school so that, if the English Department finds that these units can be fitted into your course, they will adopt them, or adapt them to your needs and fit them in. You shouldn't be able to see the join.

[Advanced Linguistics] [The Beano Unit]

"You shouldn't be able to see the join ... "

You can now see that a course is made up of units of different kinds, with different purposes and of different lengths. Obviously, the units are fitted together into the two-year course so that there is "progression in the learning outcomes". That is jargon language for the simple idea that you learn from each unit and that they demand more from you as the course continues. They get harder, if you like. They don't just do the same thing over and over again. They are intended to "stretch" you. Not literally, of course. While you probably are stretching during your third and fourth years because you are growing, the course is meant to provide for the growth of your mental powers, or, if you like, to stretch your mind.

In any unit you tackle in school, you should always know what its purpose is, what you are expected to learn during and from it, and how your work is progressing at the end of it. You should also know how it helped you, what you liked and disliked about it, what you thought could be improved or made clearer to make it better. Your teacher would like to know these things too, and most good units will include some way of letting you report what you thought of it. This is called evaluation*. Constructive criticism will always be welcome by good teachers …

We know that this is sometimes hard to do: not everyone seems to welcome criticism, especially if it is not a favourable comment. One of the central ideas of Standard Grade is to help you to be **articulate***, and that means being able and willing to talk to anyone about anything at any time — provided that you have something worthwhile to say. You must know where you are and where you are going in the course and in each unit. You must also know where you have been and what you have done and why. You should be aware of how successful you have been. You are to be responsible, too, for your learning and that means that you have to be in shared control of it. In the same way, your teacher requires control of teaching, for which he or she is responsible. The more you know about how the course works, the more confident you will be and the better your work is likely to be.

Continuous Assessment

As you've already gathered (see pages 7–8) continuous assessment does not mean that you will be sitting tests each and every day of your life in third and fourth year. School sometimes feels like that, though, doesn't it?

When I was eleven (a long time ago) and was going up from the primary school to secondary, I was telling a 14-year old friend of mine that my mum and dad were going to buy me a new bike for doing well in the exams. My experienced friend said,

"If I'd got a bike every time I passed an exam I'd be able to start a bike shop by now".

I didn't really believe her then: now I think she might have been right. Assessment of one kind or another seems more a part of life in secondary school.

The Standard Grade course in English needn't be full of exams or tests (or, as they are now called, "assessments"). It may be that in your school there are exams at the end of each term or each year, but most of the assessing (i.e., the valuing or measuring of your work) will be what is called **formative assessment**. If you look up "formative" in the dictionary you will find that it says something like:

(Adj.) serving to fashion or form.

The verb it comes from is obviously "to form", and the same dictionary will give, among other meanings of this word, "mould by discipline, train, instruct (person or faculty) ... embody or organise ... frame, make, produce ... etc.

The meaning we are interested in is "train, instruct".

We will certainly leave aside the *mould by discipline* meaning. We all know what that kind of discipline used to mean in schools, even though it went out of use in 1982, before it could happen to you. Ask your parents, though, or your grandparents. It had a lot to do with heavy leather goods usually made in Lochgelly in Fife.

In plain language, your teacher uses the opportunity when assessing or marking your work in the class to show you how it can be improved, at the same time noting what you have achieved. It is meant to teach you at the same time as recording your progress so far.

Mould by discipline

This does not have to involve an examination: any of your work whether in writing or reading or speaking or listening can be assessed in this way, painlessly for you usually. Working with you directly on your work is a most effective way of teaching and learning. Your teacher is showing you how to do it, not just telling you. You are learning by doing. As I've said already, this is an important feature of Standard Grade English.

Let's hope that your Standard Grade course isn't going to be similar to the famous satirical* poem by Alexander Scott, about education in Scotland. It's one of a series. It's very short, very clear, and very effective.

SCOTCH EDUCATION

Ah tellt ye!
Ah tellt ye!

That's the whole poem!

During the course most of what you do or produce — your performance — will be informally assessed and will contribute to another kind of assessment which is made towards the end of the course, or at various points within the course, such as at the end of a unit. This is the kind of assessment that sums up your performance overall, and deals with a larger body of work, not just with separate pieces of it. Because it sums up, it is called **summative assessment**.

This kind of assessment is rather important, because it provides information for the grades your teacher awards for the internally-assessed parts of the course (i.e., carried out within the school). The whole of the Talking element is assessed internally. Summative assessment also provides your teacher with the information for estimates of the grades he or she thinks you will get in the external examination. The SQA needs these estimates of your performance in Reading and Writing. The reasons for this are explained later in the Guide at the chapter dealing with how to survive the examinations (Chapter 5). Estimates are a kind of life-jacket for you.

Learning Groups

One of the interesting things you find out if you visit a great many schools over the length and breadth of the country is that both teachers and students tend to think that one school is much the same as any other and that it is therefore "normal". The reality is that schools are different from each other in a surprising number of ways and that it would be difficult to say which were "normal" and which were not. One way in which schools differ from each other is in how they arrange students into classes or teaching groups.

For this reason it is not possible to speak about your school and the way it arranges teaching groups. It is entirely up to the school (or even the department) to decide which way is best for its students and its teachers. Standard Grade courses, however, do depend on certain kinds of arrangements within each class or teaching section.

You probably realise that schools set up very artificial learning situations. What I mean by this is that in ordinary life outside of school, if someone wants to teach someone else how to do something, they don't usually gather together 29 other people of exactly the same age, wait for a bell to ring before starting, speak to all the people in the same way regardless of any differences among them and then stop at the sound of the next ringing bell.

Of course not … but this is a travesty*, a deliberate and generalised exaggeration of what a school is like, but I'm sure that you get the point. What schools do by way of organising learning situations is not quite like other learning situations in the world beyond school. Think of how you learned to ride a bike, for example, or how to do your make-up, or to catch fish or tie your laces. Was it really like learning Maths … or English for that matter?

Some of the methods used outwith schools can certainly be used in schools, and in Standard Grade English this is recognised. So, you will find that, for some of the time in English, you will not be one of a group of 30 or so classmates listening to your teacher teaching you all the same thing at the same time and in the same way. Sometimes you will be one of a small group discussing some topic or problem: you might be working alone or with a partner writing up information you gathered while working together on some kind of investigation. Sometimes you might not even be in a classroom — because you have had to interview someone in another part of the school: the janitor who is an expert on bee-keeping: or the headteacher because he used to live in Africa; or a teacher who was Miss Scotland in 1970, for example!

On the other hand, you alone might be being shown some particular detail of writing by your teacher. If you're in a school where co-operative teaching takes place, you might find yourself in a small group or alone with one teacher while the rest of the class works with another teacher on different work or in the library or at the computer, involved in research for information needed for the unit they are working on. If this sounds unfamiliar to you, don't be surprised. It is happening in other schools. Your school might be using methods and groupings that others don't.

Re-drafting and storing your work

One major feature of Standard Grade English is that your coursework contributes to your final award at the end of the course. In the Writing element, for instance, your grade is not simply the result of what you write on one single (usually fine and very warm) day in May when you are stuck in the examination hall and invited to be creative at 9.15 am. As a matter of fact, you will be doing something quite similar, but different (see Chapter 5) that will count for only half of your grade for writing. In the same way, the exam in Reading will count for only half of your grade for Reading.

Your coursework in Reading and Writing provides the other halves of your grades for each of these elements. These parts of your grades come from the coursework you have done and which have been sent in to the SQA at Dalkeith for external assessment by the examiners. They are submitted in a folder of work called the Folio of Coursework. What it contains is specified* by the SQA so that every student is doing the same kind of work. This is not so that they can be measured against each other, but so that they can be measured against the published criteria* designed for assessing them. The whole business of criteria is explained in Chapter 8. The detailed information on the Folio of Coursework is set out for you in Chapter 4.

It is essential that you understand exactly what is required in the Folio. Your teacher will make sure that your Folio meets the exact requirements, the specification, as it's called.

The important thing about the work in the Folio, as well as all your other written work in the course, is that it can be "re-drafted". Put simply, that means that you will be given the chance and expected to improve your work step by step until you consider it finished and polished. What you "hand in" to be assessed is your best, finished work, the version that you're happy with. There is no limit to the amount of changes and improvements you are allowed to make to the first version of your writing. You will do this yourself, on the basis of advice and information from your teacher ... formative assessment that I've already described.

Important digression*

Though this might begin to sound to you like a very easy way to produce work for assessment, there are very strict rules about it and you must obey them. Otherwise the consequences for you could be disastrous. Re-drafting your work does not mean that your teacher does it for you. It can't be done in that way because your teacher has to assess **your** work.

That would be unfair to all the other candidates who gained grades for their work honestly produced. It would be unfair and completely misleading to all those people who "use" your certificate (employers, college and university admissions, for example). And *they* would certainly find out very quickly if you can't do the things that they thought you could do by yourself in English!

Apart from anything else it would be fraud, and fraud is theft.

The whole purpose of teaching is to help you to be able to do things after the teaching that you couldn't do before you were taught. These "things" are the acquiring of skills and knowledge and understanding. This is obvious. But the purpose of the certificate is to tell others what you have been able to do, and how well.

That little digression into certification is not to mislead you into thinking that re-drafting is done only for assessment. It is one of the main ways in which you learn to write, and to write better. It's an important feature of all the work you do in class and its main purpose is to teach you about writing. It encourages you to examine more carefully and analyse what you've produced. Your teacher will use it in formative assessment.

The chapter of the Guide on the Folio will tell you more about re-drafting, naturally, but there are two main ideas to understand at this point in the information process:

1 Re-drafting is not simply making a neat copy of your original in your best writing to improve its appearance for the SQA marker.

2 The chance of your first version being perfect is a very slim one.

Virtually every piece of writing can be improved by re-drafting. The illustration overleaf shows the kind of thing I mean. The scope for improvement of the first (typed and handwritten) version is clear. The final version is actually on page 8 of the Guide, so you can now compare the two versions.

The widespread use of the "tools" facility on the word-processor in schools and in life in general has made the task of re-drafting easier to complete than it ever used to be. You will make good use of this facility. It doesn't help much with advice about what to change and improve, especially if you follow the often absurd suggestions in the spell-check and in the grammar and style checker. It just makes it easier to carry out the changes once you know what they are to be. This is where your teacher's advice and comments and your own increasing skills are required. You are allowed to use spell-checkers and the like in your coursework. You won't be able to use them in the exams though.

In the world of work, people who write for publication almost always re-draft their first attempt. Many people have their work re-drafted by others as well. I do. In my work, everything I write, including these sentences, is re-written after I've read it over and thought about it. Quite often it's re-written as a result of comments and suggestions by other people who have read the first version.

As a matter of fact, almost every paragraph in this edition of the Guide has been re-drafted and edited because I thought it was better than the first edition version. If you were able to find a copy of the first edition, you'd see the difference.

It's still my work if I make the changes. Sometimes it's re-drafted for me — but then, my writing isn't being assessed by SQA markers. Thank goodness, I'm glad to say. It is being read by 5000 English teachers though.

The writing that you do over the course will sometimes be about what you have been reading, either in class or privately, and sometimes it will be the writing of stories, reports, of your own experiences (personal writing), poems, and articles and so on. Some of it will be re-drafted, some not. It is important for you to know from the beginning of the course that this material is potentially valuable and should be kept carefully, using the storage system that your teacher will have set up so that work does not go astray. There will also be some form of labelling/recording system so that

Basically, it means that when they 'mark' your work, they
will be using the chance to ~~teach you~~ *see* how it ~~can~~ *could* be
improved ~~as well.~~ *and will then show you how to do that* You will get used to one of the main
ways of working ~~at~~ *in the* Standard Grade *English course* – the improving of 're-
dr afting' of your work. This is not simply re-writing a neat
copy of what you have ~~done~~ *written*.

> Cartoon of 'Formative Assessment Chamber'
>
> "a lot less painful than it sounds"

~~There is a section of this book about writing that deals with~~ *an example* *of*
~~redrafting and shows you what can be done to improve~~ *later in the book which*
~~almost anything you produce.~~ The sentences you are
reading have been re-drafted. *I think t* ~~T~~hey are better than the
original version, but you can judge ~~later~~ for yourself ~~how~~
~~good they are!~~ *whether the re-drafting has worked. If it*
has, the few sentences above this will be clear and understandable.

> There is an example of re-drafting later in
> ~~this~~ the book (page 24) which shows what
> can be done to improve almost anything

you and your teacher will know what you have done and will be able to identify your work. There will be a record of what you have completed and what you still have to do.

These arrangements are essential for you and for your teacher, and will become very important towards the end of the course, when you and your teacher have to decide together which pieces of your coursework are to go into your official Folio to be sent to the SQA.

There is more detail on your official Folio in Chapter 4. You should read and understand all the requirements there when you come to it. All you need to know just now is that you will be keeping your written work (not every single scrap of paper though) in some form of storage in the English Department, where it's safe and sound. Think of this as your **big Folio**: from this you and your teacher will later make the selection of pieces of writing that will go in to the SQA. That will become your **specified Folio**. Some people still call it the **slim Folio**.

Coursework

Before Standard Grade was introduced, the work you did in class in English was assessed by your teacher and figured in your school reports and in other assessments made in your school. It didn't count in national assessment by the SQA. The grade you got on your certificate was the result of what you did on the day of the examination, and that was that. Now, your class work is taken into account as well as what you do in the examination.

There are several ways in which what you do in class helps to decide the final award you gain at the end of the course in Standard Grade English. These are:

1 Talking
2 Estimates
3 The Folio
4 Appeals

Here is some brief information on each of the four items listed above, to let you see just how important the coursework is at Standard Grade.

Talking

During the whole two years of the course you will be talking. It isn't punishable. Far from it. Your teacher will expect you to talk: to her or him; to other people in your class and often to all sorts of other people not in your class as well. Sometimes you will be given times when you are expected to talk to the whole class on some subject you have chosen and thought about carefully. It could be about your CD collection or your family or the time you spent in hospital last year, or whatever.

Mostly, however, you will not find the talking occasions so obvious or structured. The talking you are involved in will be "contextualised". That isn't painful or unpleasant in any way. It simply means that most of the talking you are expected to do will be in context … that is, it will arise apparently quite naturally from the work that is going on in the class. It will often be about the reading you have done in the current unit.

Your teacher will be talking to you, listening to you, even eavesdropping on you — and assessing your talk. Your talk activities will have a purpose and your performance can be graded. Talking matters a lot at Standard Grade. Don't think, "We didn't do much work that period. We were just talking". If reading and writing are work, talking is work too.

This is recognised at Standard Grade. Talking is coursework and is worth 33% of the whole value of your award … and it's assessed internally by your teacher. So it contributes very significantly to your final overall level of award in English.

Estimates

For Reading and Writing, your teacher sends estimated grades to the SQA at the same time as your grade for Talking. These estimates are based on the evidence your teacher has of your ability in these elements. That evidence is the work you have done in class over the course, but especially towards the end of the course. Though the two estimates also take into account how well the school thinks you will do in the examinations in Reading and Writing, the coursework clearly affects what these estimates are going to be.

The estimates are used by the SQA to help at arriving at your final award on the certificate. More importantly, they are used to work for your benefit, especially if you don't do as well in the examination as expected.

So again, your coursework counts because estimates based on it add to your award.

The Folio

To avoid being boring by mentioning the Folio again, I just remind you that the Folio is simply the best of your coursework in Reading and Writing. When it's sent in and externally assessed, this coursework (folio reading and folio writing together) counts for a whole 33% of your final award.

Appeals

It may be hard to believe, but the SQA, the authority that runs the Standard Grade assessment system, is a humane and kindly organisation. Its primary duty is to make sure that you and every other student (you are called *candidates* for exam purposes) will have your work assessed fairly and suffer no disadvantage that would produce a wrong assessment.

For this reason, the school's estimates can be used to determine your award, and in certain circumstances your school is allowed to appeal against the award you have been given. Without going into detail about this (mainly because you cannot make the appeal: it has to be done by your school), there is a system that makes sure that not only what you did on the day of the exam is taken into account. Unlike many other examination boards in other countries, the SQA will look at other evidence of your ability and performance.

If you were asked to guess what that other evidence is, you wouldn't have much difficulty in coming up with the answer. Yes, it's your coursework. It's also based on how well your classmates do in relation to the estimates given by your school. Provided they have all done broadly what the school estimated (and thus demonstrated that the school's estimates are reliable), and for some reason you haven't, then your appeal could be upheld automatically.

So what you now know is that what you do in reading, writing, talking in the course all has a direct and measurable effect on what level of award you will get at the end. It certainly does not depend only on what you do on the examination day.

External examinations

When I use the word *survive* and *survival* in the Guide, it doesn't mean that you should think of Standard Grade English as some kind of disaster. When we hear the word *survivor* we mostly think of someone who experienced some terrible event and was lucky enough to come through it safely while others perished. However, in the context of a survival, course (those courses designed to train people to cope with difficult situations), survival means learning skills that will be useful later. Often these courses are military, for commandos and the SAS, but they are increasingly used by business corporations to seek out leadership qualities in their staff. They have even become a kind of entertainment on TV, with names like *Survivor*, *Castaway*, even *Big Brother*.

The Guide aims to show you how to win through and come out smiling.

Your course comes to an end with the external examinations. These are run by the SQA, not by the school, hence external — connected with the outside: in this case outside the school.

There are two of them, one in Writing and one in Reading. You will sit them in early May (most probably) in your Fourth Year. Full details of these are in Chapter 5 — The External Examinations.

Though these two exams are set and marked by the SQA and are thus completely external, don't forget that your Folio of Coursework, though written in school, will also be externally assessed, since it is sent in to the SQA to be marked there by the examiners. The jargon term for this arrangement is "internally generated/externally assessed" or "externally-assessed coursework".

The Certificate

At last, the final item of information and explanation.

You should now know quite a lot about Standard Grade English if you've been reading carefully so far. There won't be any questions afterwards about what you've read. What follows in the rest of the Guide will make better sense if you have read and understood the basics covered in these 11 points. Each of them is picked up in turn and dealt with more fully further on. You must have noticed repeated references to the Folio, the Examination, etc.

You can see a specimen of the certificate issued to those who gain an award. It's in Chapter 9. You'll notice that it covers not only Standard Grade but also National Qualifications — Access, Intermediate 1 and 2 as well as Higher levels of that qualification. It also covers Advanced Higher and a range of other qualifications, as you'll see.

The certificate that you receive will cover only Standard Grade. You don't take Higher or any of the other levels until fifth year so there won't be any mention of that. It will show the "profile" grades for the separate elements, Reading, Writing and Talking, and your final overall award for English.

The only important thing to note at this information stage is that if you:

1 attend the course and complete the work

2 submit a Folio to the SQA

3 sit the exams in Reading and Writing

you will gain a certificate. Miss out any of these and you won't gain the certificate.

In previous and other assessment systems, your certificate was gained only by passing the exam. At Standard Grade it has nothing to with passing or failing. The certificate is designed to show what you have done and how well you have done it. The numbers after each element and subject connect with the grades available from 1–7 and these grades are directly connected with (or related to) the so-called Grade Related Criteria (**GRC**). These GRC tell whoever looks at your certificate exactly what you can do. The GRC are very important for you and they are dealt with in detail in Chapter 8 of the Guide.

Those are the basic things you should know about Standard Grade, but of course there's a lot more. It's a very large subject. Now we must look at the detail of all these features mentioned so far in this information section.

> In these chapters there are references to Purposes and the GRC. I have left the information on these important aspects until later, in chapters of their own (Chapters 7 and 8) so that you can look them up as and when you need them for reference. They are not a straight read as the other chapters are.

CHAPTER FOUR

THE FOLIO OF COURSEWORK

If you've already started your Standard Grade course in English you'll probably have already heard of the Folio[1]. Even if you haven't begun the course and have read only as far as this in the Guide, you'll have seen the Folio mentioned several times already. Maybe even more than you thought necessary.

That's because the previous chapters of the Guide were giving you the broad picture and showed only how the Folio fitted into the whole arrangements. Now we are dealing with the actual details of the Folio alone.

What is it?

The Folio is one of the other obvious things that make Standard Grade English different from some of your other subjects at Standard Grade.

Although the Standard Grade English Folio was brought in as a requirement as long ago as the 1980s, that doesn't mean that all teachers are familiar with it yet. You certainly don't know enough about it yet.

Completion

The very first thing that you need to know about the Folio is that it is very important indeed for you. If you don't complete it and have it sent in to the SQA, you cannot get an overall grade for English at all. Even if you sit the external exams in Reading and Writing at the end of your course and perform brilliantly, you cannot get an overall award: the certificate you would get would not show any final grade for English. The only thing that would be on it would be your grade for the element of Talking. The reason for this, as I explained at the beginning of the Guide (Chapter 1), is that the grades for Reading and Writing are made up of half for the Folio and half

---

[1] The word *folio* comes originally from the Italian via Latin, and means *a leaf*. Later, it came to mean a large sheet of paper folded once to make two leaves and which therefore has four pages. It was carried in a *portfolio*. The name, *Folio*, is now given to the 4-page folder/container and its contents (your selected coursework in Reading and Writing) that are submitted to the SQA for each student who hopes to gain an award at Standard Grade in English.

for the two exam papers. If the Folio grades are missing, they can't be added to the exam grades and therefore there's no complete grade for those elements.

The two halves have to be present to be added together, Folio and exams. If one or the other is missing no adding takes place, and you get nothing for Reading or for Writing. The same would apply if you sent in your Folio and then decided not to bother sitting the exam, even if your Folio was the most amazing piece of work that had ever been seen by the examiners. (If you missed the exam through illness, or for some reason your Folio had not been sent in to the SQA because it had been destroyed in a fire at the school, for example, then there are special arrangements to cope with those problems, of course.)

Submission

The second important thing about the Folio is that it has to be sent in to the SQA by your school at the correct time. That means that you have to complete your Folio in good time to allow your school to make sure that it arrives at the right time. There really isn't any way in which the school or the SQA can do much for you if your Folio isn't available at the time the assessment (marking) is being done. National examinations and the arrangements for marking your work aren't at all like the kind of arrangements your teacher can make for you and your class when it comes to marking your class work. There are clear rules about this and they have to be kept.

The Folio contents

The third important thing about the Folio has to do with the contents — your work. You already know that your Folio should contain a sample of your best work, and that the sample is specified. In other words, what you have to send in is particular kinds of work for which there are clear rules. It simply has to be right.

You are the person mainly responsible for getting it right, though your teacher will advise you, naturally.

You should not simply leave everything to your teacher, especially in the matter of your Folio. For one thing, your teacher will have up to 30 other students to deal with in making sure that your Folios are right — and that's only your class. In many schools, teachers will have more than one class doing Standard Grade English. Though all teachers will check and remind you about your Folio, remember that you will have had two years of the course to produce enough work to choose from. That could amount to a great many pieces of work. It's your work and you have some say in what should go into your Folio. You are the one whose work is being assessed. It's you who will be gaining the award for the work you've done and submitted.

Even if you've read and understood the requirements set out here in the Guide and know it all backwards, you should still take your teacher's advice in making your choice of pieces to include in your Folio. Your teacher's experience will help with choosing the work that will best meet the GRC — more of that later in Chapter 8.

Let me remind you here of the pie-chart diagrams on page 6 that show you how the value of the Folio fits into the whole scheme of things in both coursework and assessment. You will already have gathered that half of the value of Reading and half of the value of Writing comes from the Folio. You can also see that the other half of the value for Reading and Writing comes from the exams in Reading and Writing. Since you also already know that Reading and Writing together make up two-thirds of the total value of the overall award (and Talking is worth the final one-third) it doesn't take a mathematical genius to work out that the Folio is therefore worth one-third of the total value of your Standard Grade award. If this sounds confusing, look again at the diagram and you'll see that it makes sense: it's just a different way of combining the various elements and sub-elements.

What is assessed by the SQA markers is a specified body of coursework. That means that the SQA has laid down a specification — a detailed list of what is required — and nothing else will do. The reason for this is not hard to understand. No arrangements have been made to mark anything other than what is specified, so coursework that doesn't fit the requirements cannot be assessed. You will see that interpretation (close reading) work isn't included in the Folio, for example. If you sent in close reading as an example of your Reading skills, the markers/examiners wouldn't be able to deal with it, because there are no marking instructions for this in the Folio, and your Folio would be defective — so no assessment. That could lead to no final award on your certificate. So let's get it right.

Sample of Coursework

It would be a pity to get your sample wrong after all your efforts with coursework leading up to this point. As you now know what would be the result, you can understand that describing it as a pity is a pretty mild description. Words like *catastrophe*, *disaster*, *cataclysm* and *tragedy* come to mind.

The work that you submit is meant to represent the coursework you have done and to show the best you can do in particular kinds of work — the kinds of work that are specified.

It is a **sample** of your finished, polished, re-drafted writing. Most of it will have been done in your fourth year class, but some of it could have come from units that you dealt with in third year, if it was particularly good.

That should be obvious when you consider that teaching is meant to make a difference to your learning. Therefore your work will be better as result of learning and teaching over the two-year course. What you do towards the end should be better than what you did before you started the course.

Think about it. What would be the point of the course if you could already do all the things being taught and learned by you before starting?

> **Teaching and learning make a difference, and that difference should be obvious and show up in assessment.**

You'll notice that I emphasised the word **sample** earlier. That is, the work in your Folio is meant to be chosen by you and your teacher from a much larger collection of pieces of work done over the whole two years of the course. The work in your Folio should not be the only work you have done in that time. This is another way of saying that you do not spend your time producing only the specified five pieces tailor-made to go into your Folio. That would be allowing the examination system to run the course, and that's a classic example of the tail wagging the dog. The course contains much more than can possibly be assessed. The course is not just about learning what is going to be assessed. Your teacher will be well aware of that particular danger and will avoid it.

Your course will deal with all sorts of other Reading and Writing activities that don't figure in the specification. Any course that neglected other kinds of reading and writing tasks wouldn't be a course at all. It would just be cramming for the exam. That is not what your education is about.

You have probably figured out that you can't know what is your best work until you have produced enough other work with which to compare it, and can then decide what is good and what isn't. That can be decided only towards the end of the course. Correct. Except that you and your teacher will be able to recognise many pieces as good early on, and therefore likely to come up later for consideration once you have a larger collection of pieces.

Folio filing

This all means that apart from the most important business of producing your work, you will have to have a system for storing it safely until it is needed for possible selection. The arrangements for storing your work are up to individual English departments in the schools, and your school will have already set up a suitable system. There may be special cupboards or filing cabinets for each class using a particular English classroom, or the work may all be stored in the English base. You might even store your finished work and drafts on floppy disks or on CDs, although hard copies will exist alongside them.

Whatever system is in use in your school, it's unlikely that they will allow much of the finished work to go out of the school. You can see why. It's absolutely essential that nobody's work gets lost before it is needed by the SQA. The system will make sure that you can get hold of your work when you need to work on it further. Sometimes your "work in progress" will be in transit between school and home and elsewhere, because you will not necessarily be drafting your early versions of pieces of writing in the classroom. You can easily guess who is responsible for it then.

Your "folder" — no matter what form it takes — will have to be taken care of, and much of the responsibility for keeping it and your work in good order will be yours. Most schools will have a contents or checklist system operating so that you and your teacher can see exactly what is supposed to be there and what stage it is at. It would be easy for you to design a checklist of this kind and use it if you find that your school or teacher has not produced one for you.

> **I have something very important to say about this matter of working on your Folio at home and elsewhere. You will find information on working on your Folio at home when you see an example of the Folio of Coursework Flyleaf printed on pages 46–47. This Flyleaf is sent to your school by the SQA, one for every candidate, and is then used to contain your work when it goes in for assessment.**
>
> **The important information I want you to see and understand very carefully is printed on the third page of that Folio Flyleaf.**

You can probably now see that it's important that all your coursework should be carefully looked after and returned for storage. If you're using a computer, then get into the habit of saving the work in progress on disk and printing out a hard copy of finished work for later consideration for the Folio. It wouldn't be wise to store it only on the hard drive of a computer, especially if it is a shared one.

If you are handwriting your work then simply store the written pages.

Folio Contents: the Specification

The Folio will contain five pieces of work selected by you and your teacher from the body of work you have produced in S3 and S4 over the whole course.

The five pieces will include:

◆ two pieces of Writing
◆ three pieces of (extended written responses to) Reading.

At the end of this chapter you will find a sample Folio made up of examples of the kind of Writing and Reading pieces referred to here. The various items in that sample

Folio are also graded to give you an idea of the standard described in the chapter on the GRC (Chapter 8).

Writing

Two pieces are required. One must be **transactional/discursive** writing and one must be **expressive/imaginative** writing.

Don't panic at the polysyllables* (big words). We need explanations, and here they are.

Transactional/discursive writing is the kind of writing which deals with the real world, rather than with the world of literature.

Transactional writing is the kind of writing that is used to convey (usually factual — but not always) information. A simple example would be a set of directions to find your way from A to B.

Discursive writing is the kind of writing used to express ideas in an orderly and formal way. A simple example of this kind of writing would be an essay on the rights and wrongs of a topic, such as marriage or school rules or solvent abuse.

You will see examples of both of these kinds of writing in the specimen Folio at the end of this chapter.

So, in the Folio, one of your two pieces of Writing must be transactional or discursive. When you come to Chapter 7 on Purposes, you'll find that the first of your two pieces of Writing must be connected with the first two of the Purposes of Writing listed there.

The second piece of Writing must be **expressive or imaginative** writing. These kinds of writing deal with your own personal world and with the world of literature.

Expressive writing deals with your own (real) experiences and feelings — what you have done or experienced and how you react to things and events. A simple example of this kind of writing would be your reflecting on the time when you went to school for the first time, or reflecting on when you had an accident and were prevented from doing something that you had really been looking forward to.

Imaginative writing, as its name makes clear, is to do with the world of imagination. The kind of writing expected from you here is in one of the forms of literature, for example, a short story, a poem, a dramatisation or a letter (but not a "business" letter!).

Again, when you come to the chapter on Purposes (Chapter 7), you will see that this second of your two pieces of Writing is connected with the remaining Purposes of Writing listed there.

All of your writing will have a clear purpose, and the task you are given to carry out should always have a clear connection with one of the purposes. This is a very important part of Standard Grade English. For this reason, you should always be absolutely certain of the purpose of your writing — what is it for, what is its audience — and if it is not clear to you, then make sure that you ask your teacher to explain this to you before you start writing. It is not possible to produce good, effective writing unless you know its purpose.

Reading

Before we move on, let me sort out a possible confusion for you.

When we talk here of **Reading** we are really talking about pieces of work that are written down. In the *Arrangements* document they are called *Extended Responses to Reading*. In plain language, it means that they are pieces of **writing about your Reading**. We can give other people information and opinions about our reading only by writing about it or talking about it. So the Folio pieces about your reading will be written down in the Folio.

This also explains why when the words *reading* and *writing* appear here in the Guide, they sometimes have capital letters, and sometimes don't. This is because when I use the capital letter, I am meaning the separate elements of Standard Grade English that have these names: when they appear without capitals, the words have the ordinary meaning for these two activities.

The requirements for Reading are much more complicated than those for Writing, and you should read this part very carefully and regard it as a reference source. It is full of exclusions — things you cannot do if you have done something else already.

Three pieces of work, all of them extended responses to reading, are required. (Note that such things as Close Reading responses are not acceptable here.)

The **first two** must be critical* evaluations*, each of a different form of literature.

That means that you must write about (criticise and evaluate) first, say, a prose text (novel, short story, biography) and then for the second piece either a poetic or dramatic text (either a poem or a play).

The **third** piece can now, **and only now**, be any one of:

i)   another critical evaluation of *any* form of literature, prose, poetry, or drama even
       if you have already written about that form of literature already
OR
ii)   a critical evaluation of a media text (film, radio or television programmes)
OR
iii)   an imaginative response* to a literary text.

Each Reading piece you include in your Folio must deal with a separate text. You may not write about the same text more than once.

The Arrangements state that "prose is regarded as a single genre". This means that if one of your pieces is about, for instance, a novel, you must not include as your other critical evaluation a piece on any other form of prose, e.g., the short story, the essay, the biography, unless you have chosen option iii) above and have offered there a third critical evaluation on poetry or drama.

Once you are more familiar with the course generally, you will find this set of rules easier to cope with. In the meantime, the main facts to keep in your head are these:

YOU MUST WRITE ABOUT **THREE** SEPARATE **TEXTS***
YOU MUST DEAL WITH AT LEAST **TWO** SEPARATE **GENRES***

Further information/advice

Text   Critical Evaluation   Imaginative Response

There's no way of avoiding using certain words and phrases connected with Standard Grade English, especially in the Folio. It's really best that you should find out what they mean and, once you have understood the meanings, use the words and phrases themselves. It will make life easier for you and your teacher if you do.

You should certainly learn and understand what is meant by the words above because they will turn up quite often in talking about your Folio … and there will probably be quite a lot of talk about your Folio.

"Text" can mean here (in the Folio specification and also in the GRC — Chapter 8) a book, or a poem, or an extract from a book, or a script or play, or film or TV programme, a short story, or a section of a novel or a whole novel. What defines it is the fact that it has been selected for study and criticism as a whole thing, an entity. This does not mean that you will always have to write about a whole novel or a whole play or whatever. If that was so, it would be difficult to write about any of the works you were studying until you had completed them. That would make the writing parts of many units impossible to deal with. Your teacher will want you to write about and talk about various things you are reading as you proceed from the earliest stages of the work.

The difference is that in the pieces you include in your Folio, the examiners will expect you to make clear that you have read whole texts, not just bits of any work. So, although it is acceptable to produce a critical evaluation of, for instance, the first scene of *Death of a Salesman*, without referring to the rest of the play in class work, you would have to expand on this if you want to include a Reading piece in your

Folio because the examiner will want to know how that scene relates to the whole play, in your opinion.

In responding to a text — that simply means writing about something you have read— you can produce two kinds of writing about your reading: the critical evaluation **or the** imaginative response. It is important to understand fully the difference between these two ways of responding to a text. The GRC chapter of the Guide explains the difference. There is also advice about your choice between these two kinds of response.

Length of Folio pieces

Whenever your teacher asks you to do a piece of writing, there is probably someone in your class (maybe it is even yourself) who immediately asks,
"How long is it to be, Miss/Sir?"
What that question often means is,
"How short can I make it? How little can I get away with?"

That's not the right question.

Mostly, however, underlying that question is a genuine question that has not been asked in the best possible way. The student means to ask what length is appropriate to the purpose of this piece of writing … in other words, asking,

"For this kind of writing, as part of the task, and paying close attention to the purpose of the writing, what length do you think would be suitable? Is there a suitable length? Can you give me some help here?"

Often there is a suitable length, but just as often it cannot be stated exactly. Usually, rough guidance as to length is what is offered. That is what the SQA has done — given guidance on length for the submitted Folio pieces. Your teacher might say, "You should be able to do this in about a page and a half". In doing this your teacher is helping you to make a decision about how the time and length taken are appropriate to the purpose he or she has in mind for this task.

The rule is always that the **length** of any piece of work in the Folio (or anywhere else for that matter) is determined by the **purpose** of the writing. For instance, you might include a one-page set of instructions on what and how to feed your goldfish or a ten-page illustrated autobiography. As long as the length fits what you are trying to do, it's fine. If it is far too short or far too long, it will be self-penalising. If a piece of writing is too long for its purpose this will probably be because it contains much unnecessary material and that it is not focused on the central point of the task. If it is too short it will be because it does not get to grips with the subject well enough to deal with the central part of the task: it does not have enough in it to allow us to make a real assessment of whether the writer can do what was asked. Either way, it does not achieve its purpose. The writing does not manage to deal properly or concisely or adequately with what the writer intended to do. Usually that is because he or she has not fully understood the purpose. This is why you must make sure that you know exactly what is expected (not only in length, of course) and you can usually make sure by asking your teacher until it is clear.

> **To jump ahead for a moment, it is worth pointing out that in a written external exam you do not have this opportunity to interact with your teacher. This is why exam tasks are very carefully worded ... and designed for you to tackle at a time in your learning when you have developed a much better understanding of tasks and their purposes.**

The kind of guidance given by the SQA for pieces submitted in the Folio is in the table. Remember, there are no penalties for pieces that are longer or shorter than the suggested length, generally speaking, but there is a **minimum** length of 100 words for **Reading** pieces at Foundation Level. You can take it that **any** piece of prose should be of that length, at least. For **Writing** at Foundation Level the same minimum length is suggested, and this allows for the possibility that a poetry piece, for instance, could be shorter than the suggested 100 words.

There is also a normal **maximum** of 800 words for **Writing** pieces at Credit Level which you should not really exceed.

The examiners are simply suggesting that there should always be enough in the Folio pieces to allow them to form some clear ideas of what you can do, so that they can assess what you offer. That is only common sense.

Because of this, it is sensible that your teachers mostly set tasks that can achieve their purpose within these broad limits, though many class work assignments can go beyond these limits without any problem. For any pieces that are to be included in your Folio, though, the purposes and the writing you do must observe the guidance given here.

FOLIO PIECES — SQA GENERAL GUIDANCE ON LENGTH	
Writing	**Reading**
Foundation	Foundation
100 words minimum suggested	100 words minimum required
General	General
"Appropriate to purpose"	300–800 words
Credit	Credit
Normal maximum 800 words	Normal maximum 800 words

Literature and Media

You will have noticed in the Reading specification that there is a distinction between a "literary text" and a "media text". The difference is simple: *literary* means printed book text (prose, poetry or drama) and *media* means film, radio or television programme(s). Notice carefully two things about the use of media texts if you intend to include any pieces based on them in your Folio:

1 For Standard Grade purposes in Reading, media texts **do not include** the printed word, so evaluations of (meaning writing about them) newspapers or magazines or film/TV scripts are not acceptable in the Folio:

2 You may include a piece about the media only if
   i) it is a critical evaluation and
   ii) you already have **two** critical evaluations of **literary** texts in your Folio.

Stage productions/performances are not considered as mass media, **so pieces about these are not acceptable either.**

Imaginative responses to media texts are not acceptable at all. **You may not offer, for instance, the diary of a character in a film you have studied. You may be doing this kind of work in class-work, and that is fine, but don't include it in your Folio. It would not be assessed and this would seriously affect your grade for Reading, and therefore your overall grade for English.**

Summary

So, using the words of the specification, your Folio could be made up in the following ways:

WRITING — 2 pieces

1 Transactional/discursive

2 Expressive/imaginative

READING — 3 pieces

1 Critical evaluation — literary
2 Critical evaluation — literary
3 Critical evaluation — literary
   OR
   Critical evaluation — media
   OR
   Imaginative response — literary
100 words minimum
3 different texts
2 different genres*
No close reading

CANDIDATE DECLARATION
TEACHER DECLARATION

Folio: Labelling of Pieces

I have tried to make clear for you how important the **purpose** of any piece of writing is and how your understanding of this purpose is crucial to your success in the writing of the piece — how you should always know clearly what the writing is for and how your teacher will set you tasks that are intended to help you meet one or more of the purposes.

It should be obvious that the person who marks your work (usually your teacher, but for your Folio, the SQA examiners) has to know the purpose too. Obviously, your teacher will know the purpose of the task if he or she sets it for you, but anyone else might not. If they don't know what you were trying to do, how could they really know whether you have succeeded or not?

For this reason, each piece of work in your Folio must have a note or label of some kind to tell the examiner what the purpose was, and exactly what the task was. Your school will have arranged some system for this and will probably use the kind of label suggested by the SQA, though not necessarily. There may be a similar label designed in the school and your teacher will probably supply such labels for you to attach to the various Folio pieces.

It is a good idea to use this system of labelling your work, not just when you are assembling your work in your Folio, but also on every piece of work you start during the course. Any one of those pieces might turn out to be the one that you will want to re-draft and later include in the submitted Folio. You will not decide that till later on. One label does for the whole set of drafts and re-drafts of any one piece, so it does not really involve labelling every scrap of paper.

I have included the kind of labels suggested by the SQA in the sample Folio at the end of this chapter, so you can have a look at them. This need for labelling the pieces is in addition to the ticked-off entries printed in the Folio Flyleaf. It can be very difficult sometimes for the examiners to work out which piece is which if they have no identifying labels attached to them.

Folio Declarations

Immediately after this section you'll find an illustration of the SQA's official Folio of Coursework Flyleaf. On one of the pages of the form you will see two things that I have kept back till now.

THEY ARE BOTH VERY IMPORTANT.

The first is your signed Declaration that the work is your own.

The second is your teacher's signed Declaration that the work is authentically yours.

Your own work

In reality, most writers have to work to deadlines, and so do you, but these deadlines and other constraints are not like the ones you face in an examination. The examiners know that everybody is stressed to some extent in exam conditions and this is taken into account in the assessment. The Folio system is meant to remove that kind of stress and allow for better and more polished work to emerge.

Your work in the Folio is usually going to be better than you can do in the exam, but it still must be a fair example of your own work.

In the Folio Flyleaf, therefore, there is a place for you to sign a Declaration that the work is your own. Because you sign that statement it becomes permissible for you to finish some of the work outwith the classroom, following your teacher's guidance. Clearly it must not be done by others, nor should you be 'helped' by parents or other well-meaning persons, particularly "tutors". Many tutors are just teachers from another school, anyway, and should already know what is permitted in the way of guidance and help. You are placed on trust in this matter. In addition, however, the SQA will check it against your exam work and your teacher will check it against your class work and your earlier drafts if there is any suspicion about the genuineness of your Folio work. If fraud were suspected and confirmed, your teacher will not sign the Declaration or include the work in your Folio, and if the examiners discover fraud, that would lead to the **cancellation of your award in English**, or even the **cancellation of your entire certificate** covering all your other subjects as well. I am not joking or exaggerating about this.

The SQA has not laid down fixed rules about exactly what support is permitted. It really isn't possible to be definite about when the work is yours and when there has been too much intervention by someone else or from another source, so what follows can only be broad advice to keep you on the right side of the line.

You have to rely on your teacher's professional judgement always. When you draft a piece of writing, there are in it many areas that could probably be improved. Some things are obvious to you or to any other reader. Usually these are superficial, that is, right there on the surface of the piece: things like the spelling and punctuation. There are much more important things than these in any piece of writing, such as the understanding of the language structure which is shown by the writer, the structure of the composition, the effective use of paragraphing and sentence formation, of linguistic and literary devices, the style and tone, the vocabulary and so on. These are some of the things you are learning in the course, though you might not know them by these names. You learn them by reading and by using them in your writing under your teacher's guidance. Neither you nor they will probably use the kind of language I used above (deliberately to make this point), but that is neither important nor necessary. Your understanding and use of these are far more important than the labels they have.

If you remember that your teacher's marking is part of the process of teaching and part of formative assessment, you will understand how far your teacher is able to go when helping with a piece of work that is to go into your Folio and then to be assessed as your own work. They cannot write on your work the correct version of something you have misspelled or mispunctuated and invite you to copy it out. They will, however, indicate to you in matters of spelling and punctuation and similar "surface errors" that there is something wrong in this or that area of your writing, and it will be your job to go and find out what, and change it for a better version. Since no one could just mark on the page when dealing with deeper and more important matters to do with structure, syntax, style, tone and the like, your teacher will be able to tell about how to make improvements to your work in general. This will be a gradual process of teaching and re-learning for you.

When you learn and change, then the work is your own. If someone else intervenes and makes changes for you that you do not understand and could therefore not have done by yourself, then that is false and pointless, and if you sign work like that intending to send it to the SQA in your Folio, then it's fraud.

It's as well to remember that work like this will be easily recognised by the examiners when they compare it with other parts of the piece or with other pieces of your work. It may be hard for you to believe this, but professional teachers and examiners can spot this kind of work straight away. You can see the joins as plainly as you can spot the spelling mistakes.

While dealing with a section entitled *Your Own Work*, you must also give some attention to an area that could cause you endless difficulty. It could also cost you your certificate if you get it wrong. This danger could be entitled *Not Your Own Work*. I would like to introduce you here to another new word and I am spelling it out for you in capital letters.

PLAGIARISM*

It has nothing to do with "plague", but its effects could be just as deadly to the life of your Folio. Plagiarism is the same as theft — it actually comes from a Latin word that means "plunder" or "kidnap". It is the theft of someone else's work followed by the pretence that it is yours.

To get an idea of how serious it is, think of the trouble companies such as Coca-Cola, Microsoft or McDonald's take to prevent others using names and products similar to theirs. Video and record production companies and publishers will go to court to protect their rights of ownership against pirate copies, or against manufacturers who use similar labels on their products, or even those who try to benefit by adopting names too like theirs.

Recently the name "Spice" resulted in court action, the use of the name "Beckham" was also a matter taken to court, and a former Rolling Stones musician has tried to prevent an American journalist whose real name is Bill Wyman from using his own name in his own articles!

Plagiarism also covers ideas which are legally referred to as "intellectual property".

Where the SQA finds plagiarism, it can and will cancel the award. As I have made clear already, that can mean the entire certificate with all other subjects included in the cancellation, not just the English. This is done, believe me.

It is not acceptable, honest or wise to try to include in your Folio pieces of work that have been copied or largely copied from someone else's work, whether that someone is a classmate or an author or a website.

This crime presents particular problems in the Folio in the "conveying information" purpose. If the information is factual, then it is probably very tempting to copy it directly from another source: a reference work in the school library, for instance, or to download it directly from a website. **DO NOT DO THIS**. There is a world of difference between seeking information, learning and understanding it and conveying it on to paper in your own words and copying it directly as if you were simply a scanner. If you think about it for a moment you will see that what the SQA is assessing is your writing — the way **you** write what **you** have to say. If you simply copy directly, there is nothing there of yours to assess. That is the value that will be put on it — nothing. With punishment added.

Remember, anyway, that a piece like that will jump out of the page as being obviously different from your other pieces, or other parts of your piece — and there's no way of hiding it from the examiners.

So do not be tempted to copy or to allow someone else to copy from your work either. When it is discovered, if collusion (people acting together and agreeing to the copying) has taken place, both the copier and the copied suffer the same penalty — cancellation of the awards.

Word Processing

Your work in the Folio may be handwritten or typed (unlikely these days) or done on a computer/word processor. The first two present no problem. There are no extra marks for typed work as opposed to handwritten. They are marked in the same way. Handwritten work is entirely acceptable, though it is appearing less and less frequently nowadays. If you are not computer-literate, do not waste your time trying to do it that way. There are no advantages. Do not believe that the word processor makes the examiners more likely to view your work favourably: the opposite can be the reality. Because we are accustomed to seeing most work in print correctly presented, we are much more aware of the weaknesses when we are faced with work that is not up to the standards of the printed publication. This can actually emphasise the flaws and imperfections in your work in a way that is not so obvious in handwritten material.

If you are going to be using the computer for your finished work, there are some points that you should note.

Almost all computers will have spell-checkers and automatic grammar/structure/style check programs built into them. At one time students were prohibited from using this software, but it was pretty well impossible to police this rule, so it was changed. Now you are free to use the computer to its full extent, but you have to realise that because of this, the examiners will expect the Folio work to be completely polished and checked, and thus to contain very few surface flaws. This is not such a miracle cure as people thought it was going to be. Spell-checkers do not make corrections: they simply suggest that changes might be needed, but do not tell you what the changes should be. To use them with certainty you have to be able to spell. This is Catch 22*.

This arrangement allows for the Folio work to be assessed straightforwardly, and your exam work, where you don't have spell-checkers etc., to be assessed with that in mind. It means as well that the two can be compared. Believe it or not, the examiners often comment that some of the exam writing is fresher and better than the Folio work from the same student, because the Folio pieces have sometimes been so well polished that instead of shining, they have lost their "sparkle", a one-time favourite word of examiners to describe writing that just had something special about it.

Teacher Declaration

The second of these two Declarations in the Folio is also a check on the authenticity of your work. You may be getting the impression that the SQA does not trust you too much. That is not really true. You can see why everything about this part of the assessment system has to be carefully checked. It would be wrong for people to be given awards that they did not deserve. Not only would their certificates be worthless, but they would make the users (employers, colleges, universities etc.) doubt the value of the certificates gained legitimately by other people. If they later saw the real ability of fraudsters, when they had no support, doubts would arise. How did anyone as poor as this at English manage to get an award in English? Can this really be of the acceptable standard? Are they all like this, then? Do not forget that since one of the other people would be you, your award would be being devalued by the cheats.

Your teacher will sign your Folio to say that "to the best of my knowledge" it is your own work. Your teacher is in the best position to know that. Your teacher knows what your work looks like and how it looks when you have re-drafted it properly. No self-respecting teacher is going to sign for work that does not seem to be your own, and schools will have arrangements in place for drafting and re-drafting that allows your teacher to keep a good check on the progress of the work. I repeat that though you might find it difficult to believe, work that has been interfered with by others or lifted from other sources really will show up, and will not go into the Folio. If the Declaration is not signed, then the SQA will want to know why, and will investigate — so that is the other check on the genuineness of your work.

The Folio of Coursework Flyleaf

Nothing to do with flies whatsoever!

This title is a bit of a misnomer. The word Folio has come to mean the contents of the folio, rather than the folded leaf of paper (folio) itself. Thus another word has been added, to mean the original cover. The word is *flyleaf*. Effectively it means exactly the same as the word folio used to mean. We'll not quibble about this any further.

During the year you are to sit the exam and send in your Folio, the SQA sends to your school copies of the 4-page form now called the Folio of Coursework Flyleaf, one for every candidate being presented (in SQA language), or for every student sitting the exam, in other words.

The form is reprinted on the following page (except for p4, which happens to be blank) so you can see it for yourself and help to make more sense of what you have been reading about the Folio arrangements in this chapter.

Your copy of the flyleaf will contain your specified coursework and will go to the SQA by 31st March in the year you are due to sit the external examination.

The form contains a reminder of all the detailed necessary information on the specification, but it is designed only as a reminder. It will not make complete sense by itself. You have to have read and understood the information that is contained in this long chapter up till this point.

You do not need to spend any time on the cover page apart from noting that you will complete it with your personal details of name, school, date of birth, etc. before it is returned by your school to the SQA at the end of March of your fourth year. Making up the Folios and checking and signing takes quite a lot of time and care, so you can expect your teacher/school/English Department to give you a deadline **earlier than that** to complete and hand in your Folio work. This is so that they have enough time to make sure it is right and that all the forms can be filled in, too. This deadline will be part of the contract you make with the school, so you simply must not be late. Remember — no Folio: no overall award!

FOR OFFICIAL USE

	0860	ST			

Grade W R

EXTERNAL ASSESSMENT
Flyleaf

NATIONAL QUALIFICATIONS
2003

ENGLISH
STANDARD GRADE
Folio of Coursework

Fill in these boxes and read what is printed overleaf.

Full name of centre   Town

BLAIRLOGIE HIGH SCHOOL   BLAIRLOGIE

Forename(s)   Surname

HARRY   GRANT

Date of birth
Day Month Year   Scottish Candidate Number

0 4 | 2 | 9 0   0 1 2 3 4 5 6 7 8

For Marker's Use

	Writing			Reading	
W1		W2	R1	R2	R3

SCOTTISH
QUALIFICATIONS
AUTHORITY

To be completed by the Centre

Folio Checklist

Writing

		(✓)				(✓)
W1	Transactional/ Discursive	☑	**Either**	To convey information	☐	
			or	To deploy ideas, expound, argue & evaluate	☑	
						(✓)
W2	Expressive/ Imaginative	☑	**Either**	To describe personal experience, express feelings and reactions	☑	
			or	To employ specific literary forms	☐	

Reading

		(✓) Poetry	(✓) Drama	(✓) Prose	(✓) Media	Name of Text
R1	Critical evaluation	☐	☐	☑		*Of mice and men*
R2	Critical evaluation	☑	☐	☐		*Assisi*
R3	Critical evaluation	☐	☐	☑	☐	*Cider with Rosie*
	or Imaginative response	☐	☐	☐		

NB
  a   Each of the three Reading pieces should deal with a **different** text.

  b   **The two critical evaluations (R1 and R2) must each be of a different literary genre.** (For the purposes of assessment, Prose, whether novel, short story or non-fiction, will be regarded as a single genre.) The further critical evaluation or imaginative response (R3) may **then** relate to any genre.

  c   A response to Media (R3) must be a **critical evaluation** and may be offered only in conjunction with two critical evaluations of **literary** texts.

  d   Interpretation/Close Reading answers are **not** acceptable.

  e   Selected pieces for both Writing and Reading should be at least 100 words in length and normally not longer than 800 words.

  f   An Imaginative Response to Literature will be assessed as evidence of Reading. The GRC for Writing and Imaginative Responses to Literature make quite separate demands.

Candidate Declaration

The enclosed pieces are my own work. I have, where appropriate*, acknowledged all sources consulted.

Signature   *Harry Grant*   Date   **20.03.05**

Teacher/Lecturer Declaration

To the best of my knowledge this Folio comprises work which is the candidate's own.

Signature   *A. Donlivii*   Date   **20/3/2005**

Note: Teachers/lecturers should be satisfied, before signing the Declaration, on the basis of their monitoring of the work, that the work offered by each candidate has not been done in whole or in part by any other person. Any Folio with an unsigned Flyleaf should not be submitted.

        All items of work received will be accepted as **bona fide** submissions.

* Acknowledgement of sources consulted may be appropriate in connection with W1, R1, R2, R3 in particular, and should be made on the relevant piece of work using any accepted convention, eg quotation marks, footnotes, bibliography.

The second page of the Flyleaf is the one that really matters. It is a checklist of the items included in the Folio. When the required item is added, then the box for it can be ticked off and a note of the title added. This page was designed to help students and teachers by making it impossible to include the wrong items — well, almost impossible. Some people still manage to find a way to get it wrong. Since there are different ways in which a Folio can be made up because of the range of options, it is essential to understand the basic requirements (explained earlier in this chapter). Then you can see how the Flyleaf reflects that set of options.

The third page contains only the two important declarations signed by you and by your teacher. Why they are important and why they must be signed has also been explained earlier in this chapter.

Sample Folio

On the next few pages of the Guide you will see a sample Folio, to give you a better idea of what a Folio might look like, complete with checklist completed to identify the items to the examiner. This sample has actually been made up of items written by a number of different students, so they are collectively called by a name I have chosen at random, as if they were just one person — Harry Grant, who was born in 1990 and is in S4 at Blairlogie High School. Your Folio will be written by just one student — you — for reasons that should now be clear.

Notice that the tasks are detailed and the purposes clear, with the items lined up against the appropriate purpose. The grades that the SQA examiners would award for these pieces are entered on the front cover and then aggregated to give a single grade for (Folio) Writing and one for (Folio) Reading. These would be later added to the grades for Writing and Reading that Harry Grant got in the two exams.

To make reading them easier for you, the pieces have all been word processed, but the spelling, punctuation, etc., have all been left as they were originally submitted. You can have some fun spotting the mistakes, but you should really start by considering all the good points and realising what Harry has actually achieved.

Each separate item in Harry's Folio has its identifying label as well, so that you can see the purpose, the task and the title of the piece. This is what the examiner needs to be able to assess Harry's work properly according to the GRC.

Presenting Centre   BLAIRLOGIE HIGH SCHOOL

Name of Candidate   Harry Grant   Date of Birth   4/12/1990

MAIN PURPOSE   To convey information   ☐

W1 Transactional   ☑   To deploy ideas etc.   ☑

W2 Expressive   ☐   To describe personal experience   ☐   (Specify

To employ specific literary forms   ☐   _____)

Detail of Task Set:

Reseach the topic of euthanasia and then write either an argumentative or persuasive essay on the topic. Be clear about the difference between the two: argumentative is where you will consider both sides of the debate and persuasive is where you begin with a committed stance on the issue.

Sources Consulted:
(if appropriate)

Euthanasia

I am going to be exploring ideas for and against voluntary euthanasia or assisted suicide because it is a topic which is often discussed but the recent media interest in Diane Pretty has brought it out into the open yet again and politicians are having to come to a decision. The definition of voluntary is acting at ones own choice, while euthanasia means good death.

There are two sides to the euthanasia debate, those who are for voluntary euthanasia and those who are against it. But there is one question we must ask ourselves, why in the United States was a doctor found guilty of second-degree murder for assisting in the suicides of 45 people, while in the Netherlands it is acceptable for a doctor to assist 3000 people each year who request assisted suicide? Shouldn't there be a law, which will allow all doctors to help assist a patient in suicide, or should all doctors that assist someone in suicide be charged with murder? Personally I think that there should be a world-wide law to let anyone who wishes to receive euthanasia because they are in so much pain living die. Although religious leaders would go against this view because all religions believe that life is sacred and you should not harm your body.

People who are pro-voluntary euthanasia would argue that people who are in the late stages of a terminal disease should be allowed to die. The main reason given for this is that the patients will have a terrible future ahead of them. Often, their organs start to fail and in some cases their minds start to deteriorate. The large amount of medication that a terminally ill person has to take can make them delirious and unaware of their surroundings. Surely it must be better to allow them to choose how their life should end and die with dignity? Pro-voluntary euthanasia groups would also argue that although modern medicine can help rid a patient of any pain, the patient will suffer mentally, as they undergo a slow death and lose the ability to have a meaningful life. I feel that the patients who have to go through this should be allowed to die. There is no point in living if you are in pain and misery, whilst not knowing what is going on around them.

Anti-euthanasia groups however would say that modern drugs to relieve pain are flexible and effective. They claim that there is no need for terminally ill patients to ever suffer pain even at the end. In their opinion **it** is society's role to help them live their lives as well as they can. They claim this can be done through counselling which helps patients come to terms with their conditions

Another argument they put forward is that legalising assisted suicide would place an unreasonable burden on doctors. Making decisions to preserve life is difficult enough without having the added burden of deciding who can and cannot die. According to the World Medical Association's Declaration of Geneva 1948 ending the life of a patient goes against all that doctors stand for.

Suicide in itself is usually classed as sad and unfortunate but it is often accepted by understanding relatives in some circumstances. Those who commit suicide are not seen as evil and committing suicide is not a crime anymore. The illegality of assisted suicide is cruel for those who are unable to fulfil their wishes because of their illness. Suicide is a lonely and desperate act usually carried out in secret. It can be devastating to remaining family who often wish that they could have done something to stop this from happening. By legalising assisted suicide, supportive families would have the chance to discuss with their relatives the issues surrounding euthanasia. This support may in itself encourage someone who is ill to continue their fight for life knowing that should things become unbearable their family would understand any decisions they made. I feel this would relieve a lot of pressure on the patient and they may live the rest of their lives happier knowing that their families are behind them.

People who commit suicide are not evil and those who attempt suicide are not prosecuted. Some believe it is a moral duty to stop people from trying to commit suicide. One argument put forward on the debatabase website was "if someone was standing on a ledge threatening to jump you wouldn't ignore them just because it is their choice; and you definitely would not assist in their suicide by pushing them". In the same way you should try to help someone with a terminal illness, not help them to die. It has been suggested that a person's family take part in any decision of assisted suicide, this could be an unbearable burden on families, who may be very scared about being involved in their loved ones death. Voluntary euthanasia also introduces the danger of terminally ill and elderly patients feeling pressured into considering it as an option to ease the burden on their families. Is there any way to ensure that this does not happen? I personally think that there is no way to stop this from happening other than having the patient go to a psychiatrist to make sure that they themselves are ready for such a decision. Euthanasia also introduces the risk that someone could get away with murdering a friend or relative by saying that the person wanted to die and asked the accused to help them die.

Two recently reported cases highlighting the euthanasia debate are that of a woman known only as Miss B and Diane Pretty. Diane Pretty was dying from a terminal disease and wished that her husband be allowed to help her die. Her case was heard in the European Court of Human Rights When her request was denied she said, "The law has taken away all my rights". However Miss B who had suffered from a burst blood vessel and was paralysed from the neck down and was being kept alive by a ventilator was allowed to refuse treatment and was allowed to die. Why is it that one woman was allowed to choose when to die and yet another is not? I am not sure that the right decision was made in Dianne Pretty's case but I would not have liked to take part in the decision.

Several opinion polls to gather information on people's views about euthanasia show that the majority have been and would be in favour of Dianne Pretty being allowed choose how her life would end. These show that support for euthanasia is continuously growing in Britain from "75% in 1984 to 82% in 1994" (British Social Attitudes Report). Even opponents of voluntary euthanasia had similar results when they commissioned an independent MORI poll in 1987, 72% of those surveyed supported "legalised euthanasia". It is interesting to see that 92% of elderly people surveyed (Yours magazine 1994) believed that "doctors should be allowed to end the life of terminally ill patients who wish to die". This goes against the theory that the elderly would be at a disadvantage if voluntary euthanasia existed.

I am pro-euthanasia because I don't see why humans have the right end a dog's life but not decide on our own death. I believe that some form of legalised euthanasia should be introduced in Britain. To ensure someone is able to make a decision about euthanasia they should visit a psychiatrist before making such an important conclusion. Hopefully in the near future, the nationwide polls, which show a vast majority in favour of legalised voluntary euthanasia, will lead to changes in the law.

Bibliography

McLean, Britton "Sometimes a small victory"

www.euthanasia.com
www.euthanasia.org
www.re-xs.ucsm.ac.uk
www.acli.org
www.transientwaters.net
www.fortunecity.com
www.slnews.com
http://society.guardian.co.uk
www.debatabase.orguk
Collins dictionary

WRITING   BLAIRLOGIE HIGH SCHOOL   CENTRE NUMBER

Name of candidate: HARRY GRANT Date of birth   4/12/1990

W1 Transactional ☐   To convey information ☐   To deploy ideas ☐

W2 Expressive ☑   To describe personal experience ☑   To employ

literary forms ☐

Specify: _____

Details of task:

Describe your favourite outdoor place. Make it clear when and why you go there, how you feel and why it is special to you. Make the writing vivid. Don't just say what you do.

_____

_____

The Woods

Behind my house, there is a wood which sprawls along past many estates. If you go to the very end of my street, a path travels up through the woods and out onto an open field. It's a really good place to take my dog for a walk as he can sniff all through the trees but then run about when we reach the top. This place can be pure green by day, fresh and buzzing with the sun glimmering through trees. But at night, the woods are evil, dark and mysterious.

I usually go up the woods when I get home from school most evenings. Then, it's light and airy and my dog can wander about freely as there's not a lot of people around. As you walk up the dusty path, stones and gravel crunch and crust beneath your feet. The trees, bushes and flowers are dense all around, their sweet, new smells rush up you nostrils, tingling you eyes with sour green foliage. Light flickers all around, like soft candles swaying in the wind. It dances on the path and bounces off the leaves, it's a ballerina with gentle feet pirouetting off each leaf.

I love this place as you feel so alive walking through it. My dog pulls on his lead, he wants to sniff every patch of grass and every tree trunk. He wants to delve into the forest and hide under all the marshy plants and get lost in the bluebells which cover the wood like a carpet in spring. When we walk through the woods, we sometimes take another route, following a path which meanders further into the forest. It gets muddier and dirtier this way and the trees are more densely packed. I can let my dog off the lead here as I have yet to meet anyone walking the same way. He'll walk along with his nose stuck to the ground and if he senses anything he'll stop, look up and sniff. There aren't as many rabbits or burrows on this path as there are on the main route, well not that I can see anyway. We reach a kind of junction when we go this way, there are another 3 paths which lead off in different directions. One will go down and out of the woods and into another housing estate, another will go straight on and onto a main road and the last will go northwards towards the fields. We take the last route as it's a better way for the dog.

Reaching the top of the woods is such a relief. Everything is open and spacious and you start to think that it's claustrophobic in the woods as the air becomes fresher and you don't feel as surrounded by the trees. My dog will run about mad for a while and I'll throw him sticks to fetch. I have to try and catch him before we can go home, he doesn't want to leave the fields but when he gets back into the woods, he goes mad again.

If I'm coming back from my friend's house at night, I go through the woods. The path is quite short and it's quicker than going all the way round the woods to get home. Now though when you walk down the path, the trees are closer, they bend and cover you, like bad men with black coats and rotting hair. Owls squawk through the trees sending sudden rushes of fear up your clammy spine. Creatures watch, you can't see them but you can feel them following you, like glass marbles rolling through the trees. The darkness goes deeper, it's soft like a blanket of silk in the midnight sky, but when seen through the trees, it's sharp and unkind. Things whisper past your eyes, the wind snakes and unravels around you, encasing you in its hot touch. I don't like walking at night, I feel insecure and it's different without walking my dog. I'm always glad to reach the road as it's only a short distance then to my house.

The woods behind my house are full of hidden places and paths and they're always magical to walk through.

Presenting Centre   BLAIRLOGIE HIGH SCHOOL

Name of candidate: HARRY GRANT Date of birth   4/12/1990

Poetry ☐   Critical Response ☑

Drama ☐   Imaginative response

Prose ☑   Name of text and author ☐

Media ☐   "Of Mice and Men"
                                 by John Steinbeck

Detail of Task Set:

Discuss the ways in which John Steinbeck made "Of Mice and Men" a
memorable yet tragic novel. In your essay you should discuss issues such as
characterisation, dramatic incident, and thematic content.

Sources Consulted: _____
(if appropriate)

OF MICE AND MEN

John Steinbeck makes "Of Mice and Men" a memorable and tragic novel in a
number of different ways…… with the use of different themes, for example,
friendships and euthanasia.

The novel tells the story of two men, (George and Lennie) who share a dream of
one day having their own little place. "Someday – we're gonna get the jack
together (money) and we're gonna have a little house and a couple of acres.
"Animals such as cows, pigs, chickens on the land and a garden with rabbits in
cages. They'll have the freedom to do whatever they want when they want and be
their own bosses without any trouble. Only thing is holding them back, money,
sometimes Lennie finds himself in trouble which leads them to flee that place and
start all over again.

This was a memorable story because of Steinbeck's interesting characterisation,
particularly Lennie Small. He is a big, strong man with wide sloping shoulders,
large pale eyes and walks heavily dragging his feet like a little bear. My first
impression of Lennie made me think he was a huge, scary and strong guy who
would be capable of doing anything but really has the mind of a child. Some of
the things he says and does are quite childlike. In his own mind, Lennie thinks he
is clever but really he hasent, some would say he has the muscles but not the
mind (which is true). Lennie stuns his friend George with his short memory
span, "Lady huh? Don't even remember who that lady was. That was your own
Aunt Clara." George is the brains behind Lennie. He is more understanding,

friendly, caring and helps Lennie understand things. Sometimes George is angry and wants Lennie to be more like him.

I would have to say that George and Lennie's friendship is strong as a rock. They like looking out for each other, "But not us! An' why? Because..... because I got you to look after and you got me to look after you, and that's why." Lennie really needs George to look after him because he really wouldent know what to do without him. They also keep each other company when the travel around. The only thing they really do have in common is the fact that they both share a dream of their own place.

Another way in Steinbeck makes the novel interesting is through including some dramatic incidents, that stick in your mind such as the fight between Lennie and Curly. Curly seems to think Lennie is laughing at him, his rage explodes. Steinbeck uses words like slashed and smashed to describe the punches. Lennie gave out a cry to George; because Lennie has been told to keep out of trouble, he wants Curly to stop so he crys out to George. "Make 'um let me alone, George." As Curley starts attacking his stomach, Slim jumps up to help Lennie but is stopped by George. "Get 'im Lennie!" "I said get him. The fist comes towards his face when suddenly Lennie reached for it. Steinbeck uses the words flopping like a fish on a line to describe Curley as his fist is being crushed by this man. Everybody tries their best to make Lennie let go but his anger is set to destroy Curley. He suddenly lets go and crouches cowering against the wall. Lennie says miserably, "You tol' me to George." In a way, everyone is happy that Lennie taught Curley a lesson but are in a bit of a shock after Lennie busted his hand. As Slim turns to whimpering Lennie, he says, "It ain't your fault." "This punk sure had it comin' to him. But Jesus! He ain't hardly got no han' left."

The most tragic part of the novel (perhaps) is the ending as George shoots Lennie. To me, I don't think George was right but he done it so that the other guys didn't catch him and put him in the nut house (mental institution). I think he felt is was right for him to kill Lennie after all they were the best of friends. It was memorable because George killed him with love. not because he hated him, but he really cared for him. Yet it was tragic because you never expected George to do something like that. I honestly thought George would defend Lennie.

I thought this was remarkable for a short book. Usually if I read a short book its not so good but "Of Mice and Men" was interesting and exciting to read. Sometimes the words weren't so easy to read but I did understand them.

Presenting Centre   BLAIRLOGIE HIGH SCHOOL

Name of candidate: HARRY GRANT   Date of birth   4/12/1990

Poetry   ☑   Critical Response   ☐

Drama   ☐   Imaginative response   ☐

Prose   ☐   Name of text and author

Media   ☐   ASSISI BY NORMAN MACCAIG

Detail of Task Set:

The poem Assisi deals with reflections on the person sitting outside the church. Explain how the poet uses imagery and structures the poem to highlight changes in his perception

_____

_____

Sources Consulted: _____
(if appropriate)

Assisi

"Assisi" by Norman MacCaig is a poem set in modern day times at the church of St Fracis in Northern Italy. The poems deal with the themes of hypocrisy and the emptiness of modern day religion. In this evaluation, I intend to explain how the poet uses imagery and how he structures his poem to highlight changes in his perception.

Stanza one describes the beggar sitting outside the church of St Francis of Assisi, the patron saint of the poor & animals. The poet uses alliteration and a comparison with a sack, "**Sat slumped** like a half filled sack" and an implied comparison with an old toy, on tiny twisted legs from which sawdust might run" to describe the pathetic and hopeless live the "broken" beggar lives, an idea that ids implied later in the stanza by saying that the only advantage the beggar has over St Francis is that he is alive and St Francis is not but with a quality of life such as he has, it is not much of an advantage.

Stanza two is a short three line stanza stating that the appearance of the beggar is that of a sly, broken individual but looks can be deceiving. "his look owed its slyness/To the fact/That he had no neck" this statement highlights the importance of first impressions to people and the prejudice people have toward the beggar.

What is implied by this is that the first impression of wrong but no one takes the trouble to find out who he is.

The theme of stanza three seems to be telling us of he grandur of the church and of the frescoes painted onto the wall by Giotto, a famous Italian artist to reveal to the illiterate the goodness/ Of God and the suffering/Of his Son" This statement questions morality by placing the word "Goodness" at the end of one line and "Suffering at the end of the next which I think shows that with the intent to do good. Suffering often goes ignored right on your doorstep. Also the grandure of the church which is mentioned earlier in the poem with the line "Three tiers of Churches" gives the impression of a lot of money spent on actually building the church that the true message of the church, which would have been compassion is lost in amongst the many paintings and frescoes.

The fourth stanza consists of a extended metaphor comparing the tourists to a flock of chickens which I think is not a positive comparison & implies that the tourists are mindless chickens swallowing everything they are told. "fluttering after him as he scatered/The grain of the word." The stanza also contains a sense of the poets persona within the poem distancing himself so he can see what is happening.

The fifth and final stanza starts on accusatory note, "It was they" towards the tourists that are so helplessly caught up in the highly ornate church that when the meaning of the church is staring them in the face they are too ignorant to even notice.

The poet uses a metaphor describes the beggar as a ruined temple which I think implies that he should be valued & is sacred but is sitting ignored ruined outside.

The poet uses similes comparing the voice of the beggar to an inoccent child which I think again demonstrates that beauty is only skin deep.

In conclusion, I think the message of the poem is that people can say they are religious easily but true religion has been lost in amongst all the decoration and the message which would have been comparison for the poor is so hidden that the crippled beggar outside goes ignored.

School   BLAIRLOGIE HIGH SCHOOL

Name of candidate: HARRY GRANT   Date of birth   4/12/1990

	(✓)		(✓)
Poetry	☐	Critical Response	☑
Drama	☐	Imaginative response	☐
Prose	☑	Name of Text and Author:	
Media	☐	CIDER WITH ROSIE BY LAURIE LEE	

Detail of Task set:

Discuss to what extent you consider that Laurie Lee romanticised the Cotswold village, that time and his own childhood. You should refer to specific events, specific times and what he says when he reflects upon that event/person/period of time.

Cider With Rosie

In this essay, I am going to discuss to what extent I consider that Laurie Lee romanticised the Cotswold village and his childhood. I will consider the overall mood and atmosphere of the book. The book is called Cider With Rosie, and it is an autobiography by Laurie Lee. It is set in the Cotswold village of Slad in the 1920's

I think that Laurie Lee did romanticise his telling of his life in the Cotswolds because if he didn't then it would make a pretty boring story. Also, if it is set so long ago, then he is surely not going to be able to remember every single detail about it. For example, the first chapter is set when Laurie was three so things like "sharp odours of roots and nettles" would have been guessed, not remembered. Also he would not have been able to remember Marjorie say "Come down 'ome and we'll stuff you with currants", so he may have to improvise and make parts up.

A bit later on in the book, when he has to go to school, and he gets told "Boys who don't go to school get put into boxes, and turn into rabbits, and get chopped up Sundays", he writes "I felt this was overdoing it rather", he puts this in for a bit of humour to enhance the story, but he wouldn't be sure that that was how he felt, so he has romanticised that part. The tone of "overdoing it rather" is adult and reveals how he, as an adult, is laughing at himself and his sisters when they were young.

When he is describing the Winters and Summers, (in the aptly named chapter "Winter and Summer") he does a lot of describing in such a way that he seems to be romanticising it, because it is unlikely that each summer was blisteringly hot and each winter was freezing cold. He has stereotyped all winters and summers into these two extremes. For example, he describes in the winter part, "quiet lumps of sheep licking the spiky grass with their black and rotting tongues which gives a vivid picture of the sheep. It suggests how jagged and frozen the usually soft grass is. He describes the winter as being literally freezing by saying "The milk in his pale was frozen solid. He had to break lumps off with a hammer". Also in the summer part he says "Bide quiet, said Mr Brown, already dripping with sweat", to paint a picture of the heat and this makes me think of when you just come out of a gig and it's been so hot in there that your tee shirt is drenched in sweat. He also describes his time grooming Brown's horse and says, "We smelt the burning of his coat, the horn of his hooves, his hot leather harness, and dung". This is most probably what it would smell like, but he describes this moment like that, to let us, the readers know exactly what it would be like.

In the village school chapter he describes Miss B, the head teacher and his feelings towards her. He describes her as "being about as physically soothing as a rake", and recalls "we did not much approve of Crabby". These parts are not romanticised because teachers in those days where like that, and you would remember things like that vividly.

I think overall, the book is slightly romanticised but only to enhance the quality of it, or just because Laurie Lee couldn't remember parts of it. I think that it is a better book, romanticised than it would be if it wasn't. I think the overall mood of the book is happy and it seems that Laurie has missed out a lot of the bad parts, to make it a more interesting story of his life, to make it seem like he had a better childhood than he actually did, or perhaps because he views life positively.

That completes what you need to know about the Folio. It has been a long chapter, but you see why, I hope. The Folio is worth one-third of your whole Standard Grade English award, so it is worth knowing about how to get it right.

CHAPTER FIVE

THE EXTERNAL EXAMINATIONS

In the basic information section of the Guide (Chapter 3) the only facts you learned about the exams were that:

1 There are two of them: Writing and Reading.
2 They take place in early May each year.
3 They are set by the Scottish Qualifications Authority.

Elsewhere in the Guide you will also have learned that how you perform, how well you do, in these two written examinations **together** makes up a further **one-third** of the total value of your award in English.

When the grade you achieve in the Writing paper is added to the grade you gained in the Writing part of your Folio, and your grade in the Reading paper is added to the grade you got for the Reading part of your Folio, the **combined** grades for all your Writing and Reading (for Folio and exams together) now make up **two-thirds** of your total award. The other one-third comes from Talking, to be dealt with later on. The pie-chart in Chapter 3 helps to clarify the words: they can sound confusing.

WRITING

The arrangements for Writing are not as complicated as those for Reading. One of the reasons for this is that in the Writing exam you are writing and it is your writing skills that are being assessed. In the Reading exam you are reading, of course, but you can show your reading skills only through your writing. Only your reading skills are being assessed, however. Your writing is not being assessed in the Reading exam.

Now that can really sound puzzling. If it does, go back and read what was said about the four modes of language — the expressive and receptive modes — in Chapter 3.

The writing you do in the exam is assessed by being directly graded 1–6, using the marking system based on the Grade Related Criteria: there is no conversion from marks as you'll later see that there is for Reading. Another thing that makes the Writing exam more straightforward is that you're already pretty familiar with the kind of things that you're asked to do in the exam. In its simplest form, it is really just asking you to choose a topic and write about it. Exams, however, can never be as simple as this. So there are quite a few points to learn and take account of. If we look now at the sample part of the Writing paper, you'll see that this exam really does try to keep it simple. I haven't printed the *whole* paper because once you have grasped the central idea of how it works, you'll understand that the rest of the paper is very similar to what you see here — except of course that the whole paper offers you a far wider choice on the day.

F
G
C

9860/407

| NATIONAL QUALIFICATIONS | MONDAY, 14 MAY 9.00 AM – 10.15 AM | ENGLISH STANDARD GRADE Foundation, General and Credit Levels Writing |

Read This First

1 Inside this booklet, there are photographs and words.
   Use them to help you when you are thinking about what to write.
   Look at all the material and think about all the possibilities.

2 There are 24 assignments altogether for you to choose from.

3 Decide which assignment you are going to attempt.
   Choose only one and write its number in the margin of your answer book.

4 Pay close attention to what you are asked to write.
   Plan what you are going to write.
   Read and check your work before you hand it in.
   Any changes to your work should be made clearly.

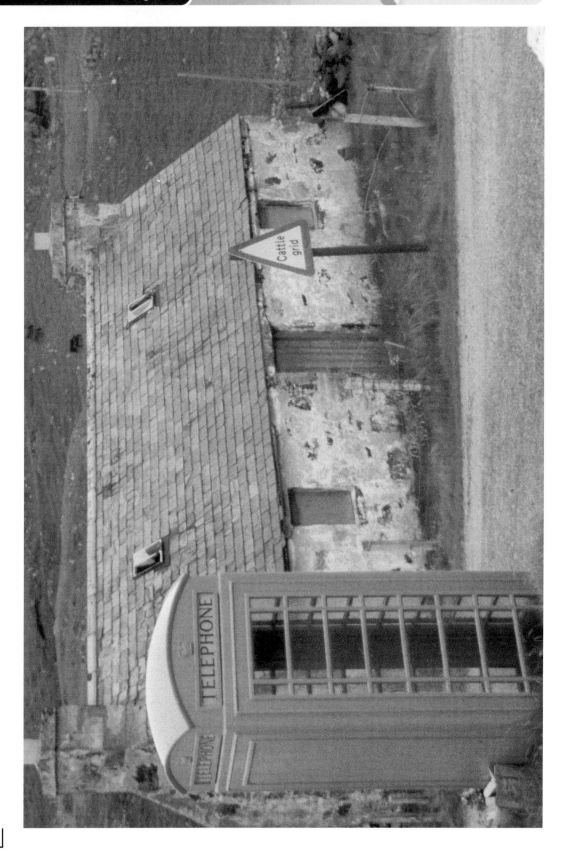

FIRST   **Look at the picture opposite.**
               It shows a semi-derelict cottage and phone box.

NEXT   Think about remote places and communications.

WHAT YOU HAVE TO WRITE

---

1.   **Write about** where you would like to live and why.

      OR

2.   "Life in quiet places is better than in the city."
      DISCUSS.

      OR

3.   **Write about** why you think so many people
      nowadays restore old buildings.

      OR

4.   Write a short story using the title:
      The Vital Phone Link.

[Turn over

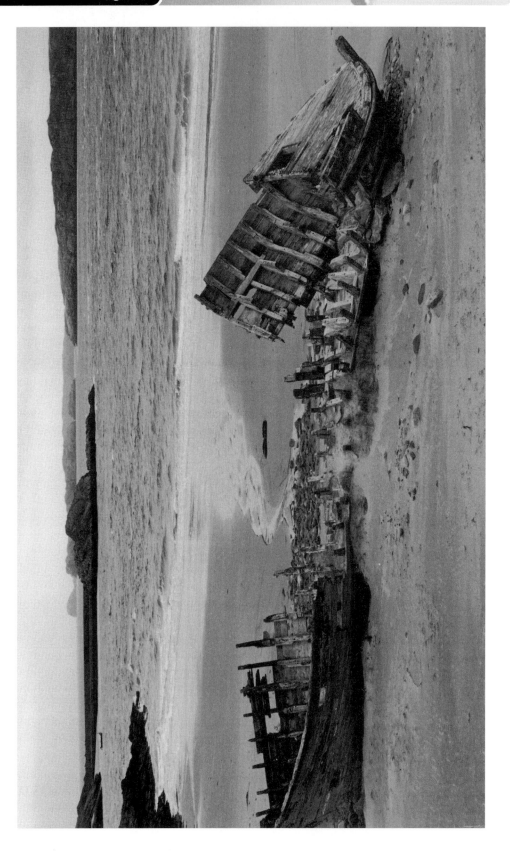

FIRST   **Look at the picture opposite.**
         It shows a wrecked boat on a beach.

NEXT   Think about the sea and its dangers.

WHAT YOU HAVE TO WRITE

---

5. **Write about** a time in your life when you were
   involved in real danger.

   OR

6. The beach at....
   Write a descriptive article for a school magazine
   about a beach you have visited.

   OR

7. "Fishing restrictions are needed to maintain fish
   stocks."
   Do you agree? **Discuss.**

   OR

8. **Write a short story** using the title:
   Saved.

[Turn over

Page five

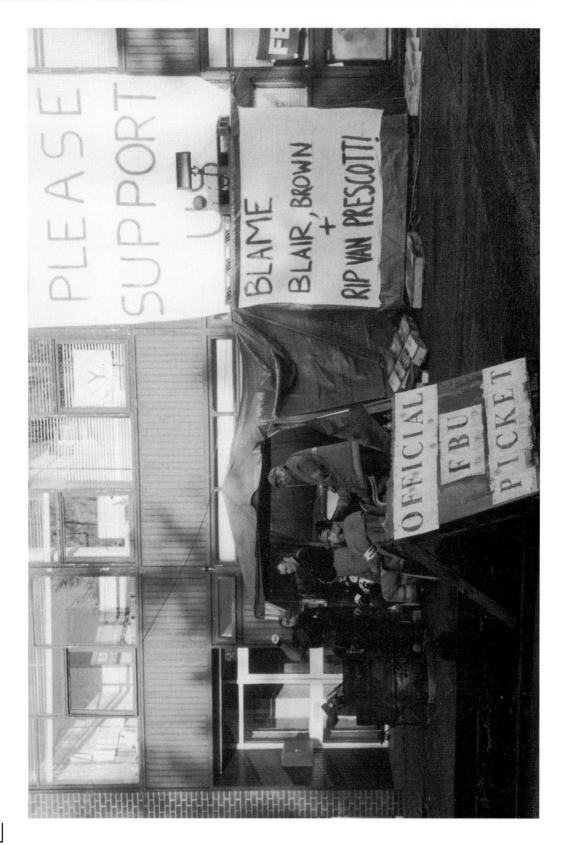

FIRST   **Look at the picture opposite.**
It shows firefighters on strike.

NEXT   Think about emergency services such as fire, police,
ambulance.

> WHAT YOU HAVE TO WRITE

9. "I could be a hero/heroine."
    Explain how you see yourself or how others may
    see you.

    OR

10. "999"
    Write about you or someone else who needed this
    service.

    OR

11. "There are some workers who should never strike."
    What in your opinion are the rights and wrongs of
    strike action?
    Discuss.

    OR

12. **Write in any way you wish** using the picture
    opposite as your inspiration.

PLEASE NOTE:
This paper is only a sample part of a Writing Paper. An actual Writing Paper would have
more pictures and assignments for you to choose from.

The design

The first thing to note is that there is a question paper like the one you have just read. It is not a question/answer booklet with spaces for the answers, as you can see. There is a separate booklet for you to write your response, the one essay you choose. That helps to make it much more like the kind of writing tasks you have been carrying out in the classroom during the course.

The second thing to notice is that although the paper contains quite a lot to read and look at, the whole paper is set out for you in the most readable step-by-step way. The reason for that is connected with the next point.

The Writing Paper is the same for everyone who sits Standard Grade English. There are no different levels of paper. This is clear from the headings: you can see at the top right the bold letters **F G C** and immediately below those the words:

ENGLISH STANDARD GRADE Foundation, General and Credit Levels.

For this reason the level of reading difficulty of the question paper is set within reach of all readers no matter what their level of ability. The instructions are meant to be completely accessible and not to create any additional task. After all, it is not a test of reading. So no matter whether you are aiming at Credit 1 or Foundation 6, you sit the same exam paper. It is what you produce in your writing that makes the difference between one grade and any other. In the Reading paper it is different, as you'll learn later on in this chapter.

The front cover of the booklet gives you all the information and the instructions that are the same every year: the detailed instructions for your particular exam year are inside the booklet.

You should always read the general instructions on the front cover first. That is why they are headed: **"Read this First"**

A particularly valuable instruction is number 4 in the list. It is there to remind you about keeping to the purpose of your writing task.

The features of the exam that are the same every year are these:

1   The exam paper is the same one for everybody at Standard Grade.

2   You can gain any grade from 1 to 6 on this paper.

3   The exam will last for an hour and a quarter — 75 minutes.

4   Across the range of questions, there are photographs, other illustrations/graphics and words as a stimulus to your writing (that simply means that you are given ideas to write about).

5   There is a large number of tasks/assignments (usually about 20+) to choose from — and you choose only ONE.

6 For each task the purpose of the writing and the form of writing required will be made clear to you.

7 The assignments will cover a range of forms of writing related to the main purposes of writing … informative, persuasive, personal, expressive, etc.

8 You may re-draft your work if you want to, and if you have time.

There is more to be said about some of the above items as we have a more detailed look at the sample Paper with its pictures, words and assignments.

The tasks and stimulus material will be different in the actual exam you sit, of course, but there are some things about them that will always be the same for you:

- the instructions will always be clearly set out like these
- there will always be choices of the kinds of writing you can do
- the choices will cover all the purposes of writing (see Chapter 7 for Purposes)
- the choices will allow you to show what you can do to meet the demands of the GRC.

Because I have already said that the kind of writing you are being asked to do in this exam is familiar to you from your classwork and from your Folio there is not a lot more to be said about it. But (there is always a but) there is some advice that can be given about your choice and about how you do your writing.

The job you are facing is more familiar than the kind of response you are expected to make in the Reading exam, but there are one or two things you have to know about and have to take care over.

Choosing your Assignment

In the Folio chapter (Chapter 4) and then in much more detail in Chapter 7, I have tried to explain about the two broad types of writing that are covered by the Writing requirements in Standard Grade English.

There is the kind of writing intended to convey information to the reader, and the kind of writing that is to express imaginative ideas or personal feelings.

The exam will offer assignments of both of these kinds of writing and they will not be difficult for you to identify. Once you have recognised them in the task and made your choice, you must keep firmly in mind the purpose of that particular kind of writing.

Long before you come to sit the exam you will have discovered for yourself (and by your teacher's commentary and guidance) which kind of writing you like best and, because of this, can do best. That is what should influence your choice.

If you look at the sample pages, you can see quite clearly that the assignments offer you the chance to write imaginatively or about your personal experience, or to write in order to convey information or argue a case — the same categories of writing that you had to produce in the coursework and for your Folio before you sit the exam. Though you cannot tell this by looking at the small sample of the Writing exam paper I have given you here, you should also know that this choice of writing tasks is generally available for each of the separate assignments (grouped around a particular picture or other stimulus) in the paper. I say "generally" because not all of the assignments in any given year will be able to offer you all of the kinds of writing. This means of course that you have to read the whole paper before making your choice. You can't choose from the stimulus alone: that stimulus might not have an assignment dealing with the kind of writing you really want. It's no good trying to write an adventure story for the stimulus if the assignments don't ask you to do that for this stimulus.

There's the famous story of the boy who had prepared an essay in advance (bad idea) on "Corporal Punishment". It was a discursive essay, arguing the advantages and disadvantages of corporal punishment. Surprise, surprise. The examiners hadn't offered such a task in the exam. So he began the adventure story instead — "The *SS Corporal Punishment* sailed out of its Caribbean harbour…" and tried to fit in all of his discursive points about corporal punishment in examples such as walking the plank, being keel-hauled and lashed by the cat o' nine tails. Not a successful adventure story, and almost completely ignored the purpose of the writing.

Though you might know in advance the kind of writing you want to do, it doesn't follow that the first assignment you come to is going to suit you perfectly. It is quite likely that there will be an even better one for you further on in the paper. For example, if you have decided in advance that you are going to be writing about personal experience and find that on the first page there is an assignment that invites you to do just that, but which is connected with a picture of, say, a football crowd, and the last thing on earth you want to write about is an experience at a football match, either because you hated it or because you've never been to one, then obviously you are not stuck with that particular personal writing assignment.

You can read further on in the question paper booklet until you find another personal writing assignment that is connected with a picture or stimulus that you can relate to. Maybe it's a scene at an airport and there is an invitation to write about a holiday that went wrong or was very enjoyable. That might be a much better choice for you if you have had such an experience. You are still choosing personal writing but are not stuck with a subject that you either don't know about or do not like very much.

> The choice has to do with combining your preferred form of writing with
> a topic or stimulus that appeals to you or that you understand or have
> experienced.

If there were no such combination in the whole paper, that would be tough, but it is
almost completely impossible. They are chosen with great care to be able to offer
choice and help to students. You may not have thought about this, but the exam is
not there to trap you or find out what you **cannot** do: its purpose is to support you
in showing how well you **can** do.

You are certain to produce much better work when you are writing
about something you know about and which really interests you.
So look for such an assignment and make your choice carefully.
When you have made your choice, make sure that you understand
the purpose of that specific piece of writing and keep to it. You will
never be offered an assignment that simply invites you to "Write in
any way you choose about any old thing that comes to mind".
Your teacher wouldn't ask you to do that kind of thing in the class
for your Folio. All your writing will have a purpose and this
purpose will be given to you in the task. It will be clear to you and
to your teacher. Though professional writers themselves choose
what they write about, their work is effective only when it has a
clear purpose and achieves it.

EXCEPTION

There is often an exception to this general rule, and there's an important point to
remember if you choose this exceptional assignment. Usually on the final page of
assignment choices there will be some grouped under the heading:

There are no pictures for these assignments

The stimulus material will typically be a quotation or an extract from a poem or
simply a title. The last of these, the simple title, will have an instruction that goes
against all I've said about the purpose being made clear in the instruction. It will say
something like:

Write in any way you wish using the title 'XYZ'

Here, you are being invited to choose your own purpose and form of writing, they
are not given to you. If you do happen to choose this option, then you must make
clear in your piece of writing what form and purpose you have decided. If you choose
to write a descriptive piece or a short story, this will be clear enough: if you choose to
write a discursive piece, you should actually state this in your introduction and make
clear what you intend to do. This is to make sure that the examiner is left in no doubt
about the form and purpose you have chosen for yourself.

Re-drafting

On the front page of the specimen exam paper (printed earlier in this chapter) you can see a note (item 4) that tells you that you may re-draft your work. You know about this in connection with your classwork and Folio. You have to be careful about this in the exam because the situation is very different to your classroom. Re-drafting your work is not just writing it out again neatly. In the class you will have had time to think about what you have written and you will have had the opportunity to discuss it with your teacher and/or others in your class or group. Re-drafting could be spread over quite a long time — several English periods or a few days or even longer, with time in between to reconsider how you want to say what you think, add new ideas and set it down carefully for the final version.

In the exam, things are very different and you do not have any of these luxuries. The main difference is the limited time available to do the writing. The other huge difference is that you will not have the chance to ask anyone else what they think of it. Your friendly teacher will be shut out of the exam room. You will be there with the other candidates and the SQA's invigilators. You are not allowed to consult any of these about your writing. In addition, the adrenalin is going.

However, by the time you come to sit the exam you will have had two years of valuable experience in re-drafting your work and you will be much better at it than you were when you first started the course.

Although you know that the kind of writing you have to do in the exam is familiar to you, the conditions under which you write are a bit different from what you do normally in the classroom. This is why the writing exam has jokingly been called "writing under stress" — only jokingly, though. It needn't be very stressful at all. When you know what you have to do, and you have the wide experience of writing and re-drafting that you have learned in the course, much of the stress connected with exams will go away.

In redrafting anything you write in the exam you do have to take account of the time available. You should not write for an hour, cancel it all out and then attempt to write a better version in the remaining 15 minutes. You can see that this would lead to disaster. Your grade for what would probably be an unfinished piece alongside a cancelled original would not be very high.

The way to proceed is to make sure that you leave enough time to re-read, re-draft and complete your work. You manage this by understanding first that the 75 minutes is not spent entirely on writing the original. You have a number of things to do in this time, and it is not all writing. Firstly, you will be thinking and choosing your assignment from what is on offer. Secondly, you should spend time on planning your work and making a written plan in note form. Then you will be writing the piece based closely on your plan. During that time, you should re-draft the wording and the surface errors section by section, paragraph by paragraph. Provided that you keep an eye on the time available, you will end up with a complete and re-drafted piece.

Alternatively you can write the whole piece and then re-draft right through once you're finished. This system makes it less easy to carry out major changes though: it is certainly more difficult to introduce changes to the structure of your piece if you now face the whole work, a complete and structured draft. It is a more complex job to tackle the whole piece at one go.

The first of the two systems is more likely to produce a polished and improved version than the second system is. It allows you to modify your original plan, and deal with such matters as a shift in the time sequence of a story, for example, or the order in which you introduce important arguments in a discursive piece of writing.

You should know that the examiners are able to cope perfectly well with your re-drafted work no matter how many changes you have made. Provided that you have deleted the first version of a word, phrase or sentence and made a careful substitution so that what you finally want to say is clear, then the actual appearance of the finished piece is not something that is going to hinder them, nor will it affect your grade because it looks untidy compared with a complete rewrite. You do not have to use correcting fluid either — simple deletion/replacement is adequate. Indeed, examiners very often see that the student has deleted something using correcting fluid and, while waiting for it to dry has gone on to the rest of the sentence/paragraph ... often, unfortunately, never to return and enter the intended change. Your final re-check of your whole piece of writing should pick this up and put it right. This is partly why the re-checking of your work is crucial. The examiners can credit you only with what you have written: not what you intended to write but never got round to.

Timing

This is brief.

Part of the job in the writing exam is to do the writing within the time set. When I lightly referred to "writing under stress", I should have mentioned that a more respectable name for it might be "timed writing". We all know that this does not have much connection with the real world. We seldom have such tight time limits set on what we write. That is not the same as having a deadline; we do quite often have these. I certainly do. Many writing projects run past their deadline, but fortunately publishers have patience ... to some extent.

The reason for the timed writing is that a national examination provides the same measurable chance for everybody who sits the exam. It is just not practicable to do anything else. The Folio writing gives you the chance to show what you can do when you are not working within the limits of time, and to offer what you choose within broader limits set by the specification. So the Folio writing and the exam writing are different from each other. They are different experiences for you and they provide the examiners with different information about your writing ability.

When you tackle the writing exam you should not think of it as simply writing for the whole of the time available. The task has several parts and these each need time set aside for them. This is what to do, step by step:

1 Arrive prepared, having made your probable choice of **FORM** of writing.
2 Read the instructions carefully and calmly.
3 Complete the details on the answer book cover.
4 Read the assignments carefully and look at the stimulus materials.
5 Choose your assignment with form and topic matching the question.
6 Check the time available.
7 Think about the task and make your written plan.
8 Write the first draft, keeping to the plan and/or amending as you proceed.
9 Check the time left.
10 Read over your work carefully and thoughtfully.
11 Re-draft it in detail and in general.
12 Check it again.
13 Enter the assignment number in the margin.
14 Cancel your plan and notes.

There is no special merit in writing more than everybody else. Most of the assignments can be covered in about two or three pages of the exam book … and the lines in the exam book are generously spaced apart from each other.

This system means that you might not start the actual writing for a good ten minutes into the exam. When you do start writing it will be the planning rather than the actual essay. You will not still be scribbling furiously when the invigilator tells you to stop.

Part of the time will be spent reading what you have written, part of it thinking about your plan and about your ideas and the best way of expressing these ideas. What is very important is that you leave a good five minutes to check finally and correct what you have written. This is almost as important as the actual first draft writing. You would be astonished at the number of daft mistakes you make when you are in this situation — wrong words (e.g., "the" instead of "that"), wrong spelling and punctuation that you know perfectly well, repetitions, important omissions, etc.

If you firmly understand that your aim when the exam comes to an end is to be either calmly and carefully reading and finally checking, or to have already finished everything, then you will get the timing right.

READING

Close Reading

The first point about the Reading exam is that it deals with a completely different kind of Reading from what was called Reading in the Folio. Here we are into what is called **Close Reading**. Another name for it is Interpretation.

In the Folio we were dealing with Reading, but it was actually concerned with your critical evaluations of literature. You wrote short essays giving your opinions of the works of literature you had been reading, and showing your knowledge of these texts, whether of prose or poetry or drama or media. These responses to the literature were in the form of extended pieces of writing, as they're called in Standard Grade English.

For the kind of Reading you will face in the exam, you are given a short **unseen** text or extract from a text and you respond to it by answering specific questions about it, with short answers, not extended essays. The questioning is concerned (mostly) with specific points and details. You are therefore obliged to read closely and show by your answers that this is what you have done. This is why it is called Close Reading.

The second major point about Close Reading is that your responses are assessed individually by gaining marks for each one. Folio Reading was assessed by being directly graded. That is, the whole extended piece was assessed against a set of GRC, using published grade descriptions. You can see these descriptions later on in the GRC chapter. The grade descriptions do what they say: they describe a piece of work as a whole, and there is description for a typical piece of writing that is worthy of a particular grade. (There is therefore a description linked to each grade of writing from Grade 1 to Grade 6.)

This system cannot really be applied to close reading. It would involve comparing your overall set of answers with a grade description, and this just is not workable. So what happens instead is that the examiners provide a text of suitable reading difficulty for each level and design questions that allow you to show your understanding at that level, encouraging a response at that level. The examiners take account of the Grade Related Criteria in setting the text and designing the questions, so that a performance meeting the requirements will attain that level and grade. Each separate response to the questioning is assigned a mark, and when these are added up, the total mark reflects your performance. This is called indirect grading. It is complicated, but fortunately you do not have to worry too much about the technicalities of this arrangement.

Levels of examination: Presentation

By the time you have reached the middle of the course's second year, your teacher will have formed a fair idea of the standard of close reading work you are capable of producing, and this is a fair guide to you both about how you should best tackle the Reading exam.

During the course you will have been learning about close reading. Don't think that you do close reading just to prepare for the exam, it's a very important part of the course learning. You might already have seen old exam papers, and your teacher might even have used them in the teaching process. This is not the only way you learn how to do close reading. The learning is insidious, meaning that it is not right up there in the front and very visible. It goes on all the time that you are studying texts and responding to them both in writing about them and talking about them in the class. Everything that you do in class is preparing you to be able to study texts closely, to understand the language of interpretation and to grasp the meaning of language where it is close and specific to extract meaning. This is the nitty-gritty of reading. By the time you come to the exam you will see that all the exam is asking you to do is to show a sample of your learning and understanding of the details of language, with its style, register, tone and modifying qualities that affect the meaning of what a writer has intended.

The external exam in Reading is offered at three levels: Foundation, General and Credit. You will understand this easily if you have understood the opening three paragraphs of this section on Reading.

In each of the exam levels there is a passage for close reading and questions to match. Each passage and its set of questions is set at a level of difficulty to match the GRC for that level (see Chapter 8). They are set like this to give you the chance to show what you can do in whatever level of question paper you attempt. There are restrictions about what levels of the papers you can sit.

> **The SQA allows you one of the following options:**
>
> **EITHER**
> i) the Foundation and General papers
> **OR**
> ii) the General and Credit papers.

Your school "presents" (enters) you for one of these options in advance (provisionally about November of – usually – your fourth year and then confirms or changes this in about January of the exam year). This entry is based on your level or standard of work up till that time and making an allowance for what improvement you could reasonably be expected to achieve from then until the time of the exam in May.

> **You should take your teacher's advice about which papers to sit, they are the best people to guide you in this.**

Your teacher will always present you for the papers that will allow you to do your best on the day. Your teacher will decide which combination of papers you are able to cope with. This choice will be based on matching the demands of the papers with your known ability as demonstrated by your work throughout the course, and will give you the possibility of achieving the best grade possible. You should never be sitting papers that are too difficult … or attempting a level that is too easy. You must attempt the levels that allow you to show the **best** you can do.

This is how it works.

If your work in Reading seems to be mostly fitting the GRC at Foundation Level, but sometimes shows the standard described by the GRC for General Level, you should sit the first of the options — Foundation and General.

If your work in Reading is mostly at General Level with occasional Foundation Level, then the best option for you is again the first of the two options — Foundation and General.

If your work is mostly achieving General Level and occasionally achieving Credit Level, you should sit the second option — General and Credit Level.

If you consistently produce work at Credit Level, you should sit the second of the options — General and Credit.

As you can see from this, everybody will be sitting the General Level Reading paper. There's a very good reason for this.

At any part of Standard Grade, because everything is based on GRC, you can gain an award only for what you have actually achieved. As already explained, for the Folio in Reading and Writing, the grade and level are based on what you actually produce. The same applies to the Writing exam and also to Talking, which we're coming on to later.

However, in the Reading exam you cannot get an award for anything you did not sit. In assessment-speak, there is "no enhancement and no compensation". This means that if you only sat the Credit level exam (you're allowed to do this — to be presented for the General/Credit papers but on the day sit only one of them: the same for Foundation/General — but it would be very unwise to do this) and if you did not score enough marks to gain the Credit award, you would **not** be given an award at General as compensation for a narrow miss. You would drop right down to Grade 7. The same would happen for the other option. If you sat only the General paper on the day and didn't gain enough marks, you would **not** get an award at Foundation as compensation. Once again, you would drop right down to Grade 7. You wouldn't be given a Foundation award as compensation. There's no evidence so there is no compensation.

It works the other way round, too. You cannot get a General award by sitting only the Foundation paper and doing very well in it — even if you gained all the marks available in the exam. Your grade would be either Grade 5 or Grade 6 because that is all that the Foundation paper tests. There's no evidence to justify a General award. Similarly, you can't get a Credit award if you sat only the General paper, no matter how well you did. There's no evidence to match the GRC. There is no enhancement in the system.

The reason for this is that the GRC say that you "can do" various things, and there has to be clear evidence showing that you can do them. Each level of exam is designed to produce only the evidence that would justify the GRC statements for that level. They don't produce any evidence for any other level. It is not quite the same as expecting to get an award in Physics because you did very well in Chemistry. But it is close.

I have said that you should pay very careful attention to your teacher's advice both on the presentation levels for the Reading exam, and on what papers you should sit on the day. Actually, the level of presentation will probably be decided by your teacher and it will be difficult to disagree with it because you will be quite aware of your ability by that time. There is room for advice and flexibility about what you should actually sit on the day of the exam, though. In that, you should pay heed to your teacher's advice, keeping in mind that you can get an award only for what you sit. At the same time, you should not be facing an exam at a level which is beyond you. That is not a lot of fun, and can be quite depressing.

These rules apply only to the Reading exam.

They do not apply for the other parts of the assessment system — the Folio, the Writing exam and the Talking element. Those parts of the assessment system are designed to offer you and everyone else the same chance of producing evidence of a performance at any point, right across the range of levels and grades, from Grade 6 at Foundation to Grade 1 at Credit.

The Question Papers

This Guide is not about how to sit the Reading exam and how to practise, though there is quite a lot of advice about this coming. Actually, the work of the course is much more important and is the best preparation for the exam. In the exam you should be displaying a sample of what you can do. You should never think of the course as just a way of practising to sit exam papers.

I have already explained to you that the exam in Reading deals only with Close Reading (interpretation) and this is why Close Reading doesn't have any place in the Folio. Although I've said it's the same as interpretation, it's a little more than that. Think of it as "super-interpretation": what you do when you really get down to examining in close detail what you read. Reading under the microscope, if you like.

Taking an adapted version of one of SQA's recent Reading exam papers (at General Level only) you can study it to see how it works and what is expected of you. Here is the whole paper: the instructions, the rubric, the passage and the questions.

I have decided to show you only the General Level paper. That is not just to save paper and costs, but is because the three levels of the paper are very similar in appearance. The only real differences among them are in two areas. These two areas are just as you'd expect:

◆ the relative reading level of the passage
◆ the relative difficulty and demand of the questions.

It is pretty obvious that the Foundation paper is a bit easier than the General, and that the Credit paper is harder than it. Otherwise, they are the same, and everything that is said about the General paper applies exactly to the other two levels of paper. Take some time now to read the passage, then go on to what is said about it, before you turn to the questions.

The exam paper is in two parts. There is the text itself inside a four-page booklet. The front page of the booklet contains very little other than the name of the exam. At the top right is the identifying letter for the level of examination, in this case **G** for General Level. Immediately below this it is spelled out:

ENGLISH
STANDARD GRADE
General Level
Reading
Text

Inside, there is simply the text printed in numbered paragraphs. This text is accompanied by a photograph. In any given year there might be an illustration or other graphic material, or just the text alone.

G

0860/403

NATIONAL QUALIFICATIONS 2002	TUESDAY, 7 MAY 1.00 PM – 1.50 PM	**ENGLISH** STANDARD GRADE General Level Reading Text

Read carefully the passage overleaf. It will help if you read it twice. When you have done so, answer the questions. Use the spaces provided in the Question/Answer booklet.

SCOTTISH QUALIFICATIONS AUTHORITY

MCB 0860/403 6/70170

1   The kettle switched itself off the boil with a sharp click. The young man filled the teapot with the steaming water and dropped in a teabag to add to the one already there. He sat the full pot on the formica-topped breakfast bar and made a silly face at his five-year-old daughter who was perched on a stool slowly getting through a bowl of milky porridge. Hearing his wife coming down the stairs from the bathroom he began to refill her mug but instead of entering the bright warm kitchen she lingered in the hall. He could hear her pulling on her heavy coat. She came in saying she had no time, she'd be late for her lift, her heels clattering on the tiled floor. She kissed goodbye to daughter and husband then was off in a whirl of newly-applied perfume and the swish of her clothes and the front door slamming.

2   He sat down on his stool and poured himself another mug of tea. He asked the child how she was doing, was the porridge too hot? She told him gravely that it was OK and went on making a show of blowing on each hot spoonful as she had been shown.

3   He picked up the newspaper that was lying folded open at the Situations Vacant pages. One advert was targeted in a ring of red felt-tip pen. The introduction was in big bold italics: ***"This time last year I was made redundant. Now I own a £150,000 house, drive a BMW and holiday in Bali. If you . . ."*** He opened out the paper and refolded it to the front page to check the headlines. The date he knew already but there it was: exactly one year he had been out of work.

4   Father and daughter chatted brightly as they strolled hand in hand down Allison Street heading for school. She was a talkative child and he would egg her on in her prattle for his own amusement. It was now well into the rush hour: traffic gushed by or fretted at red lights and urgent pedestrians commanded the pavements and crossings. It was bitter cold. He looked down at the girl to reassure himself that she was warmly enough dressed, but there was no need; he was well used to getting her ready. Her round reddened face was the only prey to the cold air and she beamed up at him, quite content.

5   At the last corner before the school's street they both halted in an accustomed way and he squatted down to give her a kiss. She didn't mind the ritual but not outside the gates: her pals might see and that would be too embarrassing. He tugged her knitted hat a little further down her forehead and tucked in a couple of strands of her long reddish hair. They could hear the kids' voices laughing and shouting from the playground. They waved cheerio at the gate and he stood watching until she was inside and with her friends, then he turned away. He was vaguely aware of one or two mothers doing likewise and one or two car doors slamming. With both gloveless hands shoved into the pockets of his cream-coloured raincoat he made for home. Behind him the bell began to sound above and through the high excited voices.

* * * * *

6   He finished writing the letter and signed his name with a brisk underline, printing it in brackets below, just in case. Picking up the CV from the coffee table he glanced over the familiar details of his education and career. It looked good, he thought, organised, businesslike. His wife had managed to get a couple of dozen of them run off on her word processor at the office. It was the contents that struck him as pointless. What use was it to anyone to know what he had done at school? It was the grown man, someone with work experience, who was on offer, not the schoolboy. Not the kid who'd scuffed along, neither brilliant nor stupid, not the football-daft apprentice smoker who'd put his name to those long-forgotten exam papers then sauntered out carefree into the world. Well, maybe not carefree: he could still

[0860/403]   *Page two*

remember some of the burdens and terrors of adolescence that he'd laugh at now. Then there was his five years of selling for the one firm. No problem there; those were good years. Their fruits were holidays abroad, marriage, the house, the baby. Plain sailing until the company had gone bust. Now he was no longer young and upwardly mobile. Not even horizontally mobile: stopped, stuck.

7   Referees. He always wanted to write the name of a football referee but didn't. What did people expect to hear from the names he always supplied—"Don't touch this character, he's a definite no-user"? It was just wee games, this form-filling. He believed it was the interview that would count, if only he could land one.

8   He arranged the letter and CV together, tapping sides and tails until there was no overlap, then folded them in half and in half again. The envelope was ready, briskly typed by his wife on the old manual machine she used for home typing jobs. As he made ready to lick the stamp he stopped suddenly. He'd done it again, folding the sheets in half twice. That was clumsy, unprofessional-looking. The way she'd shown him was much better: folding one third then another so that you only had two folds instead of three. Gingerly, he tried to reopen the envelope but it was stuck fast and the flap ripped jaggedly. He'd have to type another one himself in his laborious two-fingered style. His first go had two mistakes and so he typed another one, slowly, making sure he got everything right.

* * * * *

9   He kept walking, on past the pillar-box at the corner of their street. That one was definitely unlucky: nothing he had ever posted there had brought good fortune. No, he would carry on to Victoria Road whose offices and air of industry made it feel a more hopeful point of departure. As he reached the main thoroughfare he saw a mail van pull up at the postbox he was heading for and he quickened his pace. He watched the grey-uniformed driver jump down and unlock the red door; he broke into a run. The pillar-box yielded a bulky flow of mail to the driver's hand combing it into his big shapeless bag. The young man handed over his letter with a half-smile although his heart had sunk. One letter in all that flow of paper. And how many were job applications piled randomly, meaninglessly on top of one another? His own would soon be lost in that anonymous crowd. It seemed to him now more than ever like buying a raffle ticket, like doing the football coupon every week. What chance had you got?

10   But it was easy standing here to recall the bustle of business life. It came to him how much he wanted it, that activity. It was more than just something you did to make money: it was the only life he knew and he was missing out on it, standing on the sidelines like a face in the crowd at a football game. If it wasn't for the child, he thought, he wouldn't have the will to keep on trying. He checked his watch: the kids would soon be coming out.

* * * * *

11   He waited at their corner, hands deep in pockets, his shoulder to the dirty grey sandstone wall. The bell was ringing and he could hear the children streaming out into the playground. When she spotted him she broke into a trot and he retreated round the corner a little to swoop suddenly with a mock roar, bearing her laughing wildly up into his arms. As he set her down he asked quite formally what kind of morning she'd had. She began to speak, and her enthusiasm breathed upwards into his smiling face and beyond in the chill air.

Adapted from the short story "Application" by Michael Munro

[END OF PASSAGE]

[0860/403]   *Page three*

FOR OFFICIAL USE

G

Total
Mark

0860/404

NATIONAL
QUALIFICATIONS
2002

TUESDAY, 7 MAY
1.00 PM – 1.50 PM

ENGLISH
STANDARD GRADE
General Level
Reading
Questions

Fill in these boxes and read what is printed below.

Full name of centre

Town

Forename(s)

Surname

Date of birth
Day Month Year   Scottish candidate number   Number of seat

**NB Before leaving the examination room you must give this booklet to the invigilator.
If you do not, you may lose all the marks for this paper.**

SCOTTISH
QUALIFICATIONS
AUTHORITY
©

MCB 0860/404 6/70170

QUESTIONS

Write your answers in the spaces provided.

Look at Paragraphs 1 to 3.

1. Why did the young man have time to make breakfast for his wife and daughter?

   _____

   2 ■ 0

2. From the last sentence in Paragraph 1, **write down two separate words** which suggest his wife was in a hurry.

   2 1 0

3. (a) In Paragraph 1, why is "**perched**" a particularly suitable word to describe how the five-year-old girl sat on her stool?

   _____

   _____

   2 1 0

   (b) Give **two** pieces of evidence to show that the daughter treated the business of eating her breakfast seriously.

   (i) _____

   _____

   2 1 0

   (ii) _____

   _____

   2 1 0

4. Why do you think one advert in the newspaper was "targeted in a ring of red felt-tip pen" (Paragraph 3)?

   _____

   _____

   2 1 0

Marks

PAGE
TOTAL

Marks

Look at Paragraphs 4 and 5.

5. What did the young man enjoy about the walk to school with his daughter? **Answer in your own words.**

_____

_____   2 | 1 | 0

6. The writer uses a colon (:) in Paragraph 4 (after "rush hour") and in Paragraph 5 (after "outside the gates").

    Tick (✓) the box to show which you think is the correct reason for its use in each case.   2 | 1 | 0

	Paragraph 4	*Paragraph 5*
To introduce a quotation		
To elaborate on an idea		
To introduce an explanation		

7. Write down **two** examples of **separate words** the writer has used to convey the idea of "rush hour".

    [   ]   [   ]   2 | 1 | 0

8. "It was bitter cold." (Paragraph 4)

    Explain clearly how later in Paragraph 4 the writer makes the cold air seem alive.

_____

_____   2 | 1 | 0

[Turn over

PAGE
TOTAL

Marks

9. (*a*) Why is the father's kiss described as a "ritual" (Paragraph 5)?

_____

_____ | 2 | 1 | 0 |

(*b*) Which expression earlier in Paragraph 5 helps you to understand the meaning of "ritual"?

_____ | 2 | ■ | 0 |

10. ". . . but not outside the gates . . ." (Paragraph 5)

Using your own words as far as possible, explain why the daughter made this condition.

_____

_____ | 2 | 1 | 0 |

Look at Paragraphs 6 and 7.

11. (*a*) What did the man think "looked good" about his CV?

_____

_____ | 2 | ■ | 0 |

(*b*) What **two** things about "this form-filling" did he think were "pointless"?

In each case explain **why** he thought so.

(i) _____

_____ | 2 | 1 | 0 |

(ii) _____

_____ | 2 | 1 | 0 |

PAGE
TOTAL

Marks

Look at Paragraph 8.

12. (*a*) Why did the man not put the stamp on the envelope?

_____

_____ | 2 | 1 | 0

(*b*) "Gingerly, he tried to reopen . . . flap ripped jaggedly."

How does the structure of this sentence emphasise the man's care in reopening the envelope?

_____

_____ | 2 | 1 | 0

(*c*) **Write down** the **two** expressions the writer uses in this paragraph to show the contrast between the man's typing skills and his wife's. | 2 | 1 | 0

(i) _____

(ii) _____

Look at Paragraphs 9 and 10.

13. Explain clearly why the man chose to post his letter in Victoria Road.

_____

_____

_____ | 2 | 1 | 0

14. Explain clearly why "his heart had sunk" (Paragraph 9) when he handed over his letter.

_____

_____ | 2 | 1 | 0

[Turn over for Questions 15 to 17 on *Page six*

PAGE
TOTAL

Marks

15. " . . . standing on the sidelines like a face in the crowd at a football game."
(Paragraph 10)

Explain how effective you find this simile.

_____

_____   2 1 0

Think about the passage as a whole.

16. Throughout the passage, the man is shown to be thoughtful and caring about his
daughter.

What evidence is there of this:

(a) in Paragraph 11?   2 1 0

(i) _____

(ii) _____

(b) elsewhere in the passage?   2 1 0

(i) _____

(ii) _____

17. Overall, do you feel the story conveys a sense of **hope**, or of **despair**?

Tick (✓) the box to indicate your choice.

Hope	
Despair	

Justify your choice by detailed reference to the text.

_____

_____

_____

_____   2 1 0

[END OF QUESTION PAPER]

FOR OFFICIAL USE

The Text

This passage is carefully chosen to make sure that it is of the right level of reading difficulty for General Level, matching the demands of the GRC. In any given year, the passage might be a piece of prose or poetry or drama. Though it is most often prose from a novel or story, or from non-fiction or from a newspaper or magazine, you must be prepared for any of the other forms instead. It might be illustrated or not. It might be a little longer or a little shorter, though not by much either way. The language could be formal or colloquial in style. In other words there is no guarantee that the question paper you will face will look exactly like this one although it will be of the same standard of difficulty.

For the reasons already given, you will most probably be sitting a General Level paper along with one of the other two, either Foundation or Credit. So you will either already have taken the Foundation paper when you see the General paper, or you will be going on to sit the Credit paper immediately afterwards.

The Questions

Now have a look at the question paper.

The front page is similar to the text booklet's front page, but has the word "Questions" instead of "Text", and then below that the area where you provide details of yourself. There is also a note printed in bold about remembering to hand in the paper when you have finished. Inside, there is a question/answer booklet where you write the answers in the spaces provided.

The Answers

The spaces are carefully planned to help you. The spaces for your answers are of different types and are there to give you some guidance as to the kind of answer (its length, the number of sections, etc.) the examiners expect you to write. The Reading paper is not a test of writing, and the quality of the language in your answers is not being assessed here.

> **This is not the case if you go on to sit the Higher English exam later. There, not only what you answer, but how you say it, matters.**

Quite often the briefest of answers is all that is required — indicated by a single line, or several lines, or a box, or even by a small "tick-box" for your answer in a multiple-choice question. The examiners do not expect short essays as answers, nor should you waste time and effort by repeating the stem of the question in your answer. Your answers should always be full, making sure that you have responded to all the points being asked about, but they should also be concise, not rambling or repetitive. You must convey your meaning clearly but without over-elaboration. When the examiner wants your answer in your own words, this will be clearly indicated either in the wording of the question or at the beginning of the paper, or both.

The Marking System

Down the right-hand side of each page of the question paper there is a section headed *Marks*. It has three columns, as you can see. This column is important for you as well as for the examiner. For you it provides a further indication of the kind of answer you are expected to give: for the examiner it provides a fail-safe marking system that helps them to mark accurately and prevents them from making mistakes, both in awarding marks and adding them to arrive at your total.

There are two kinds of questions, broadly speaking:

1 Questions where there is an answer worth either 2 marks or 0 marks. In the part of the columns opposite this type of question you can see the entry

2   0

You can gain 2 marks for the right answer. No other mark is available. Questions like this are called dichotomous*, that is, capable of right or wrong only. There is no partial credit. It's either right or wrong.

Question 1 in this paper is an example of this kind of question, though Question 9b is a clearer example, since only the single exact word asked for will do as the correct answer.

2 Questions where the answer may be right, or partly right, or wrong.

In the part of the column opposite this type of question you can see the entry

2   1   0

You can gain 2 marks for the right or full answer, 1 mark for a partly correct or less full answer and, of course, 0 marks for a wrong or unacceptable answer.

There are many examples of this type of question, but question 7 is the clearest. You can gain 2 marks by providing two correct words, 1 mark for providing one correct word, or 0 marks for providing no correct words.

This coded information can be valuable to you in helping you to decide the kind of answer expected. At the same time, it helps the marker and the examiners. The markers simply circle the mark awarded. They do not have to spend a long time deciding what to do about your answer here because they are following a detailed marking system with an answer key. This is why there is a black box in the dichotomous questions. It prevents the marker from accidentally awarding partial credit in that type of question.

You will have noticed that all the questions have the same **maximum** value (i.e. 2 marks) as each other. The difference between them is in the way you can gain credit for each one: all or nothing for the first type, the dichotomous; all, part or nothing for the second type. This is one of the ways in which the examiners distinguish between the upper and lower grades at each level of examination.

While the marking system and how it works is not necessarily very interesting for you, you can see that understanding it could be very important in how you gain your marks and therefore what grade you ultimately achieve. If you do understand it and follow it, it will have a definite effect on how well you perform in this particular part of the assessment system.

How marks become grades

These Close Reading papers are the only part of the Standard Grade English assessment system where your work is assessed using marks. All the other parts are directly graded, as you already know. As explained earlier, close reading cannot be directly graded. The separate questions have to be marked and the marks totalled carefully — very carefully. That is why at the foot of each page of the question paper there is a sub-total and at the end of the paper a cross-checking of the total marks you have gained in the paper. This total mark is then converted into a grade so that it can be aggregated with your other grades from the other elements and sub-elements (the Folio Reading and Writing, the Writing exam and the Talking) to arrive at your final grade for English. How this is done is not simple, but it is valuable for you to know about it.

When the question paper is constructed, the passage, the questions and the marking scheme are arranged very carefully to allow you to "demonstrate performance", as the *Arrangements* document says. In plain English this means that it helps you to show what you can do. The whole package is designed using the purposes of Reading and the GRC which are described in Chapter 7. The examiners calculate what scores (number of marks) in that paper are needed to gain the upper and lower grades available for the paper in question. These scores are called "cut-off scores" or "cutting scores". The actual cut-off scores for a particular paper will not be the same as for all other papers. The reason for this is that the cut-off score is calculated on a **percentage** of the total marks available for the paper, and that total number of marks available can vary a little from year to year. It depends on the passage and the number of questions that can reasonably be asked about it.

The cut-off score is calculated before the exam is taken. But what is more important is that it is checked again after a large sample of the papers has been marked by the examiners and then again after all the papers have been marked. This is because students do not always do what the examiners think they will do. Particularly, the examiners' expectations of the difficulty of the questions is often modified by what they find when they are able to see what all the students together have done. Sometimes some of the questions turn out to be generally more difficult or easier for the students than the examiners anticipated. If this happens, the cut-off scores can be altered up or down as the case may be.

As a general rule, the cut-off score for the upper grade (in the General paper that is Grade 3) is set at 70% of the total marks available: the cut-off score for the lower grade (in the General paper that is Grade 4) is set at 40% of the total marks available. This percentage figure remains constant from year to year and across all levels of paper. It is the total marks available that can change each year, and other things also affect the actual cut-off scores. The changes that I have mentioned are to make the exam fair for all students who sat it.

So, if you had a General Level paper with 30 questions, the maximum number of marks available would be 60 (2 marks available for each question). The cut-off score for Grade 3 would be 70% of 60, which is 42 marks. Notice that you don't have to get all of the marks available to get the grade. The examiners realise that, though strictly speaking it would seem that you should get all the marks by getting all the questions correct because the GRC say that someone who gets that grade can do all of the things mentioned there, the exam actually samples these and tests them several times over in the exam. The people who sit exams are human beings who make mistakes and are not always consistent anyway. The 70% rule allows for this.

You can get a total mark by any combination of marks for answers to 2 0 questions and 2 1 0 questions. For example, you could get 21 questions worth 2 marks each, or 12 questions worth 2 marks and 18 questions worth 1 mark each. Each of these scores would get the same grade. Notice too that you would have to get at least 12 2-mark questions fully correct before you could reach the upper grade in this example. That is quite a high proportion of the total number of questions, 12 out of 30, especially when you have to get another 18 1-mark questions at least. If you dropped even one of those marks you would gain the lower grade, not the upper. So although you can gain the upper or lower grade by different combinations of answers, you don't get either of these grades for nothing. The sums work.

The cut-off score is affected by a number of factors, but you can take it that the principle is always the same. It makes sure that those who gain the grades do so on the basis of what they can do, as described by the GRC. The percentages I have been talking about have nothing whatsoever to do with the number of people who sit the exams. There is no pre-determined percentage of candidates who gain awards at any level. If you can do what the GRC demand, you get the award regardless of what other people do.

This is because the assessment system is based on what we call criterion-referencing and not on what we call norm-referencing. It sounds complicated but it isn't.

Just for information, you might want to know that the examiners mark the higher level of your two papers first. If you reach the cut-off score for a grade at that level, then they don't need to mark your other paper, the one at the lower of the two levels you attempted.

The GRC are the criteria, and everyone who meets them gets the award, regardless of numbers of candidates. So the awards are connected with (refer to) the publicly-stated, up-front criteria or judgement points. That is criterion-referenced assessment.

In norm-referencing, the calculation is quite different. The percentage score for each grade is pre-determined and, when the quota number of candidates for each grade is filled by the expected percentage of candidates arranged in rank order, then the next batch of candidates get the next lower grade, and so on. This is norm-referencing. The reference is to what is called the norm*. In this system, the rank order is usually based on a marks system, and therefore each candidate is compared with (referred to) all other candidates. This can be done because large numbers of candidates follow a norm of performance: they fall broadly into categories and this phenomenon* is used to assign grades.

Aggregation

Health Warning!

Time has been taken in this chapter to explain how marks are arrived at and how grades for Reading are calculated from them to become grades. Because of that, and because you have now dealt with the whole of the Folio and the whole of the external examinations, this might be the place to explain how the complete element grades for Reading and Writing are calculated. It's not completely necessary for you to understand this aggregation system, so if you don't feel you want to know about it at this stage, skip on to the next chapter on Talking, and you can always come back to this when you think you would like to know about it.

Calculation of overall grades

You could gain a different grade for each of the separate parts of Standard Grade English, at least in theory. In practice most people will be much more consistent than that and will tend to get grades that are broadly similar for the various elements and sub-elements. Because everyone has the possibility of gaining different grades for different skills and knowledge and understanding in the range of elements, however, the different elements are assessed separately. Someone who gains a Grade 1 for Reading and Writing might not achieve anything as good in Talking, for instance. This is why the elements are reported separately on your certificate as a "profile", and then aggregated to produce an overall grade for English. This can show your strengths and weaknesses — if you have any, of course.

Some examples will help to make this clearer. In the table below, the headings are for the various elements and sub-elements of Standard Grade English that are added together to make up your final award. Let's start with an easy one.

READING		WRITING		TALKING
Folio	Close	Folio	Exam	Whole course
3	3	4	4	2
= Reading 3		= Writing 4		= Talking 2

Final award = 3 + 4 + 2 = 9/3 = 3

Now a slightly more complicated mixture of grades to show you that the same arrangement works and still produces a final grade that reflects overall performance and shows a profile at the same time.

READING		WRITING		TALKING
Folio	Close	Folio	Exam	Whole course
5	3	6	5	2
=Reading + 3 + 5 = 8/2 = 4		= Writing 5 + 6 = 11/2 = 5.5 = 5		= Talking 2

Final award = 4 + 5 + 2 = 11/2 =3.6 = 4

So, how it works is that all the sub-grades for the elements are added (for example, Folio Reading 5 + Close Reading 3 gives 8) the mean is found (the average of the two) by dividing by 2. (The answer is 4.) If the answer is not a whole number it is rounded up to the higher of the grades on either side. Thus, in the second example, Folio Writing 6 and Exam Writing 5 gives 11. Dividing by 2 produces 5.5. The grades on either side are obviously 5 and 6. Of these 5 is higher, so the grade you get is 5. The final award in that example is based on a raw total of 3.6. That is nearer 4 than 3, so the final grade is 4.

Once you have the grade for each element, they are added and the mean is calculated in the same way. The only slight difference is that since there are three elements and they are all equal in value, you divide by 3 to get the final grade for English.

You can see that the level of the paper you sit in Reading doesn't fix what grades you can get for the other parts of the assessment system. It does have an effect on the overall grade, naturally, since the highest grade you can get for Reading depends on which level of the Reading paper you sat.

CHAPTER SIX

TALKING

This chapter gives you some advice about dealing with talking in the classroom. That is where the activity takes place and that is where the assessment of it takes place too. You know that Talking is all internally assessed — by your teacher in the classroom. There is no exam in Talking, and there is no Talking item to be included in the Folio either.

Background

Long ago, when Standard Grade English was first being piloted in about 20 different schools all over Scotland, there was the idea that every student would keep an "electronic jotter" of Talking activities and send in their cassette tape with the Folio which would be externally assessed by examiners.

Trials of this idea took place, and there was an amazing archive of fascinating talk from students from all over the country, from Stornoway to Eyemouth, from Aberdeen to Glasgow and schools in between. There were wonderful accounts of building bikes from scrap-yard salvage, gralloching* stags illegally poached from the hill, weird stories that would have done well in a ceilidh house, interviews with interesting people, and much more, in all sorts of accents. The work was often excellent, but the problem of assessing it was too great. Too much that makes up real talk was missing because it was not live. The assessment could not cover the valuable Talking/Listening skills involved in Discussion, as it was impossible to work out who was really talking and what other talk behaviours they were using. As well as this, the time taken for the job was unacceptable and so external assessment was dropped as a result of the trials.

For you, assessment of Talking is done internally by your teacher and is worth one-third of the whole value of your award. It has the same value as Reading and the same value as Writing, as you now know.

In some schools, the assessment of individual talking may begin to look like an exam because it is "set up" to take place at fixed times. This is not how it was intended to be done, and I hope that it is not always going to be like that in your school. Talking is supposed to be assessed as it happens naturally in the course, arising from the normal work of your class. Occasionally your teacher may have to "stop the world" and create time for some or all students to give a talk to the whole class. You can understand this, because the whole class can hardly get on with other activities and be an audience for a talk at the same time. The audience for your talk can be other groupings though: such as a small group of four or five or even a single individual. There is no need for every single person to take their turn addressing the whole class. This kind of arrangement is what could make the internal assessment feel very much like an exam, where you get one shot at it.

Talking in the Course

Your teacher has to assess what you can do. He or she must hear you in Individual Talk and in Discussion on several occasions over the two years, with most of the actual assessments that will count towards your final grade taking place nearer the end of the course rather than nearer the beginning. You will be better at talking at the end of S4 than you were at the start of S3. You have to admit that teaching does have an effect on you.

During the course, you will be taught about talking and you will learn how to improve by practising. Trial and error, it's called. This is why the learning and formative assessment takes place earlier in the course, and why assessment takes place towards the end. Talking is one of the important ways in which learning is carried forward. Talking over your ideas, plans and opinions is one of the main ways in which you really learn about things — or, as someone said, "I don't know what I think until I hear what I say". This is perhaps not as profound a statement as the famous one made by the French philosopher, René Descartes, when he pronounced, *Cogito, ergo sum* (I think, therefore I am). When you spend much of your time in the course talking to your group or teacher or class, you are learning.

Discussion is especially valuable in confirming your learning. It not only advances your skills in the actual business of discussion, negotiating language with others, but it also serves to test your ideas and opinions against those of other people. It helps to consolidate your learning of the subject you are discussing, whatever it is. This helps you to learn more about the subject of the discussion, whether it is differing views about genetic experimenting, or the character of Macbeth or the role of skinny supermodels in our world.

Talking certainly is one way to learn how to talk better (I do not mean elocution: I'm coming to that), but is also how you learn to think both logically and imaginatively (they are not opposites). From talking you also learn about reading, listening and certainly about writing. Remember that writing is the mode of language that is closest to talking. These two modes of language are the "expressive" modes, the ones that allow you to express your thoughts, ideas, opinions, information, and to communicate with others.

Never underestimate the importance of talking. It is seldom "just talking". If you think you learned to talk without any effort, you're wrong. It takes an enormous amount of effort and hard work to learn what language you have by the age of five, and you learn almost everything you know by that age by listening and talking. You certainly didn't learn it by reading, did you?

Talking and language do not just happen. If you had been born and lived in another country, say Hungary, you would know all about the problems of learning English, the language you probably take for granted. It would be just the same as you trying to learn to speak the Hungarian language now. That is not easy. A major reason for people thinking that talking does not have to be learned and refined is that we know that almost all 5-year olds can talk when they start school, but very few can read or write and have to be taught to do so. This obscures two facts:

◆ 5-year olds have spent five years learning to talk
◆ learning to talk does not stop when you start school.

One of the Scottish kings tried an experiment to settle this mystery of talking and language. There was a notion that a child just spoke naturally, without teaching or learning, as if it were built in genetically, in the same way as your teeth and height are. He also thought that the "natural language" would be Gaelic. In his bizarre experiment he sent a baby to live on an island in the River Forth in the sole care of a deaf and dumb nurse. However, his idea that the baby would grow up and speak the "language of Heaven" (Gaelic) was disproved. The child did not learn to speak any language at all. It didn't have anyone to teach it to talk. That might sound daft, but it would be funny if it were not so tragic. Talking and language have to be learned, and that learning does not stop when you come to school and **appear** to be spending all your time learning to read and write and count.

In your Standard Grade English course, you should be a little more aware that the teaching of language is going on all the time, even if there is a sneaking suspicion that some teachers still seem to believe that it just happens. I hope that your teacher is not one of them.

That situation has arisen because, although almost all teachers recognise the importance of talking, a very large number have difficulty because its assessment is very time-consuming. Many still don't give it an equal place alongside reading and writing. The assessment of talking concentrates on the individual student talking and it has to happen "in real time", so it is not like reading and writing, where the formal assessment of a whole class can take place at the same time.

Activities and Talk Behaviours in the Course

There are two kinds of Talking being assessed:

◆ Individual Talk

◆ Discussion

and we will take them in turn.

Individual Talk

You will be taking part in several different kinds of talk activities in your class. In Individual Talk, you might find that as part of a unit you are asked to give a talk to the whole class. Since you are the only one talking at that time it can feel very much like a test. As I've said, not all such talks have to be counted towards your final grade for Talking. The assessments that count will come towards the end of the course. All assessment should take place after the learning that is being assessed, not the other way round. Think of early talk activities as part of the learning and teaching process, and the assessment is to measure what you have learned: not what you know before you have had any teaching. That's obvious, isn't it? Your earlier attempts help you and your teacher to improve your performance.

Other activities in Individual Talk will include:

◆ reporting a discussion to the class

◆ taking part in debates, either formal or informal

◆ talking on a subject of your choice to your small group

◆ being a member of a panel

◆ talking briefly in response to questions from an audience.

Whatever activity you carry out will have a clear purpose and this means that it can be assessed.

Role Play

The word "performance" has been mentioned a few times already in the Guide. It simply means "what you do" and how well you do it. It has nothing whatsoever to do with acting, as in a stage performance of a play, or standing up to do a song. This leads us to a matter that has to be cleared up for you.

Sometimes when you are carrying out a talk assignment, you will be asked to do it *in role*. Your teacher will set you a task and tell you that you are, for example, one of a group of people in a lifeboat after a shipwreck. There is no food, and everybody is slowly starving to death, so you have to find food somehow. Setting aside the morality of this, they have all decided that the only way they can survive is by eating one of the people in the boat. Each person has to argue how valuable they are to society if they are rescued, and that they should not be the person who has to become their dinner. We leave aside the horrible little detail of cannibalism and get on with the task, the purpose being to make the best case you can for avoiding being turned into food, because of your value to society.

Each person in the group is given a "role". One is an international footballer, one is a film actress, another is a teacher, another is a doctor, one is a joiner and the final role is of a young pop star.

I know, I know, you've already decided who has to go!

The main thing to notice is that you are not being asked to **act** the part of being any one of these people. They do not even have names. You are not being asked to impersonate an actual real person. The point is that you don't act: you **talk**. How well you do in talking depends on how well you can put forward the point of view of that role as valuable to society. It is really not about the people in the lifeboat. It is about the value of the contribution to society of, say, doctors or footballers or any of the others. You can figure out that even after the various points of view have been put, they have to decide who is for the chop. Outside the range of the assignment, the poor souls in the lifeboat would have to do it.

Unless some bright spark thought of fishing instead, of course.

If you were asked to **act** the part of the doctor, or the pop star or whoever, and to make the character come to life as it were, that would require a completely different assignment, and it wouldn't be part of Standard Grade English because there are no GRC in English for assessing acting. You could do it in Standard Grade Drama, though, where there are GRC for it.

Talking to a Group

The task you are most likely to be asked to carry out is to talk to a small group of classmates. You will be told the purpose of the talk, but it is usually up to you to decide on the exact subject.

For such a talk you will typically sit with a small group of no more than four or so other students, and it's best if you can do this without large areas of desks or tables separating you from them. You will choose the language suitable to the occasion: not the kind of language you might use if you were making a speech in Parliament or preaching a sermon. Those would be inappropriate styles for this situation.

The talk will be best if you have a clear plan in your head of what you want to say, but you should try not to deliver a prepared speech. You may use brief notes. The headed sections that follow have much more to say about the details of giving such a talk.

Learning resources

One of the best ways of seeing how giving a talk can be done is to ask your teacher to show you the various videotapes of students talking that have been supplied to your school over many years by the SQA. They show students of all levels of ability talking to small groups and to the whole class. The videos are supported by printed commentaries on the talks and they are also graded using the GRC, and with explanations of the grades awarded. These videos and the other material were provided to help teachers with the job of grading talk: they were also intended to be used as teaching and learning resources for students. So you should expect to see them. You should ask.

In the chapter dealing with the GRC, you will find out how talk is graded, with attention paid to all the talk behaviours that you can use as targets. The information speaks of what should be done, and how well it should be done. You can use these criteria and the videos together to learn what to do and what not to do.

You will also learn about talking to a group, how to do it and what to avoid, because it will form part of the teaching and learning that goes on in the classroom during the course. You will learn by doing it.

Confident talking

You may feel that talking to a group or to a larger audience is a terrible prospect. You may feel that you will dry up, that you'll be too embarrassed, or that you're too shy, or that you just won't ever be able to do it. Like a great many other things you thought were going to be awful or impossible before you had done them (riding a bike? kissing? being alone in the dark?), once you start doing it you will wonder what all the fuss was about.

It may be that you have already had some experience of this kind of work in school, and are therefore pretty confident that you can do it, and that you can get better and better at it. This is certainly true. If there has been what teachers call a "wash-back effect" from Standard Grade in your school then you have a major advantage. The "wash-back effect" is when, because certain things are happening further up the school, they gradually start to happen further down the school too, in anticipation of the time when they become a requirement. So you may have already been doing some talk activities in first or second year as a wash-back effect from Standard Grade Talking. I hope so.

Accent

Another area of talk behaviours that you should be quite clear about from the start is the business of accent. Standard Grade English does not assess accent, there are no criteria for its assessment. This means that your talking can be done in any accent: whatever accent you normally speak in, that is.

The course is not about elocution — that means, literally, "speaking well". You may have heard some people calling it "speaking posh" or "speaking properly". This is a different matter altogether from Talking at Standard Grade. The GRC for Talking have nothing to say about it, and that means that it is not being assessed in Standard Grade English, and therefore can have no effect on the grade you might gain. All of the talking you do will be carried out in the accent you have.

Most accents are derived from the place where you live and were brought up, very few are associated with social class rather than with any regional factors. You may have noticed that though everybody in your class speaks English, they don't necessarily all speak it with the same accent. They don't all sound the same as you. We all know that most foreign speakers of English have an obvious accent, and you can often work out which country they come from. We hear them every day on radio and TV. We are also familiar with the accents of speakers of English from other English-speaking countries, such as American accents (there are many different American accents) and of Australian accents. Surprisingly, we are less familiar with accents used by people who live in different parts of Scotland. If you live in Glasgow, for instance, you might not hear people from Dundee or Aberdeen or Lerwick very often. They have very distinctive accents. So do you.

> **Watching the videos I have recommended will let you hear people of your own age talking in a wide variety of accents from across the country … even if some of them in the most recent videos are affected by the execrable intrusion of the Californian fad, "Like", in almost every sentence. Is this showing my age?**

And spilling over into Register …

Accents are mostly to do with intonation and the pronunciation mainly of vowel sounds in your normal speech. They have nothing to do with correct grammar or syntax, so the language people use can be perfectly grammatical, but be spoken in a wide range of accents, including yours. Most people have local accents, and there is nothing wrong or surprising about that.

You will be expected to speak in an appropriate register, however. Put simply, that means choosing the appropriate kind of language for the situation. Most people know how to do this and generally choose correctly without giving it much thought. It's a very complicated area, and is easily misunderstood if you just read about it. You would know what set of language to use if you were speaking to your best friend about your boy/girlfriend one minute and then had to speak to someone else in a completely different situation (maybe talking to the Head about why you have to be off school tomorrow). You would not change your accent (it is actually quite difficult to do this) but you would want to change the register. You would want to be less familiar, possibly more formal, and you would also think more carefully about getting your grammar and word-choice right. All you would be doing would be using the appropriate register for the occasion.

Provided the register is appropriate and the formal rules of spoken English are applied, the accent of any one part of the country is no better and no worse than any other. So if you speak with the accent of Inverness or Langholm or Pittenweem, your accent is entirely acceptable. There is no need to alter your accent, to try, for example, to speak in the accent called "RP" — Received Pronunciation. It was originally modelled on the accent of a particular social class in the South-East of England and took on some **social** importance when it was adopted by the BBC as the voice of broadcasting when that first started in the 1920s. It still lingers on as what many people think of as proper English, but this is a mistaken idea. The broadcast media now present their programmes in accents from all over the country and indeed from all over the world. It should be said that if you **do** happen to speak RP — it is not really a **local** accent any more — then that is perfectly acceptable too.

The educational world has learned that if you set out to attack and destroy people's speech, you are attacking their very culture too, their roots and family. It's like insulting them and telling them that their way of life is not as good as the one with which you want to replace it.

Illustrated Talk

If you want to give a talk to your class or group and to support what you have to say with what we call visual aids, you must remember that your purpose is to **talk**, not just to point to things and make comments, or to show pictures. Visual aids can include such things as overhead transparencies, slides, video, diagrams, books or real objects. The illustrative material, whatever it is, should support your talk, not replace it. The GRC deal with how you succeed in communicating by talking, so you will only be successful if the aids fit into and back up, clarify or illustrate your talk. They can easily overwhelm it if you're not careful.

I once witnessed a brilliant visual aid totally wasted. The anonymous student showed us a video she had made of her brand-new baby sister being born in hospital (not the details) and it was very good indeed … as video. Unfortunately she didn't have anything very much to add in the way of talking about that special event, so there was nothing there to assess. The video isn't assessed in Standard Grade Talking, so this "talk" added nothing much except experience to that student's assessment.

Another student wanted to bring her pet into the classroom to illustrate what she had to tell us about how she took care of it. I thought I'd best check with the Rector about whether we could have pets in the school for this purpose. He agreed it was fine, but that was because I didn't mention that Lorna's "pet" was her very large horse. Her talk went fine though, with Trigger looking in through the classroom window while she talked about him and showed us her care routine.

Lorna and her horse . . . as it turned out

Demonstrating

This particular kind of talk is really no more than a sub-set of the illustrated talk. The simple difference is that there is more support for you in the structure and sequence of your talk because the very thing you are talking about is there in front of you to remind you at every stage what you intend to say. If you remember all the time while you are showing or demonstrating how something is done that your most important concern is what you have to **say** about it, not what you might choose to **do**, then your work will be talking, not just doing and pointing.

You might for example want to demonstrate how to mend a puncture or make pancakes, for example, and you would have the necessary equipment or ingredients with you. These would be clear markers for the next step of what you wanted to say about the whole process. Provided that you really did keep on providing step-by-step, continuous information on the task, this would be a talk and could be assessed as such. Again, the GRC don't deal with pointing or nodding at objects in silence. The talking is all that matters. For this kind of talk, your real knowledge of the process and the physical presence of the visual aids combine to make sure that your talk is structured in sensible order, that you begin at the beginning and go on confidently until the conclusion. You can see that this could be a very helpful and secure way for you to convey information, one of the main purposes of Talking.

Using Notes

When you are giving an individual talk you are allowed to use notes. You are absolutely not allowed to read aloud from a prepared script or essay. Reading aloud is not one of the skills assessed by the GRC for Standard Grade English, so by doing that you just simply disqualify yourself and your efforts cannot be assessed.

Reading aloud is a valuable but particular skill that is wonderful when it is mastered. You can hear very enjoyable and interesting performances using this skill from such masters of the art as Alastair Cooke in his long-running "Letter from America" or Stephen Fry or Alan Bennett reading stories and tales on tape and radio. Broadcasting gives us fascinating accounts from correspondents in far-away places, and these are delivered with such skill that it's often difficult to know whether they are speaking *ad lib** or are in fact reading from a script. Though this is a skill that we should all strive to achieve, the fact remains that it isn't one of the skills that is assessed in Standard Grade.

Standard Grade English assessment, like all other examination systems, only samples the content of the course that leads to an examination. If we had assessment that tested everything that was in a course — everything you learned — then the course would consist of only what was in the examination. Courses would be very restricted in their scope if they were to contain only what can be assessed. You are not taking the course in order to sit an examination: you are taking the course in order to learn and to build an education.

> This Guide lays a lot of emphasis on what is assessed at the end of the course and rather less on what is contained in the whole learning and teaching in the course. This is because no guide can hope to provide you with a whole course in a book: that is what your teacher does in the classroom.

What can you do about notes? You can certainly have notes, but these must be no more than headings to remind you quickly of your next point. They are best written quite large on something no bigger than a postcard so that you can see your point at a quick glance and carry on talking. If they are lengthy, and written small, you will rely on them too much, burying your head in them and losing eye contact with your audience — perhaps doing more reading than talking. Everybody can tell the difference between reading and talking. Relying too much on notes means that you will do relatively badly in your talk, and if you rely on them completely your talk won't be counted at all.

Memorising

Another related problem is in the use of a memorised "talk". You should realise that talking at Standard Grade is concerned with *ex tempore** talking. This phrase has a similar meaning to *ad lib*: they both mean speaking freely, saying what is in your mind at that moment. Memorising and recounting a "talk" is very close to reading aloud and also to acting or performing and is not talking in the sense that is required at Standard Grade. A memorised performance isn't even going to sound like talking, unless you have reached the level of skill of the best actors, or the broadcasters I have mentioned, and that is very rare. There is nothing more likely to confuse you than trying to remember a memorised script. You must have seen on TV the programmes based on "out-takes", the versions of prepared, pre-recorded broadcasts that were never used because the performers made a complete mess of what they were supposed to say. Most of them go wrong because the performer/actor forgets the exact wording and tries over and over again to get it right. It's exasperating, because you really want the person just to say something very similar and get on with it. But they're stuck with the version they tried to memorise and can't actually think how simple it would be just to move on.

In the kind of talk you are required to give, there isn't a fixed script: you say what you have to say using your head at the time, and from knowing the gist of the message you want to convey to your audience. Memorised "talks" have no place in Standard Grade.

By the end of the course, you will have had the chance to carry out talk activities on many occasions, you will be able to say what you have to say without notes, or maybe with just a few postcard reminders of what you want to include. The thing that makes this possible is that you will know what you are talking about, and you will be fully aware of the purpose of what you are doing. It's easier to talk about something you know inside out than to talk convincingly about something you have just begun to pick up from "research". Talking about something within your own experience is always going to be better supported (by your unique knowledge, your real interest, your actual memory of events) than trying to deliver a talk on a subject where you are no better informed than your audience. Personal experience topics are always going to be easier to handle than conveying information, or expounding an argument. When you think about it, if you are talking about your own experience or knowledge, you are the expert and probably know more about it than anyone in the room, including your teacher. That must be a bonus. Much depends on your own particular ability to organise what you know and how you can convey it so that you have an effect on your audience.

Discussion

A prominent feature of your course will be the discussions you will carry out with your group. Most discussions will take place on a topic and for a purpose clearly set out by your teacher. This is different to an individual talk, where often the topic and the purpose can be decided by you yourself.

All the members of a group discussion are required to take part and to contribute by talking. You must not sit quietly with your lips zipped. You must talk, but not just for the sake of talking. Discussion is not a competition to see who does the most talking and prevents the others from talking. Anybody who did that would get a very low grade for discussion because they would actually have ruined the discussion and failed to achieve the purpose.

Working together

Discussion is a collaborative project where those taking part are trying to achieve a common goal. They are trying to reach a consensus or agreement, even if that agreement is no more than agreeing to disagree. Most discussions will have an issue in the topic, that is, the topic contains the possibility of various ways of looking at a question and coming up with differing views and opinions based on arguments for or against. Other discussion topics will be more open and the purpose will be to explore the knowledge and views of the participants and consider how these might be brought together, or reconciled. Essentially, discussion is meant to be amicable and civilised.

How these purposes are achieved is by the individuals' exchange of views, information, opinions, feelings and attitudes on a topic. They will support the views of other people by adding ideas and evidence; they will challenge opinions and facts presented by others; they will take turns in speaking either when asked, or when the moment is opportune, even if that means politely interrupting another person; they will try to make sure that everybody is encouraged to speak and advance the discussion in some way. They will also keep to the point of the discussion and remind others to do the same. Occasionally they might need to recap the progress of the discussion, or even to take on the role of organising the discussion so that it doesn't stray from the point and purpose. This last point would apply when no one has been formally designated as the chairperson for the discussion. There are brownie points to be won for informally taking on this role and subtly directing the discussion along the lines it is supposed to take according to the purpose and topic.

Talk behaviours

There are several other points that will help you in your performance in every discussion. You should always be listening and must always be seen to be listening. Always pay close attention to the person speaking and note whatever points you may want to contribute immediately in response to that person's view.

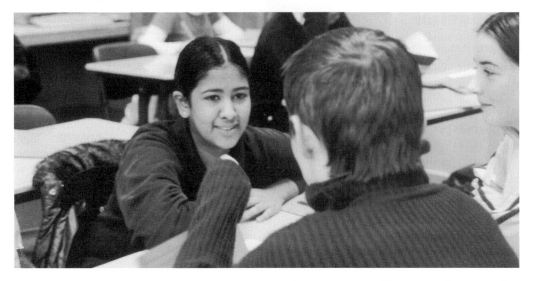

Keep good eye contact

When you are speaking, make sure that you keep good eye contact with the others, and do not address your remarks only to the chair or to any one other person. Remember, you are trying to persuade all of the others.

Use body language, especially your hands and posture, to strengthen what you have to say and to indicate how you are responding to others. For example, using open hands when you're making a point makes it not only more expressive, but also much more convincing and acceptable to your listeners. As a negative example, don't sit with you arms folded when someone else is speaking: that sends a clear signal to them that you are not interested, bored, or not in agreement or convinced.

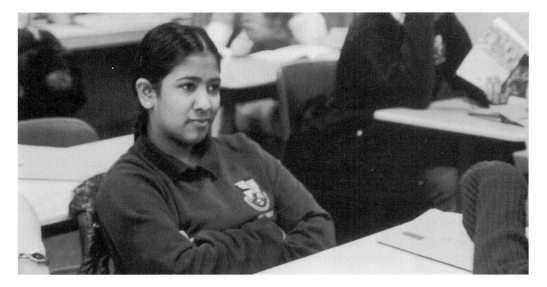

I hear what you're saying. It's really interesting. Not.

Our body language is something that we do naturally, without thinking, but it reflects our feelings and thoughts, whether we are aware of it or not. Your listeners get the message without necessarily thinking about it either; it gets through without words. For this reason, you should always try to be aware of your body language when you are communicating with other people.

An Exercise

The second paragraph under the heading 'Working together' (beginning, "How these purposes…") has been written in a fairly impersonal style, using "they" and the passive voice. Go back through it and carry out a transformational exercise — changing it into the active and second person singular, so the first sentence becomes: "You need to make discussion a collaborative project, where you're trying to achieve a common goal". And so on. Doing this will reinforce the message to you. The message is that YOU are the person who has to do all these things in discussion.

Chairing a Discussion

Some discussions will have a "chair" or chairperson. This person (and it may be you) has certain additional duties in any discussion. If you are chairing the discussion you will have to:

◆ introduce the topic
◆ state the purpose of the discussion
◆ start off the discussion by stating a view
◆ invite comment on that view
◆ share out the time among participants
◆ control over-loquacious (too-talkative) members
◆ encourage the reticent to speak
◆ regularly confirm the state of the discussion's progress
◆ move the discussion along in the relevant direction
◆ recap arguments and positions
◆ summarise
◆ conclude the discussion fairly.

It is your job to give everyone a chance to speak and to encourage them by asking them what they think. Though each person is responsible for their own performance, some people will do much better when they are given a relaxed and welcoming opportunity to enter the flow.

Most importantly, the chair is not just a referee or umpire or observer. He or she must take as much a part in the discussion as anyone else, perhaps even a little bit more, by doing not only all the things listed above, but by contributing views, support, challenges and so on in the same way as all the others in the discussion.

If this idea strikes you as a great way of having more power over the others, forget it. Your teacher will make sure that everybody gets a turn at being the chair, so any injustices you commit could backfire on you in a later discussion.

Assessment

There is assessment of both Individual Talk and Discussion in roughly equal balance. Near the end of the course, your grades for the two kinds of Talking are aggregated using the record of assessment that your teacher has been keeping and a single grade for Talking is sent in to the SQA at the same time as the Folio.

You will see and know that assessment of Talking is taking place in the classroom. This will be most obvious when there are set piece individual talks and when you are taking part in discussions in the class or in your groups. This might be a little less obvious to you, but your teacher will be assessing the performance of individual students in the discussion. You won't know whether it's you or one of your classmates at any particular discussion, but this is a good reminder that you should be trying to do your best in every discussion. This could be the one that matters most. Your teacher won't sit there with clipboard and the GRC for Talking, and won't take part in the discussion either. He or she will be quite discreet but will be watching the talk behaviour and listening carefully to all that is being said.

Moderation

Your teacher's assessments will be moderated by the SQA. Every teacher taking a Standard Grade class in S4 will be trained and tested by the SQA. This process is used to make as sure as can be that the grades from every teacher in your school and in every other school will be using the same standard — the GRC — and will be interpreting these criteria in the same way. That's very important. To make even more sure that things are transparent and fair in every possible way, a sample of all schools across the country is visited by moderators from the SQA after the grades are submitted. This moderation is not as easy to carry out as it would be if the work of students was actually written material, instead of being oral evidence that vanishes as soon as the talking is over. It is as secure a system as can be devised, however, and you should not think that other schools produce better grades overall than your school does.

The arrangements made by the SQA are applied to any element where there is internal assessment, so your grade should be the same in value as the work of any comparable student in any other school in the country. Your certificate will have the same value no matter where you attend school.

Audio-visual help for you

The training material used by the SQA is in the form of videotapes, with students from all over the country carrying out typical assignments in Talking. These are both in Individual Talk and in Discussion. The printed material that comes with these videotapes gives the grades that were awarded and explains exactly how this grade was arrived at using the GRC. There is also general commentary on the students' performances and on the use of the particular kind of Talking activities shown on the tapes.

Your teacher will have access to this material so you should ask your teacher to let you view the videos and read the commentaries on the performances, because this will help you to learn. It supports what your teacher is doing in teaching Talking and setting assignments.

CHAPTER SEVEN

PORPOISES AND PURPOSES

At the start of Standard Grade English long ago, there was a lot of jokey talk about PORPOISES and their central importance. Why were these apparently fun-loving aquatic animals so important? Well, they weren't. It was their close relations, the PURPOSES that really mattered. Examiners are easily amused by puns or paronomasia* or malapropisms*, evidently.

Purposes really are fundamental to Standard Grade English. I did not discuss them in detail in the early information chapter where I listed the features. That was because I wanted to stress their importance to you in most of the course and assessment system.

The purposes of RWTL

RWTL isn't a complex codified mystery: it's just an unpronounceable acronym* for Reading, Writing, Talking and Listening — the four elements.

Everything you do in your coursework and again in the examinations will have a purpose and, while you are doing any piece of work in class or exams, you have to know what its purpose is. Equally, while your work is being assessed, the assessors (your teacher, the SQA examiners, the markers, sometimes your classmates and sometimes you yourself) can only do that job properly if they know what the purpose of your work was. They must be able to see whether and how well you have achieved the thing you set out to do — to fulfil the purpose.

The Chocolate Fireguard

The four modes of language — Reading, Writing, Talking and Listening — each have a number of purposes.

These purposes are the reason why language activities are carried out. What and **for what purpose** we are trying to produce when we read, write, talk and listen.

> Sometimes you have to be cruel to be kind, or exaggerate to make a point more obviously. Winston Churchill's famous response to complaints that his ending a sentence with a preposition was poor style and ungrammatical was both brief and witty: "This is the sort of English up with which I will not put", thus showing what happens when you stick too closely to the rules on every occasion, suitable or not.

Every piece of communication in language is intended to achieve a result. We have to know before we start what result we intend. Otherwise the communication doesn't work properly. It's vague, or irrelevant, or even meaningless, if there is no real purpose.

To try to make this clearer, look at this example taken from the physical world rather than from the world of language. Everyday objects that we use in our daily lives always have a purpose or intended function. We design and make them for our use. Another way of putting it is to say that we expect them to do what we made them for and why we designed them that way. They have a function. That function can be to serve as tools or as entertainment or as decoration, and so on. Everybody knows this and we judge how well they function by using them, and by knowing what they were supposed to do for us.

If the true purpose of an object such as a chair or table, or a compass or pair of trainers isn't made clear to the designer/maker/artist/craftsperson then it probably won't fulfil its purpose. So if you need a fireguard its purpose must be clear in the mind of the person designing it and the person making it. If the maker, following only the design but not informed of its purpose, believes that it is an ornamental item and decides to make it out of milk chocolate, then it will not meet the intended purpose of a fireguard. It looks like a fireguard, but it doesn't fulfil the purpose of a fireguard, since one of the functions is to contain the heat of the fire and not be seriously affected by it, to withstand the heat. Different designs of fireguard do this more or less effectively: chocolate ones don't. Hence we currently have the saying, "About as useful as a chocolate fireguard".

There was a breakdown between the purpose and the product. If there is no clear purpose for a language communication, the same result occurs.

Look at this list:

- Each assignment is based on
- The units are based on
- The courses are constructed around
- The examinations are set on
- The Folio specification depends completely on
- The assessment system rests on
- The GRC are founded on

PURPOSES

That should give you a fair idea of the important place the purposes of the language modes have in Standard Grade English. You need to know more about purposes for that reason. It is crucial for you to know how they fit into the whole scheme of things, and how they affect you directly at several important stages in your course and exams.

1   The first of these points isn't really a stage, but is present all the time in all the work you do in class. The purpose of what you are assigned to produce in your work across the four elements has to be built in at the start of each piece and has to be understood by both you and your teacher. Each task will be introduced by making clear its purpose, and clarified further by having a description of the detailed task. This arrangement will be the same whether your assignment is in Reading or Writing or Talking.

2   The second stage is when you come to assemble and submit your Folio. Each piece has to fit within one of the purposes of Reading or Writing. If your class work has been organised with clear purposes, then this requirement will already have been taken care of. All that is required is the labelling that describes the task, and the ticking of the appropriate boxes in the Folio Flyleaf to indicate the particular purpose of the piece.

3   The third place where you must understand the purpose of a task is in the exams. This is especially true in Writing, where the possible assignment choices cover the range of the purposes of Writing. The essay choices allow you to write for a selection of different purposes. This will always be made clear in the question and you will write in response to that purpose of your choice.

In the Reading exam the questions are also based on different purposes, but less obviously. You can work out what these are by reading the keywords carefully. You will find questions asking for information, questions on the writer's craft, and so on. These connect with the purposes of Reading.

Indeed, in the marking keys that the assessors use, these purposes are identified by code letters with each question, so that they can gauge whether your answer meets the purpose. At Higher English in Close Reading, the actual questions on the students' question paper have these code letters to make sure that students know what kind of question is intended. Unfortunately, these helpful clues don't figure on Standard Grade exam papers … yet.

Purposes and tasks

All your work is going to be better if you have the answers to key questions about the task such as, "Why?", and "For what or whom?", and "How?". That applies to any single piece of work you may face in English, although it appears most obviously in Writing. If your teacher asks you simply to 'Write a letter' it is impossible to fulfil the purpose if that is all you know about the task. If your teacher meant you to write a letter to a friend in Canada telling her about what you had been doing (but didn't tell you that) and you wrote a letter to the local paper arguing for better facilities for young people then quite a lot has gone wrong here. The purpose of one letter is very different from the purpose of the other. When it came to assessing your work you and your teacher would be at cross purposes, and your writing would be regarded as missing the purpose. That situation would be absurd. You must both know the real purpose in detail. Only then can the piece of writing be assessed fairly against the criteria.

In case you are thinking that the only reason you ever do work in school is so that someone can mark it, it should be said that (almost) everything we do in school or outside has a purpose. If we know what we are doing and what we are doing it for, and what we hope to achieve by doing it, the chances are that it will be better, more effective than otherwise.

In short, both you and your teacher should know exactly what you are being asked to do so that, amongst other things, when it is finished it can be properly assessed for what it is. As a matter of fact, unless you both know the purpose and the task, you won't even know whether it is finished or not. Nor will your teacher be able to teach you what you need to know next about it.

Each of the four modes of language has a set of purposes; they set out what we hope to achieve in studying the language in any mode. You should know what they are, and it's a good idea with all your work (not just your written work) to look at what you have been asked to do, or have chosen to do — the task — and try to match it against one of the purposes for the mode you're working in. You'll find that some pieces of work involve more than one purpose for any particular task. If you look at the list below you should see that there is a strong continuing linkage in what you do. The list is a kind of Lego structure of Standard Grade English to show how it starts with deciding the purposes of language communication and leads on through the whole system.

> **Purposes for each language mode decided**
>
> GRC for each mode based on purposes
>
> Course design with units with purposes
>
> Units designed with activities related to purposes
>
> Tasks with detailed purposes constructed
>
> GRC used in assessing work against purposes
>
> Folio specification addressing set purposes
>
> Examinations set with tasks and purposes
>
> GRC used in assessing work against given purposes

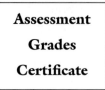

Assessment

Grades

Certificate

The highlighted **purposes** in the box are connected with everything else. The exact order of the items in the list changes depending on which part of the system you are starting from, but always the **purposes** and the GRC have important and strong connections with all the other parts.

The four modes each have clear main purposes. The two "expressive" modes, Writing and Talking, have similar purposes to each other. The two "receptive" modes, Reading and Listening, have similar purposes to each other.

For that reason, I have run the purposes together, not to save space and avoid repetition, but to emphasise the connections.

The main purposes of the expressive modes, Writing and Talking.

We write and talk to:

i) convey information

ii) deploy* ideas, expound*, argue and evaluate*

iii) describe personal experience, express feelings and reactions

iv) employ specific literary forms (for example, short story, letter or poem) (in Writing); create particular effects (in Talking).

The main purposes of the receptive modes, Reading and Listening.

We read and listen to:

i) gain overall impression/gist of a text (R)
    gain overall impression/gist of a message (L)

ii) obtain particular information from a text/message

iii) grasp idea or feelings implied in a text/message

iv) evaluate the attitudes, assumptions and arguments expressed

v) appreciate the writer's craft (R)
    appreciate the techniques used (L)

vi) enjoy and obtain enrichment from a text/message.

Though there are words here that might not be familiar to you, you can look them up in the Glossary at the end of the Guide, or you can ask about them. Even without fully knowing these words, you can understand what the purposes are doing here.

> **Purposes set down our basic reasons for doing anything in the study and use of English.**

Whenever you are reading, writing, talking or listening, and whether it's in the teaching or the learning, one or more of these purposes is there. They are the reason that you are doing English. They help your teachers to decide what and how to teach you; the activities your teacher asks you to carry out in the course are designed to help you meet these purposes, and the assessment system is designed to find out whether you can do this or whether you need more teaching and learning. The GRC help to measure how well you can do them both during and at the end of the course.

Note that the GRC are based on these purposes. You can actually follow step by step through the various statements of each set of GRC in the next chapter and connect each one directly with the purpose statements listed previously. Every task you undertake should fit with one of these purposes, and sometimes with more than one. So check.

The minor exception here is in the Listening purposes. Since Listening is not now being assessed separately the Listening purposes appear in the GRC for Talking under Discussion. Listening is still very important, however. You can't do well in Discussion without listening to the others in the group. It is also, of course, one of the main sources of learning. Much of what you learn comes through talk, and that is why you have to listen to learn.

If you understand the place and the importance of the purposes in the whole system of Standard Grade English, you will be much more likely to produce a better performance all round. Each time your teacher sets you a task from one of the units you have been dealing with, it will be clearer to you what you are expected to do. This will help you to stick clearly to the purpose of what you are doing. It will also make for sensible assessment of your work. That matters a great deal in the assessment of your work, not only in your coursework, but in your Folio and in your final exams.

CHAPTER EIGHT

THE GRADE RELATED CRITERIA (GRC)

You can treat this chapter as a straight read, but you will use the actual GRC grids mainly **for reference** when you need them to consider your work and what grade it might achieve.

We come at last to the Grade Related Criteria in detail, though they have been mentioned often. I say "they" and "them" because "criteria" is a plural: the singular is "criterion"; one criterion, two criteria. The word means the standard upon which a judgement or assessment may be based, a point of reference for valuing something. It would probably be best for you to think of them as the descriptions against which your performance is measured. That is one of the fundamental things about Standard Grade. Your work is not compared with the work of other students in your class or anywhere else for that matter; only against the GRC.

That is why they are central to Standard Grade English. Almost everything else depends on them.

Criterion is a very popular name for pubs and hotels. If you have seen such a place and wondered about the name, now you know. By choosing that name the owners are saying that this is the pub or hotel against which all others are measured: it sets the standard.

GRC are not some kind of deadly bacteria or virus, though the name makes them sound as if they could be. They are just descriptions of what a student can/should be able to do in the four language modes. If you think of them like this you don't have to bother with the awkward jargon name. Just call them the GRC.

GRC is one term that can't be avoided.

For Standard Grade they are essential. They are the public statement of the standards required for each of the grades of award possible for each of the four elements of English. They are used by your teachers and by the SQA to assess your work and arrive at the grade you have achieved. They are also meant for all the "users" of your certificate — employers, parents, other schools, colleges, universities and so on. They are also important for you since both you and your teacher can use them as the targets for you to aim for, both during and at the end of the course.

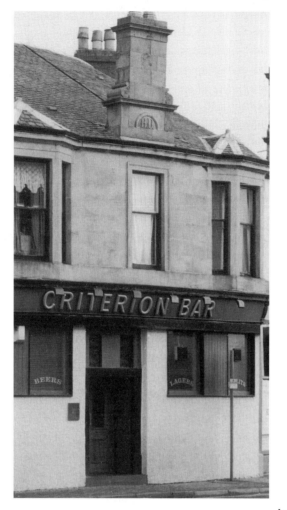

It sets the standard

The Summary GRC

The GRC come in two forms: the Summary GRC and the Extended GRC.

The Summary GRC are brief and describe in general the performance (what a student has produced) required for each of the possible levels of award. When you read them you can see exactly what your work has to be like to gain a grade at Foundation, General or Credit Level. You will find this most easily by looking at the table of Summary GRC for each of the elements, Writing, Talking and Reading. They give you the general idea.

SUMMARY GRC

Writing

Credit Level (grades 2, 1)
In finished work the candidate communicated meaning clearly at a first reading. Formal errors were insignificant and sentence construction was accurate. There was some distinction in ideas and language. The work demonstrated a detailed attention to the requirements of the task. Where appropriate, the candidate sustained the quality of the writing at some length.

General Level (grades 4, 3)
In finished work the candidate communicated meaning at a first reading. There were some formal lapses but sentence construction was mostly accurate. Ideas and language were on the whole adequate and the work demonstrated a reasonable attention to the requirements of the task. The candidate was able to write at a length appropriate to the task.

Foundation Level (grades 6, 5)
In finished work the candidate managed to communicate meaning largely at a first reading despite formal errors and weaknesses. The writing was limited in ideas and language, but showed a few signs of awareness of the requirements of the task. Where appropriate, the candidate was able to sustain a length of at least 100 words.

Talking

Credit Level (grades 2, 1)
In discussion and individual talk the candidate conveyed substantial and relevant ideas readily; expression was fluent. The candidate was consistently aware of the purpose and situation of the talking. In discussion close account was taken of others. In individual talk language was varied and accurate and there was little or no prompting.

General Level (grades 4, 3)
In discussion and individual talk the candidate conveyed relevant ideas adequately; expression showed some traces of variety. On the whole, the candidate was aware of the purpose and situation of the talking. In discussion account taken of others was reasonably regular. In individual talk language was generally accurate; some support was needed through prompting and questioning.

Foundation Level (grades 6, 5)
In discussion and individual talk the candidate managed to convey a few simple ideas; weaknesses in expression did not prevent communication. There were a few signs of awareness of the purpose and situation of the talking. In discussion account taken of others was intermittent. In individual talk the candidate used a

limited range of language and needed substantial support through prompting and questioning.

Reading

Credit Level (grades 2, 1)

The candidate demonstrated in writing a good understanding of whole works and extracted passages. These passages went beyond what was readily understandable or related to personal interests: they sometimes featured unfamiliar, abstract ideas and complexity of structure and tone. Grasp of ideas was firm and there was sound appreciation of the author's purpose and technique. The candidate made a perceptive and developed statement of personal response to what had been read.

General Level (grades 4, 3)

The candidate demonstrated in writing a fair understanding of whole works and extracted passages. These passages were on the whole readily understandable, were mainly related to personal interests and dealt with relationships or ideas in a straightforward way. Grasp of ideas was on the whole adequate and there was appreciation of some obvious aspects of the author's purpose and technique. The candidate made a reasonably developed statement of personal response to what had been read.

Foundation Level (grades 6, 5)

The candidate demonstrated in writing some evidence of understanding whole works and extracted passages. These passages were brief and readily understandable, were related to personal interests and dealt with relationships or ideas in a straightforward way. Grasp of ideas and appreciation of the author's purpose and technique were rudimentary. The candidate showed traces of a personal response to what had been read.

These are descriptions for each of the three Levels and are intended to be used by the general public to help them understand what your award broadly means. The "candidate" who is mentioned frequently, by the way, is YOU. In school or college you are a pupil or a student: in the examinations, you become a candidate.

The Summary GRC are not hard to understand because they are written straightforwardly in plain English. They are meant to be read and easily understood by you, by the users of certificates and by the general public. They are meant to explain simply what the grades on your certificate mean. These are not the GRC used by your teachers and by the SQA assessors for assessing your work. For that, the Extended GRC are used.

The Extended GRC

When we come to the Extended GRC, the more detailed versions intended to be used in assessment, things become more complicated.

First of all, there is the more specialised language, or jargon. Jargon is, however, quite appropriate. After all, it is merely a form of shorthand. Every job or profession has its own jargon. That is unobjectionable, for it is no more than using technical terms whose meaning is well-known to the professionals reading it. These GRC are meant to be used by teachers and by the SQA for assessment, and that is their job.

The whole purpose of the Guide is to let you understand as much as possible about Standard Grade. The more you know about what you are expected to do (the GRC) the better you will be able to do it. The GRC are as hard to grasp as some other jargon. Take this example of jargon from the world of sociology:

"the cognitive-affective state characterised by intrusive and obsessive fantasising concerning reciprocity of amorant feelings by the object of the amorance."

This is just another (jargon) way of describing what is all you need — according to the Beatles — and can be said in one word:

LOVE

which was what the sociologist who used the jargon was trying to define. No doubt there's a place for this language, and other sociologists probably knew what she was talking about. If graffiti suddenly appeared on the wall at the back of the bike shed at school saying,

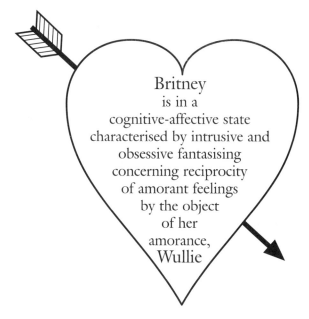

Britney
is in a
cognitive-affective state
characterised by intrusive and
obsessive fantasising
concerning reciprocity
of amorant feelings
by the object
of her
amorance,
Wullie

and if all that the writer had meant was,

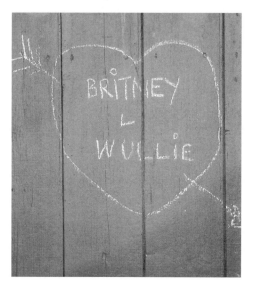

people would be a bit surprised. They'd also be puzzled. Compared with that kind of jargon, the GRC won't look so bad, you'll see.

If we take the most straightforward set of GRC first, things will become clearer more quickly.

The GRC for Writing

Keep your finger in the page with the Writing GRC on (page 127) as you read on here. This will make it easier to find and understand the various points referred to as we go along.

These GRC for Writing are not too obscured by jargon, though you might have to look up some of the words in the Glossary.

The Task

Quite a lot of what is being said in the GRC makes more complete sense if you read them together with the advice being given in the Folio and Examination chapters earlier in the Guide. The "task" mentioned will be given to you by your teacher if the writing is coursework and by the SQA examiners if it's in the Writing exam. The same GRC are used to assess these, as I've already said. Wherever the task comes from, it will make clear what you are to do, what is expected, and it will be related to a purpose of Writing. In other words, whatever you are asked to do, it will have been designed to give you the opportunity to produce a piece of writing that can be assessed/measured against one or more of the purposes of Writing and that means that the GRC will be used to do the job of assessing.

It's important for you to know exactly what the task is, exactly what is required. Whether you have managed to do what was required and how well you have managed are the main things used to determine the grade — how close you have come to fulfilling the demands of the GRC in making your work match the purpose. Any task you are given will thus be chosen to allow you to carry out the task in line with the particular purpose or purposes, and the parts of the GRC which connect with that purpose will be used to assess your work.

> If you understand the GRC and use them as targets for your writing, they
> will help you to make the whole package (task, purpose and GRC)
> complete. This will clearly improve your chances. Put simply, you'll know
> what you are doing.

The Writing GRC are laid out in much the same way as all the other GRC.

At the top of the grid, there is a broad description for pieces of work at each of the levels, Foundation, General and Credit. At the lowest part of the grid you can see the "Differentiating Factors". These provide a closer focus to show the differences between the two Grades for each level, Grades 2 and 1 at Credit Level; Grades 4 and 3 at General Level; Grades 6 and 5 at Foundation Level.

At the left-hand side of the grid you can see the statement that tells you how the GRC are used in assessment: only those that apply to the task are used for any one piece of writing.

In the centre of the grid you'll notice another statement: a combination of these qualities may be called for by any one writing task, a reminder that a task might cover more than one purpose.

WRITING GRC

	CREDIT	GENERAL	FOUNDATION
	The work displays some distinction in ideas, construction and language. This is shown by a detailed attention to the purposes of the writing task; by qualities such as knowledge, insight, imagination; and by development that is sustained. Vocabulary, paragraphing and sentence construction are accurate and varied.	The work shows a general awareness of the purposes of the writing task. It has a number of appropriate ideas and evidence of structure. Vocabulary is on the whole accurate, but lacks variety.	The work shows a few signs of appropriateness and commitment to the purposes of the writing task.
AS THE TASK REQUIRES, THE CANDIDATE CAN	convey information, selecting and highlighting what is most significant;	convey information in some kind of sequence;	convey simple information;
	marshal ideas and evidence in support of an argument; these ideas have depth and some complexity; he/she is capable of objectivity, generalisation and evaluation;	order and present ideas and opinions with an attempt at reasoning;	present ideas and opinions in concrete personal terms;
	give a succinct account of a personal experience; the writing has insight and self-awareness;	give a reasonably clear account of a personal experience with some sense of involvement;	convey the gist of a personal experience;
	express personal feelings and reactions sensitively;	express personal feelings and reactions with some attempt to go beyond bald statement;	make a bald statement of personal feelings or reactions;
	display some skill in using the conventions of a chosen literary form, and in manipulating language to achieve particular effects.	use some of the more obvious conventions of a chosen literary form, and occasionally use language to achieve particular effects.	display a rudimentary awareness of the more obvious conventions of a chosen literary form, and occasionally attempt to use language to achieve particular effects.

A combination of these qualities may be called for by any one writing task.

| INTELLIGIBILITY AND CORRECTNESS | Writing which the candidate submits as finished work communicates meaning clearly at a first reading. Sentence construction is accurate and formal errors will not be significant. | Writing which the candidate submits as finished work communicates meaning at first reading. There are some lapses in punctuation, spelling and sentence construction. | Writing which the candidate submits as finished work communicates meaning largely at first reading; however, some further reading is necessary because of obtrusive formal errors and/or structural weaknesses, including inaccurate sentence construction and poor vocabulary. |

	GRADE 1	GRADE 2	GRADE 3	GRADE 4	GRADE 5	GRADE 6
LENGTH	When it is appropriate to do so, the candidate can sustain the quality of writing at some length. Pieces of extended writing submitted in the folio of coursework should not normally exceed 800 words in length. The overriding consideration is, however, that the length should be appropriate to the purposes of the writing task.		Length is appropriate to the purposes of the writing task.		100 words is to be taken as a rough guide to the minimum length expected for each finished piece of work, but the overriding consideration should be that the length is appropriate to the purposes of the writing task.	
DIFFERENTIATING FACTORS	The finished communication is not only clear; it is also stylish. Attention to purpose is not only detailed; it is also sensitive. Writing shows overall distinction in ideas, construction and language. Vocabulary is apt and extensive, and paragraphing and sentence construction are skilful. In these respects performance transcends the level of accuracy and variety acceptable at grade 2.	Evidence of one or more of the qualities of distinction in ideas, construction or language is present but these qualities are less well sustained and/or combined than at grade 1. In the main writing is substantial, accurate and relevant, but it lacks the insight, economy and style which characterises achievement at grade 1.	Writing is characterised by overall adequacy of communication. It conveys its meaning clearly and sentence construction and paragraphing are on the whole accurate. There is a reasonably sustained attention to purpose, and structure shows some coherence. Where appropriate there is a measure of generalisation and objectivity in reasoning.	Writing approaches the qualities of adequacy required for grade 3 but is clearly seen to be impaired in one of the following ways: there are significant inaccuracies in sentence construction, or the work is thin in appropriate ideas, or the work is weak in structure.	Writing rises a little above basic intelligibility and rudimentary attention to purpose. Formal errors and weaknesses are obtrusive but not as numerous as at grade 6. Attention to the purposes of the writing task is weak but the quality of the writer's ideas is perceptibly stronger than at grade 6.	Writing contains many formal errors and structural weaknesses but they do not overall have the effect of baffling the reader. The conveying of simple information is marked by obscurities and extraneous detail, and the presentation of ideas, opinions and personal experience is somewhat rambling and disjointed.

The middle section of the grid covers two other areas of your work. The first is the general description of the control of language shown by the candidate. That is you, of course. It is concerned with how well you can write in grammatically correct sentences, with a command of punctuation and spelling. The second section gives details of the required length of pieces of work for the different levels.

The final section, at the bottom of the grid, sets out the differences between the grades, already mentioned.

There is not much jargon here, but you might like to look up some words in the Glossary, such as:

Distinction	Conventions	Economy
Insight	Bald	Sustained
Marshal	Gist	Coherence
Objectivity	Rudimentary	Intelligibility
Evaluation	Obtrusive	Extraneous
Succinct	Transcends	Rambling

If you already know these words, then that's good. If not, look them up in the Glossary.

I said at the beginning of this chapter that the GRC for Writing are more straightforward and would make the others easier to follow. I hope you agree so far. You might like to attempt some self-assessment. You should be able to take one of your own pieces of writing and try assessing it against the Writing GRC. This will help you to see how the GRC can be used as targets. If you can assess your work as it is now, you can tick off those areas where it matches the GRC and at the same time note where it doesn't. Any single piece of work might meet the GRC at one level for some qualities, and match the GRC for some other qualities at a different level. Your ticks in the different columns will show a pattern, however, and you can use this pattern to show you where improvements could be made. Your teacher will be able to identify these areas with you and to reinforce the improvements needed.

You should also know that where a piece of writing does not match the descriptions completely at any one Level, it is given the Grade where it most consistently matches the description. So, if most of the ticks are in the General Level and a few in the Credit Level, it will be assessed as General Level, Grade 3.

The one remaining problem with the GRC is that they use words to describe performance, and everyone who reads the description thinks that he or she knows exactly what is meant. That is until two people are faced with the same piece of work and each reckons that it exactly matches one description — but they disagree about which particular level description it fits. The words of the GRC are capable of different interpretations. To resolve this problem, we need examples of work which we can say are clear examples of the descriptions in the GRC. The SQA has provided examples of this kind and your teacher probably still has them. To help further with this problem, I have supplied real examples of students' writing in the illustration of the Folio in the Folio chapter earlier on. These pieces have been graded as they would be by the SQA and therefore give a good idea of the standard of work that is being described in each section of the GRC grid. You can match yours against them.

It should have become clear now that there is an unbroken connection in Standard Grade English between the GRC and the teaching and learning.

GRC for Talking

So far, not everything has been said about the place of Talking at Standard Grade. Its place in the course is very important. In the assessment system as a whole it is worth one-third of the total value of your work. In the course, talking comes into everything you do, not just in talk activities but in all the preparation work you do for reading and especially writing.

There are two sets of GRC for Talking. The first covers Discussion and the second set covers Individual Talk. These don't need to be explained at any great length since they are plainly enough stated. But why do we need two sets of GRC? Don't think of these activities as different from each other simply because of the number of people involved. That would be quite a natural way of thinking of the difference, but it is only partly right (individual talk means only one individual person talking; discussion means many people talking).

It will be more helpful to you in understanding if you follow this line of thinking.

Talking is thought of as a "continuum of interaction". Not a familiar phrase, and more jargon, but it contains an idea that I'm sure you already know. Think of the continuum as a line, a scale of measurement where the gradations (the lines between one area and the next) are unmarked or vague: the sections merge into one another at the edges. At one end of this scale there is 'pure' listening: at the other end there is 'pure' talking. The scale measures 'interaction' — the amount of exchange of talking and listening that goes on between those taking part in the talk activity. This diagram will help you to visualise the idea.

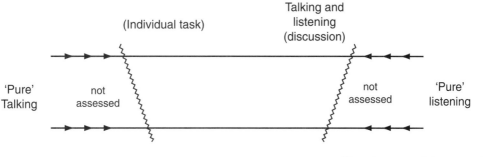

Continuum of interaction

You're probably wondering why we're referring to listening in this section of talking. Just a reminder, then, that discussion has to involve listening. You can't have discussion unless those taking part listen to others and then talk because of what they have listened to. So the continuum is like a line and the extremes of the line (the very end points) aren't used to measure anything we do at Standard Grade. It's only the central part of the line that is used to measure or assess. This central part includes talking and listening to some degree or another. Somewhere about the middle of the central part of the line there is the mixture of talking and listening that makes up discussion. When you are in a discussion, you have to listen to what others say, and behave in such a way that you take full account of their contribution. Without this, you are not doing what we call discussion. Ignoring others' contribution makes your contribution more like individual talk, and therefore fails as discussion when we apply the GRC for Discussion.

Towards the left-hand edge of this central part of the line is the area that makes up individual talking. In this area there is far less listening than there is for discussion, but still enough to recognise that even in individual talk there is a need on the part of the individual talker to recognise the needs of the audience — and that involves a form of 'listening'. While you give your individual talk, you 'listen' to how it is being received by your audience, and take account of that in what you say next. Though your audience doesn't talk, they send you messages that you can 'hear'. This is a part of individual talking that is assessed by the GRC for Individual Talk.

So, somewhere slightly to the left of the middle area of the continuum that you're probably fed up hearing about (some re-drafting needed, perhaps?) is the line that divides the two forms of talking. We cannot assess Individual Talking in a discussion, and we cannot assess Discussion in an individual talk: that is why we have to have two completely separate sets of GRC for these two forms of talking. In plain English, if you gave an individual talk in the middle of a discussion, you would ruin the discussion for yourself and others; if you became involved in discussion during your individual talk you would ruin your own chances of doing at all well in the individual talk assessment.

They are separate activities, so don't believe anyone who tells you that, for instance, you could be assessed for an individual talk you gave during a discussion.

To the far right of the continuum is an area that covers listening alone, as if it were separated completely from the talking itself. This is an area that is no longer assessed separately in Standard Grade English, so for the time being we can forget about it altogether.

In the GRC, the distinction made above is assumed to be a clear one, so that once it has been agreed what is going on, either Discussion or Individual Talk, the appropriate GRC are used for the assessing. The separate sets cannot be used interchangeably. They can each apply only to the one activity for which they are designed. The task that has been set is what decides which GRC are to be used in assessing your performance. A discussion task will always be quite clearly different and separate from a task in individual talking. Incidentally, even if the individual talk is followed by questions from the audience to which the speaker responds, this part is not assessed at Standard Grade. You will find no reference to such an activity in the GRC. The only thing that you will find there in connection with questioning of this kind is an indication that if the speaker has to be helped along by prompting or questioning, then this is something that the assessor would take into account in assessing the talk. It would actually affect the grade achieved — by lowering it. There is no way in which it could improve the grade. What the GRC say is what is assessed, and how.

When you look at the GRC for Talking you can see that what you are actually expected to do is much the same at all three Levels, but that the quality of performance, i.e., how well you actually do it, is different. The main thing to notice in the GRC for Discussion is that there are special requirements for how you deal with other people in the discussion. It is the only activity in the course where your performance — what you do in the discussion — and therefore also your grade, can be affected by what other people do or fail to do.

The reason for this is that discussion is a co-operative task and activity. Look back to the chapter on Talking for more details on this. Think of any other co-operative or team activity — playing football or dancing, for instance, or being a member of a relay team or an acrobatic troupe in a circus or stage show. These activities all depend on you working with others and on others working with you. Whether an individual performance is good or not is not the question. If the members of the team do not co-operate with each other, then the whole event can end in disaster. Your part in a discussion cannot be as good as it might have been if the others do not understand

TALKING (Individual Talk) GRC

	CREDIT	GENERAL	FOUNDATION
CONTENT	Expresses ideas of quality, relevance and interest. Links ideas clearly to each other and to main purpose of task.	Expresses appropriate ideas. Links ideas with some skill.	Expresses obvious and simple ideas. Displays little skill in linking ideas.
PURPOSE (as appropriate)	Conveys information, highlighting what is most significant. Marshals ideas and evidence in support of argument. Gives succinct and coherent account of personal experience, with sensitive expression of feelings and reactions. In storytelling, achieves effect through creative use of structure, tone, timing, vocabulary and characterisation.	Conveys information in an orderly sequence. Orders and presents ideas and opinions with some attempt at reasoning. Gives a reasonably coherent account of a personal experience, expressing feelings and reactions with some sense of involvement. In storytelling, sets the scene, sustains narrative to its climax and conveys some sense of character.	Presents simple facts, ideas or opinions with little attempt at sequencing. Gives a simple account of personal experience with a limited sense of involvement. In storytelling, sets the scene and outlines the narrative.
LANGUAGE	Uses varied and accurate vocabulary. Uses an appropriately wide range of spoken language structures. Uses a register appropriate to topic and audience.	Uses vocabulary and spoken language structure which are largely accurate. Shows some awareness of appropriate register.	Uses a limited range of vocabulary and spoken language structures. Is restricted in register.
EXPRESSION	Is consistently audible and clear. Is consistently fluent. Adjusts pace to suit purpose. Varies intonation to point up meaning.	Is largely audible and clear. Displays some fluency. Shows some signs of ability to vary intonation to point up meaning or to adjust pace to suit the purpose.	Is, in part, audible and clear.

	CREDIT	GENERAL	FOUNDATION
AWARENESS OF AUDIENCE	Takes due account of the requirements and reactions of the audience. Makes appropriate use of eye contact, facial expression and gesture. Requires little or no prompting.	Shows awareness of requirements and reactions of audience. Occasionally makes appropriate use of eye contact, facial expression and gesture. Requires some support through prompting and/or questioning.	Shows limited awareness of the requirements and reactions of audience. Requires substantial support through prompting and/or questioning.
DURATION	Sustains talk at considerable length, as appropriate to purpose.	Sustains talk at some length, as appropriate to purpose.	Shows a limited ability to sustain talk, as appropriate to purpose.

	CREDIT		GENERAL		FOUNDATION	
DIFFERENTIATING FACTORS	**GRADE 1**	**GRADE 2**	**GRADE 3**	**GRADE 4**	**GRADE 5**	**GRADE 6**
	Distinguished by a consistent and alert attention to purpose and combines some of the following features: high quality in content and language; confidence of expression; sensitive awareness of situation and audience. Overall, characterised by consistency of quality.	Sound attention to purpose, but lacks some sophistication, insight, fullness. Performance is generally good, but is less rich/ less confident/ less sensitive/ less consistent than at grade 1.	Attention to purpose, is intermittent but adequate and combines some of the following features adequate content; adequate accuracy of language adequate expression; adequate awareness of audience.	Attention to purpose, though impaired in some significant way, just achieves the adequacy required for General Level. Despite weaknesses, the combination of qualities of content, language expression, awareness of audience just achieves overall adequacy.	Shows a few signs of attention to purpose and combines some of the following features: several items of content, though weakened by irrelevance and/or obscurity; intelligible language, weakened by inaccuracy; some limited awareness of audience; expression reasonably audible and clear.	Communicates a few intelligible ideas at least one of which is to the point.

TALKING (Discussion) GRC

	CREDIT	GENERAL	FOUNDATION
SUBSTANCE AND RELEVANCE OF CONTRIBUTION	Is substantial in quality and relevant to purpose of discussion. Provides a good number of relevant ideas/responses/opinions/experiences. Supports ideas with evidence. Questions and answers relevantly.	Contributes some relevant ideas/responses/opinions/experiences and EITHER occasionally supports these with evidence/reasons OR occasionally questions and answers relevantly.	Contributes a few ideas/responses/opinions/experiences and these are only tenuously relevant.
ACCOUNT TAKEN OF OTHER CONTRIBUTIONS	Takes account of what others have to say in several of the following ways: by analysing/summarising/using/expanding/supporting/challenging/refuting their contributions.	On the whole, takes some account of what others have to say in one of the following ways: by summarising/using/expanding/supporting/challenging their contributions.	Shows a few signs of taking account of what others have to say, in one of the following ways by repeating/using/supporting/challenging their contributions.
AWARENESS OF SITUATION	Behaves in a way appropriate to the situation by: acknowledging the status of chair, leader, interviewer, etc.; allowing/encouraging others to have their say; speaking readily, but not excessively; using language suited to the listener(s).	Behaves in a way appropriate to the situation by two of the following: acknowledging the status of chair, leader, interviewer, etc.; allowing/encouraging others to have their say; speaking readily, but not excessively; using language suited to the listener(s).	Shows a few signs of attempting to behave in a way appropriate to the situation by one of the following: acknowledging the status of chair, leader, interviewer, etc.; allowing/encouraging others to have their say; speaking readily, but not excessively; using language suited to the listener(s).
CONTROL OF EXPRESSION	Is consistently audible and clear and shows some skill in varying intonation to point up meaning and in adjusting pace to suit circumstances.	Is largely audible and clear and shows some signs of varying intonation to point up meaning or adjusting pace to suit circumstances.	Is in part audible and clear.

DIFFERENTIATING FACTORS	GRADE 1	GRADE 2	GRADE 3	GRADE 4	GRADE 5	GRADE 6
	Consistent, alert attention to purpose	Sound attention to purpose, but lacks some shrewdness, tenacity, subtlety.	Attention to purpose, is adequate	Attention to purpose, though impaired in some significant ways, just achieves adequacy required for General Level	Shows a few signs of attention to purpose	At least one audible intelligible attempt to contribute relevantly
	and		and	and	and	and
	combines some of the following features:	Performance is generally good, but is less fertile/less confident/less sensitive/less consistent than at grade 1.	combines some of the following features:	combines some of the following features:	combines some of the following features:	shows some signs of willingness to co-operate in the discussion.
	high quality in contributions and taking account of what others say;		adequate substance and relevance of contribution;	substance and relevance of contribution;	a few contributions though weakened by irrelevance;	
	confidence of expression;		adequate account taken of other contributions;	account taken of other contributions;	some limited account taken of others;	
	tactful awareness of situation.		adequate awareness of situation;	awareness of situation;	some limited awareness of situation;	
	Overall, characterised by consistency of quality.		adequate control of expression.	control of expression.	reasonably audible and clear expression.	
				(One or more of these is impaired in some way but the combination just achieves overall adequacy.)		

that co-operation is what makes the discussion successful. If you do not co-operate, your performance is poor, and the performance of the others is downgraded as well.

The GRC for both Discussion and for Individual Talking are set out in much the same way as for the Writing GRC, but allowing for the differences in the two elements, as you would expect. You can see the broad description for the three separate Levels, set against the different features of the two forms of Talking. These features you find in the left-hand column. Then, at the bottom of the grid, the same "differentiating factors" section to mark the grades within these three Levels, as in the Writing GRC.

Once again, there is a certain amount of complex/technical language that shows that the grid is aimed at teachers and examiners, rather than at students. I have already said that if you know and understand well what the GRC say and use these statements as targets for your work, you will do far better in Standard Grade English than if you knew nothing about the GRC. For that reason, it would be good to know what the technical/jargon language actually means.

You may have to look up some of the words they use, and you will find most of the rather obscure terms in the Glossary. These words might include the following in the Discussion GRC:

Analysing	Pace
Refuting	Tenuously
Status	Irrelevance
Intonation	

In the GRC for Individual Talk, many of the technical terms used have already been used in the GRC for Writing or in the GRC for Discussion, so you will not need to look them up separately. The few others that there are might include:

Tone	Facial expression
Characterisation	Gesture
Register	Climax

Your teacher will be using these GRC grids to assess your work in Talking. The obvious problem in assessing talking is that it is over when it is over, and there is no lasting record of it. Your teacher cannot sit down with your talk and 'mark' it in the same way that he or she can deal with a piece of writing. Even though we can make an audio or video recording, these do not capture all that there is in a talk situation. It is not just about the sounds you make. Look at what the GRC have to say about other aspects: *awareness of situation, allowing, acknowledging, account taken, facial expression* and so on. These and other aspects should make it clear to you that there is more to it than just talking in any way that you happen to choose. Discussion, especially, is something that has to be taught and learned, and you have to know what you are expected to do when talking or discussing. The GRC will play a part in that teaching/learning process as well.

GRC for Reading

The GRC for Reading look more complicated, but that is mainly because there are three separate grids this time, one for each of the three separate forms of reading. As explained earlier for Talking, we need a separate set of GRC for each of these forms, just as for Individual Talk and Discussion. The three forms of reading covered in Standard Grade English are:

◆ Critical Evaluation

◆ Imaginative Response

◆ Close Reading.

The first two are similar in that they are what we call extended responses to reading. In other words, they involve a lengthy piece of writing.

The first of these is the kind of writing (in response to reading) where you are writing about a text you have read (or heard or seen/viewed if it is a media text). The purpose of the writing about the text is to criticise and evaluate it in a personal response. This kind of writing has already been explained and described at length in the Folio chapter, and this would be a good time to look back at that chapter.

The second kind of writing (in response to reading) has also been explained and described in the Folio chapter. Here you produce a piece of writing in which you respond imaginatively to a text. What this means in practice is that your piece of writing is based on a text you have studied and your writing attempts to create an imaginative piece that could take several forms: a continuation or altered ending; a diary supposedly written by one of the characters; an account of an incident in the text from the point of view of a different character, re-setting the story in a different time and place, and so on.

The third kind is what is sometimes called interpretation. Here the response is not extended but is in the form of short answers to questions on a short text (usually an extract from a longer text). You will do this kind of reading in class and certainly in the Reading examination set by the SQA at the end of the course. Work of this kind does not go into your Folio, however. You can figure out for yourself how difficult it would be to include such work, with the need for many different text extracts, responses, marking instructions etc., from schools and colleges all over the country.

N.B. You won't find these Close Reading GRC written down anywhere else in the grid form you see here. The reason for this is that they are used only as a design blueprint for the examination paper by the examiners who set the paper. The exam is marked using detailed marking instructions for each separate year's examination. The reason for this is very similar to the reason for there being no Close Reading included as part of the Folio.

READING — Extended Responses to Text

Critical Evaluations

In what follows the term "text(s)" should be taken to refer to poetry, drama and prose (both fiction and non-fiction) and also to films and radio and television programmes.

The quality of the text(s) chosen should allow the candidate to demonstrate the following skills.

	CREDIT	GENERAL	FOUNDATION
AS APPROPRIATE TO THE PURPOSE THE CANDIDATE	Displays a thorough familiarity with the text(s): this appears, e.g., in the analysis of its main ideas and purposes and through detailed reference to relevant areas of content. Shows an ability to relate significant detail to the overall context of the work(s) studied.	Displays an acceptable familiarity with the text(s): this appears in a statement of its main ideas and purposes and through reference to some relevant areas of content. Shows some ability to relate detail to the overall context of the work(s) studied).	Displays some familiarity with the text(s): this appears in the statement of one or two of its main ideas and/or purposes and through reference to one or two relevant areas of content. Shows a little ability to relate detail to the overall context of the work(s) studied.
	Gives a perceptive and developed account of what s/he has enjoyed in/gained from the text(s): this clearly conveys the sense of a genuine personal response and is substantiated by reference to pertinent features of the text(s).	Makes a reasonably developed statement about aspects of the text(s) which have affected him/her: this conveys the sense of a genuine personal response and is accompanied by some reference to pertinent features of the text(s).	Makes a statement about at least one aspect of the text(s) that has affected him/her: this conveys traces of a genuine personal response.
	Demonstrates awareness of technique by analysis, using critical terminology where appropriate: this appears in full and perceptive explication of stylistic devices substantiated by detailed reference to the text(s) and, where appropriate, apt quotation.	Identifies individual features of technique and explains their effects, using basic critical terminology where appropriate: this involves the brief explication of obvious stylistic devices and is accompanied by some reference to the text(s) and/or quotation.	Identifies one or two features of technique which contribute to some obvious effect: this is accompanied by some reference to the text(s) and/or quotation.

	CREDIT		GENERAL		FOUNDATION	
AS APPROPRIATE TO THE PURPOSE THE CANDIDATE	Organises the response in such a way as to reflect, accurately, the purpose and nature of the assignment: this appears in an ability to select what is relevant in the text(s) and give due weight and prominence to what is important; the response is a substantial one but not normally exceeding 800 words.		Organises the response so as to take some account of the purpose and nature of the assignment: most of what is selected from the text(s) is relevant and adequate attention is given to what is important; the response is a reasonably extended one, probably between 300 and 600 words.		Displays some signs of awareness of the purpose and nature of the assignment: some of what is selected from the text(s) is relevant and a degree of attention is given to what is important; the response is at least 100 words in length.	
DIFFERENTIATING FACTORS	GRADE 1	GRADE 2	GRADE 3	GRADE 4	GRADE 5	GRADE 6
	Analysis of main ideas/purposes is thorough-going and precise.	Analysis of main ideas/purposes is full but less penetrating than at grade 1.	Statement of main ideas/purposes is reasonably comprehensive and accurate.	Statement of main ideas/purposes is less complete/less correct than at grade 3.	Statement of main ideas/purposes displays a basic grasp.	Grasp of main ideas/purposes is tenuous.
	The account of personal reaction displays a high level of sensitivity and self-awareness.	The account of personal reaction is discerning but less fully realised than at grade 1.	Statement of personal reaction displays a degree of insight.	Statement of personal reaction is more superficial and generalised than at grade 3.	Statement of personal reaction is brief but clear.	Statement of personal reaction lacks clarity but conveys a recognisable stance in relation to text(s).
	Use of critical terminology is confident and accurate.	Use of critical terminology is generally accurate but occasionally lacks the sureness of touch characteristic of grade 1.	Use of basic critical terminology is reasonably assured.	Awareness of critical terminology falters on occasion.	Awareness of technique is conveyed explicitly in simple non-technical language.	Awareness of technique is detectable but tends to appear implicitly.
	There is an overall proportion and coherence in the structure of the response.	Everything is relevant to the purpose of the assignment but there is some disproportion of constituent parts.	There is clear reference throughout to the purpose of the assignment.	Sense of the purpose of the assignment is present but not explicitly acknowledged throughout.	There is at least one explicit reference to the purpose of the assignment.	Awareness of purpose appears briefly/implicitly.

READING — Extended Responses to Text

Imaginative Responses

In what follows the term "text(s)" should be taken to refer to poetry, drama and prose (both fiction and non-fiction).

The quality of the text(s) chosen should allow the candidate to demonstrate the following skills.

	CREDIT	GENERAL	FOUNDATION
AS APPROPRIATE TO THE PURPOSE THE CANDIDATE	Displays, as appropriate, a thorough familiarity with the text(s) through	Displays, as appropriate, an acceptable familiarity with the text(s) through	Displays, as appropriate, some familiarity with the text(s) through
	detailed allusion to relevant areas of content,	allusion to some relevant areas of content,	allusion to one or two relevant areas of content,
	sustained attention to the main ideas and purposes,	some attention to the main ideas and purposes,	and recognition of one or two of the main ideas and purposes.
	and sensitive evocation of mood and tone;	and occasional evocation of mood and tone;	
	awareness of technique appears through skilled deployment of appropriate stylistic devices.	some awareness of technique appears through the use of more obvious stylistic devices.	
	Organisation accurately reflects the purpose and nature of the assignment.	Organisation takes some account of the purpose and nature of the assignment.	There are some signs that account has been taken of the purpose and nature of the assignment.

141

DIFFERENTIATING FACTORS	GRADE 1	GRADE 2	GRADE 3	GRADE 4	GRADE 5	GRADE 6
	The candidate is confident and accomplished in the use of the chosen literary medium.	There are occasional lapses in control of the chosen literary medium.	The candidate displays some skill in using the chosen literary medium.	The candidate is less confident in using the chosen literary medium.	The candidate displays limited skill in using the chosen literary medium.	The candidate displays very little skill in using the chosen literary medium.
	The writing consistently demonstrates:	The writing demonstrates a high level of:	There is clear evidence of:	There is some evidence of:	There is little evidence of:	There are fleeting signs of:
	familiarity with the text(s);	familiarity with the text(s);	familiarity with the text(s);	familiarity with the text(s);	familiarity with the text(s);	familiarity with the text(s);
	awareness of technique;	awareness of technique;	awareness of technique;	awareness of technique;	awareness of technique;	awareness of technique;
	powers of organisation.	powers of organisation.	powers of organisation.	powers of organisation.	powers of organisaton.	powers of organisation.

READING — Extended Responses to Text

Close Reading

	CREDIT	GENERAL	FOUNDATION
TEXTS	Go beyond what is immediately accessible or related to personal interest and experience. Some feature unfamiliar, abstract ideas and complexity of structure and tone.	Accessible as a whole, mainly related to personal interest and experience, dealing with concrete human relationships or containing clearly presented ideas.	Brief and readily accessible, related to personal interest and experiences, dealing with concrete human relationships or containing clearly presented ideas.
THE CANDIDATE CAN	Make a clear concise statement of the main concerns of the text and show awareness of their relationships;	Make a clear statement of the main concerns of the text;	State the main concerns of the text;
	state accurately in his or her own words (where appropriate) and collate as required, items of information retrieved from the text;	state accurately in his or her own words (where appropriate) individual items retrieved from the text;	state accurately individual items of information from areas of the text which have been clearly defined;
	draw a precise inference from a key statement or statements, and substantiate this from evidence in the text;	draw a precise inference from a key statement in the text;	draw an acceptable simple inference from a key statement in the text;
	comment relevantly on some aspects of the author's point of view, and show some skill in justifying the comment from personal experience and knowledge and from evidence in the text;	comment relevantly on a clearly defined aspect of the author's point of view, and justify the comment from personal experience and knowledge and from evidence in the text;	comment simply and intelligibly on an aspect of the author's point of view that has been clearly defined and relate it to personal experience and/or knowledge;
	demonstrate some awareness of the author's technique by analysis, using critical terminology where appropriate.	identify individual features of the author's technique and explain their effects.	identify a feature (or features) of the author's technique which contributes to some clearly defined effect.

	GRADE 1	GRADE 2	GRADE 3	GRADE 4	GRADE 5	GRADE 6
DIFFERENTIATING FACTORS	The candidate demonstrates a sureness and sensitivity of understanding and appreciation in responding to particular questions on the various aspects of purpose. The responses are more consistent, more perceptive and more substantial (as required) than at grade 2.	While displaying as appropriate the characteristics essential for Credit Level, the candidate's responses are less consistent, less clear in perception and less full in explanation than at grade 1. Overall the performance is more uneven than at grade 1.	The candidate demonstrates a clear under-standing and a sound appreciation in responding to particular questions on the various aspects of purpose. The responses are more consistant, more relevant and more successful in retrieving, paraphrasing, explaining and justifying than at grade 4.	While displaying as appropriate the characteristics essential for General Level, the candidate's responses are less consistent, less apt in illustration and explanations are less successful in retrieving, paraphrasing, explaining and justifying than at grade 3. Overall the performance is more uneven than at grade 3.	Demonstrates understanding and some appreciation in responding to particular questions on the various aspects of purpose. The responses are more consistent, more comprehensible and more specific than at grade 6.	While displaying as appropriate the characteristics essential for Foundation Level, the candidate is less consistent, less clear and more ambiguous in communicating responses than at grade 5. Overall the performance is more uneven than at grade 5.

You already know that half of your Reading grade comes from the Folio and the other half from the examination in Reading. This arrangement is designed to give you the best situation for each of the two broadly different kinds of response to reading: extended responses in the Folio and Close Reading in the examination.

Turning back to the GRC grids now, you can see once again that the way they are laid out is much the same as for Writing and Talking, allowing for the differences across the three elements.

You can also see some additional notes that did not appear in the two earlier GRC grids. The "texts" used for response are defined, and there is a note about the quality of the texts. This is there because though it would be possible for a very able student to write at Credit Level about almost any text (a poster for a pop concert or the current page of Oor Wullie in the *Sunday Post*, for example) it would be much more likely to be successful for most students if the text had what is called literary merit: in other words, if it contains what we expect to be present in works of good literature. There has to be something substantial in the text to write about, so that the student has material to work on. This is a delicate balance where the depth of the text and the ability of the student have to be matched. There is no point in struggling with the work of James Joyce or Fyodor Dostoevsky if you don't have a clue about their writing. Equally pointless is trying to write a critical evaluation of a thin romantic story or blood-and-guts macho-action tale with little literary value in either.

The note about the quality of texts for the Close Reading GRC is useful to the examiners who will always make sure that the texts chosen in the examination will meet this requirement.

The three sets of GRC can again be read following the general advice given for Writing GRC. There are the same broad statements at the three levels fewer entries though for special aspects set out down the left-hand column, and at the foot of each grid the same layout of differentiating factors for the grades at each level.

Most of the technical jargon in the GRC has already been used in previous grids, but you might have to consult the Glossary for a few, such as:

Critical	Explication
Evaluation	Stylistic devices
Context	Explicit
Perceptive	Stance
Pertinent	Implicitly
Critical terminology	

I want to close this chapter on the GRC with a few further notes on the three forms of response. They will be brief, because quite a lot has been said about them elsewhere in the Guide.

1 Critical Evaluations

When you evaluate something you are simply placing a value on it, saying what significance it has, usually after some careful study and thought. 'Critical' is a word clearly connected with 'criticise', a much misunderstood word. It does not mean simply to complain about the faults of someone or of some situation. It means, as used here, to judge. The word comes from a Greek word κριτεφ (kriteo) meaning 'I judge'. So does 'criterion', the word we spent some time on earlier when explaining about 'Grade Related Criteria' (GRC). So to criticise means to consider the merits and the faults of the work, both sides of the case — judging. A critical evaluation of a work of literature (or media) is a piece of writing which judges the merits and demerits of a work and comes to a conclusion based on careful study and appraisal. Despite this, most tasks will ask you to say how much you enjoyed the work. Very seldom will you be asked to say why you absolutely hated it.

"Make a statement about at least one aspect of the text(s) that has affected him or her ..."

You are quite familiar with this kind of writing. Your teacher will have asked you to produce such work before, though it is unlikely that you were asked to "write a critical evaluation of" whatever you have been reading in class. Although the term is another piece of shorthand, you should really get into the habit of using it, once you have understood what it means. You will find it useful to use this jargon in any discussion with your teacher on the subject of your Folio work. Unbelievably, it will be good to use it when you are talking about classwork and Folio work even with your classmates. It helps to simplify and clarify things.

In producing this kind of work, one important reminder: the examiners are looking for your personal response to the work. The evaluation consists not only of what you have learned or read about other people's opinions of the work, but also and importantly, your own opinion and reactions.

2 Imaginative Responses

You've done this kind of work too, but perhaps not heard it called by that name. As for critical evaluations, it helps if you can begin to use the term used in the *Arrangements*. I said that the jargon was the everyday usage of insiders at Standard Grade English: you have become one of these insiders by being a student on the course and should use this term to describe the kind of writing intended.

Once you've read a work of literature and studied it for some time in a unit, your teacher might ask you, for example, to imagine that you are a character in the work and to write a diary or a letter by that character. It might be a letter from Daisy Buchanan to her friend Jordan Baker after the death of Jay Gatsby in *The Great Gatsby*, or Lady Macbeth's diary entries after she learns of her husband's murder of Banquo. You might be asked to write a different ending to a story in the same style as the original, or to write a short poem based on one you have studied, but with an updating to bring in into a 21st century situation.

To tackle any of these or similar tasks effectively you need a good knowledge of the text and an understanding of the writer's purpose. It is another way of showing that you have read and understood the work and it is thus an indirect way of commenting on it. In addition, you apply your creative imagination to the writing.

You should be reminded again that there are very clear rules about the conditions under which you can include an imaginative response in your Folio. Ignoring these rules can have serious consequences: having your work disqualified and therefore not graded or counted towards your award because it did not meet the Folio specification. So if you think that you might want to include an imaginative response in your Folio, check the rules very carefully in the Folio chapter of the Guide and double-check with your teacher. I say this because producing an imaginative response is a very popular classroom activity and you might be asked to produce many over the course, but there are defined limits to the part it can play in the assessment of your work. You might also like to re-read the advice about this form of Reading response in the chapter of the Guide dealing with Reading.

3 Close Reading

Look now at the GRC for Close Reading. The layout is generally simpler than the other GRC, for the reasons already explained, and these GRC are used differently from the others. If you use them as targets they will help you both in the exam, where there is the close reading paper, but do not forget that though close reading will not feature in your Folio, you will still be doing quite a lot of it (sometimes called interpretation) during class work. This is another way of studying texts, usually shorter and unseen, and you must be able to respond to these texts in such a way that the examiners and your teacher can see that you have understood and appreciated what the text contains. Some people think that the only reason for doing close reading in the class is to practise for the exam. Nothing could be further from being true.

You should pay attention to words that are used in the GRC frequently. The words I mean are not the ones I listed as technical terms for you to look up and learn from the Glossary, but words that are there to remind you of the kind of attention you should be paying to answering questions in the way expected by the examiners: words like "clear", "concise", "relevantly", "justifying", "accurately", and "evidence in the text".

I end this chapter by agreeing with you that the GRC look pretty boring. I hope though that you realise that it is indispensable to you, to know and understand what they say, because they set down both the targets for learning and the means by which your work will be assessed.

Perhaps boring, but crucial to you.

CHAPTER NINE

THE CERTIFICATE

The only purpose of this short penultimate* chapter is to let you see what the certificate looks like.

What you see is just a scanned-in image of part of it, for it can't be shown here in all its glory, unfortunately. It is slightly larger than this page and is printed in colour and has a laminated cover to protect it from dust and dirt, and also from interference or alteration once it has been issued to you.

The version of the certificate you see is only a specimen for information and issued to a fictitious candidate from an equally fictitious school. The word "SPECIMEN" is all over it to make sure that no one is left in any doubt about whether it is a real certificate or not.

So this is the paper qualification that you will have worked hard for two years to gain, and it is worth it.

You can see the subjects this candidate sat and the awards that she gained. You can see the overall award for English and the 'Profile of Performance' that shows what grades she achieved in each of the elements of Standard Grade English.

Perhaps you think it does not look like much in return for all that work. Certainly if it were **all** you had gained, it wouldn't be much. You know, however, that the certificate is merely a symbol of your achievements. The real reward is the satisfaction you will have achieved from the course and from having done as well as you can, whatever level of award you will have gained.

I hope that you will get much satisfaction and benefit from your Standard Grade English course, that you will succeed to the best of your ability and gain a certificate like this one.

SCOTTISH
QUALIFICATIONS
AUTHORITY

Ref code	Qualification title	Level	Grade	Date
Units contributing to the award of Higher Mathematics				
D321 12	Mathematics 1	Higher		08/2003
D322 12	Mathematics 2	Higher		08/2003
D323 12	Mathematics 3	Higher		08/2003
Units contributing to the award of Intermediate 2 Physics				
D380 12	Electricity and Electronics	Higher		08/2003
D383 12	Mechanics and Properties of Matter	Higher		08/2003
D384 12	Radiation and Matter	Higher		08/2003
National Units				
D339 12	French: Language	Higher		08/2003
D342 12	French: Extended Reading/Viewing	Higher		08/2003
D01D 11	Information Technology	Intermediate 2		08/2003

Standard Grade Elements

			Grade	Date
Elements for Standard Grade English				
	Reading		1	08/2002
	Writing		1	08/2002
	Talking		1	08/2002
Elements for Standard Grade Business Management				
	Knowledge and Understanding		1	08/2002
	Decision Making		1	08/2002
	Practical Abilities		1	08/2002
Elements for Standard Grade Drama				
	Knowledge & Understanding		2	08/2002
	Creating		2	08/2002
	Presenting		2	08/2002
Elements for Standard Grade French				
	Reading		1	08/2002
	Listening		4	08/2002
	Speaking		1	08/2002
	Writing		3	08/2002
Elements for Standard Grade Mathematics				
	Knowledge & Understanding		2	08/2002
	Reasoning & Enquiry		2	08/2002

SPECIMEN

Reference: Candidate Sophie - SCN 007119550   Page 2   Issued: 12 August 2003

Notes:
1   Where column is blank, the information in the column does not apply to that qualification.
2   For qualifications marked * or + see the section of this Certificate entitled 'Supplementary'.
3   Results marked with a # indicates that these units can only be achieved at a Pass.

CHAPTER TEN

HIGHER ENGLISH

If you achieve a Grade 1, 2 or 3 award in Standard Grade English and move into S5, you will start a new course leading to Higher English.

If you have enjoyed the ways of working at Standard Grade, you will be well prepared for the course at Higher.

Since the introduction of the new Higher English and subsequent changes to it, the *Arrangements* have made the transition from Standard to Higher even more smooth than it was before. An obvious connection has been made by the fact that there are now several levels of courses and examinations rather than just one, as previously. I have mentioned these in the Guide, as far back as the Introduction, and outlined how they connect with Standard Grade. Indeed, the two lower levels, Intermediate 1 and Intermediate 2, have the equivalent value of Standard Grade at Credit and General respectively. That means that you may already have achieved one of these levels and can go on to the one above. The uppermost level is, of course, called Higher English.

The courses are formed of units, with internal assessment and then external exams. So it is familiar. Since you would always be taking a course at a level higher than the one you may have achieved (at least in equivalence), the demands will always be greater, and there is definitely a major increase in the standard required at Higher from Standard Grade.

The exams cover critical evaluation and close reading, so you already know about that.

I hope that this Guide will go some way to helping you survive the Standard Grade course and assessment and to come out of it successfully, prepared and fit to tackle Higher English.

GLOSSARY

Acronym A word formed from the initial letters of other words, e.g., NATO (from North Atlantic Treaty Organisation)

Ad lib Speak or perform without formal preparation

Analysing Finding or showing the essence or structure of (a book, music)

Articulate Able to speak fluently and coherently (adj.) or to explain and express fluently and coherently (verb)

Assessment Estimate or measure of the quality of something

Bald Blunt or unelaborated (e.g. statement)

Catch 22 A dilemma from which there is no escape from incompatible conditions. In Joseph Heller's novel *Catch 22*, the hero wants to escape combat duty. To do so he has to be judged insane; but since anyone wishing to avoid combat duty is obviously sane, he must be fit for duty — Catch 22

Characterisation Creation of character(s) in a literary work

Climax Point of greatest intensity: a series arranged in order of increasing importance

Coherence Demonstrating consistency

Context The parts of something written or spoken that immediately precede or follow a word or passage and clarify its meaning

Conventions Accepted methods or rules

Criteria The standards by which a thing is judged

Critical Making or involving comments or judgements

Critical terminology The system of words or terms used in literary criticism

Curriculum The subjects that are studied or prescribed for study in a school

Deploy Bring arguments into effective action

Dichotomous With a sharply defined division into two (e.g., yes or no)

Digression	A temporary departure from the main subject
Distinction	Great excellence
Economy	Sparing or careful use (of language)
Elements	Basic component parts
Evaluation	Assessment, placing a value on something
Ex tempore	Without preparation, on the spur of the moment
Explication	Development of the meaning or implication of an idea
Explicit	Stated in detail, expressly stated
Expound	Set out in detail, explain or interpret
Extraneous	Irrelevant or unrelated to
Folio	A sheet of paper folded once to make two leaves of a book (within the context of Standard Grade English it is a compilation of course work)
Genre	A kind or style of literature or art
Gesture	A movement of the body or limbs to express feeling or thought
Gist	The substance or essence or central meaning of something
Gralloching	Disembowelling or gutting (specifically a deer but sometimes used in a more general context)
Imaginative response	A written or spoken creation based on or extending a literary original
Implicit	Implied though not plainly expressed
Insight	The ability to understand hidden truths, especially of character or situations
Intelligibility	Understanding, comprehensibility
Intonation	Modulation or moderation of the voice
Irrelevance	Not applicable to the subject being written or discussed
Malapropism	Use of a word in mistake for one sounding similar (e.g., *Porpoises* for *Purposes*) from a character Mrs Malaprop in Richard Sheridan's play, *The Rivals*
Marshal	Arrange in due order
Norm	A standard or type or pattern
Objective	Uncoloured by feelings or opinions
Obtrusive	Unduly (or often unpleasantly) noticeable
Pace	Speed or tempo

Paronomasia	A play on words, a pun
Penultimate	Second last
Perceptive	Sensitive, discerning, observant
Perspective	A mental view of the relative importance of things
Pertinent	Relevant, to the point
Phenomenon	A fact or occurrence that appears, especially one whose cause is in question
Plagiarism	The taking and using the thoughts, writings, inventions, etc., of others as one's own
Rambling	Disconnected, incoherent
Refuting	Proving a statement false or erroneous
Register	Each of several forms of a language (colloquial, literary, formal, etc.)
Rudimentary	Basic, fundamental
Specified	Clearly defined (requirements)
Stance	A standpoint, an attitude
Status	Position in relation to others
Stylistic devices	Particular arrangements of words, terms, etc., used in literary style
Succinct	Briefly expressed, concise
Sustained	Maintained continuously for a long period
Tenuously	Slightly, thinly, barely relevantly
Text	In Standard Grade usage, a book or a single work or an extract for study or comment, a literary work: or a work in a medium other than print, e.g., film, television, oral format
Tone	Modulation of the voice expressing a particular feeling or mood
Transcends	Goes beyond, surpasses, excels
Vicarious experience	Experience in the imagination through another person or character
Weighting	an additional value applied to certain components or situations over others

Medical Terminology and Clinical Procedures

Edition **3**

Mary Bird SRN RN FAMS

Former Chief Examiner (Medical Aspects) for AMSPAR
(The Association of Medical Secretaries,
Practice Managers, Administrators and Receptionists)

MAGISTER
CONSULTING

Published in the UK by
Magister Consulting Ltd
The Old Rectory
St. Mary's Road
Stone
Dartford
Kent DA9 9AS

Copyright © 2005 Magister Consulting Ltd
Printed by Ethos Productions Ltd

ISBN 1 873839 58 8

Contents

Contents

Contents

Contents

The role of the foreword writer is to inform the reader what it is that makes the book in question special, and what separates it from others in the field. That being so, writing the foreword for this book does not present a challenge, for I know of no other book of this kind. The word 'unique' is frequently misused to mean only 'slightly different' from something else, whereas in fact it should define a total difference – a 'one-off', and Mary Bird's book is just that.

This is not a book one reads; it is a book that one uses. Those who purchase the book will find it will become indispensable, and well-worn! It is an essential guide and companion for anyone setting out on a medical career, whether as a medical secretary, practice manager, nurse or therapist. Within it are tools to make sense of any sort of medical discourse. Whether one is trying to understand a paper, text or a conversation on anything medical, then one should consult this guide.

In truth I am not sure where else to find such an eclectic mix of information; a dictionary may contain definitions, but this book goes further than that in many instances. Not long ago books such as this were deemed unfashionable, being strongly influenced by the 'medical model'. Nowadays I hope we have matured enough to acknowledge the worth and usefulness of guides like this, which do not set out to declaim, critique or analyse, but simply explain the words that medical professionals use.

I am full of admiration for the sort of writer who can carry out this expert task in the way that Mary Bird has here, for I cannot imagine even starting to compile a volume like this. I recommend it to you to use – it will be a good companion!

Sue Hinchliff MSc BA RN RNT
Head of Continuing Professional Development and Accreditation
Royal College of Nursing of the United Kingdom

Mary Bird was born in Dorset, attended the local grammar school in the immediate post war period and began registered nursing training locally, upon leaving school. She gained wide experience in all branches of nursing, (including medical, surgical, orthopaedic, paediatrics, ophthalmology, neurology, ENT and theatre) during this period and had the benefit of the influence of a charismatic matron, with extremely high standards. Awarded numerous prizes for differing specialities, she gained the equivalent hospital 'Gold Medal' award, (the Sanderson Wells Award), as the best student nurse of her year.

Qualifying as an SRN in 1957 and marrying in the same year, she moved to Devon. Mary gained further experience in the casualty department and medical wards prior to the birth of her first child in 1960. Her second child was born in 1962. A period of time out from nursing between 1960 and 1964, enabled Mary to spend important time with her family prior to returning in a part time capacity as a District Nursing Sister and later in Intensive Care.

In 1971, Mary together with her family, moved to Essex where she continued nursing, including a period as an Industrial Nursing Sister and also as a School Nurse at a busy comprehensive school. She also gained invaluable experience as a Practice Nurse for a busy general practice.

In 1976, Mary commenced lecturing in medical terminology, anatomy and physiology at a College of Further Education. Among her students were pre-nursing cadets, community care students and AMSPAR medical secretaries and receptionists.

Eventually she became the Course Director for AMSPAR students, including those students who were studying for the Diploma for Practice Managers. Mary was appointed by AMSPAR, first as an Examiner and then, in 1989, as Chief Examiner for the Medical Aspects section. Involvement in NVQ training and assessing led to her appointment as an OCR/AMSPAR External Verifier. Retiring from college teaching in 1994, Mary continued with providing independent training for various Health Authorities and hospitals, under the name of Medicus Enterprises. She continues this at the present time as well as her role of Examiner for the AMSPAR Medical Terminology Certificate, of which she is author. She was awarded an AMSPAR Fellowship in 1997, in recognition of her contribution to AMSPAR.

Involvement in teaching and examining for the Voluntary Aid Societies, St John Ambulance and the British Red Cross, are also important aspects of her life and in 1965 was presented with the Royal Humane Society Award for the resuscitation of a youth from drowning.

Both of her children have chosen medical subjects for their careers; her daughter is a well-known psychologist and her son is a Professor of Molecular Endocrinology, in the USA. She and her husband, a retired solicitor, enjoy their grandchildren and hobbies of gardening, swimming and reading – now that there is time to do so!

This book is intended to provide an insight into medical terminology and the common clinical procedures met in the everyday work of health workers, including secretaries, receptionists, administrators and managers, as well as students in many other disciplines.

The breakdown of medical words into the basic prefixes, roots and suffixes, aims to help unravel the mystery of medical language and enable the reader to build a vast vocabulary in a surprisingly short time. Basic anatomy and physiology of the body have been included in order to provide further explanation and interest for the reader. Medical terms and abbreviations are grouped together with the appropriate body system, wherever possible, eg: 'Angina pectoris' and 'Blood pressure' are explained in Chapter 5: The Cardiovascular System.

At the end of each chapter you will find lists of abbreviations, terminology, diseases and disorders, as well as procedures and equipment related to that body system. The index at the end of the book contains all the full terms mentioned in the text. The appendices provide further lists of prefixes roots suffixes, abbreviations and eponyms.

Chapters on drugs and preventive medicine, including immunisation schedules and notifiable diseases are included. Areas concerning the work of the pathology and imaging/X-ray departments are intended to provide more knowledge of the principles of common tests performed on patients.

In this new edition, numerous procedures have been added to the text in an attempt to keep up with the ever growing changes in medical procedures and investigations.

At the outset of my career, I was encouraged always to remember that the welfare of the patient was the priority. I express the hope that this book, by giving a better understanding, will enable all those involved in patient care to deal more effectively with that most important person – the patient!

Mary Bird
July 2004

Acknowledgements

This book is dedicated with grateful thanks to:

All my AMSPAR students, *past and present,*
from whom I have learnt so much.

Olga de Souza, *my predecessor as*
AMSPAR Chief Examiner, for her very high standards,
which I have tried my best to maintain.

Michael, **Susan**, **Ian**, **Beth** and **Iain**,
for all their support and encouragement,
without which this book would never have been written!

And with love to my grandchildren
James, **Sarah**, **Jennifer** *and* **Christopher**.

Mary Bird

Chapter 1

Understanding terminology

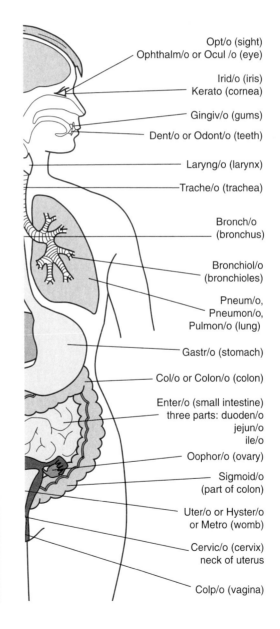

Opt/o (sight)
Ophthalm/o or Ocul /o (eye)

Irid/o (iris)
Kerato (cornea)

Gingiv/o (gums)

Dent/o or Odont/o (teeth)

Laryng/o (larynx)

Trache/o (trachea)

Bronch/o
(bronchus)

Bronchiol/o
(bronchioles)

Pneum/o,
Pneumon/o,
Pulmon/o (lung)

Gastr/o (stomach)

Col/o or Colon/o (colon)

Enter/o (small intestine)
three parts: duoden/o
jejun/o
ile/o

Oophor/o (ovary)

Sigmoid/o
(part of colon)

Uter/o or Hyster/o
or Metro (womb)

Cervic/o (cervix)
neck of uterus

Colp/o (vagina)

The origin and construction of medical terms

To the uninitiated, medical terms can seem frightening and unintelligible. As with any specialty, a language has developed which separates those 'within' from outsiders, conveying a mystique which appears hard to penetrate. However, it is necessary to have a precise language to describe a medical condition or procedure, in order that other members of the medical profession may accurately interpret diagnoses etc. Most medical words are derived from Greek and Latin sources – international languages until the eighteenth century. Some Arabic, Anglo-Saxon and German origins are also involved. Understanding and following some basic rules can reveal the mystery of medical terminology.

Basic construction of medical terms

Medical terms consist of the following parts:

- a **prefix**
- a **root** or **stem**
- a **suffix**
- a **combining vowel**.

Prefix

This part of the word is found before the stem and qualifies, (i.e. tells us more about), the stem.

e.g. **poly** – meaning 'many'.

Not all words have a prefix.

Root or stem

This is the main part of the word, which gives the information about that which is being described.

e.g. **neur** – meaning 'nerve'.

Suffix

This part of the word is found following the stem and gives further information about the stem.

e.g. **-itis** – meaning 'inflammation of'.

All medical terms have a suffix.

e.g. **polyneuritis**

Prefix		Root/stem		Suffix
poly	/	**neur**	/	**itis**

Combining vowel

This is a vowel which is added to the stem, when necessary, to allow easy pronunciation; it is usually an **o**.

If the suffix begins with a vowel then it is not required.

e.g. **poly/neur/itis** meaning 'inflammation of many nerves' where the suffix **-itis** begins with a vowel and so does not require a 'combining vowel'

Some further examples

En/cephal/o/gram

means 'a recording of brain waves'.

As there is no vowel in the suffix, **o** is inserted between the stem and suffix.

> **en-** is a prefix meaning 'within'.

> **-cephal-** is a stem meaning 'head', i.e. the brain.

> **-gram** is a suffix meaning 'a tracing or writing'.

Peri/card/itis

meaning 'inflammation of the pericardium' (the layer of tissue around the heart).

> **peri-** is a prefix meaning 'around'.

> **-cardi-** is a stem meaning 'heart'.

> **-itis** is a suffix meaning 'inflammation'.

However, there is a vowel at the end of the stem **cardi** as well as a vowel **i** at the beginning of **itis**. One of the **i**s is dropped to form the word 'pericarditis'. No added **o** is necessary.

The letter **h** is also treated as a vowel sound and is dropped when combining with another vowel, or where the pronunciation would be clumsy:

An/aem/ia

literally means 'lack of blood', but in medical terms it is the reduction of red cells or haemoglobin content in the blood.

> **an-** is a prefix meaning 'absence of'.

> **-haem-** is a stem meaning 'blood'.

> **-ia** is a suffix meaning 'condition of'.

The **h** of the stem is dropped as 'anhaemia' is difficult to pronounce.

Leuc/o/rrhoea

meaning 'white discharge'.

leuc- is a stem meaning 'white'.

-o- is a combining vowel added to the stem.

-rrhoea is a suffix meaning 'running or discharge'.

By following the rules illustrated above, many terms can be understood or constructed. Some examples are given below:

Examples of common prefixes

a- or an-	meaning absence of
anti-	meaning against
ante-	meaning before
dys-	meaning difficult/ abnormal/painful
endo-	meaning inside
haemo-	meaning blood
hypo-	meaning under/low
hyper-	meaning above/high

Examples of common suffixes

Surgical procedures

-otomy	meaning cutting into or dividing, e.g. **osteotomy** meaning cutting into bone
-ostomy	meaning making an artificial opening, e.g. **tracheostomy** meaning making an artificial opening into the trachea

N.B. Note the difference between tracheotomy and tracheostomy. In a tracheostomy the hole is left open, whereas a tracheotomy is a simple cutting into and then closing.

-orrhaphy	means a sewing or repair, e.g. **herniorrhaphy** meaning repair of a hernia
-ectomy	means surgical removal, e.g. **appendicectomy** meaning surgical removal of the appendix
-pexy	meaning fixation, e.g. **orchiopexy** meaning fixation of an undescended testicle

Other surgical and procedure suffixes

-oscopy	meaning examination with a lighted instrument
-plasty	meaning reshape or form
-tripsy	meaning crushing
-centesis	meaning puncturing and drawing off (tapping)
-gram	meaning record/picture
-graph	meaning instrument that records
-graphy	meaning procedure of recording
-opsy	meaning looking at
-stasis	meaning stopping
-clasis	meaning breaking

Examples of other important suffixes

-ia, -iasis	
-osis, -ism	all meaning condition of
-itis	meaning inflammation of
-pathy	meaning disease of
-genic	meaning produced from or originating from
-al, -ic, -iac	meaning pertaining to
-oid	meaning shape or form
-ology	meaning scientific study of
-cyte	meaning cell

Common roots or stems

The following is a list of common roots or stems together with combining vowel. Some have two different stems, one from the Greek and one from the Latin, e.g. **phleb/o** (Greek) and **ven/o** (Latin) both meaning 'vein'.

Stem	Meaning
abdomin/o, lapar/o	abdomen/abdominal wall
aden/o	gland
adipo	fat
amyl	starch
an/o	anus
andr/o	man

Roots for body parts and organs

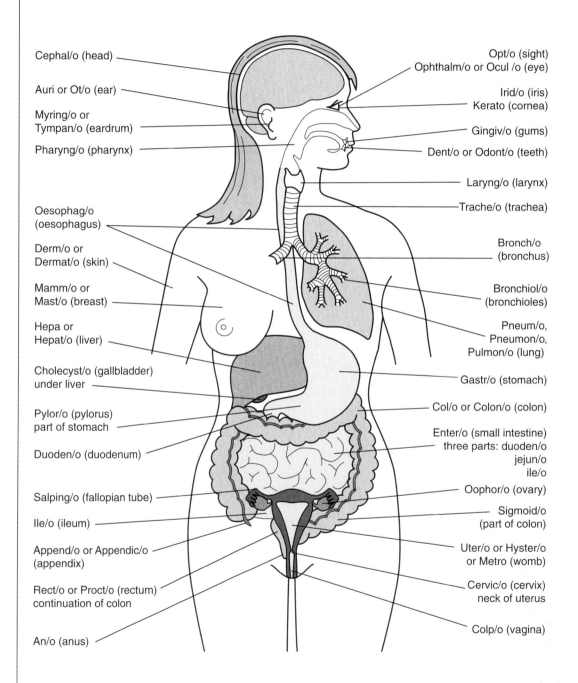

Cephal/o (head)

Auri or Ot/o (ear)

Myring/o or
Tympan/o (eardrum)

Pharyng/o (pharynx)

Oesophag/o
(oesophagus)

Derm/o or
Dermat/o (skin)

Mamm/o or
Mast/o (breast)

Hepa or
Hepat/o (liver)

Cholecyst/o (gallbladder)
under liver

Pylor/o (pylorus)
part of stomach

Duoden/o (duodenum)

Salping/o (fallopian tube)

Ile/o (ileum)

Append/o or Appendic/o
(appendix)

Rect/o or Proct/o (rectum)
continuation of colon

An/o (anus)

Opt/o (sight)
Ophthalm/o or Ocul /o (eye)

Irid/o (iris)
Kerato (cornea)

Gingiv/o (gums)

Dent/o or Odont/o (teeth)

Laryng/o (larynx)

Trache/o (trachea)

Bronch/o
(bronchus)

Bronchiol/o
(bronchioles)

Pneum/o,
Pneumon/o,
Pulmon/o (lung)

Gastr/o (stomach)

Col/o or Colon/o (colon)

Enter/o (small intestine)
three parts: duoden/o
jejun/o
ile/o

Oophor/o (ovary)

Sigmoid/o
(part of colon)

Uter/o or Hyster/o
or Metro (womb)

Cervic/o (cervix)
neck of uterus

Colp/o (vagina)

Figure 1: Gyne (woman). Anterior view showing intestinal tract, female reproductive organs, lung and airway *Redrawn after Prendergast A: Medical Terminology, 2nd edition, Addison-Wesley, 1983.*

Stem	Meaning
angi/o, vas/o	vessel
appendic/o	appendix
arteri/o	artery
arthr/o	joint
aur/i, ot/o	ear
bili	bile
bronch/o	bronchus
bronchiol/o	bronchiole (small termination of bronchial tubes)
cardi/o	heart
carpo	wrist
cephal/o	head
cerebr/o	cerebrum (part of brain)
cheil/o	lip
cheir/o	hand/surgery
chole	bile
cholecyst/o	gallbladder
choledoch/o	common bile duct
chondr/o	cartilage
col/o	colon (large intestine)
cost/o	rib
crani/o	cranium (skull containing brain)
cyst/o	bladder
cyto	cell
dacryo	tear
dactyl	finger
dent/o, odont/o	tooth
derm/o, dermat/o	skin
duoden/o	duodenum (part of small intestine)
encephal/o	brain
gastr/o	stomach
gingiv/o	gums
gloss/o, lingu/o	tongue
glyco	sugar
gynaec/o	woman

Stem	Meaning
hep/o, hepat/o	liver
histo	tissue
hydro	water, fluid
hyster/o, metr/o, uter/o	womb/uterus
iatro	physician
ile/o	ileum (part of small intestine)
ili/o	ilium (bone of pelvis)
irid/o	iris (of eye)
karyo	nucleus
kerat/o	cornea of eye
lacrim/o	tear
lacto	milk
lamina	part of vertebra
lip/o	fat
lob/o	lobe (e.g. of lung)
lympho	lymphatic
mast/o, mamm/o	breast
metro	measure, uterus
my/o, myos	muscle
myco, myceto	fungus
myel/o	bone marrow/spinal cord
myring/o, tympan/o	eardrum
nas/o, rhin/o	nose
nephr/o, ren/o	kidney
neur/o	nerve
oesophag/o	oesophagus
onycho	nail
oo	egg/ovum
oophor/o	ovary
ophthalm/o	eye
orchi/o, orchid/o	testicle/testis
oro	mouth
oste/o	bone
paedo	child
pancreat/o	pancreas
patho	disease
pharmaco	drugs/chemist

Roots for body parts and organs

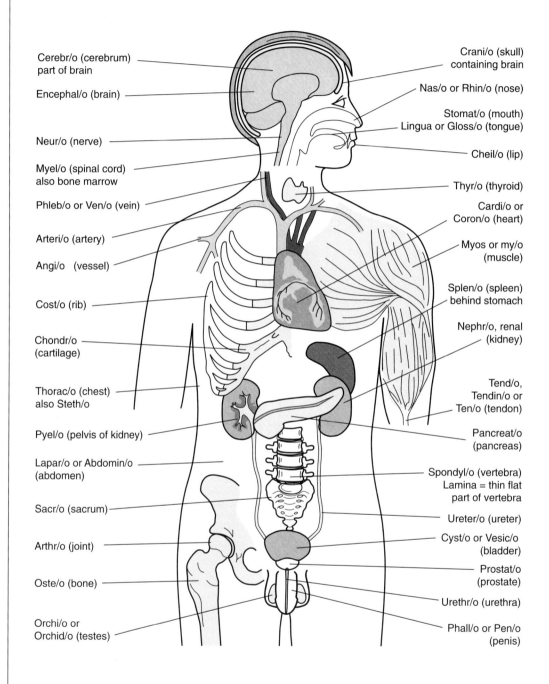

Cerebr/o (cerebrum) part of brain

Encephal/o (brain)

Neur/o (nerve)

Myel/o (spinal cord) also bone marrow

Phleb/o or Ven/o (vein)

Arteri/o (artery)

Angi/o (vessel)

Cost/o (rib)

Chondr/o (cartilage)

Thorac/o (chest) also Steth/o

Pyel/o (pelvis of kidney)

Lapar/o or Abdomin/o (abdomen)

Sacr/o (sacrum)

Arthr/o (joint)

Oste/o (bone)

Orchi/o or Orchid/o (testes)

Crani/o (skull) containing brain

Nas/o or Rhin/o (nose)

Stomat/o (mouth)
Lingua or Gloss/o (tongue)

Cheil/o (lip)

Thyr/o (thyroid)

Cardi/o or Coron/o (heart)

Myos or my/o (muscle)

Splen/o (spleen) behind stomach

Nephr/o, renal (kidney)

Tend/o, Tendin/o or Ten/o (tendon)

Pancreat/o (pancreas)

Spondyl/o (vertebra)
Lamina = thin flat part of vertebra

Ureter/o (ureter)

Cyst/o or Vesic/o (bladder)

Prostat/o (prostate)

Urethr/o (urethra)

Phall/o or Pen/o (penis)

Figure 2: Andro (man). Anterior view showing male reproductive organs, urinary tract, heart, spleen, pancreas, hip joint and some shoulder muscles
Redrawn after Prendergast A: Medical Terminology, 2nd edition, Addison-Wesley, 1983.

Stem	Meaning
pharyng/o	pharynx
phleb/o, ven/o	vein
phren/o	diaphragm
pleuro	pleura/rib/side
pneumo	air
pneumon/o, pneum/o	lungs
podo	foot
proct/o	rectum/anus
prostat/o	prostate gland
psycho	mind
pyel/o	pelvis of kidney
pylor/o	part of stomach
pyo	pus
pyro	fire, heat
radio	radiation
rect/o	rectum
sacr/o	sacrum (part of vertebrae)
salping/o	fallopian tube
sial/o	salivary gland
splen/o	spleen
spondyl/o, vertebr/o	vertebra
steato	fat
stomat/o	mouth
tarso	foot, eyelid
ten/o, tendin/o	tendon
thermo	heat
thorac/o, steth/o	thorax (chest)
thrombo	blood clot
thyr/o	thyroid gland
tox, toxico	poison
trache/o	trachea (windpipe)
trich/o	hair
ureter/o	ureter (urinary system)
urethr/o	urethra
uro	urine
vaso	vessel

Common prefixes

The following is a list of common prefixes for combining with stems and suffixes.

Prefix	Meaning
a- or **an-**	absence of, without
ab-	away from
acro-	extremity
ad-	towards
ambi-	both
ana-	up, excessive
aniso-	unequal
ante-	before
anti-	against
auto-	self
bi-	two
bio-	life
brady-	slow
centi-	hundred
chrom-	colour
circum-	around
co-/con-	together with
contra-	against
cryo-	cold
crypto-	hidden
cyano-	blue
de-	away from/reversing
demi-	half
dextro-	to the right
di-	two
dia-	through
dys-	difficult, painful
ecto-	without, outside
endo-	within, inside
epi-	upon
ery-/erythro-	red
eu-	good, normal
ex-	out
extra-	outside
flavo-	yellow

Prefix	Meaning
gen-	referring to birth or producing
haemo-	blood
hemi-	half
hetero-	different, other
homeo-	like
homo-	same
hyper-	above, in excess of normal
hypo-	below, under, less than normal
idio-	peculiar to the individual
in-	in
infra-	below
inter-	between
intra-	within
iso-	equal, same
kypho-	humped, rounded
leuco-	white
macro-	large
mal-	bad, abnormal
mega-	big, enlarged
melano-	black, dark, pigment
meta-	beyond
micro-	small
multi-	many
narco-	stupor
neo-	new
nocto-/nycto-	night
oligo-	scanty
ortho-	straight
os-	opening, bone
pachy-	thick
pan-	all
para-	alongside, close to
ped-	foot, child
penta-	five
per-	through
peri-	around
polio-	grey
poly-	many
post-	after

Prefix	Meaning
pre-/pro-	before
proto-	first
pseudo-	false
quadri-	four
retro-	behind
sub-	below
supra-	above
syn-	with, union
tachy-	fast, rapid
tetra-	four
tri-	three
ultra-	beyond
uni-	one
xantho-	yellow
xer/o-	dry

Roots used as prefixes and suffixes

Some root word parts may also be used as prefixes if they are used at the beginning of a word to qualify or describe a following root word part.

e.g. **haem/o/thor/ax**
blood in the thoracic (chest) cavity

haem meaning blood, used here as a prefix referring to **thor**, the root for chest cavity

o combining vowel

thor root for chest cavity

ax suffix for the singular ending of the noun.

e.g. **hist/o/path/ology**
study of the disease of tissues

hist meaning tissue, used here as a prefix, referring to **path** the root for disease

o combining vowel

path root for disease

ology suffix for the 'study of'

Common suffixes

Suffix	Meaning
-aemia	blood
-aesthesia	sensibility
-al	pertaining to
-algia	pain
-an	pertaining to
-blast	immature cell
-cele	swelling/protrusion/ herniation
-centesis	puncture, drawing off
-cide	killing, destroying
-cision	cutting
-clasis	breaking
-coccus	round cell, type of bacteria
-cyte	cell
-derm	skin
-desis	binding together
-dynia	pain
-ectasis	dilatation
-ectomy	removal of
-form	having the formation or shape of
-genesis	forming or origin
-genic	producing or forming
-gram	a picture
-graph	a machine which records
-graphy	the procedure of recording
-iasis	condition of/state of
-iatric	pertaining to medicine/physician
-ism	condition of
-itis	inflammation of
-kinesis	movement, activity
-lith	stone
-lithiasis	condition of stones
-lysis	breaking down (keep splitting)
-malacia	softening
-megaly	enlargement

Suffix	Meaning
-meter	measure
-oid	likeness, resemblance
-ology	scientific study of
-oma	tumour
-opia	condition of the eye
-ose	sugar
-osis	condition of
-ostomy	making an opening (to remain)
-otomy	to cut into, divide
-ous	like, similar to
-paresis	weakness
-pathy	disease
-penia	lack of, decreased
-pexy	fixation of
-phage	eating, ingesting
-phagia	swallowing
-phasia	speech
-philia	loving, affinity for
-phobia	irrational fear of
-phylaxis	protection, prevention
-plasia	formation
-plasty	form, mould, reconstruct
-plegia	paralysis
-pnoea	breathing
-poiesis	making
-rhythmia	rhythm
-rrhage	to burst forth (heavy bleeding)
-rrhaphy	sewing, repair
-rrhexis	rupture of
-rrhoea	flowing, discharge
-sclerosis	hardening
-scope	lighted instrument used for examination
-scopy	examination with lighted instrument
-somatic	pertaining to the body
-stasis	cessation of movement/flow

Suffix	Meaning
-staxis	dripping (blood)
-stenosis	narrowing
-sthenia	strength
-taxia	co-ordination, order
-tome	cutting instrument
-tripsy	crushing of stones
-trophy	nourishment
-uria	condition of urine

Common plural forms

The following rules apply when forming plural words:

Singular	Plural
-us	**-i**

e.g. staphylococcus / staphylococci

-a	**-ae**

e.g. vertebra / vertebrae

-um	**-a**

e.g. atrium / atria

-is	**-es**

e.g. diagnosis / diagnoses

-oma	**-omata**

e.g. stoma / stomata

-ix	**-ices**

e.g. cervix / cervices

-ax	**-aces**

e.g. thorax / thoraces

-on	**-a**

e.g. ganglion / ganglia

Americanisms

In American versions of medical terms, spellings are altered in the following ways. It is common to drop the silent double vowels (diphthong) as used in English spellings, e.g. **ae** becomes **e.**

The English stem **haem**, in American spelling is **hem** (meaning blood).

Other examples include:

English	American
anaemia	**anemia**
anaesthesia	**anesthesia**
oedema	**edema**
dyspnoea	**dyspnea**
leucocyte	**leukocyte**
paediatric	**pediatric**

With the advent of word checks on computers, American style spellings of medical words is increasing in use. However, the English interpretation is used throughout this book.

The structure and function of the human body

Anatomy and physiology

Anatomy   is the study of the structure of the body.

Physiology   is the study of the function of the body.

The basic elements

The human body is an incredibly complex creation, much of which is still not fully understood. In order to appreciate its complexity, the basic elements must be examined. The following are the main structures of which it is composed:

cells, tissues, organs and **systems**

Cells

The human body is composed of billions of tiny living materials known as cells. Cells vary in form and size, each type being adapted in structure to the function it performs.

The cell is composed of **protoplasm** containing numerous inclusions. It is surrounded by a selective semi-permeable membrane; i.e. it will allow some substances in and out through the membrane, but not others.

Figure 3: The human cell

At some stage in every cell's life, there is a **nucleus** surrounded by a similar membrane known as the nuclear membrane (*see Figure 3*). It is here within the nucleus that the chromosomes are found, consisting of **DNA** (deoxyribonucleic acid). Each human cell normally contains 23 pairs of **chromosomes**, and it is upon these structures that the genetic blueprint is found, known as **genes**. These determine the individual characteristics of each cell.

The sex cells (**gametes**) of the ovum from the female and the spermatazoon from the male contain only 23 single chromosomes, which upon fusion at fertilisation enables the mixing of the genetic materials to form a new unique human being.

Tissues

Similar types of cells are grouped together to form tissues (*see Figure 4*). Each type of tissue has a particular function.

Abbreviations

Ca	carcinoma
SA	sarcoma
TNM	tumour nodes metastases
T	tumour

Types of tissues

There are four main types of tissue in the human body:

1. Epithelial
covering and lining of organs and cavities, (known as endothelium when lining internal organs).

2. Connective
supporting tissue, includes fibrous and elastic fibres, ligaments, cartilage and bone-blood.

3. Muscle
voluntary muscle (skeletal) attached to the skeleton; involuntary muscle (smooth) forming many internal organs, e.g. the stomach; **cardiac muscle** is a specialised muscle found only in the heart.

4. Nerve
a highly specialised tissue containing neurones forming the central, autonomic and peripheral nervous systems as well as special sensory organs, e.g. retina of eye (see Chapter 13).

Organs

Differing types of tissues are grouped together to form organs which perform special functions.

Systems

Organs working together to perform particular functions are known as systems. In health, each system normally works in harmony with others to maintain the body in its correct state (homeostasis).

Tissue cells

A EPITHELIUM

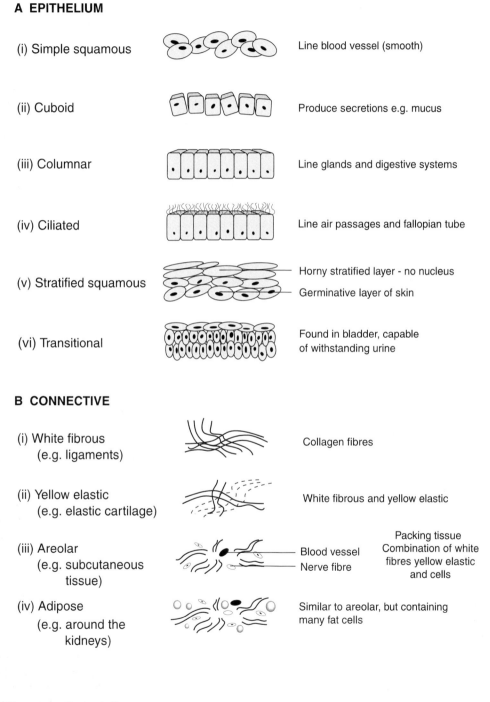

(i) Simple squamous — Line blood vessel (smooth)

(ii) Cuboid — Produce secretions e.g. mucus

(iii) Columnar — Line glands and digestive systems

(iv) Ciliated — Line air passages and fallopian tube

(v) Stratified squamous — Horny stratified layer - no nucleus / Germinative layer of skin

(vi) Transitional — Found in bladder, capable of withstanding urine

B CONNECTIVE

(i) White fibrous (e.g. ligaments) — Collagen fibres

(ii) Yellow elastic (e.g. elastic cartilage) — White fibrous and yellow elastic

(iii) Areolar (e.g. subcutaneous tissue) — Blood vessel / Nerve fibre — Packing tissue Combination of white fibres yellow elastic and cells

(iv) Adipose (e.g. around the kidneys) — Similar to areolar, but containing many fat cells

Figure 4: Tissue Cells

Properties of living organisms

All living organisms, as opposed to non-living matter, have the following qualities:

Respiration
the process of producing energy in order to carry out all the metabolic processes required. In humans, this involves the absorption of oxygen for use in the cells together with glucose, and the production of waste products for excretion of carbon dioxide and water.

Nutrition
the process by which food is obtained for use as energy for growth or repair of the body.

Excretion
the process by which the body eliminates the waste products of metabolism.

Growth and repair
the ability to increase in size and repair damage to cells as well as producing new, similar cells (by **mitosis** division).

Reproduction
the process by which new individuals are produced (by **meiosis** division).

Sensitivity
the ability to detect changes in the environment.

Movement
capability of some movement.

Non-living materials

The following materials are also present in the body and are essential to life:

Water
- H_2O forming the largest component of all.

Mineral salts including
- Sodium   Na
- Potassium   K
- Calcium   Ca
- Magnesium   Mg
- Iron   Fe
- Phosphates, carbonates, chlorides and other trace elements.

The balance of salts in the body is vital to life, and the electrolytes or electrolytic balance (balance of ions or mineral salts) are often measured in blood tests.

Metabolism

Metabolism is the basic working of the body cells. It concerns the continuous chemical changes that occur to sustain life. Energy is produced as a by-product of the reactions.

Osmosis

This is the passage of fluid across a semi-permeable membrane, which allows equalisation of the concentration of solutions either side of the membrane. Tissue fluid is drawn back into the venous capillaries of the body by the presence of large plasma proteins, after it has given up its nutrients etc. to the tissue cells.

Glands

These are structures which produce and secrete their own substance. There are two types:

1. Exocrine glands (with ducts)
These pour their secretions through ducts to another organ, or directly upon the surface of a membrane, e.g. mucus secretions from epithelial tissue, or **bile** from the liver to the bile-duct.

2. Endocrine glands (ductless)
These produce secretions known as **hormones**, which are secreted directly into the blood supply for stimulation of another target organ (see Chapter 15, Endocrine system).

Membranes

These are special tissues covering and lining areas of the body. There are three types:

1. Mucous membranes
tissue containing mucus-secreting cells which moisten and lubricate surfaces.

2. Serous membranes
a double-layered tissue composed of smooth, simple squamous epithelial cells which secrete

a thin fluid between the two layers known as serous fluid, e.g. **pleura** covering the lungs and **peritoneum** covering abdominal organs.

3. Synovial membranes

a single membrane which produces a thick glairy fluid known as synovial fluid, found at freely moveable joints preventing friction and wear.

Anatomical position and planes

The body is described facing forwards, feet apart, arms at sides and palms facing forward, as illustrated in Figure 5.

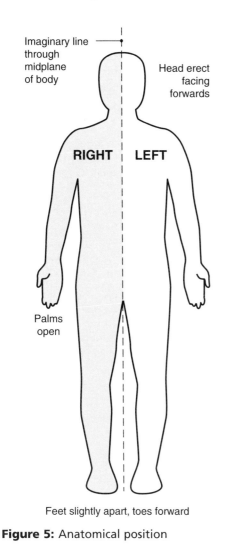

Imaginary line through midplane of body

Head erect facing forwards

RIGHT | LEFT

Palms open

Feet slightly apart, toes forward

Figure 5: Anatomical position

The following terms are used to describe anatomical positions:

Superior	above
Inferior	below
Anterior	front or in front
Posterior	back or back of
Medial	midline towards centre
Lateral	side or away from midline
Proximal	nearest to a point of origin
Distal	furthest from a point of origin
Superficial	nearest body surface
Deep	away from surface
Ventral	front
Dorsal	back
Cortex	outer region, e.g. of kidney
Medulla	inner region, e.g. of kidney
Peripheral	relating to the outer surface or circumference
Plantar	referring to sole of foot
Palmar	referring to palm of hand

The following terms are used to describe anatomical planes *(see Figure 6)*:

Sagittal	lengthwise (vertically) from front to back
Frontal or coronal	lengthwise (vertically) from side to side dividing body into ventral and dorsal sections
Horizontal or transverse	divides body across into upper and lower parts
Cranial	head or upper section
Caudal	tail or lower section

Cavities of the body

The main cavities of the body are the:

- **thoracic cavity**

- **abdominal cavity**

- **pelvic cavity**

Regions of the abdomen

The abdominal and pelvic areas of the trunk are divided into **quadrants**, as shown in Figure 7.

The abdomen is also divided into the **regions** shown in Figure 8.

Terminology

Anaplasia	abnormal cells without a regular nucleus (malignant)
Atrophy	wastage of an organ
Cortex	outer portion of an organ
Cytology	study of cells
Dysplasia	formation of abnormal cells
Fundus	the area of a hollow organ, which is opposite the main opening, e.g. of the uterus
Genome	a map of the genetic material of the species
Hilum	a depression on the surface of an organ where blood and other vessels, and ducts enter and leave
Histology	study of tissues
Hypertropy	enlargement of an organ with its own tissue
Infarct	a wedge-shaped area of tissue deprived of its blood supply
Interstitial	type of supporting tissue
Ischaemia	lack of blood to a part
Medulla	inner portion of an organ
Metaplasia	type of cell growing beyond where usually found
Oncology	study of tumours
Viscus	organ

Anatomical planes

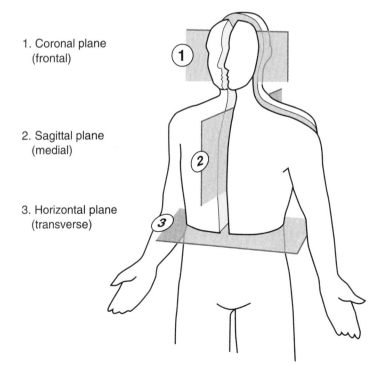

1. Coronal plane (frontal)

2. Sagittal plane (medial)

3. Horizontal plane (transverse)

Figure 6: Anatomical planes

Diseases and disorders

Adenoma	tumour of a gland
Benign	favourable for recovery, opposite of malignant
Carcinoma	cancerous, abnormal malignant cells growing in the body
Chondroma	benign tumour of cartilage
Chondrosarcoma	malignant tumour of cartilage and bone

Contusion	bleeding beneath the skin (bruise)
Embolism	obstruction of a blood vessel by a detached, travelling particle of blood, fat or air
Embolus	blood clot, fat or air detached from another place and travelling in the blood stream

Quadrants of the abdominopelvic regions and regions of the abdominal cavity

Figure 7: Quadrants of the abdominopelvic regions of the body

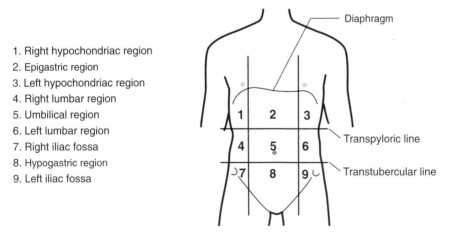

1. Right hypochondriac region
2. Epigastric region
3. Left hypochondriac region
4. Right lumbar region
5. Umbilical region
6. Left lumbar region
7. Right iliac fossa
8. Hypogastric region
9. Left iliac fossa

Figure 8: Regions of the abdominal cavity

Epithelioma	tumour of epithelial tissue (lining and covering organs), e.g. of the epidermis
Fibroma	tumour of fibrous tissue
Fibrosis	formation of scar tissue
Haematoma	swelling containing blood
Ischaemia	deficiency of blood supply to a part
Keloid scar	abnormal overgrowth of fibrous tissue in the healing of a wound
Lesion	morbid (abnormal) change in tissue
Lipoma	tumour composed of fat
Malignant	virulent/dangerous, likely to have a fatal outcome (disease or tumour)
Myalgia	painful muscles
Myasthenia gravis	disease causing abnormal fatigue and weakness in voluntary muscles
Myoma	tumour composed of muscle
NG	new growth
Necrosis	death of tissue
Necrotising fasciitis	destruction of soft tissue by overwhelming infection, usually post-operatively, by haemolytic streptococcus bacteria (Group A)
Neoplasm	new growth or tumour
Oedema	free fluid in the tissues
Papilloma	wart-type benign tumour
Peritonitis	inflammation of the peritoneum (the lining of the abdomen and pelvic cavities)
Pleurisy	inflammation of the pleura (the covering of the lungs)
Sarcoma	cancer arising in the connective tissue, e.g. bone, blood
Sebaceous cyst	swelling caused by blockage of sebaceous gland duct in the skin

Procedures and equipment

Biopsy	removal of a portion of living tissue for microscopic investigation

Classification of diseases

Acquired	acquired after birth
Acute	rapid onset and progress
Allergic	hypersensitivity to foreign proteins
Chronic	slow onset and progress
Congenital	present at birth
Cryptogenic	of doubtful or hidden origin
Endocrine	associated with hormone dysfunction
Familial	occurs in families
Functional	no anatomical abnormality demonstrated but associated with dysfunction
Iatrogenic	a disease produced by the treatment given for a primary illness
Idiopathic	peculiar to the individual
Infectious	caused by micro-organisms readily passed on to other people
Local	involving an area or one part of the body only
Metabolic	disorder of basic working (physiology) of the body
Neoplastic	associated with development of new growths (e.g. malignant or benign tumours)
Nosocomial	infection acquired from hospital, e.g. MRSA
Organic	structural abnormality demonstrated
Silent	no symptoms apparent or obvious signs
Systemic	involving the entire body
Traumatic	involving injury

Chapter

The locomotor system

The locomotor system

The locomotor system consists of the bones, muscles, ligaments, cartilage and tendons. It is mainly concerned with movement.

Bone

There are two different types of bone structure known as:

- **Compact** (hard)
- **Cancellous** (spongy)

Cancellous bone tissue forms the red bone marrow. All bones are covered in a membrane known as the **periosteum**, which provides nourishment.

Hyaline cartilage tissue is found at the ends of long bones where joints are formed, preventing wear. In fetal life, bone is generally developed from cartilage tissue by the laying down of calcium salts by specialised bone cells. This continues after birth and is known as **ossification.**

Vitamin D and **calcium** are essential for healthy bone formation. There are 206 bones in the adult human body.

Descriptive terms of bones

Articulation	a joint between two bones
Border	edge separating two surfaces of bone
Condyle	rounded enlargement at the ends of bone
Crest	elevated ridge on a bone
Facet	a small articulating surface
Foramen (pl: -mina)	hole or opening in a bone
Fossa	depression or hollowed out area on the surface of a bone
Lamina	thin plate or layer (usually of bone)
Process	projection from a bone
Trochanter	large, rough eminence on a bone
Tuberosity	large protuberance on a bone
Tubercle	small rounded prominence

The skeleton

This is made up of five classifications of bones:

1. long bones
forming limbs and having a cavity

2. short bones
having no cavity, found in the hands and feet

3. flat bones
forming the cranium and scapula

4. irregular bones
face bones and vertebrae

5. sesamoid bones
formed in a tendon, e.g. patella and hyoid bones

The bony framework of the body (*see Figure 9*) has the following functions:

Support	provides a framework for the body and gives shape
Leverage	provides levers for muscle attachment allowing movement and articulation
Protection	protects organs, e.g. brain within the cranium
Storage	stores calcium salts
Production	manufactures blood cells in the bone marrow

There are two parts to the skeleton:

1. The axial skeleton
formed from the skull, vertebrae, rib cage and breast bone - made up of 80 bones

2. The appendicular skeleton
consisting of 126 bones forming the limb bones and their girdles.

Some unusual adjectives of bones

Clavicular	relating to the clavicles
Coccygeal	relating to the coccyx
Femoral	relating to the femur
Fibular	relating to the fibula
Humer	relating to the humerus
Phalangeal	relating to the phalanges
Scapular	relating to the scapula
Ulnar	relating to the ulna

The skeleton

1. Skull
2. Maxilla
3. Cervical vertebrae
4. Humerus
5. Lumbar vertebrae
6. Pelvis
7. Carpals
8. Metacarpals
9. Phalanges
10. Patella
11. Tarsals
12. Metatarsals
13. Phalanges
14. Tibia
15. Fibula
16. Femur
17. Ulna
18. Radius
19. Ribs
20. Sternum
21. Clavicle
22. Mandible
23. Frontal bone

Figure 9: The skeleton

The skull

This includes the bones of the face and the bones which form the **cranium** containing the brain and beginning of the spinal cord (*see Figure 10*). The lobes of the **cerebrum** (part of brain) are named by the bones under which they lie.

Bones of the cranium

These consist of the following individual bones:

- One **occipital**
- Two **parietal**
- Two **temporal**
- One **frontal**
- One **sphenoid**
- One **ethmoid**

Fontanelles

The uniting of the cranial bones by **sutures** (fibrous immovable joints) occurs after birth. Because the bones are not united in the fetus, moulding of the skull to aid delivery is able to occur during childbirth.

The anterior fontanelle is a 'soft spot' which can be felt until its closure at approximately 18 months. The 'soft spot' allows the skull bones to continue to grow to accommodate the increasing size of the brain.

The posterior fontanelle closes at approximately three months (*see Figure 11*).

Bones of the face

These consist of the following individual bones:

- One **mandible**   lower jaw
- Two **maxilla**   upper jaw
- Two **malar** or
  zygomatic   cheek bones
- One **nasal**   part of nose
- One **vomer**   part of nasal septum
- Two **lacrimal**
  (lacrymal)   bony orbit
- Two **palatine**   hard palate in mouth
- Two **turbinate**   inside nose

Bones of the skull

1. Parietal*
2. Sphenoid*
3. Temporal*
4. Occipital*
5. Mastoid portion of
   temporal lobe
6. Mandible
7. Malar or zygomatic
8. Maxilla
9. Ethmoid*
10. Nasal
11. Lacrimal
12. Frontal*

   * form the cranium

Figure 10: Bones of the skull

Fontanelles of the skull

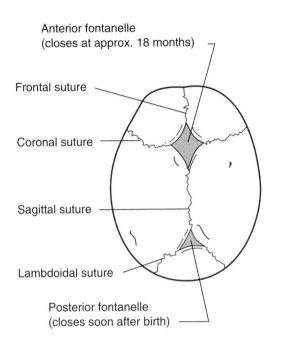

Anterior fontanelle
(closes at approx. 18 months)

Frontal suture

Coronal suture

Sagittal suture

Lambdoidal suture

Posterior fontanelle
(closes soon after birth)

Figure 11: Fontanelles of the skull

Air sinuses of the skull

These are cavities containing air within the bone tissues which lighten the skull. They are lined with mucous membrane which may become infected. They are found in the following bones:

- **Frontal**

- **Maxillary**

- **Ethmoid**

- **Sphenoid**

Hyoid bone

The **hyoid** bone is a small bone to which the tongue is attached. It is often found to be fractured in cases of strangulation.

Vertebrae

There are 33 irregular bones in the vertebral column or **spine**, stacked one upon the other and bound together by strong ligaments. The spine combines great strength with mobility. Its function is to:

- Provide a framework for attachment of other structures

- Protect the spinal cord and nerves

- Provide locomotion

- Absorb shock

- Form strong joints

Vertebrae are in groups and are named after the region in which they are situated. They become larger and heavier in size as they descend, although the neural or vertebral **foramen** (hole through which the spinal cord travels) becomes smaller.

The vertebrae are described as **typical** (having similar features) or **atypical** (not having the typical features).

Typical vertebrae

A typical vertebra (*see Figure 12*) contains the following features:

- A **body**

- Four **articulating processes** (surfaces) – forming joints with the vertebrae above and below

- Two **pedicles**

- Two **transverse processes**

- Two **lamina**

- A **spinous process** – formed from the uniting of the lamina

- Two **intervertebral notches** – through which spinal nerves travel from each side of the spinal cord

- A **vertebral (neural) foramen** – through which the spinal cord travels

Vertebrae

Figure 12: A typical vertebra

Figure 13: The atlas and axis (anterior view)

Atypical vertebrae

These consist of the **atlas** and **axis** (the first and second cervical vertebrae), and the **sacrum** and **coccyx** which are formed of fused vertebrae. They do *not* possess the typical features described above.

The atlas forms a joint (**articulates**) with the occipital bone of the skull above, and allows the movement of nodding the head. The atlas and axis form a pivot joint which allows movement of the head from side to side *(see Figure 13)*.

Intervertebral discs

Between the bodies of each vertebra are the intervertebral discs, pads of cartilage filled with a fluid. These act as shock absorbers, preventing damage to the structure.

Regions of the vertebral column

- **cervical**   seven bones
- **thoracic**   12 bones
- **lumbar**   five bones
- **sacral**   five fused bones
- **coccyx**   four fused bones

Curvatures

The curvatures of the vertebral column are initially formed in fetal development, while the developing fetus is curled up in the mother's uterus. These are the **thoracic** and **sacral** curvatures *(see Figure 14)*.

After birth, the **cervical curvature** is formed when the baby is able to support its own head, from approximately three months. The lumbar curvature forms when the child stands and supports his/her body at 12-18 months.

Rib cage (thoracic)

This is made up of the following structures *(see Figure 15)*:

- One **sternum** (breast bone)
- 12 pairs of **ribs**
- 12 **thoracic vertebrae**

Sternum

This flat bone forms the front (**anterior**) part of the rib cage, and it is to this that the ribs and collar bone (**clavicle**) are attached. It is composed of three parts known as the **manubrium**, **body** and **xiphoid** portions. Beneath this bone lies the heart, and it is this bone which is depressed in the rendering of **cardiopulmonary resuscitation** (**CPR**).

The ribs form the bony lateral walls of the chest cavity and form joints (**articulate**) with

Vertebral column and curvatures

ANTERIOR   **POSTERIOR**

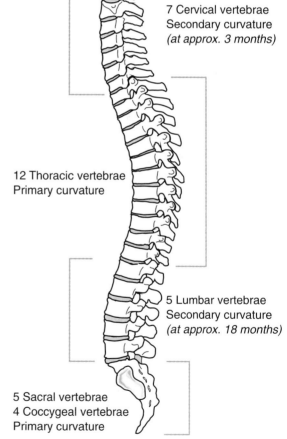

7 Cervical vertebrae
Secondary curvature
(at approx. 3 months)

12 Thoracic vertebrae
Primary curvature

5 Lumbar vertebrae
Secondary curvature
(at approx. 18 months)

5 Sacral vertebrae
4 Coccygeal vertebrae
Primary curvature

Figure 14: The vertebral column and curvatures

the **thoracic vertebrae** at the rear (**posteriorly**). The first 10 pairs of ribs are attached to the sternum **anteriorly** by the attachment of **costal cartilages**, the first seven directly and the lower three indirectly as shown in Figure 15. The last two pairs of ribs are known as **floating ribs** as they remain unattached to the sternum.

The rib cage protects the organs lying within it: heart, lungs, oesophagus, major blood vessels etc.

Intercostal muscles are attached to the ribs between the rib spaces and are involved in the process of **inspiration** and **expiration**. The rib cage swings outwards and upwards on inspiration, which increases the capacity of the thoracic cavity, allowing expansion of the lung tissue (see Chapter 7).

Pelvis

This structure is composed of the following bones:

- Two **innominate bones**

- **Sacrum** (part of the vertebrae)

These structures are bound together by ligaments to form the pelvic basin (*see Figure 16*). The innominate bone is composed of three separate bones which are fused together:

- **Ilium**

- **Ischium**

- **Pubis**

The rib cage

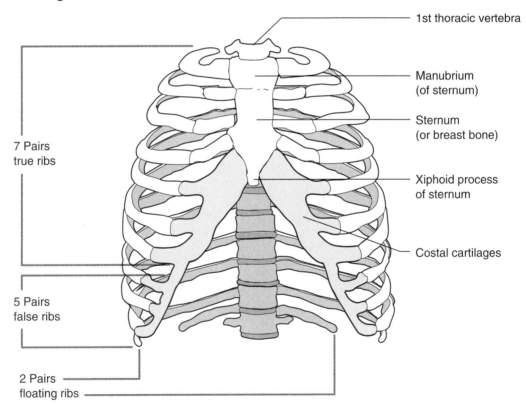

Figure 15: The rib cage

The pelvis

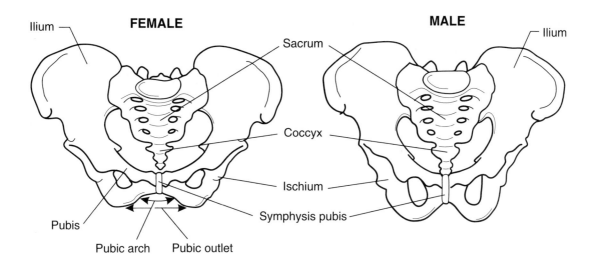

Figure 16: The pelvis

The area within the pelvis is known as the **pelvic cavity** and contains important structures, such as the intestine, rectum and anus, bladder, ureters, urethra, prostate gland, some organs of the male reproductive system, female reproductive organs, blood vessels, nerves etc., which are protected by the bony frame.

The hand

The hand comprises a number of small bones (shown in Figure 17).

The foot

The foot comprises a number of small bones (shown in Figure 18).

Joints

Joints are formed wherever two or more bony surfaces are attached to each other.

Types of joint

Fixed joints
formed of fibrous tissue where no movement is possible, e.g. sutures of cranium

Slightly moveable
cartilaginous joints which allow only slight movement, e.g. intervertebral joints between the bodies of vertebrae

Freely moveable synovial joints
which allow free movement according to the shape of the joint. *(see Figures 19 and 20)*

Synovial joints are lined with a synovial membrane which produces synovial fluid, a thick glairy fluid which acts as a lubricant preventing friction and wear. The ends of the bones which form these joints are covered in **hyaline cartilage** *(see Figure 20)*.

Bones of the hand and foot

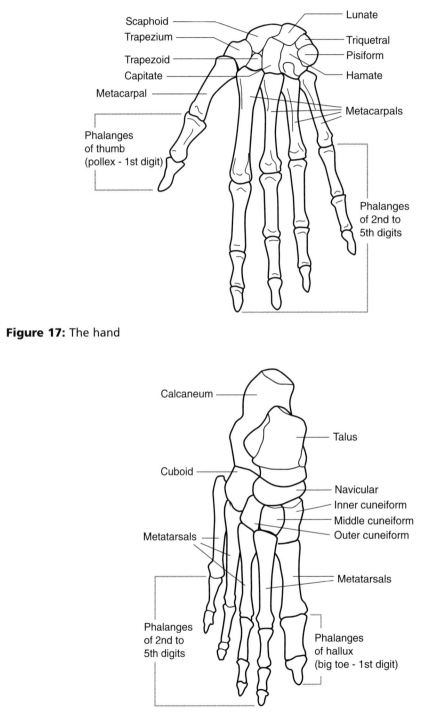

Figure 17: The hand

Figure 18: The foot

Body movements and positions

Figure 19: A sample of terms used to describe body movements and positions
Redrawn after Prendergast A: Medical Terminology, 2nd edition, Addison-Wesley, 1983

A synovial joint

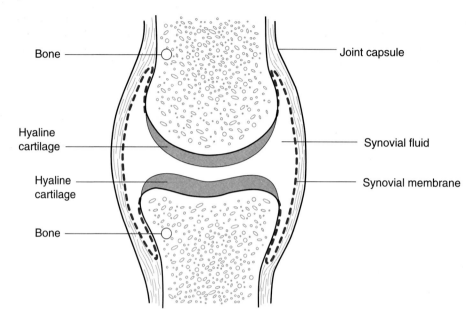

Bone — — Joint capsule

Hyaline cartilage — — Synovial fluid

Hyaline cartilage — — Synovial membrane

Bone —

Figure 20: A synovial joint

Bursa

This is a sac lined with synovial membrane containing synovial fluid, usually found between a tendon and a bone near the surface of the body in order to prevent friction on movement. Inflammation of these is common in conditions such as **housemaid's knee**.

Ligaments

These are composed of tough fibrous tissue and bind bone to bone.

Muscles

These are strong elastic tissue, well supplied with blood (vascular), capable of contraction and relaxation. In life, muscles are always partially contracted, and this is known as muscle tone.

Types of muscle

There are three types of muscle in the body:

1. **Voluntary (striated)**
   attached to the skeleton and under control of the will

2. **Involuntary (unstriated)**
   smooth and controlled automatically by the autonomic nervous system; these form the walls of major organs, e.g. stomach

3. **Cardiac (myogenic)**
   special muscle exclusive to the heart, forming its walls; controlled by the autonomic nervous system. It's capable of independent contraction causing quivering of the heart if the nerve supply within is interrupted.

Skeletal or striated muscle is often named from its shape, e.g. **deltoid** (triangular), or the number of heads it has, e.g. **triceps**. Muscles usually work in groups and in co-ordination.

Diaphragm

This is an important muscle which divides the **thoracic** (chest) cavity from the abdominal cavity. It is essential for the act of **respiration** (breathing). Also involved are the **intercostal muscles** which move the rib cage (see Chapter 7).

Tendons

These are specialised fibrous bands found at the ends of muscles which attach muscle to bone, or muscle to muscle.

Energy

Muscles require a good blood supply to provide oxygen and nutrients. Glucose is converted and stored in muscle tissue ready for its release when required. Cramp occurs when there is insufficient oxygen available for the chemical reaction to occur and **lactic acid** is produced. The remedy for cramp is to extend the muscle.

Hernia

This condition arises from a weakness in the muscle which allows part of an organ to **prolapse** through the space created by the weakness.

Types of hernia

Inguinal hernia
This is common in men. It arises in an area known as the **inguinal canal**, which is a tunnel in the abdominal muscles where the spermatic cord and testis travel to descend into the scrotum in fetal life. Protrusion of the intestine through this area can occur and may lead to strangulation, i.e. the blood supply to this intestinal area becomes deprived.

Femoral hernia
This is a condition where the weakness is in the groin where the **femoral artery** travels to the leg. Hernias in this area are more common among women.

Hiatus hernia
This is a condition where the weakness is in the diaphragm. Part of the **oesophagus** (gullet) and/or the stomach travels through the space created by the weakness causing symptoms of 'heart burn' due to gastric juices affecting the oesophagus.

Umbilical hernia
In this condition, the weakness is in the area of muscle through which the umbilical cord travelled in the fetus and may give rise to an intestinal protrusion.

Abbreviations

BI	bone injury
C1, C2 etc	cervical vertebrae
CDH	congenital dislocation of the hip
CPT	carpal tunnel syndrome
L1, L2 etc	lumbar vertebrae
NBI	no bone injury
OA	osteoarthritis
PID	prolapsed intervertebral disc (can also mean pelvic inflammatory disease)
RA	rheumatoid arthritis
RTA	road traffic accident
T1, T2 etc	thoracic vertebrae
THR	total hip replacement
TKR	total knee replacement

Terminology and roots/stems

acetabul/o	acetabulum, area where femur/thigh bone, forms joint with innominate bone
arthr/o	joint
articul/o	joint
carp/o	carpals, hand bones, wrist
chondr/o	cartilage
clavicul/o	clavicle, collar bone
cost/o	rib

coxyg/o	coxyx, part of spine/rudimentary tail
crani/o	cranium (skull containing brain)
disc/o	disc between vertebrae
ethmoid/o	part of cranium
femor/o	femur, thigh bone
fibul/o	fibula, lower leg bone
front/o	frontal bone part of cranium
humer/o	humerus, upper arm
ischi/o	ischium, part of innominate bone
ili/o	ilium (bone of pelvis), part of innominate bone
intra-articular	directly into a joint, e.g. injected
lacrim/o	lacrimal bone of eye orbit/socket
lamin/o	lamina, arch of vertebra, thin sheet of bone
mal/o	malar, cheek bone
mandibul/o	mandible, lower jaw
maxill/o	maxilla, upper jaw
menisc/o	meniscus, cartilage of knee
metacarp/o	metacarpals, hand bones
metatars/o	metatarsals, foot bones
my/o (myos)	muscle
myel/o	bone marrow (also spinal cord)
nas/o	nasal bone, part of skull
occipit/o	occipital, part of cranium
olecran/o	part of elbow joint
orbit/o	orbital, part of eye socket
oste/o	bone
palat/o	palatine bones (in roof of mouth)
pariet/o	parietal, part of cranium
patell/o	patella, knee cap
phalange/o	phalanges, fingers/toes
pub/o	pubis, part of innominate bone
radi/o	radius, main lower arm bone
sacr/o	sacrum, part of spine

scapul/o	scapula, shoulder blade
sphenoid/o	sphenoid, part of cranium
spondyl/o (vertebr/o)	vertebra/spine
stern/o	sternum, the breast bone
synov/o	synovial
tars/o	tarsals, foot bones
tempor/o	temporal bone, part of cranium
ten/o, tendin/o	tendon
tibi/o	tibia, lower leg bone
turbin/o	turbinate bones in the nose
uln/o	ulna, lower arm bone adjective: ulnar
vertebr/o	vertebra
zyg/o, zygomat/o	cheek bone

Diseases and disorders

Ankylosing spondylitis	fixation of the vertebrae with fibrous tissue causing loss of movement
Ankylosis	immobilisation and solidification of a joint
Arthritis	inflammation of a joint
Arthrodynia	pain in a joint
Bursitis	inflammation of the pad of synovial membrane protecting a bone near the surface of the body, e.g. the elbow or knee
Callus	an outgrowth of partly bony tissue produced in the body's process of the mending of bones
Exostosis	an overgrowth of bone
Genu valgum	knock knee
Genu varum	bow legged
Hallux valgus	bunion/deviation of the large toe joint
Kyphosis	hunchback/excessive curvature of the thoracic vertebrae

Lordosis	'sway back'/excessive inward curvature of the lumbar spine
Luxation	complete dislocation of a joint
Osteoarthritis	degenerative disease of ageing – large joints of knee, hip etc.
Osteoma	tumour of bone
Osteomalacia	rickets – softening of bone due to lack of vitamin D and deposit of calcium salts
Osteomyelitis	inflammation of the bone marrow
Osteoporosis	brittle bones due to ageing and lack of oestrogen hormone which affects the ability to deposit calcium in the matrix of bone
Polyarthritis	arthritis involving many joints
Rheumatoid arthritis	disease causing inflammation of small joints, usually hands and feet
Scoliosis	a lateral S-shaped deformity of the vertebrae
Spina bifida	failure of the spinous processes to unite in fetal development, causing various degrees of deformity, with or without the meninges (covering of spinal cord) and/or spinal cord protruding through to the surface of the body
Spondylitis	inflammation of one or more vertebrae
Spondylosis	degenerative disease of the spine, crumbling occurs
Still's disease	a form of rheumatoid polyarthritis in children
Subluxation	partial dislocation of a joint
Synovitis	inflammation of a synovial (moveable) joint
Talipes	club foot deformity
Valgus	deviation outwards
Varus	deviation inwards

Procedures and equipment

Arthroclasia	surgical breaking of a joint to provide movement
Arthrocentesis	puncture of a joint cavity to remove fluid
Arthrodesis	surgical stiffening of a joint
Arthroplasty	reshaping or moulding of a joint
Arthroscopy	examination of a joint with a lighted instrument
Bursectomy	removal (excision) of bursa
Laminectomy	surgical removal of the lamina of a vertebra to relieve pressure in 'slipped disc'
Meniscectomy	surgical removal of the semi-lunar cartilage of the knee joint
Open reduction	using surgery to reduce a dislocation of a joint or fracture as opposed to a closed reduction where manipulation alone is used
Osteotomy	cutting or dividing of bone
Prosthesis	artificial part or replacement, e.g. hip, leg or breast
Synovectomy	surgical removal of synovial (lining) membrane
Tenotomy	surgical dividing or cutting of a tendon

Fractures

Fracture	a break in the continuity of the bone – includes cracks as well as complete breaks (*See Figure 21 for types of fracture*)
Avulsion	fragmented bone at the site of a ligament or tendon attachment
Colles'	fracture of the wrist, both the radius and ulna are fractured and cause the typical dinner fork deformity

Comminuted	a fracture where there are several breaks in the bone		is not as ossified (hardened with mineral salts), but is rather like a green branch of a tree in its splitting – heals quickly
Complicated	fracture in which there is associated damage to vital neighbouring structures		
Compound/open	a break in a bone where there is communication with the outside air through the skin – danger of infection	**Impacted**	a fracture where the ends of the bone are forced into one another
		Oblique	fracture that is not directly across the axis of the bone
Depressed	fracture of the skull with depressed segments	**Pott's**	fracture of the ankle involving both the tibia and fibula
Greenstick	type of fracture in children where the bone does not completely break as it	**Transverse**	fracture at right angles to the axis of the bone

Types of fracture

Greenstick

Open

Complicated

Potts's

Comminuted

Transverse

Oblique

Impacted

Avulsion

Depressed

Spiral

Colles' **(i)** lateral
(ii) posterior(dinner fork appearance)

Figure 21: Types of fracture

Chapter

The blood

Function

The function of blood can be summarised as both the transportation of substances throughout the body and also a defence system.

Structure

Blood consists of a slightly alkaline (*pH* 7.35) straw-coloured fluid known as plasma that contains blood cells suspended within it. It is the main transport system of the body, travelling within a closed system of blood vessels.

An adult has five to six litres (eight to10 pints) of blood.

Plasma

The fluid which forms 55% of the blood and contains numerous substances, including:

- **Water** (91%)
- **Mineral salts**
  including sodium chloride,
  the largest component at 0.9%
- **Food materials**:
  - amino acids (proteins)
  - glucose
  - fats known as lipids
- **Plasma proteins**
  albumin, globulin and the clotting factors fibrinogen and prothrombin
- **Waste materials**
  carbon dioxide in solution, urea and uric acid
- **Antibodies** and **antitoxins**
- **Vitamins**
- **Hormones**
- **Enzymes**
- **Oxygen** – in solution.

Serum

When the clotting factor fibrinogen has been removed from plasma, it is known as serum.

Cells

These consist of three main groups (*see Figure 22*):

- **Red cells** known as **erythrocytes** (around 5 million per cubic millimetre – *see Tables 1 and 2*)

- **White cells** known as **leucocytes** (around 8,000 per cubic millimetre)

- **Platelets** known as **thrombocytes** (around 350,000 per cubic millimetre).

Erythrocytes

These are smaller than the white cells and have no nuclei. This gives them a biconcave shape and enables them to carry more **haemoglobin** (an orange-coloured substance containing iron, which combines with oxygen in the blood contained in the capillary network of the lungs). This is then carried in the blood stream, ready to supply the tissues where oxygen is released. Their function is to carry oxygen, and they are small enough to travel within the capillaries.

Haemoglobin combines with oxygen to form **oxyhaemoglobin**:

$$\text{Haemoglobin} + O_2 \longleftrightarrow \text{oxyhaemoglobin}$$

(reversible)

Erythrocytes are manufactured in the bone marrow, live for approximately 3 months and are destroyed by the spleen and liver. The part containing iron is stored by the liver and the residue is excreted as bile pigments (bilirubin) in the faeces, and it is this pigment which gives the faeces their colour.

Anaemia

Anaemia may be defined as a condition in which there is an insufficient amount of oxygen-carrying capacity in the blood. It may be caused by too few normal erythrocytes or by red blood cells not being mature and fully

Table 1: Meaning of pathology values for red blood cells

Term	Meaning of term
Erythrocyte count	Number of red blood cells per litre or per cubic millimetre of blood
Haemoglobin	Weight of haemoglobin in whole blood expressed as grams per decilitre
Mean cell volume	Average volume of cells expressed in femtolitres
Mean corpuscular (cell) haemoglobin	Average amount of haemoglobin in each cell expressed in femtolitres
Mean corpuscular (cell) haemoglobin concentration	Amount of haemoglobin in 100 ml (1 decilitre) of blood
Packed cell volume or haematocrit	Volume of red cells in 1 litre (100 millilitres) of whole blood

charged with haemoglobin. Varying conditions of anaemia may give rise to erythrocytes which are large and pale (**macrocytic**) or small (**microcytic**).

Certain factors are necessary for the production of mature red blood cells. These include iron and trace elements as well as vitamin C and folic acid. **Vitamin B$_{12}$** is also essential and is known as the **extrinsic factor**. These are all provided in the diet.

Pernicious anaemia

However, a further substance known as **Castle's intrinsic factor**, found within the gastric juice produced by the stomach, is essential for the absorption of vitamin B$_{12}$ necessary in the diet. If this is not present, a condition known as **pernicious anaemia** will result where large pale immature red cells (macrocytic), unable to carry much oxygen, occur. Treatment is by giving regular B$_{12}$ injections.

Iron deficiency anaemia

Iron deficiency anaemia is very common and occurs when there is insufficient iron or other necessary factors in the diet, or when there has

been a loss of blood through haemorrhaging (bleeding), either severe or as a constant, slight loss, e.g. a slowly bleeding peptic ulcer. The condition of **menorrhagia** (heavy periods) is a common cause of this type of anaemia in women. The erythrocytes are pale (**hypochromic**) and small (microcytic).

Leucocytes

These white cells are composed of two main types:

1. Granulocytes (polymorphonuclear leucocytes): 65–75% of white cells

2. Non-granular leucocytes (mononuclear leucocytes): 25–35% of white cells.

The life-span of white cells is approximately 3 weeks or less and is dependent on the state of infection in the body.

Granulocytes (polymorphonuclear leucocytes)

These cells are manufactured in the bone marrow and are concerned with the defence of the body. They are mainly **phagocytes**, i.e. capable of changing their shape and ingesting (eating) bacteria and foreign matter. They are larger than the red cells but by changing their

Blood cells

Average number
per cubic millimetre
of blood

RED CELLS (Erythrocytes)   5,000,000

Biconcave discs
(contain no nucleus)

WHITE CELLS (Leucocytes)   8,000

Polymorphonuclear leucocytes
(or granulocytes)

Monocytes (mononuclear leucocytes
or non-granular leucocytes)

Lymphocytes
(large or small)

PLATELETS OR THROMBOCYTES   350,000

Fragmented cells

Figure 22: Blood cells

shape (**amoeboid action**) are able to squeeze out of the capillary walls to reach the tissues. Named after the stains which they will take up in the laboratory, they consist of three types:

- **Neutrophils** (60–70% of white cells)

- **Basophils** (0.5–2% of white blood cells)

- **Eosinophils** (2–4% of white blood cells).

The majority of phagocytes are neutrophils and their numbers increase greatly in response to bacterial infection.

Non-granular (mononuclear) leucocytes
These blood cells consist of:

- **Lymphocytes** (representing 20–30% of blood cells) and

- **Monocytes** (accounting for 4–8% of blood cells)

and are developed in the bone marrow and lymph tissue.

Lymphocytes
These blood cells are concerned with immunity and when activated produce antibodies, so protecting the body from foreign materials e.g. viruses. These antibodies assist the other body defences to overcome infection. Lymphocytes form the majority of the non-granulocytes and are found in lymph tissue throughout the body.

Monocytes
These blood cells are also concerned with immunity and are capable of phagocytic and amoeboid action. They work in close association with lymphocytes and their numbers are greatly increased in certain infective conditions, e.g. glandular fever.

Thrombocytes
These are fragmented cells, with no nucleus, and are concerned with clotting. They are also manufactured in the bone marrow.

Table 2: Normal values of erythrocytes

Abbreviation	Sex	Normal value *for meanings of the units used here, see Chapter 17*	
Erythrocyte count	Female	**4.0–5.5** x10^{12}/l	**4.0–5.5** million/mm^3
(RBC – red blood cells)	Male	**4.5–6.5** x10^{12}/l	**4.5–6.5** million/mm^3
Haemoglobin	Female	**11.5–16.5** g/dl	
(Hb)	Male	**13.5–18.0** g/dl	
Mean cell volume	Female	**80–100** fl	
(MCV)	Male	**80–100** fl	
Mean corpuscular (cell)	Female	**30–36** g/dl of cells	
haemoglobin concentration (MCHC)	Male	**30–36** g/dl of cells	
Packed cell volume (PCV)	Female	**0.37–0.47** l/l	**37% - 47%**
or Haematocrit (HCT)	Male	**0.40–0.54** l/l	**37% - 54%**

NB: There are variations of normal values with different laboratories.

Clotting

The process of blood clotting requires many factors including **thrombocytes (platelets)**. The clotting factors **prothrombin**, **fibrinogen** (manufactured in the liver) and **vitamin K** are essential.

Also necessary is **factor VIII**, a substance which is absent from the blood of patients suffering from **haemophilia**. Spontaneous bleeding occurs into joints with this condition. Factor VIII is given artificially by injection when necessary.

Blood groups

These are genetically determined. There are many different groups. The main classification is the Landsteiner ABO type (agglutinin) present in the red cells.

- **Type A:** contains factor A in cells, anti-B in serum

- **Type B:** contains factor B in cells, anti-A in serum

- **Type AB:** contains factor A and B in cells, no anti-A or anti-B in serum.

- **Type O:** contains no factor in cells, anti-A and anti-B in serum.

Therefore the serum of group A blood, containing anti-B, will cause group B red blood cells to be destroyed and vice versa. The serum of group O blood will destroy A, B and AB. However, group AB blood will not react with any of the groups as it has no anti-factors in its serum to do so.

The Rhesus factor

A further factor present in the plasma of the blood is the Rhesus factor (anti-D) present in 85% of the population. When present the type is known as **Rhesus positive** (Rh +ve). When absent it is known as **Rhesus negative** (Rh -ve).

The Rhesus factor must always be considered, particularly in the case of females, where the giving of Rhesus-positive blood to someone who is Rhesus negative, will cause antibodies (anti-factors) to be produced by the person's immune system. Subsequently, in pregnancy, these can damage the blood of the fetus if it is Rhesus positive.

Compatibility

In a blood transfusion, if the blood given to a patient (**recipient**) from a **donor** contains a factor in the cells to which the patient's (recipient's) blood serum will react, the donor's blood will be destroyed, causing clumping together of the red cells (**agglutination**) which can be fatal. Therefore blood is normally 'cross-matched' for compatibility before transfusion is given. In extreme emergencies, the **'universal donor'** group is given, i.e. O Rhesus -ve, before any investigations are done.

In normal circumstances the same group as the recipient is given.

- **Group AB Rh +ve is the universal recipient.**

- **Group O Rh -ve is** the universal donor.

Abbreviations

AIDS	acquired immunodeficiency syndrome
ALL	acute lymphocytic leukaemia
AML	acute myeloid leukaemia
APT	activated prothrombin time
APPT	activated partial thromboplastin time
BUN	blood urea nitrogen
CLL	chronic lymphocytic leukaemia
CML	chronic myeloid leukaemia
CO$_2$	carbon dioxide
ESR	erythrocyte sedimentation rate
FBC	full blood count
Hb	haemoglobin (pigmented protein which carries oxygen)
HDL	high density lipoprotein
Ig	immunoglobulin

INR	international normalised ratio (prothrombin time)
LDL	low density lipoprotein
MCH	mean corpuscular haemoglobin
MCHC	mean corpuscular haemoglobin concentration
MCV	mean corpuscular volume
O_2	oxygen
PCV	packed cell volume
RBC	red blood count
TIBC	total iron-binding capacity
WBC	white blood count
WBC & diff.	white blood count and different percentages present

Units used in biochemistry

SI	international system (Système International)
IU or U	international unit
mmol	millimole
mmol/l	millimole per litre
nmol	nanomole
µmol	micromole
µg	microgram
g	gram

Terminology

Coagulation	clotting of blood
Ery-, Erythro-	red
Gamma-globulin	plasma proteins which include antibodies
Haem-, Haemato-	stem for blood
Haemostasis	stopping bleeding
Immunoglobulin	plasma proteins which are antibodies
Leuco-	white
Thrombo-	clot

(see also Chapter 17 on pathology.)

Diseases and disorders

Agranulocytosis	large decrease in number of white granulocytes (cells which fight against infection)
Anaemia	amount of oxygen carrying capacity is reduced due to either too few red blood cells or too little haemoglobin
Epistaxis	nose-bleed
Haemolysis	destruction of blood cells
Haemophilia A	hereditary disease caused by lack of clotting factor (VIII) in the blood
Haemophilia B	hereditary disease caused by lack of clotting factor (IX) in the blood
HIV	human immunodeficiency virus
Hypercholester-olaemia	raised blood cholesterol (lipid or fat levels)
Hyperlipidaemia	raised blood fat levels
Hypochromic anaemia	anaemia associated with pale, small red cells due to insufficient iron
Infectious mononucleosis	glandular fever – increase of white cells called monocytes present in blood
Leucocytosis	a normal increase of white blood cells in response to infection
Leucopenia	a decrease in the number of white blood cells in the blood
Leukaemia	a cancer of the blood – abnormal white cells increase
Pernicious anaemia	inability of body to manufacture normal red blood cells due to a missing factor
Polycythaemia	too many red and other blood cells present in the blood
Sickle-cell anaemia	anaemia associated with people of African ethnic origin, red cells have sickle shape
Thalassaemia	anaemia associated with people of Mediterranean origin

Procedures and equipment

Cryoprecipitate   use of very low temperatures to separate required factors from blood

Paul-Bunnell test   blood test for glandular fever

Plasmapheresis   taking blood from a donor, removing the required factor and returning the remainder to the donor's circulation

Chapter **5** | The cardiovascular system

Structure and function

The cardiovascular system consists of the heart and blood vessels, and is responsible for the transportation of blood throughout the body.

Organs forming the system are the:

- **Heart**

- **Blood vessels**

The heart

Structure

This heart is a hollow muscular organ, the size of the owner's fist, situated in the **mediastinal space** (between the lungs) of the **thoracic** (chest) cavity. It is tilted to the left and its base rests upon the diaphragm.

It is composed of three layers of tissue:

Pericardium	a specialised fibrous sac, lined with serous membrane, covering the heart and preventing friction
Myocardium	composed of cardiac muscle forming the chambers and septum
Endocardium	a smooth endothelial lining which also forms the valves.

The heart is a double pump. It consists of two thin-walled upper chambers known as **atria** and two thick-walled lower chambers known as **ventricles**, the left ventricle having the thickest wall. It is divided into left and right sides by a muscular septum. Blood contained in the left chambers has no communication with that in the right *(see Figure 23)*.

Valves of the heart

The upper and lower chambers are separated by non-return valves which prevent the backflow of blood – the **tricuspid valve** between the right chambers and the **bicuspid** or **mitral** valve between the left chambers.

Specialised nerve supply to the heart

The **vagus nerve** supplies the heart as well as fibres from the **sympathetic chain** of the **autonomic nervous system (ANS)** (see Chapter 13).

There are also specialised areas of nerve fibres within the heart muscle. These are the:

- **sinu-atrial node** in the wall of the right atrium (pacemaker)
- **atrioventricular node** in the wall at the junction of the atria and ventricles
- **bundle of His** in the ventricular septum of the heart.

Function

The cardiac cycle

The two upper chambers (atria) receive blood from the veins and, on contraction, force blood through the valves into the lower chambers (ventricles). This impulse is controlled by the sinu-atrial node. As the atria relax, blood is automatically sucked in from the attached blood vessels to refill these chambers.

As the atria relax, so the ventricles contract (at an impulse from the atrioventricular node, conducted down through the bundle of His), pumping blood into the attached arteries through one-way valves which guard their openings. The ventricles relax and the cycle recommences.

Blood flow

The right side of the heart contains deoxygenated blood, returned from the body via veins; the left side contains oxygenated blood returned from the lungs where gases have been exchanged. The left ventricle, the thickest walled chamber, pumps blood to the body via the main artery, the **aorta**.

Heart sounds

Two sounds, which are produced by the closing of valves, can be clearly heard during the cardiac cycle: 'lubb' and 'dup'.

'**Lubb**' a long, dull sound is produced at the closing of the valves between the upper and lower chambers of the heart (**atrioventricular**

The heart

1. Aortic arch
2. Left pulmonary artery
3. Left pulmonary veins
4. Left atrium
5. Ascending aorta
6. Pericardium
7. Mitral valve
8. Aortic valve
9. Atrial septum
10. Myocardium
11. Left ventricle
12. Right ventricle
13. Descending aorta
14. Endocardium
15. Ventricular septum
16. Inferior vena cava
17. Tricuspid valve
18. Pulmonary valve
19. Right atrium
20. Pulmonary artery
21. Right pulmonary veins
22. Right pulmonary artery
23. Superior vena cava

Blood flow ➡ De-oxygenated blood ▭

Figure 23: The heart

valves), whilst '**dup**', a sharp, short sound is produced by the closing of the valves guarding the arteries arising from the ventricles (the **pulmonary valves** and **aortic valves**).

It is these sounds which are known as the heart sounds. Abnormality may be caused by disease of the heart valves (as in cases of **rheumatic fever**) and the sounds produced are then known as '**murmurs**'.

Blood vessels

These form a completely closed system which transports blood, containing various substances, to and from the heart via all the tissues of the body.

They consist of:

- **Arteries** (*see Figure 24*)

- **Veins** (*see Figure 25*)

- **Capillaries**

Arteries

Arteries, varying in size, are vessels travelling from the heart and (apart from the **pulmonary artery** travelling to the lungs which contains de-oxygenated blood) contain oxygenated blood. They contain muscle and elastic tissue in their walls to allow for contraction and relaxation with the contraction of the heart. They have a very smooth lining to prevent clotting. The smallest arteries are known as **arterioles**.

Veins

There are more veins than arteries in the body. Veins, varying in size, carry deoxygenated blood (apart from the **pulmonary veins** containing oxygenated blood) returning to the heart. They have a similar structure to arteries, but the walls are thinner and much less elastic (Figure 26). If a vein is cut it collapses, but an artery remains open and spurts blood rhythmically. Veins possess one-way valves to prevent backflow of blood. It is these which become damaged in the condition of **varicose veins**. The smallest veins are known as **venules**.

Main arteries of the body
(carrying blood away from the heart)

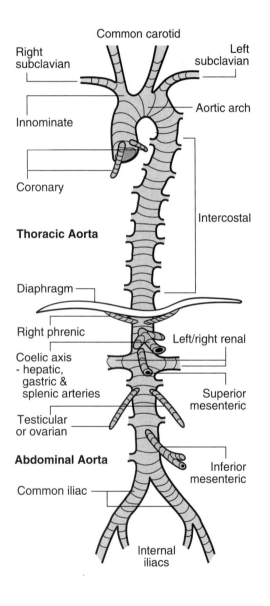

Figure 24: Main arteries of the body

Capillaries

These are fine, hair-like vessels, consisting of one-cell-thick coats. It is from these structures, because they are only one cell thick, that fluid (**tissue fluid**) containing oxygen, nutrients and other substances, is able to flow into the tissues, so supplying the individual cells with their requirements.

These blood vessels are the only ones where substances are able to leave the blood stream. Large proteins remain behind in the blood vessels, as they are too large to pass through the capillary walls. These proteins enable some of the fluid to be attracted back into the venous capillaries by osmosis. The remaining fluid (lymph) is returned to the circulation via the lymphatic system (see Chapter 6).

Main blood vessels:

Aorta	main artery of the body, stems from the left ventricle to supply the body with oxygenated blood
Pulmonary artery	takes blood to the lungs for oxygenation and removal of carbon dioxide
Superior vena cava **Inferior vena cava**	main veins of the body returning blood from the body to the right atrium
Pulmonary veins	return oxygenated blood to the left side of the heart for distribution to the body via the aorta.

Blood circulation

Systemic	supplies the main body; the main artery is the **aorta** from which other large arteries arise; all organs have their own blood supply
Pulmonary	supplies the lungs for oxygenation of the blood and removal of carbon dioxide – oxygenated blood is returned to the left atrium

Portal   supplies the liver and is concerned with the transport of food substances from the intestine for assimilation by the liver; the liver has two blood supplies from the hepatic artery and the portal vein.

Blood pressure (arterial)

This is the force, or pressure, that the blood is exerting against the walls of the blood vessels in which it is contained. This pressure varies during the cardiac cycle.

Systolic pressure

This is the pressure felt when the ventricles of the heart are contracting and pumping blood through the arteries via the main aorta. This is also known as the **systole**. It is the higher reading.

Diastolic pressure

This is the pressure felt when the heart chambers are at rest as the heart relaxes. This is also known as the **diastole**. It is the lower reading.

Factors affecting normal blood pressure:

- **Cardiac output** – the pumping of the heart
- **Volume** of the blood circulating
- **Peripheral resistance** of the blood vessels – the **calibre** (diameter) of small arteries away from the centre of the body – this is also affected by hardening and narrowing caused by age and fatty deposits (**atherosclerosis**)
- **Elastic recoil** of large arteries
- **Viscosity** (thickness) of the blood.

Pulse

This is a wave of distension and recoil, which can be felt in the wall of an artery as it passes over a bone near the surface of the body. It reflects the pressure transmitted from the aorta at the beating of the heart.

Main veins of the body
(carrying blood back to the heart)

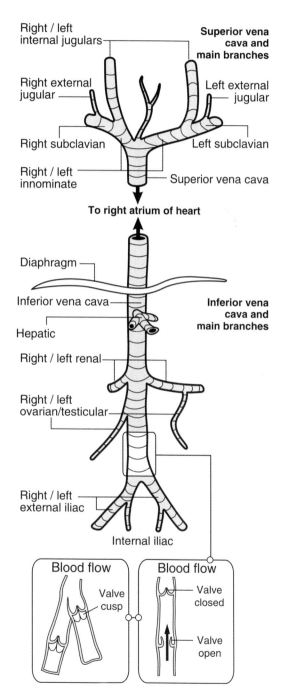

Figure 25: Main veins of the body

Normal pulse range
(number of beats per minute)

In the newborn	**140**
Infants	**120**
Children at 10 years	**80 - 90**
Adults	**60 - 80**
	(average 72)

Emotion, exercise, age and health will all affect the pulse rate.

Abbreviations

AS	aortic stenosis
ASD	atrial septum defect
ASHD	arteriosclerotic heart disease
AST*	aspartate transaminase (cardiac enzyme)
BP	blood pressure
CABG	coronary artery bypass graft
CABS	coronary artery bypass surgery
CAD	coronary artery disease
CCF	congestive cardiac failure
CCU	coronary care unit
CHF	congestive heart failure
CPK*	creatine phosphokinase (cardiac enzyme)
CPR	cardiopulmonary resuscitation
CVP	central venous pressure
CVS	cardiovascular system
DVT	deep vein thrombosis
EBT	electron beam tomography, a way of scanning the heart
ECG	electrocardiogram (records the electrical impulses of the beating of the heart muscle)
EOF	end organ failure, e.g. kidney failure, caused by high or very low blood pressure
GOT*	glutamic-oxaloacetic transaminase (cardiac enzyme)
HCM	see HoCM

Structure of artery and vein

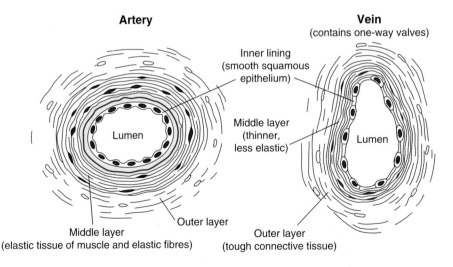

Figure 26: Structure of artery and vein

HI	hypodermic injection
HoCM (or HCM)	hypertrophic (obstructive) cardiomyopathy, a genetic disease of the heart muscle which tends to show itself during development in adolescence
HS	heart sounds
ICU	intensive care unit
IM	intramuscular injection
ITU	intensive therapy unit
IV	intravenous injection
LD*	lactate dehydrogenase (cardiac enzyme)
MOF	Multiple organ failure, e.g. all major organs do not work properly, caused by septicaemia, toxic shock syndrome etc.
NT-pro BNP	blood test for heart failure, enables early diagnosis
PAT	paroxysmal atrial tachycardia
PTCA	percutaneous transluminal coronary angioplasty
PVC	premature ventricular contraction
TC	total cholesterol (LDLs and HDLs)
TMR	transmyocardial revascularisation
TOE	trans-oesophageal echocardiography: a procedure where a scan of the heart is performed with the equipment used, placed into the gullet (oesophagus). The computerised picture is produced by the bouncing back of sound waves. Used particularly in the diagnosis of hypertrophic cardiomyopathy and other heart conditions
VSD	ventricular septal defect

* These enzymes also indicate metabolism of other organs

Terminology

Angi/o	stem for blood vessel
Arteri/o	stem for artery
Blood pressure	normally referring to the force of blood felt against the artery walls on the contraction and relaxation of the left ventricle (chamber of heart), measured in millimetres of mercury (mmHg)
Cardi/o (Coron/o)	stem for heart
Cardiology	study of the heart
Diastole	the relaxation phase of the heart cycle where chambers fill with blood – this is the lower reading of blood pressure
Endocardi/o	stem for endocardium, lining of the heart
Myocardi/o	stem for myocardium, muscle layer of the heart
Pericardi/o	stem for pericardium, outer covering of the heart
Phleb/o (Ven/o)	stem for vein
Pulse	a wave of distension and relaxation felt where an artery crosses a bone near the surface of the body
Sinus rhythm	the heart beating in normal rhythm
Systole	the contraction phase of the cardiac cycle – the force felt when the left ventricle contracts, forcing blood through the aorta to supply the body with its blood supply
Vascular	referring to blood vessels.

Diseases and disorders

Aneurysm	a weakness in the wall of an artery (can cause ballooning and rupture)

Angina pectoris	pain in the chest and left arm caused by insufficient blood to the heart muscle, usually on exertion or excitement
Angioma	tumour of blood vessels, usually capillaries
Arrhythmia	abnormal rhythm of the heart
Arteriosclerosis	hardening of an artery
Arteritis	inflammation of an artery
Atheroma	fatty deposits in the wall of an artery
Atherosclerosis	narrowing (with fatty deposits) and hardening of an artery
Atrial fibrillation	disorder of the heart beat, no co-ordination between atria and ventricles
Bradycardia	an abnormally slow heart beat
Cardiac arrest	cessation of the heart beat
Cardiac asthma	breathlessness caused by right-sided failure of the heart, usually at night
Carditis	inflammation of the heart
Coronary occlusion	a sudden blocking of an artery supplying the heart muscle, e.g. thrombosis (formation of a blood clot)
Coronary thrombosis	a blocking of an artery by a blood clot in the coronary (heart) circulation
Cyanosis	blueness of the skin and mucous membranes due to lack of oxygen
Diastolic murmur	abnormal sound heard during relaxation phase of the cardiac cycle
Dyspnoea	laboured or difficult breathing
Embolism	sudden obstruction of a blood vessel by an embolus
Embolus	a detached and travelling particle of fat, air or blood clot
Endocarditis	inflammation of the lining of the heart (endocardium)

End organ failure (EOF)	e.g. kidney failure, caused by high or very low blood pressure
Fibrillation	a quivering of the heart chambers, an ineffective action of pumping blood
Haemorrhoids	varicose veins of the rectum
Hypertrophic (obstructive) cardiomyopathy (HoCM)	a genetic disease resulting in abnormal heart muscle
Hypertension (hyperpiesis)	high blood pressure
Intermittent claudication	painful condition of the leg caused by lack of blood supply
Mitral incompetence	disordered function of the mitral valve of the heart (between the left chambers of the heart)
Mitral stenosis	narrowing of the mitral valve
Multiple organ failure (MOF)	e.g. all major organs do not work properly, caused by septicaemia, toxic shock syndrome etc.
Myocardial infarct	death (necrosis) of a wedge-shaped area of heart tissue when the artery supplying it becomes blocked
Myocarditis	inflammation of the muscle of the heart
Occlusion	blockage of blood vessel
Oedema	excess fluid in the tissues
Palpitations	rapid forceful beating of heart of which the patient is aware
Pancarditis	inflammation of all structures of the heart
Patent ductus arteriosus	failure of the ductus arteriosus (artery bypassing lungs in fetus) to close at birth
Pericarditis	inflammation of the outside covering of the heart
Phlebitis	inflammation of a vein
Phlebolith	stone in a vein (calcium deposits)

Pulmonary stenosis	narrowing of the valve between the right ventricle and pulmonary artery
Systolic murmur	abnormal sound heard during contraction phase of cardiac cycle
Tachycardia	a rapid heart beat
Thrombo-phlebitis	inflammation of the wall of a vein causing a blood clot to form (thrombus)
Thrombosis	a condition where a thrombus has formed
Thrombus	a blood clot in a blood vessel
Varices	varicose veins
Varicose veins	presence of thickened and twisted veins caused by incompetent valves
Ventricular fibrillation	a quivering of the ventricles of the heart instead of contracting forcefully.

Procedures and equipment

Angio-cardiography	demonstration of heart and major blood vessels using an opaque medium injected into the circulation
Angiogram	special X-ray of arteries using radio-opaque medium (dye which shows up in X-rays)
Angioplasty	reshaping or forming a blood vessel
Aortograph	recording of a pulse on a graph demonstration of aorta by use of opaque medium
Arteriotomy	cutting into an artery
Auscultation	listening to sounds for diagnostic purposes, usually with a stethoscope
Cardiac catheterisation	a fine hollow tube (catheter) is inserted into heart chamber to measure

Stent

Figure 27: Before and after x-rays of a stent insertion *(with kind permission of Peter Woodford)*

	gases and pressure/radio-opaque dye is introduced
Defibrillation	restoring the heart rhythm to normal sinus rhythm by means of electrical shock from defibrillator
Electron beam tomography (EBT)	a way of scanning the heart
Electrocardio-gram (ECG)	records the electrical impulses of the beating of the heart muscle
Endarterectomy	surgical removal of deposits (e.g. fat, blood clots) from the lining of arteries
Exercise tolerance test	test (ECG) on the heart during exercise
Haemorrhoid-ectomy	surgical removal of haemorrhoids
Injection of varicose veins	treatment of varicose veins – an injection is given of a substance which will cause the vein to sclerose, i.e. seal up
Intravascular thrombolysis	an agent which destroys/dissolves clots is infused into the blood vessels to clear a blood clot (thrombus)
Ligation of varicose veins	surgically tying off parts of a varicose vein to divert the blood supply through healthier veins
Pacemaker	referring to:
	a) an artificial implant of an electrical mechanism to replace the damaged sinu-atrial node
	b) the sinu-atrial node of specialised nerve tissue in the wall of the right atrium which initiates the contraction of the heart
Percutaneous transluminal coronary angioplasty	a procedure where an occluded (blocked) blood vessel is dilated using a ballon catheter; guidance is provided by a monitor which shows the position of the catheter within the body by fluoroscopy

Phlebotomy	cutting into a vein
Phonocardi-ography	the heart sounds of the cardiac cycle (contraction and relaxation of the chambers) are displayed as graphic images on a monitor; an ECG is displayed simultaneously
Sphygmoman-ometer	instrument used for measuring blood pressure
Stent (see figure 27)	small instrument/structure inserted into the blood vessel to keep it open in cases of lack of blood to an organ (ischaemic heart disease, etc.)
Stethoscope	instrument used for listening to sounds of the body
Stripping of varicose veins	surgical procedure where varicose veins are removed
Thallium scan	procedure of injecting radioactive thallium to demonstrate the condition of the blood vessels (coronary arteries) supplying the heart muscle (see Chapter 21 on Miscellaneous Tests: Electrocardiography)
Transmyocardial revascularisation	a procedure where smal holes are made in the cardiac muscle in order to stimulate growth of new blood vessels to increase blood supply to damaged heart muscle
Valvectomy	surgical removal of a valve
Valvotomy	cutting into a valve, by custom referring to the heart
Varicotomy	cutting into a varicose vein
Venepuncture	insertion of a needle into a vein
Venesection	cutting down into a vein for purposes of transfusion or insertion of drugs
Venogram	X-ray of a vein using an opaque medium.

Chapter

The lymphatic system

Function

The lymphatic system is a transport and defence system.

Lymph is the remains of **tissue fluid** after it has passed through the tissues from the capillaries and given up its nutrients and gases to the cells. It has gathered waste products and is returned to the circulation via the lymphatic system.

Structure

The lymphatic system consists of the following (*see Figure 28*):

- **Lymph**
- **Lymph capillaries**
- **Lymph vessels**
- **Lymph nodes (or glands), superficial and deep**
- **Main lymph ducts**
- **Specialised lymph glands.**

Lymph capillaries

These are similar in structure to the blood capillaries, but start in the tissue spaces and are open-ended tubes; they are not continuous.

Lymph vessels

These are similar in structure to veins, but have many more valves in their walls giving a beaded appearance.

Lymph nodes or glands

These act as filters between the returning lymph fluid and the vessels, trapping debris and bacteria, and are part of the defence system of the body. Cancer cells are also filtered here, but unfortunately some of these cells manage to reach the main blood stream and secondary deposits of these malignant cells occur in distant tissues (**metastases**).

They also manufacture some types of white blood cells (**lymphocytes** and **monocytes**).

The lymphatic system

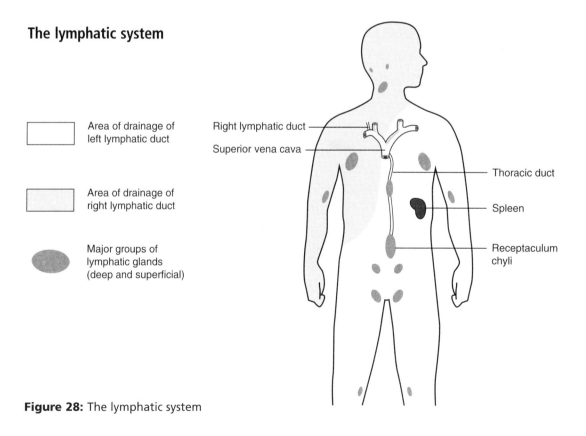

Figure 28: The lymphatic system

Main lymph ducts

These consist of:

- **Right lymphatic duct**
- **Thoracic duct**

The right lymphatic duct drains lymph from the right upper trunk, head and right arm.

The thoracic duct receives lymph from the rest of the body. It also receives fat absorbed from the **ileum** of the small intestine.

The contents of both of these ducts empty into the main veins of the body for circulation.

Specialised lymph glands

These include:

- **Tonsils** and **adenoids**
- **Peyer's patches** in the ileum
- **Appendix** in the large intestine
- **Spleen** in the abdominal cavity.

They act as defence mechanisms and also manufacture some types of white blood cells (**lymphocytes**).

Peyer's patches become infected in cases of **typhoid fever**.

The **spleen** also controls the volume and quality of blood circulating, destroys worn out red blood cells and produces **antibodies**.

Terminology

Aden/o	stem for gland (any)
Antibody	an immunoglobulin protein which is produced in response to the presence of an antigen or foreign protein, specific to the antigen. The production of antibodies is essential to immunity and the overcoming of infections such as measles, etc
Antigen	a substance which is capable of producing sensitivity/immunity of the body
Antitoxins	these neutralise poisons produced by micro-organisms
Lymph/o	stem for lymph
Lymph	fluid draining from the tissues to be returned to the circulation
Lymphangi/o	stem for lymph vessels
Lymphocyte	white blood cell which is manufactured in lymphatic tissue and fights infection by producing antibodies and antitoxins
Splen/o	stem for spleen

Diseases and disorders

Adenitis	inflammation of a gland
Adenoma	tumour of glands
Anasarca	widely spread oedema
Ascites	free fluid in the peritoneal cavity
GVHD	graft versus host disease (in transplants)
Hodgkin's disease	malignant disease of the lymphatic system caused by a virus
HVGD	host versus graft disease
Infectious mononucleosis	glandular fever
Lymphadenoma	tumour of lymph gland
Lymphangitis	inflammation of lymph vessels
Lymphocythaemia	excessive number of lymphocytes in the blood
Lymphocytopenia	deficiency of lymphocytes in the blood
Metastasis (pl. metastases)	secondary deposit(s) of malignant cells from a primary tumour or source (usually through the lymph channels)
Oedema	free fluid in the tissues (fluid is not draining back to circulation)
Splenitis	inflammation of the spleen
Splenomegaly	enlargement of the spleen

Procedures and equipment

Adenectomy	surgical removal of a gland
Lymphangiogram	special X-ray of the lymph vessels with an opaque dye
Paracentesis abdominis	drawing off of free fluid from the abdominal/ peritoneal cavity
Paracentesis thoracis (or **thoracentesis**)	drawing off of fluid from the chest cavity (thorax)
Paracentesis tympani	drawing off of fluid from the middle ear
Splenectomy	surgical removal of the spleen
Splenogram	special X-ray of the spleen using opaque dye

Chapter **7**

The respiratory system

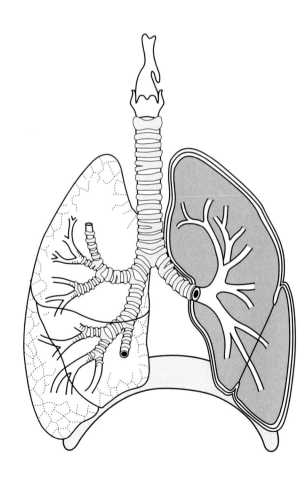

Function

The respiratory system is concerned with the vital function of external respiration, the exchange of gases – taking in oxygen from the air and the excretion of carbon dioxide and water vapour as waste products.

Structure

The structure of the respiratory system consists of the following organs:

- **Nose**
- **Nasopharynx** ⎤
- **Larynx** ⎦ upper respiratory tract

- **Trachea**

- **Bronchi** (two) ⎤
- **Bronchioles**
- **Alveoli** ⎦ lower respiratory tract
- **Lungs**

Nose

The nose is made up of bone and cartilage and is connected to the **sinuses** (spaces of air). Its function is to receive, moisten, warm and filter air. It is also the organ of the sense of smell which is closely linked with taste (see Chapter 14).

Pharynx

This extends from the back of the nose to the larynx, and the **nasopharynx** is the area at the back of the nose. The **eustachian tube** from the middle ear enters here. Both air and food pass through the pharynx.

Larynx

The larynx (*see Figure 29*) is also known as the **voice box** as it contains the **vocal cords** (*Figure 30*), two delicate folds of membrane which vibrate to produce sound.

The larynx is composed of several irregular-shaped cartilages:

- **Epiglottis**
- **Thyroid cartilage**
- **Arytenoid cartilages** (two)
- **Cricoid cartilage**

The **thyroid cartilage**, also known as the **Adam's apple** is found at the anterior of the larynx. The cricoid cartilage is shaped like a signet ring, whilst the **arytenoid cartilages** are attached to the vocal cords.

The entrance to the larynx, known as the **glottis**, is guarded by a flap of cartilage called the **epiglottis**. This structure prevents food or fluid passing into the air passages. This occurs automatically by a reflex action when the person is conscious. *However, in a state of unconsciousness this reflex does not occur and blockage of the airway can easily result.*

The larynx

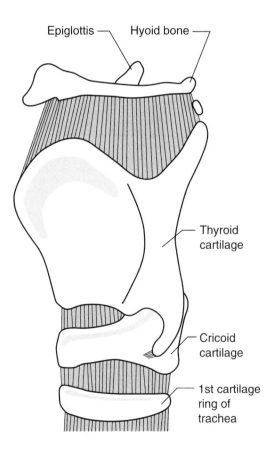

Figure 29: The larynx (lateral view)

Vocal chords of the larynx

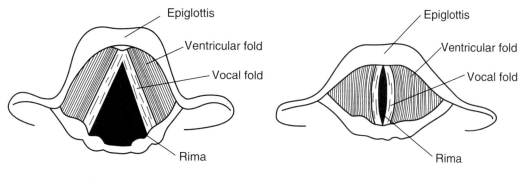

A - relaxed   **B - in speech**

Figure 30: Vocal chords of the larynx

Trachea

This is known as the **windpipe** and is continuous with the larynx and extends to the bronchi. It is composed of several C-shaped rings of cartilage, which keep the structure open to allow air to pass down into the lungs.

Bronchi

These are two short tubes, the right and left bronchi, continuous with the trachea and containing cartilage and muscle. The bronchi enter the lung at an area known as the **hilum**. The bronchi divide into numerous branches known as **bronchioles** – smaller tubes of similar structure to the bronchi, but which contain more muscle tissue in their walls. These take air to the delicate air sacs at their terminations known as **alveoli**.

Lungs

These are two pink, spongy, cone-shaped organs lying in the thoracic cavity (the chest), one either side of the heart and great blood vessels. The base of each lung rests upon the **diaphragm** and the apex lies just below the level of the **clavicle** (collar-bone). The right and left lungs consist of lobes, covered in a serous membrane known as the **pleura**. The right lung, which is larger, has three lobes, the left lung has two. These are further divided into **lobules**, each being complete in itself, and including blood vessels, lymphatic vessels, elastic connective tissue, bronchioles and alveoli *(Figure 31)*.

Alveoli

These are tiny, delicate, one-cell-thick air sacs surrounded by a capillary network from the pulmonary circulation. This membrane is moist and it is only here that the exchange of gases occurs. All other parts of the respiratory tract or airway convey air to the air sacs for this vital purpose.

Ventilation

This consists of **inspiration** (breathing in) and **expiration** (breathing out). The muscles of respiration are essential for this process; these are the **diaphragm** and the **intercostal muscles** (between the ribs).

Inspiration

The chest cavity expands as the muscles of respiration contract, swinging the rib cage out and the diaphragm down. The action is similar to a pair of bellows and air (containing oxygen) is sucked in through the nose/mouth to fill the expanding lungs.

Respiratory system

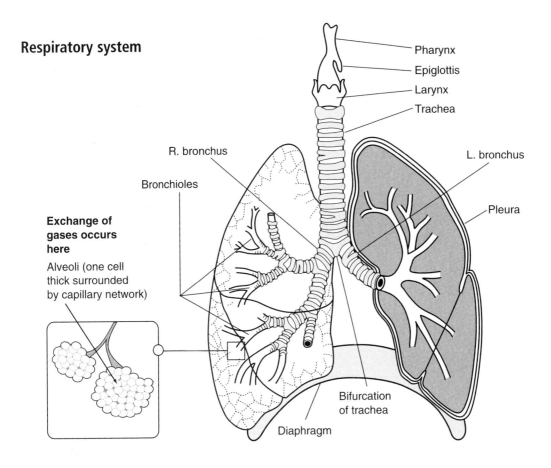

Pharynx
Epiglottis
Larynx
Trachea

R. bronchus

L. bronchus

Bronchioles

Pleura

Exchange of gases occurs here

Alveoli (one cell thick surrounded by capillary network)

Bifurcation of trachea

Diaphragm

Figure 31: Respiratory system

Expiration

When these muscles relax it has the opposite function to inspiration, decreasing the size of the chest cavity and forcing out expired air through the airway, removing waste gases (including carbon dioxide) and water vapour. Figures 32 and 33 show instruments designed for measuring peak expiratory flow.

Air content

Inspired air contains **21% oxygen** and **0.04% carbon dioxide**.

Expired air contains **17% oxygen** and **4% carbon dioxide**.

In **cardiopulmonary resuscitation**, the presence of oxygen in the expired air provides sufficient oxygen for the patient's requirements. The higher level of carbon dioxide present can, in certain situations, also stimulate the **respiratory centre** in the brain to start spontaneous respiration

Respiration

Breathing is an automatic process, although it can be controlled by the will. It is controlled by the respiratory centre in the brain which responds to the level of carbon dioxide in the blood. Oxygen is vital for every cell and the brain cells have the greatest requirement. If they do not receive a supply of oxygen for three to four minutes brain damage will occur and death will usually result. If the person is resuscitated after this time period, there is likely to be permanent damage to the brain.

Exchange of gases

Pressure of oxygen in inspired air in the air sacs is high while the oxygen pressure within the capillary blood surrounding these sacs is low. Therefore the oxygen passes through the membrane into the blood, combining with the **haemoglobin** of the red cells to be carried back to the heart for distribution to the body.

Pressure of carbon dioxide in the air sacs is low, while the pressure of it within the capillary blood is high. Therefore carbon dioxide passes through the membrane into the air sac and is breathed out of the lungs on expiration.

Respiration rate

The rate of respiration will vary with the individual, increasing with exercise, emotion, certain diseases and fever.

Normal rate per minute

Newborn (first four weeks)	40
Infants (four weeks to one year)	30
Children (up to five years)	24
Adults	12 – 18

Abbreviations

AP	artificial pneumothorax
COAD	chronic obstructive airway disease
COLD	chronic obstructive lung disease
COPD	chronic obstructive pulmonary disease
CPR	cardiopulmonary resuscitation
FB	foreign body
IPPB	intermittent positive pressure breathing
LRTI	lower respiratory tract infection
NSCLC	non-small cell lung cancer (slow growing type of lung cancer)
PCP	*Pneumocystis carinii* pneumonia (associated with AIDS)
PE	pulmonary embolism
PEFR	peak expiratory flow rate (see also vital capacity)
PND	paroxysmal nocturnal dyspnoea
RD	respiratory disease
RDS	respiratory distress syndrome
SCLC	small cell lung cancer (fast-growing, aggressive type of cancer also known as 'oat cell')
SMR	submucous resection (altering the structure of the nasal septum, i.e. cartilage division, or correcting crooked septum)
SOB	shortness of breath
Ts & As	tonsillectomy and adenoidectomy
TB	tuberculosis
URI	upper respiratory infection
URTI	upper respiratory tract infection
VC	vital capacity

Terminology

Adenoids	specialised lymphatic tissue behind the nose (naso-pharynx)
Bronchioles	the smallest tubes of the lungs between the bronchi and the alveoli
Bronch/o	stem for bronchus(i)
Bronchi/o	stem for bronchioles (smaller tubes)
Epiglottis	flap of cartilage which guards the entrance of the glottis to prevent food being inhaled into the larynx (reflex action in the conscious person)

Figure 32: Mini-Wright standard range peak flow meter (for adults)
Reproduced with kind permission from Clement Clarke International Ltd

Laryng/o	stem for larynx (voice box)
Nasal	referring to the nose
Nas/o	stem for nose.
Pharyng/o	stem for throat
Pleura	membrane covering lobes of lungs
Pleur/o	stem for pleura, covering of lungs
Pneum/o (pneumon/o)	stems for lungs
Pnoe-	stem for breathing
Pulmon/o	stem for lung
Rhin/o	stem for nose
Tonsill/o	stem for tonsils
Trache/o	stem for trachea (windpipe)

Vital capacity	amount of air which can be breathed out on a forced expiration following a forced inspiration (as on a peak expiratory flow meter)

Diseases and disorders

Apnoea	cessation of breathing
Asphyxia	lack of oxygen in the blood and thus in the tissues
Asthma	inflammatory disease of the bronchial tubes due to hypersensitivity to foreign proteins (allergy) resulting in narrowing of airway as the result of bronchial constriction

Figure 33: Peak flow meter in use
Reproduced with kind permission from Clement Clarke International Ltd

Atelectasis	failure of the lungs to expand, e.g. at birth, or collapse of the alveoli (air sacs)
Bronchiectasis	over dilatation of the bronchioles due to fibrous tissue
Bronchitis	inflammation of the bronchial tubes
Cheyne–Stokes respiration	irregular breathing with periods of cessation of breathing (apnoea) and overbreathing (hyperventilation); this is due to change in pH of the blood passing through respiratory centre in the brain resulting from levels of urea build up in body as

	kidneys fail – this usually results in death
Cor pulmonale	right ventricular heart failure caused by lung disease
Coryza	the common cold
Crêpitations	fine crackling which can be heard
Cyanosis	blueness of the skin and mucous membranes due to lack of oxygen
Dyspnoea	difficulty in breathing
Epiglottitis	inflammation of the epiglottis
Epistaxis	nose-bleed
Haemoptysis	coughing up of blood from the lungs, usually bright red and frothy

Hypoxia — insufficient oxygen in the blood

Laryngeal stridor — harsh sounds on inspiration – can be due to spasm

Laryngitis — inflammation of the larynx

Laryngostenosis — constriction (narrowing) of the larynx

Lobectomy — surgical removal of a lobe of lung

Nasal polyp — pedunculated tumour of the lining of the nose (tumour with a stalk)

Non-small cell lung cancer (NSCLC) — less aggressive and slower growing type of lung cancer

Oat cell — small cell lung cancer (SCLC) fast-growing, aggressive type of cancer

Orthopnoea — only able to breath when sitting upright

Pharyngitis — inflammation of the throat (pharynx)

Pleurisy (pleuritis) — inflammation of the pleura, with effusion, producing fluid

Pneumonia (pneumonitis) — inflammation of the lungs

Pneumothorax — air in the pleural cavity causing collapse of lung

Pulmonary emphysema — abnormal distension of the alveoli (air sacs) of the lungs in chronic respiratory disease, e.g. bronchiectasis

Pulmonary empyema — presence of pus in the pleural cavity

Râle — abnormal rattling sound heard – present in bronchitis and pneumonia

Rhinitis — inflammation of the nose

Rhinorrhoea — discharge from the nose

Rhonchi — abnormal sounds in the bronchial tubes on listening with a stethoscope (auscultation)

Sinusitis — inflammation of the lining of the cavities of the nasal and skull bones

Sleep apnoea — periods of cessation of breathing during sleep, particularly in men

Small cell lung cancer — fast-growing, aggressive type of cancer also known as 'oat cell'

Spontaneous pneumothorax — collapse of the lung spontaneously

Stertorous — noisy breathing, as in snoring, due to obstruction, e.g. tongue falling to back of throat

Tachypnoea — rapid breathing, as in pneumonia

Tonsillitis — inflammation of the tonsils (specialised lymphoid tissue)

Tracheitis — inflammation of the trachea

Tuberculosis — an infection of the lung or other organs by the bacteria tubercule bacillus (unfortunately this is increasing)

Procedures and equipment

Adenoidectomy — surgical removal of the adenoids

Antral puncture — puncture of the antrum (sinus) in the maxillary bone of the face through the nose in order to drain pus and washout the cavity (antral washout)

Artificial pneumothorax — collapse of the lung by the deliberate introduction of air into the chest cavity

Auscultation — listening to sounds with a stethoscope

Bronchogram — special X-ray of the bronchial tubes using an opaque medium

Bronchoscopy — examination of the bronchi with a lighted instrument

Heaf test — skin test for tuberculosis

Intubation — introduction of a tube into air passages to allow

	air into the lungs (as in anaesthesia)
Kveim test	skin test for sarcoidosis
Laryngectomy	surgical removal of the larynx
Laryngoscope	a lighted instrument used for examination of the larynx
Laryngoscopy	examination of the larynx with a lighted instrument
Lobectomy	surgical removal of a lobe of the lung
Mantoux test	skin test for tuberculosis
Pharyngoscopy	examination of the pharynx with a lighted instrument
Pneumonectomy	surgical removal of the lung
Rhinoplasty	reshaping the nose

Rhinoscopy	examination of the nose with a lighted instrument
Spirogram	measurement of respiratory movements with a special machine – spirograph
Tine test	skin test for tuberculosis
Tracheostomy	making an artificial opening into the trachea (allowing air to enter the bronchi and lungs to relieve obstruction to breathing)
Tracheotomy	cutting into the trachea
Underwater seal drainage	the removal of air from the chest (thoracic) cavity by the insertion of a tube placed under water in a special drainage bottle

Chapter

The digestive (gastrointestinal) system

Function

This system is concerned with the intake, breakdown and absorption of food substances for use and storage by the body cells.

Food is taken into the mouth, chewed, mixed with saliva and formed into a **bolus** which, on swallowing, is passed into the **oesophagus**. From here it travels through the remainder of the alimentary canal by means of **peristalsis** (alternate waves of contraction and relaxation of the muscular walls of the hollow organs). It mixes with the various digestive juices, secreted from glands situated in the lining of the stomach and small intestine. These juices contain enzymes which allow the chemical process of digestion to occur. Other substances are also received into the small intestine for this purpose, from the liver and pancreas, via ducts.

Digestion

This is both:

physical
by means of chewing (mastication), peristalsis and churning (by muscular action of the stomach and intestinal walls) which reduce the food to smaller particles,

and

chemical
by the presence of chemicals, including substances known as **enzymes**. These allow chemical changes to occur enabling more simple compounds to be absorbed through the lining of the organs, especially in the ileum of the small intestine where most food substances are absorbed.

Structure

The following organs form the system and are known as the **alimentary canal** (*see Figure 34*):

- **mouth** or **buccal cavity**
- **oral pharynx** (throat)
- **oesophagus** (gullet)
- **stomach**

- small intestine:
    - **duodenum**
    - **jejunum**
    - **ileum**
- large intestine:
    - **caecum**
    - **appendix**
    - **ascending colon**
    - **transverse colon**
    - **sigmoid colon**
    - **rectum**
    - **anus**

Oesophagus

This is a strong muscular tube, situated in the thoracic cavity, extending from the pharynx above to the stomach below. It penetrates the diaphragm at its junction with the stomach.

Stomach

This is the most dilated part of the alimentary canal, containing numerous glands, secreting enzymes and also mucus to protect its own tissues from digestion.

Gastric juice is produced, which includes enzymes, starting the digestion of protein, and hydrochloric acid aiding digestion. Absence of hydrochloric acid is common in **pernicious anaemia**.

The stomach is guarded at the junction to the oesophagus by a weak sphincter muscle (**cardiac sphincter**). At its junction with the duodenum is a stronger sphincter known as the **pyloric sphincter**. These regulate the entrance and exit of, the now liquid, food substances known as **chyme**.

Sphincter muscles

A sphincter muscle consists of a ring of circular muscle which guards the entrance or exit of certain structures of the body. By its contraction or relaxation it controls the passage of various substances.

Digestive system

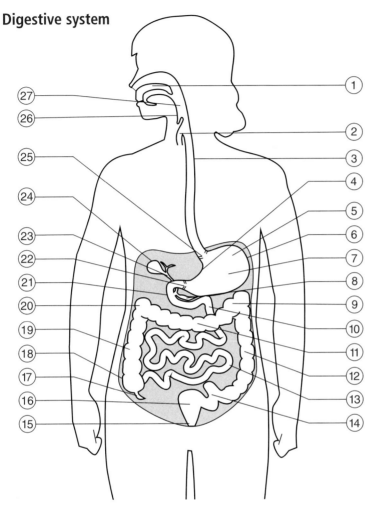

1. Buccal cavity
2. Larynx
3. Oesophagus
4. Lesser curvature
5. Fundus
6. Greater curvature
7. Stomach
8. Pancreatic duct
9. Splenic flexure
10. Jejunum of small intestine
11. Transverse colon
12. Descending colon
13. Ileum
14. Sigmoid colon
15. Anus
16. Rectum
17. Appendix
18. Caecum
19. Ascending colon
20. Hepatic flexure
21. Duodenum
22. Pyloric sphincter
23. Common bile-duct
24. Gallbladder
25. Cardiac sphincter
26. Epiglottis
27. Pharynx

Figure 34: The digestive system

Small intestine

This consists of the **duodenum**, **jejunum** and **ileum**, each of which contributes to the mechanical and chemical digestion of food substances.

Numerous tiny projection-type structures, known as **villi**, are found in the lining of the small intestine, the most numerous being found in the ileum. It is through these specialised structures that most of the food substances reach the blood stream and fats, as fatty acids (**lipids**), are absorbed directly into the **lymphatic system** as **chyle**.

Ileocaecal reflex

Whenever food or liquid is swallowed and passes into the stomach, a reflex action occurs known as the ileocaecal reflex. This involves the passing of the liquid food substances from the last part of the ileum of the small intestine, into the **caecum** through the **ileocaecal valve**, a one-way valve.

Large intestine

This is also known as the **colon**. It consists of a long muscular tube, starting at the caecum, to which the **appendix** is attached, extending to the **anus** below. It is concerned with the reabsorption of water, mineral salts and vitamins, and the breakdown of indigestible matter (cellulose from plants) into faeces. At the act of defecation this is eliminated from the body via the anus. The anus is guarded by a voluntary sphincter muscle.

Certain vitamins, e.g. **vitamin K**, are manufactured here by the action of bacteria, naturally present in the bowel. Treatment with extended courses of oral antibiotics interfere with this function.

Accessory organs of digestion

These consist of the following structures:

- **teeth**
- **tongue** — in the mouth
- **salivary glands**

- **pancreas**
- **liver** — in abdominal cavity
- **gallbladder**

Teeth

There are 32 **permanent teeth** and 20 **primary** or **deciduous teeth** which are replaced in childhood and adolescence by the permanent or **secondary teeth**.

Tongue

The tongue, also involved in speech and perception of taste (see Chapter 14), is concerned with formation of a **bolus** (a ball of food mixed with saliva), which is moved to the back of the pharynx and swallowed (**deglutition**), travelling into the oesophagus. Difficulty with swallowing is known as **dysphagia**.

Salivary glands

The salivary glands secrete **saliva** which starts the digestion of cooked starches.

Pancreas

The pancreas is a gland producing **insulin**. It secretes **pancreatic juice** containing several enzymes which are carried via ducts to the duodenum where it aids in the digestion of proteins, starches and sugars.

Liver

The liver secretes bile which emulsifies fat ready for digestion and absorption. There are many other functions of the liver, including:

- The removal of nitrogen from proteins which are to be eliminated from the body (**deamination**)

- The breakdown of drugs and poisons ready for excretion by the kidneys (**detoxification**)

- Production of numerous enzymes

- Production of clotting factors, including **prothrombin**, **fibrinogen** and anti-clotting factor **heparin**

- Storage of essential vitamins, including **vitamins A, B, D and K**

- Storage of **iron** from worn out blood cells, and the conversion of pigments into bile pigments (**bilirubin**) which colour the faeces in which they are excreted

- Breakdown of many fatty acids (**desaturation**) ready for storage or use by the body

- Conversion and storage of glucose ready for release into the blood stream

- Production of heat for distribution via the blood stream to the rest of the body – the numerous chemical reactions occurring in the body produce heat.

Gallbladder

The gallbladder is an elongated sac located below the liver. It stores and concentrates bile which it receives from the liver via ducts, ready for release into the duodenum of the small intestine to mix with other enzymes secreted by the intestinal walls.

Abbreviations

ABC	aspiration, biopsy, cytology
abdo	abdomen/abdominal
Ba E	barium enema
Ba M	barium meal
BM	bowel movement
BO	bowels open
D&V	diarrhoea and vomiting
DU	duodenal ulcer
ERCP	endoscopic retrograde cholangiopancreatography
GI	gastrointestinal
GU	gastric ulcer
HCl	hydrochloric acid
Hp	*helicobacter pylori* (bacteria responsible for gastric ulcers)
IBS	irritable bowel syndrome
IUC	idiopathic ulcerative colitis
IVC	intravenous cholangiography
LIF	left iliac fossa
LIH	left inguinal hernia
LLQ	left lower quadrant
LUQ	left upper quadrant
N&V	nausea and vomiting
NG	new growth/nasogastric (tube)
OGD	oesophago-gastroduodenoscopy
ORD	oesophageal reflux disease
PR	per rectum
PU	peptic ulcer
RIF	right iliac fossa
RIH	right inguinal hernia
RLQ	right lower quadrant
RUQ	right upper quadrant
UC	ulcerative colitis
UGI	upper gastrointestinal

Terminology

Abdomino/o	stem for abdomen
An/o	stem for anus
Appendic/o	stem for appendix
Caec/o	stem for caecum
Chol/e	stem for bile
Cholangi/o	stem for bile/biliary vessels
Cholecyst/o	stem for gallbladder
Choledoch/o	stem for common bile duct
Col/o	stem for colon (large intestine)
Dent/o	tooth
Duoden/o	stem for duodenum
Gastr/o	stem for stomach
Gingiv/o	stem for gums
Gloss/o	stem for tongue
Hepat/o	stem for liver
Herni/o	stem for hernia/rupture/protrusion
Ile/o	stem for ileum (part of small intestine)
Jejun/o	stem for jejunum
Lapar/o	stem for abdominal wall/flank
Odont/o	tooth
Oesophag/o	stem for oesophagus
Pancreat/o	stem for pancreas
Phag/o	swallow/eat
Proct/o	rectum
Pylor/o	part of stomach (pylorus)
Rect/o (proct/o)	stem for rectum
Sial/o	stem for salivary glands
Sigmoid/o	stem for sigmoid colon
Stomat/o	stem for mouth
Atresia	without a natural opening
Biliary	concerning bile
Caries	dental disease
Deciduous teeth	primary/first teeth (20)
Orthodontal	concerned with the correction of dentition (teeth)
Orthodontist	specialist in correction of teeth
Permanent teeth	secondary teeth (32)

Diseases and disorders

Achlorhydria   absence of hydrochloric acid secretion in the stomach

Acholia   absence of bile

Adhesions   fibrous tissue formation causes abnormal joining of two organ surfaces

Anal fissure   painful crack in the mucous membrane of the anus

Anorexia   loss of appetite

Anorexia nervosa   loss of appetite due to emotional states

Appendicitis   inflammation of the appendix of the intestine

Ascites   free fluid in the peritoneal cavity

Barrett's oesophagus   disease of the gullet where, in response to reflux of acid stomach contents, similar tissue to that which lines the stomach has grown to line the gullet (metaplasia). Danger of cancer arising from this condition

Cholecystitis   inflammation of the gallbladder

Choledo-cholithiasis   condition of stones in the bile duct

Cholelithiasis   condition of stones in the gallbladder

Cirrhosis   hardening of an organ, usually the liver

Coeliac disease   disease in which the protein gluten is not properly broken down – characterised by fatty stools (steatorrhoea) and failure to gain weight when it occurs in early childhood

Colic   spasmodic waves of pain due to contraction of muscles in tubular organs

Colitis   inflammation of the colon

Crohn's disease   chronic inflammation of the last part of the ileum (small intestine)

Diverticulitis   inflammation of a pouch formation in the lining of the intestine

Diverticulum   an abnormal pouch formation in the lining of a hollow organ, e.g. intestine

Faecal vomiting   present when all bowel movements have ceased – obstruction, paralytic ileus – vomit consists of liquid faeces

Fistula   abnormal communication between two organs or an organ with the skin

Gastritis   inflammation of the stomach

Gastroenteritis   inflammation of the stomach and intestine

Gingivitis   inflammation of the gums

Haematemesis   vomiting of blood from the stomach

Haemorrhoid-ectomy   surgical removal of haemorrhoids

Haemorrhoids   varicose veins of the rectum ('piles')

Helicobacter pylori   bacteria which live and reproduce in the gastric secretions of the stomach and may cause gastric ulcers

Helminthiasis   infestation with intestinal worms

Hepatitis   inflammation of the liver

Hepatoma   malignant tumour of the liver

Hepatomegaly   enlargement of the liver

Hernia   abnormal protrusion of an organ or structure through a weakness in a muscle

Hiatus hernia   protrusion of the stomach wall through a weakness in the diaphragm – allows regurgitation of acid contents

Intestinal obstruction   an acute abdominal emergency – contents of intestine are unable to pass along due to obstruction, e.g. strangulated hernia

Intussusception	the pushing of one part of the intestine into the lumen (space) of another part immediately adjacent to it; causes obstruction – common in children – an acute abdominal emergency
Malocclusion	badly aligned teeth when closing mouth
Malnutrition	deficiency of quantity or quality of food eaten
McBurney's point	area on the abdominal wall in the right iliac fossa where pain is felt when pressure is applied when diagnosing appendicitis
Melaena	black, tarry stools due to presence of digested blood (bleeding occurring)
Metaplasia	type of cells that have grown beyond the area where they are usually found
Occult blood	hidden blood, not visible to the naked eye (in stools)
Oesophagitis	inflammation of the oesophagus (gullet)
Paralytic ileus	no bowel sounds heard with stethoscope indicating no movement (peristalsis)
Periodontal	area around the tooth
Peritonitis	inflammation of the peritoneum (the membrane covering and nourishing the abdominal organs)
Pilonidal sinus	an abnormality consisting of an infolding of skin containing hair over the coccygeal area which has formed a space (sinus) and can become infected
Plaque	tartar upon the teeth causing caries etc.
Proctalgia	pain in the rectum
Pyloric stenosis	narrowing of the pyloric sphincter of the stomach (muscle fibres fail to relax sufficiently to allow passage of food from stomach into duodenum) – causes projectile vomiting, common in first-born male babies
Pyorrhoea	discharge of pus from the tooth cavity
Steatorrhoea	abnormal fatty stools
Stomatitis	inflammation of the mouth
Strangulated hernia	an acute abdominal emergency in which a portion of the alimentary canal protrudes through the muscle and becomes constricted, losing its blood supply – without intervention, gangrene will occur
Ulcerative colitis	chronic inflammatory disease of the colon which causes diarrhoea, blood and mucus in the stools
Volvulus	twisting of intestine upon itself, causing obstruction

Procedures and equipment

Abdominoperineal excision	surgical removal of rectum and part of colon and a colostomy created
Anastomosis	surgical joining of two hollow organs
Appendicectomy	surgical removal of the appendix
Barium enema	X-ray where barium compound (opaque medium) is inserted into the bowel via the rectum for diagnostic purposes
Barium meal	as above, but taken by mouth
Barium swallow	as above, but the swallowing process is also screened
Cholecystectomy	surgical removal of the gallbladder
Colectomy	surgical removal of all or part of the colon
Colostomy	making an artificial opening of the colon onto the abdominal wall

Endoscopic retrograde cholangio-pancreatogram	special X-ray of gall-bladder and pancreas using fluorescent dye which is inserted into ampulla of Vater ducts from duodenum using a duodenoscope with a catheter attached. It allows investigation of bile and pancreatic ducts and their contents. Cytology and biochemistry tests are performed
Endoscopy	examination of a hollow organ with a lighted flexible tube – fibre optics
Extraction	removal of (e.g.tooth)
Gastrectomy	surgical removal of the stomach
Gastrojejunostomy	anastomosis (joining together) the stomach and jejunum having removed or bypassed the duodenum; similar anastomosis terms follow this form
Gastroscope	lighted instrument used to examine the stomach
Gastroscopy	examination of the stomach with a lighted instrument
Gastrostomy	an artificial opening into the stomach, usually for feeding purposes
Gastrotomy	cutting into the stomach
Herniorrhaphy	surgical repair of a hernia
Ileostomy	making an artificial opening of the ileum onto the abdominal wall
Laparoscopy	examination of the abdomen with a lighted instrument through the abdominal wall
Laparotomy	incision into the abdominal wall for exploratory purposes
Oesophagectomy	surgical removal of the oesophagus
Proctoscope	lighted instrument for examination of the rectum

Figure 35: A gastrointestinal fibrescope

Reproduced with kind permission from Keymed (Medical and Industrial Equipment) Ltd

Figure 36: Hysteroscopy *Reproduced with kind permission from Keymed (Medical and Industrial Equipment) Ltd*

Proctoscopy	examination of the rectum with a lighted instrument
Ramstedt's operation	cutting into tight muscle fibres of pyloric sphincter of stomach and reshaping the stomach wall (for pyloric stenosis in babies)

Endoscopy

Endoscopy is the examination of a canal or hollow organ with a lighted instrument *(Figures 35 and 36)*. The conventional **endoscope** is rigid and non-flexible which has been widely replaced by the flexible fibre-optic variety. The

Table 3: Examples of endoscopies

Procedure	Examination	Description
Oesophagoscopy	Oesophagus	Use of oesophagoscope for visual examination of oesophagus or removal of foreign body.
Gastroscopy	Stomach	Visual examination of stomach using a gastroscope inserted via the mouth and oesophagus. Biopsy and aspiration are performed.
Duodenoscopy	Duodenum (part of small intestine)	Visual examination of duodenum via mouth, oesophagus and stomach. Biopsy and aspiration are performed.
Colonoscopy	Large intestine	Visual examination of colon via rectum using a colonoscope. Polyps may be removed and a biopsy performed.
Sigmoidoscopy	Sigmoid area of large intestine	Visual examination of the sigmoid colon via the rectum using a sigmoidoscope. Polyps may be removed and a biopsy performed.
Proctosigmoidoscopy	Rectum and sigmoid area	Visual examination using proctoscope or sigmoidoscope. Polyps may be removed and a biopsy performed.
Endoscopic retrograde cholangiopancreatography	Bile and pancreatic ducts	X-ray by insertion of dye into ampulla of Vater via catheter attached to endoscope inserted into duodenum.

endoscope is inserted into a hollow organ or tube such as the alimentary canal. Visual examination is performed and photography, biopsy and aspiration are carried out in appropriate cases *(Table 3)*.

Commonly, an **oesophagogastroduodenoscopy (OGD)** is performed which examines all three areas of the alimentary canal. Any lesion or abnormality can be seen and samples can be taken for histology.

Other common endoscopies

Procedure	Examination of
Laryngoscopy	larynx (voice box)
Tracheoscopy	trachea (windpipe)
Bronchoscopy	bronchial tubes
Laparoscopy	lower abdominal cavity via the umbilicus (also used for biopsy of ovaries and female sterilisation)
Colposcopy	vagina
Culdoscopy	through the recto-uterine pouch of pelvic peritoneum (pouch of Douglas) to view pelvic cavity
Hysteroscopy	cavity of uterus
Cystoscopy	bladder
Retinoscopy	retina of eye
Rhinoscopy	nasal cavities
Otoscopy	ear canal

Chapter

The urinary system

The urinary system is concerned with the removal of waste products from the body and the maintenance of correct water and **electrolyte** (ion) levels.

Function

The kidneys remove the nitrogenous content from the protein food substances which have not been utilised by the body, after they have been broken down for excretion by the liver (deamination). Protein cannot be stored by the body. Drugs and toxins are also removed in this way.

The kidneys act as filters and also selectively secrete and reabsorb substances from the blood to maintain the correct balance of salts, water and other substances. This is an example of **homeostasis**, whereby the body is kept in the correct state for functioning. A sufficiently high blood pressure is necessary for this to occur and any prolonged condition of extreme **hypotension** (abnormally low blood pressure) can cause permanent damage to the kidneys.

Structure

It comprises the following organs (*see Figure 37*):

- Two **kidneys**
- Two **ureters**
- **Bladder**
- **Urethra**

Kidneys

Kidneys are brown/purple bean-shaped vascular organs which are divided into **lobules.** They lie on the posterior part of the abdominal cavity deeply embedded in fat, and are surrounded by a capsule consisting of an outer portion, the **cortex**, and an inner portion, the **medulla**. The medulla shows striations called **pyramids**; these project into the **pelvis of the kidney** which is continuous with the **ureter**. On the upper pole of each kidney is the **adrenal** or **supra-renal** gland.

Microscopic structure of kidneys

The complex structures forming the kidneys are called **nephrons**, of which there are approximately 1 million in each. A nephron consists of a structure called a **Malpighian body** (in which **filtration** occurs) and various tubules, where substances are either secreted from or reabsorbed into the blood. Nephrons have a very rich blood supply.

Nephron

The nephron consists of the following microscopic structures:

- **Glomerulus**, collectively known as Malpighian body or **glomeruli** apparatus
- **Bowman's capsule**
- **First convoluted tubule (proximal)**
- **Loop of Henle**
- **Second convoluted tubule (distal)**
- **Collecting tubule**

Malpighian body or glomeruli apparatus

A Malpighian body, also known as the glomeruli apparatus, consists of the **glomerulus** and a cup-shaped tubular structure called the **Bowman's capsule**. The glomerulus consists of a tuft of capillaries tightly packed into the Bowman's capsule, which is the expanded commencement of a '**uriniferous**' or **kidney tubule**.

The small arteries leading into the glomerulus (**afferent vessels**) are wider than the arteries leaving the glomerulus (**efferent vessels**), thus back-pressure arises to allow filtration of substances from the blood to occur in the Bowman's capsule.

Tubules

The first convoluted tubule (**proximal tubule**) is coiled and continuous with the Bowman's capsule, the loop of Henle which dips down into the medulla of the kidney, and the second convoluted tubule (**distal tubule**) which joins the collecting tubule, also situated in the medulla.

Urinary system

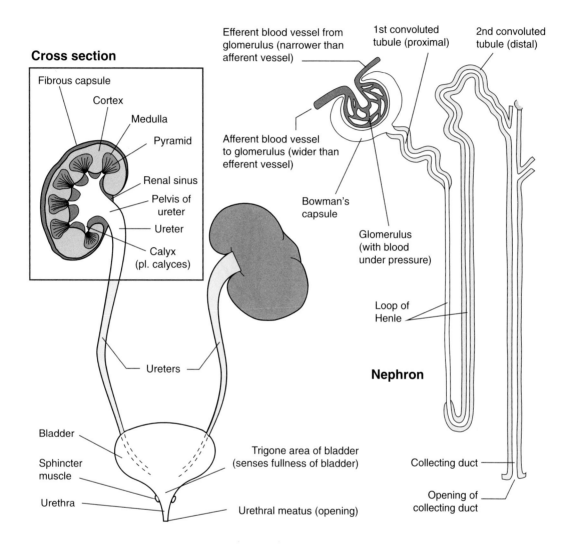

Figure 37: The urinary system

The collecting tubule terminates at a cup-shaped structure called the **calyx** (plural **calyces**) which opens into the pelvis of the kidney.

The Malpighian bodies and convoluted tubules are found in the **cortex** of the kidney where they are richly supplied with blood.

Formation of urine

Urine is formed by the following processes:

- **Filtration** – Non-selective

- **Secretion** – Selective

- **Reabsorption**

Filtration

Filtration is a non-selective process which takes place in the Malpighian bodies. Water, salts, glucose, **urea**, **uric acid** and toxins are filtered from the blood in the glomerulus into the Bowman's capsule (pressure in the glomerulus is high due to the efferent arteries being narrower than the afferent vessels). The capillary walls are more permeable than those elsewhere in the body. The fluid produced in the Bowman's capsule by this pressure is known as **filtrate**.

Secretion

Secretion occurs mainly in the first and second convoluted tubules. Special secretory cells line the tubules and **selectively** secrete substances from the blood which are at a high level, e.g. glucose in cases of **diabetes mellitus**. Foreign substances such as drugs and toxins will also be secreted. Similarly, any waste products of metabolism which have not already been filtered will be secreted into the tubules.

Reabsorption

Harm would occur if all the fluid, salts and food substances (such as glucose) filtered from the blood were allowed to leave the body. Specialised cells **selectively** reabsorb the necessary factors. In the loop of Henle most of the water is reabsorbed and the salt balance is restored mainly in the second convoluted tubule. The 'renal threshold' (whereby the level of various substances retained or excreted by the kidneys is governed by the requirements of the body) is another example of homeostasis.

Hormones influence reabsorption; **aldosterone** secreted by the adrenal cortex stimulates the sodium/potassium reabsorption or secretion by the second convoluted tubule. The action of the pituitary hormone, **anti-diuretic hormone (ADH)**, influences the amount of water reabsorbed.

After all these processes the end product is urine which is acid in reaction. This passes to the collecting tubules and then into the pelvis of the kidney. Approximately 1 litre of urine is secreted in 24 hours.

Kidney damage

Any damage or disease to the kidney will obviously affect the processes of filtration, secretion and reabsorption, resulting in many beneficial factors, such as the **protein albumin** being lost from the body. Not all harmful substances and waste products will be excreted. If the damage is sufficient, then the resultant renal failure may require **dialysis** (the removal of waste products by artificial means) or a kidney transplant.

Erythropoietin and renin

The kidneys also secrete a hormone known as erythropoietin which affects the production of red blood cells. In patients on permanent dialysis these red blood cells can become depleted, causing anaemia. The hormone **renin** is also produced by the kidneys and helps to maintain blood pressure. It acts by converting one of the blood proteins into **angiotensin** which causes constriction of the arterioles, thus raising blood pressure.

Pelvis of the kidney

The dilated portion of the kidney, which acts as a funnel for the collection of the secreted urine from the tubules, is known as the pelvis of the kidney. Urine passes through this on its way to the ureters.

Ureters

These are two muscular tubes which convey urine from the kidneys to the bladder. They are joined obliquely to the base of the bladder at an area known as the **trigone**.

Bladder

This is a hollow, pear-shaped muscular sac where urine is stored before micturition (passing of urine) through the urethral **meatus** (opening). It is capable of great expansion and rises in the abdomen as it fills. Micturition is a reflex action which, after infancy, is normally controlled at will. In **incontinence** this property is lost.

Normal content of the bladder is approximately 150 ml, but it can hold up to 350-400 ml. A **sphincter muscle** guards the bladder opening.

Urethra

This is a muscular tube through which the urine is passed to the outside of the body. It is short in the female - one to two inches in length – and seven to eight inches in the male. It is guarded by a **sphincter muscle**.

Composition of urine

Normal urine has the following composition: straw-coloured acid fluid pH 5-7, containing –

Water	96%
Solids	2% salts
Nitrogenous products of urea and uric acid	2%
Creatinine – waste product of cell metabolism	

Abbreviations

AGN	acute glomerulonephritis
BNO	bladder neck obstruction
CAPD	continuous ambulatory peritoneal dialysis
C&S	culture and sensitivity (to grow any micro-organisms and determine the antibiotic to which they are sensitive)
CSU	catheter specimen of urine
EMU	early morning urine
ESL	extracorporeal shock-wave lithotripsy
GU	genitourinary
HPU	has passed urine
HNPU	has not passed urine
KUB	kidney, ureter, and bladder (X-ray)
MSU	midstream specimen of urine
NAD	no abnormality detected/demonstrated
NOAD	no other abnormality demonstrated

IVP	intravenous pyelogram
IVU	intravenous urogram
pH	acid/alkaline balance
RGP	retrograde pyelogram
UA	urinalysis
UTI	urinary tract infection
VCU	voiding cystourethrogram
VCUG	voiding cystourethrogram

Terminology

Cyst/o	stem for bladder
Glomerul/o	stem for glomerulus (part of nephron)
Nephr/o (pyel/o, ren/o)	stem for kidney
Pyel/o	stem for pelvis of kidney
Ur/o	stem for urine
Ureter/o	stem for ureter
Urethr/o	stem for urethra
Urin/o	stem for urine
-uria	suffix for condition of urine
Genitourologist	specialist in the treatment of sexually transmitted diseases
Glomerulus	small tuft of capillaries found within Bowman's capsule, forming part of the nephron
Micturition	the act of passing urine
Urologist	specialist in diseases of the urinary system
Urology	study of the urinary system

Diseases and disorders

Albuminuria	the abnormal presence of albumin in the urine (protein)
Anuria	suppression of urine secretion from the kidneys – renal failure
Bilirubinuria	presence of bile pigments in the urine
Biluria	presence of bile salts in the urine

Cystalgia	pain in the bladder
Cystitis	inflammation of the bladder
Cystocele	protrusion of the bladder, usually into the vaginal wall
Cystolithiasis	condition of stones in the bladder
Diuresis	increase in the production of urine
Dysuria	difficulty/pain in passing urine
Enuresis/ eneuresis	bedwetting
Glomerulo- nephritis	any of a group of kidney diseases involving the glomeruli
Glycosuria	presence of glucose in the urine
Haematuria	presence of blood in the urine
Hydronephrosis	backlog of urine in the pelvis causing pressure and damaging the kidney
Incontinence	inability to control the passing of urine or faeces
Ketonuria	presence of acetone in the urine
Nephritis	inflammation of the kidney
Nephrolith	a kidney stone (calcium salts)
Nephrolithiasis	the condition of stones in the kidney
Nephropathy	degenerative disease of the kidney
Nephrosis	disease of the kidney
Nephrotic syndrome	extensive signs and symptoms of kidney disease; can be caused by a variety of disorders, usually glomerulonephritis
Nephrotomy	cutting into the kidney
Nocturnal enuresis /eneuresis	bedwetting at night
Oliguria	scanty production of urine
Papilloma	a simple benign tumour of the bladder lining – can become malignant
Phenylketonuria (PKU)	presence of abnormal breakdown of protein in urine in hereditary disease of PKU; screened for at birth as causes mental deficiency if not treated
Polydipsia	excessive thirst
Polyuria	passing large amounts of urine
Pyelitis	inflammation of the pelvis of the kidney
Pyelonephritis	inflammation of the kidney and its pelvis
Pyuria	presence of pus in the urine
Renal calculus	kidney stone
Renal colic	severe spasmodic pain caused by presence of kidney stones in the renal system (kidneys or tubules)
Renal failure	the kidneys fail to produce sufficient urine to remove waste substances from the blood
Urethral stricture	narrowing of the urethra
Uraemia	high levels of urea (the waste part containing nitrogen) in the blood
Ureteritis	inflammation of the ureters
Ureterolith	stone in the ureter
Ureterolithiasis	condition of stones in the ureters
Urethritis	inflammation of the urethra
Urethrocele	protrusion of the urethra, usually into the anterior vaginal wall

Procedures and equipment

Catheterisation	the withdrawal of urine from the bladder by the insertion of a catheter (fine hollow tube) into the urethra

Continuous ambulant peritoneal dialysis (CAPD)	removing toxins and waste products from the body in kidney failure by passing the peritoneal fluid through a bag (containing chemicals) attached to the abdomen
Cystectomy	surgical removal of the bladder
Cystoscope	instrument used to examine the bladder
Cystoscopy	examination of the bladder with a lighted instrument
Dialysis	artificial filtration of the blood to remove waste products by machine or by chemical means (peritoneal dialysis)
Extracorporeal shock-wave lithotripsy	see lithotriptor
Intravenous pyelogram	special X-ray demonstrating the shape and condition of the kidneys, ureters and bladder by intravenous injection of an opaque dye into the veins of the arm
Lithotripsy	the breaking up of kidney stones (calculi) by a lithotriptor
Lithotriptor	a machine which is used to break up stones by use of shock waves (pieces are then passed in the urine)
Micturating cystogram	special X-ray of the bladder when passing urine to demonstrate any weakness in muscles
Micturition	act of passing urine
Nephrectomy	surgical removal of the kidney
Peritoneal dialysis	artificial removal of waste products from the blood by means of passing peritoneal fluid from the abdominal cavity through a chemical (externally)
Retrograde pyelogram	special X-ray of the kidney pelvis ureters and bladder by the insertion of fine catheters via the urethra and insertion of an opaque dye
Ureterotomy	cutting into the ureter
Voiding cysto-urethrogram	see micturating cystogram. Urethra is also demonstrated.

The
skin

The skin is a vital organ which covers the whole of the body surface and is continuous with the mucous membranes.

Structure

It is composed of (*see Figure 38*):

- **Epidermis**

- **Dermis**

- Appendages of **hair** and **nails**

Epidermis

This is the uppermost layer of the skin and consists of several layers of stratified squamous epithelial-type cells. The top layers have no nucleus and are flattened and scaly. This is known as the horny layer or **keratin scales**. They are constantly being rubbed away and shed. These areas are thicker in various areas of the body which have to withstand friction and pressure, e.g. soles of feet.

The bottom layer of the epidermis, known as the **Basal (Malpighian) layer**, is the germinative layer from which these cells originate. It is here that the pigmentation (**melanin**), which gives rise to the colour of the skin, is found. There are no blood vessels in this layer and it is nourished by **lymph**.

Dermis

This is the layer found beneath the epidermis. It is composed of dense connective tissue containing elastic fibres and numerous structures:

- **blood vessels**

- **sensory nerve endings**

- **hair follicles** attached to small muscles

- **sweat glands**

- **ebaceous glands**

Blood vessels are numerous and are concerned not only with nourishment and delivery of vital substances to the skin, but also with the control of body temperature.

Sensory nerve endings are concerned with the relay of messages to the brain concerning touch, pressure, pain and temperature changes.

Sweat glands

These are concerned in the production of **sweat**, which excretes waste substances of water and salts from the body and also aids in the control of body temperature by loss of heat through **evaporation**.

Sebaceous glands

These produce a substance known as **sebum** which keeps the skin and hairs supple. Blockage of the duct of the gland produces a condition known as a **sebaceous cyst**.

Appendages

The hairs and nails are found in the dermis but are really outgrowths of the **epidermal** layer, as are sweat and sebaceous glands. Nails are protective and are outgrowths of the horny layer of the epidermis.

Beneath the dermis is a **subcutaneous layer** of connective tissue containing fat which helps to prevent heat loss.

Function

Control of body temperature

This is one of the main functions of the skin and is under the control of the brain. Special cells in the brain centre are triggered by the temperature of the blood flowing through it which, when the body temperature is becoming too hot, cause dilatation of the blood vessels in the skin, thus bringing more blood closer to the surface of the body. Sweat glands are stimulated to produce more sweat, excreting it through the pores onto the body surface where it evaporates.

Evaporation is a very efficient form of heat loss. **Radiation**, **convection** and **conduction** from the body surface also contribute to loss of body heat.

Structure of the skin

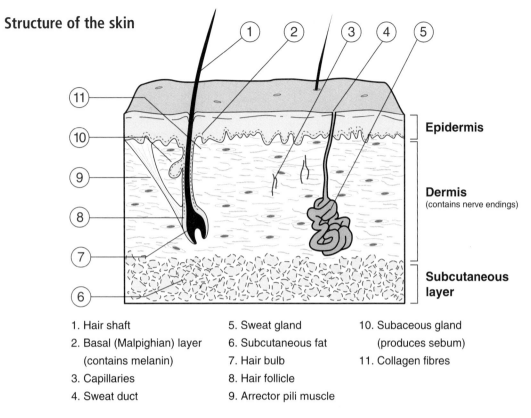

1. Hair shaft	5. Sweat gland
2. Basal (Malpighian) layer (contains melanin)	6. Subcutaneous fat
3. Capillaries	7. Hair bulb
4. Sweat duct	8. Hair follicle
	9. Arrector pili muscle
10. Subaceous gland (produces sebum)	
11. Collagen fibres	

Figure 38: Structure of the skin

Conversely, blood vessels constrict causing a transfer of blood to the centre of the body (core) and less heat is lost. Small muscles attached to hairs make them erect and cause 'goose pimples' which are an attempt to produce heat and allow hairs to trap air to provide insulation of the body, when it is cold. This is a remaining reflex from a more primitive form of life in evolution, when the body was covered in hair.

The average body temperature is 37°C, but varies during the day being lower in the morning.

Summary of other functions

- **Protection** by preventing micro-organisms entering the body and causing infection

- **Preservation** of body fluid

- **Conveys sensations** of touch, temperature, pain and pressure to the brain

- **Produces sweat** and excretes waste products by this action

- **Produces sebum**

- Converts a substance known as **ergosterol**, present in skin, to **vitamin D** in the presence of ultraviolet light in sunshine. This vitamin is necessary for healthy bones and teeth

- It is capable of **absorbing** some drugs, e.g. anti-inflammatory drugs

- It gives origin to the **hair** and **nails** which continue to grow for a short time after death

Abbreviations

DLE	disseminated lupus erythematosus
SLE	systemic lupus erythematosus

Skin lesions

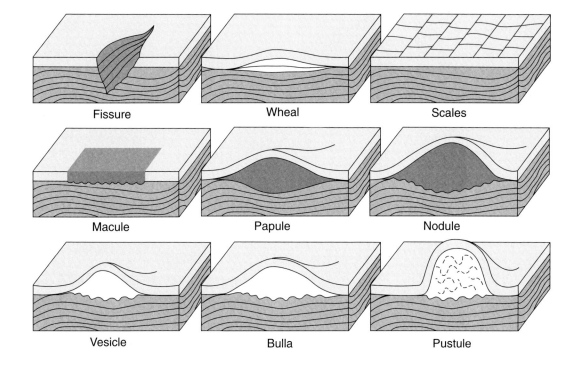

Fissure	Wheal	Scales
Macule	Papule	Nodule
Vesicle	Bulla	Pustule

Figure 39: Skin lesions *Redrawn after Glylys BA (1995) Medical Terminology: A Systems Approach, 3rd edn. FA Davis.*

Terminology

Cutane/o	skin
Derma/to	stem for skin
Hidr/o	sweat
Kerat/o	stem for scaly, horny
Onych/o	stem for nail
Pil/o	hair
Trich/o	stem for hair
Ungu/o	nails
Dermatologist	medical specialist of skin diseases
Percutaneous	through the skin (infusions)
Subcutaneous	under the dermis layer of the skin

Diseases and disorders *(see Figure 39)*

Abscess	collection of pus in a cavity
Acne rosacea	skin disease due to thinning of the skin producing acne- like spots – can be caused by excessive use of steroid skin applications
Acne vulgaris	skin disease – inflammation of sebaceous glands causing papules (red spots) and pustules to form – common in adolescence
Bullae	large (fluid containing) blisters

Carcinoma of the skin	
Basal cell	cancer of the basal layer
Melanoma	cancer of the pigmented layer (invasive)
Squamous cell	cancer of the middle layer of the epidermis (invasive)
Cellulitis	inflammation of the sub-cutaneous layer of the skin
Chancre	an ulcer-type sore – primary stage of syphilis
Comedone	blackhead
Contusion	bruise – bleeding beneath the skin
Cyst	membrane – encapsulated sac containing fluid or other materials
Decubitus ulcer	bed sore (pressure sore)
Dermatitis	inflammation of the skin
Dermatosis	disease of the skin
Dermoid cyst	cyst present at birth containing embryonic materials – skin, nails, teeth etc; usually found in the ovary
Eczema	inflammatory skin disease due to allergy, usually against food; common in flexures of skin
Erosion	rubbing away of tissues
Erysipelas	acute contagious condition of the skin causing pain, fever and local inflammation of skin, usually on the face (caused by haemolytic streptococcus bacteria)
Erythema	reddening of skin
Excoriation	injury worsened by act of friction (scratching)
Exfoliation	scaling of skin tissue in layers
Fissure	a split or cleft
Folliculitis	inflammation of a hair follicle
Furuncle	a boil – an infection of the tissue around a hair follicle
Haemangioma	birth mark (e.g. port wine type)

Herpes simplex	virus causing skin infection, usually cold sores
Herpes zoster	painful shingles skin eruption along nerve path due to chicken pox virus
Hidrosis	sweating
Hirsuitism	excessive amount of body hair
Hives	(also known as urticaria) weal-type spots due to allergy, as in nettle rash
Hyperhidrosis	excessive production of sweat
Hyperkeratosis	thickening of the horny layer of the skin
Impetigo	acute contagious disease pro-ducing pustules and scabs
Keloid scar	overgrowth of scar tissue
Lesion	any abnormal change in tissue
Lupus erythematosus	inflammatory dermatitis characterised by 'butterfly' lesion over nose and cheeks; may become widespread and destroy vital tissues
Macule	spot or discolouration of skin not raised above the surface, e.g. measles rash
Malignant melanoma	virulent cancerous invasive type of melanin- (pigment-) producing cells
Melanoma	pigmented mole of melanin-producing cells
Morbilliform	describing a type of rash – similar to measles rash
Naevus	birth mark
Nodule	a small node (protuberence or swelling)
Onychogryphosis	thickened deformed nails
Pachydermatous	thickened skin
Papilloma	simple tumour (not malignant)
Papule	spot – small raised solid elevation
Paronychia	infection of a nailbed (whitlow)

Pediculosis	infestation with lice
Pemphigus	blister-like eruptions which can be acute or chronic
Petechiae	small purplish patches under skin due to fluid escaped from small blood vessels – can be sign of recent asphyxiation or pressure
Prodromal rash	a fleeting rash which appears before the true rash of an infectious disease
Pruritus	irritation of the skin
Psoriasis	chronic skin disease characterised by scaly patches of unknown cause
Pustule	pus-filled small elevation of the skin
Roseola	a rose-coloured rash as in secondary syphilis
Scabies	infestation with the parasite scabies mite producing itching and soreness
Scales	compact layers of epithelial tissue shed from the skin
Seborrhoea	overactivity of the sebaceous glands which produce excessive sebum
Tinea pedis	athlete's foot

Trichosis	any abnormal state of hair
Ulcer	an open sore of skin or mucous membranes
Urticaria	nettle rash, an allergic reaction
Vesicle	small fluid-filled blister
Vitiligo	patchy white depigmentation of the skin
Wart (verucca)	an epidermal tumour of viral origin, or any benign hardening
Wheal	an acute reaction of the skin in nettle rash/urticaria/hives
Xeroderma	abnormally dry skin

Procedures and equipment

Débridement	surgical cleaning of wounds by removing dead tissues
Dermatology	scientific study of the skin
Dermatome	instrument used to cut very thin layers of skin for skin grafting
Escharectomy	removal of scar tissue
Escharotomy	dividing burn-scar tissue (to prevent scarring)

Chapter 11

The female reproductive system, pregnancy and childbirth

Introduction

This chapter is concerned with women's reproductive health. It is presented in two sections:

Gynaecology:

The branch of medicine that deals with disorders of the female reproductive system

Obstetrics:

The branch of medicine that deals with **pregnancy**, **childbirth** and the **puerperium** (the first six weeks after giving birth)

Note on spelling: Fetus or foetus

In recent years, **'fetus'** has become the accepted UK spelling in medical and scientific publishing and has been adopted in this text. However, readers should be aware that some organisations prefer to use the old spelling **'foetus'**.

Candidates for examinations should find out which spelling is preferred by their examiners. If in doubt, candidates should make it clear that they recognise both spellings.

Gynaecology

The female reproductive system

Structure

The female reproductive system is concerned in the reproduction of the species (*see Figures 40 and 41*). It is composed of both internal and external organs.

Internal organs

- Two **ovaries**
- Two **fallopian tubes** ⎫ situated in the
- **Uterus** ⎭ pelvic cavity
- **Vagina**

Ovaries

The ovaries, situated in the pelvic cavity, are the female **gonads** and produce **ova** (eggs) after **menstruation** starts (**menarche**). They are under the influence of the hormones from the **pituitary gland** and produce the female sex hormones **oestrogen** and **progesterone** at different stages of the menstrual cycle.

Oestrogen is responsible for the development of the female sexual characteristics, while progesterone, produced in the second phase of the menstrual cycle, supplements the action of oestrogen by thickening the lining of the uterus ready for the possible implantation of a fertilised egg. Progesterone also stimulates the breasts, preparing them for **lactation**. The female is born with all the eggs (immature) present at birth. Normally only one egg (**ovum**) ripens and is released each month.

At the **menopause (climacteric)**, egg production and hormonal secretion cease, although the adrenal gland cortex continues to influence the production of sex hormones at a lower level.

Fallopian tubes

These are situated one each side of the uterus, and attached to the ovaries by fine, finger-like strands. They are composed of muscle and are hollow tube-like structures which carry the released ovum along into the uterus ready for embedding, or shedding if fertilisation has not occurred. **Fertilisation** occurs when the male **spermatazoon** fuses with the ovum in the fallopian tube.

Female reproductive system

1. Fallopian tube
2. Ovary
3. Uterus
4. Bladder
5. Perineum
6. Vagina
7. Cervix
8. Rectum
9. Vertebrae

Figure 40: The female reproductive system (side view)

1. Fimbria
2. Endometrium (lining of uterus)
3. Myometrium
4. Cervical canal
5. Cervical os
6. Vagina
7. Uterus
8. Ovary
9. Fallopian tube

Figure 41: Female reproductive system (front view)

Uterus

This consists of a muscular pear-shaped hollow organ partially covered in a layer of membrane known as the **peritoneum**. It normally slopes forwards (**anteverted**).

The three layers are the:

- **peritoneum**
- **myometrium**
- **endometrium**

The neck of the uterus is known as the **cervix** and protrudes into the **vagina** which envelopes it.

The endometrium, the lining of the uterus, is under the influence of the female hormones and is the site for the embedding of the fertilised ovum. If fertilisation and embedding do not occur, the lining is shed in monthly menstruation.

Vagina

This is a muscular tube-like structure of vascular, **erectile tissue** extending from the cervix of the uterus above to the **vulva** externally below. Its function is for the deposit of the male spermatazoa, a passage way for menstruation

and the birth of a baby. Its walls are convoluted to allow for expansion.

External organs

Collectively these are known as the vulva (*see Figure 42*). They consist of the:

Bartholin's glands	two glands, one in each of the labia minora providing a secretion lubricating the vestibule
Clitoris	a rudimentary penis of erectile tissue (becomes engorged with blood)
Hymen	thin membrane guarding the entrance to the vagina
Labia majora	large outer lips
Labia minora	smaller inner lips
Mons veneris	pad of fat upon the pubis
Perineum	area of skin and muscle extending from the vagina to the anus (in the male the area from the scrotum to the anus)
Vestibule	opening containing entrance to vagina and urethral meatus (opening)

External genital organs

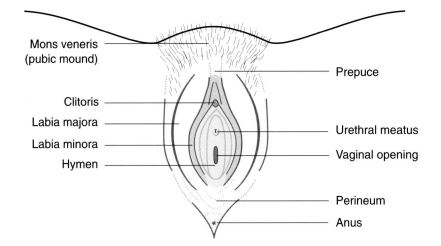

Figure 42: The external genital organs

The breast

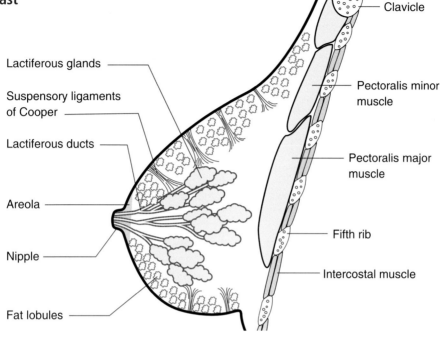

Clavicle

Lactiferous glands

Suspensory ligaments of Cooper

Lactiferous ducts

Pectoralis minor muscle

Pectoralis major muscle

Areola

Nipple

Fifth rib

Intercostal muscle

Fat lobules

Figure 43: The female breast

The breasts

The breasts, or **mammary glands**, are the accessory glands of the female reproductive system. They are rudimentary in the male. Their function is to produce milk for feeding the newborn baby.

Development

At puberty they enlarge and develop in the female, being under the influence of the female hormones. In pregnancy they increase in size and are stimulated ready to produce milk following delivery. They atrophy in old age.

Structure

The milk-secreting glands are found in **lobes** grouped together in **lobules**, separated by fibrous connective and fatty tissue. Each lobule opens into tubules, known as **lactiferous ducts**, which unite to form the main ducts terminating at the **nipple** (*see Figure 43*).

Hormone influence

The influence of the female hormones, **oestrogen** and **progesterone**, secreted by the ovaries at puberty and the start of menstruation, causes the enlargement and development of the breasts ready for future suckling.

In pregnancy, the production of progesterone by the **placenta** also influences further enlargement and development.

Prolactin (LTH), a hormone secretion of the anterior part of the **pituitary gland**, stimulates the production of milk. **Oxytocin**, from the posterior part of the pituitary gland, stimulates the **ejection** (or let down) of milk from the breast. Suckling encourages more milk to be produced.

Milk

This is a complete food for the newborn and is the most suitable nourishment for the human baby, having the correct proportions of nutrients.

Cow's milk contains a larger proportion of protein which is not easily digestible, being very complex. Numerous **antibodies** produced by the mother are also present and help to prevent infection occurring in the baby.

Colostrum

During the latter part of pregnancy, a yellowish clear fluid, known as **colostrum**, containing sugar and protein, is produced. The milk production does not normally occur until the second or third day following birth. This substance provides nourishment and also acts as an **aperient** to remove secretions present in the newborn's intestine.

The menstrual cycle (28 days)

This monthly cycle, occurring regularly in females every 26 days to 30 days throughout the child bearing period (approximately 36 years in total). Stimulated by changes in the concentration of hormone production, it is concerned with the release of the **ovum** and the preparation of the woman's womb (**uterus**) for **conception**.

The menstrual cycle (*see Figure 44*) can be divided into the:

- **Proliferative phase**

- **Ovulation**

- **Secretory phase**

- **Menses**

Proliferative phase (10 days)

This is under the influence of the **anterior pituitary hormone**, known as the **follicle stimulating hormone (FSH)**, which stimulates an immature follicle (**graafian follicle**) in the ovary to mature and ripen, resulting in the release of an egg (**ovum**), ready for fertilisation. Oestrogen is produced by the follicle, which stimulates the rapid growth (**proliferation**) of the lining of the womb (**endometrium**).

Ovulation

The egg (ovum) is released from the ripened follicle of the ovary, on approximately the 14th day from the first day of the last menstrual period. There is a corresponding rise in body temperature just before this occurrence. Sometimes there is a small amount of blood shed at this time, which can irritate the tissues and cause some women regular monthly pain.

The ovum is wafted into the **fallopian tube** (**oviduct**), by the movement of the specialised, **ciliated epithelium**, lining the tubes. One egg is usually released each month from the onset of periods (**menarche**) to the menopause (**climacteric**).

Secretory phase (14 days)

This phase is under the influence of the anterior pituitary hormone known as the **luteinising hormone, (LH)** in the second part of the menstrual cycle. This hormone stimulates the follicle to develop into the **corpus luteum** (yellow body), which then begins to secrete the hormone, progesterone.

This second phase is concerned with preparing the lining of the womb for the implantation of the embryo and supplying the correct environment for the embryo to grow. Under the influence of progesterone, numerous glands begin to secrete watery mucus, which is thought to assist the **spermatazoa** in their passage through the uterus to reach the fallopian tubes, to fertilise the ovum. There is a similar increase in the secretion of mucus from the glands in the **cervix** (neck of the womb) and the fallopian tubes.

The ovum probably remains able to be fertilized for only about 8 to 12 hours; the spermatazoa capable of doing so, for about 24 hours, although they may survive for several days.

The menses (4 days)

If the ovum is not fertilized, the corpus luteum in the ovary, withers and stops producing progesterone. The sudden drop in the levels of this hormone causes the **shedding** of the lining of the womb, as a **period** (the **menses**). The corpus luteum withers and eventually becomes scar tissue upon the surface of the ovary.

Hormone control

The hormones of the menstrual cycle are governed by feed back mechanisms of **homeostasis,** in that as levels rise there is a corresponding drop in the hormone stimulating its production and vice versa. Overall, hormone production is governed by the part of the brain known as the **hypothalamus** (see Chapter 15 on the endocrine system).

The menstrual cycle

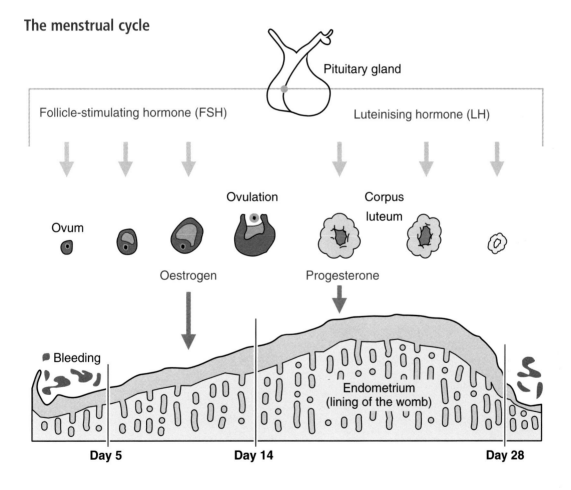

Figure 44: The menstrual cycle

Obstetrics

Pregnancy, childbirth and puerperium (the first six weeks after giving birth)

Stages of pregnancy

The stages of development in pregnancy include:

- **Gamete**
- **Fertilisation**
- **Zygote**
- **Conception and implantation**
- **Embryo**
- **Fetus**

Gonads

This is the proper name given to the sex organs which produce the **sex cells**, i.e. the **ovum** in the female and **spermatazoon** (plural: **spermatazoa**) in the male. The female gonads are the **ovaries**; the male gonads are the **testes**.

Gamete

This is the name given to the primitive sex cell, i.e. the egg or ovum in the female and the spermatazoa in the male. By process of reduction division (**meiosis**) the nucleus of each gamete contains only 23 single **chromosomes**. One of these will be the sex chromosome.

The chromosome from the ovum will always be an **X chromosome**. The chromosome from the male spermatazoon may be an **X** *or* **Y chromosome**. If the ovum is fertilised by sperm carrying a Y chromosome the fetus will be **male (XY chromosomes)**; if with an X it will be **female, (XX chromosomes)**. It is therefore the male spermatazoon, which determines the sex of the developing fetus.

Zygote

This is the name given to the **fertilised egg**. Only one spermatazoon is able to penetrate each egg.

Fertilisation

During **intercourse**, the male spermatazoa are deposited into the vagina at ejaculation. Fertilisation occurs in the **fallopian tube** (**oviduct**), when the successful spermatazoon, having travelled up through the **cervix** into the **uterus** and then the fallopian tube, penetrates the egg (ovum) and invades its nucleus, causing the mixing of the 23 single chromosomes of each gamete (i.e. ovum and spermatazoon) to form 23 pairs. It is this mixing of the genetic material, which makes each person unique.

On fertilisation many changes occur in the zygote and a hollow ball of cells is formed known as a **morula** (mulberry). These contain the **stem** cells. They divide into approximately 100 cells, by the time **implantation** occurs. They differentiate to form two distinct layers:

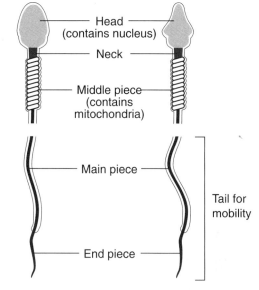

Figure 45: Spermatazoa

- the outer layer, which burrows into the uterine lining and will form the **choroid, placenta** and **amnion;**

- and the inner one divides again into three layers, to form the tissues and organs of the developing fetus.

At the time of **implantation** this ball of cells is known as a **blastocyst.**

Conception and implantation

This occurs when the fertilised egg (ovum) embeds in to the lining of the uterus (**implantation**).

Corpus luteum

If **conception** occurs, the **corpus luteum** (see the menstrual cycle earlier in this chapter) of the ovary continues to produce the hormone **progesterone**, which helps to maintain the

pregnancy until the placenta is fully formed and able to produce sufficient of its own **chorionic gonadotrophic hormone (HCG)**. It is this substance which forms the basis of chemical pregnancy testing. (An early morning urine sample will show a greater concentration of this substance). A negative test is not necessarily proof of non-pregnancy. It is the influence of these hormonal changes, which prepare the mother's body for child birth.

Embryo

The embedded fertilised egg is known as the **embryo** for the first 8 weeks of the pregnancy.

Fetus

At 8 weeks of pregnancy the embryo starts to resemble a human being, having all its rudimentary organs and is now known as a **fetus.**

Fertilisation, conception and implantation

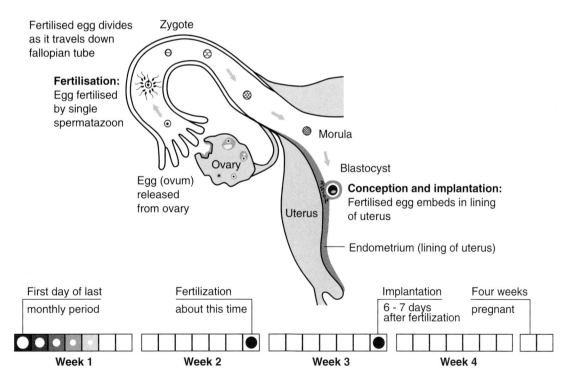

Figure 46: Fertilisation, conception and implantation

The duration of pregnancy (gestation)

The duration of pregnancy is normally 40 weeks. The **expected date of delivery** or **confinement** (**EDD** or **EDC**), is calculated from the first day of the last menstrual period. Nine months plus 7 days is added, to estimate the relevant due date.

The developing embryonic membranes

The structures of the developing membranes consist of:

- **Chorion**
- **Placenta**
- **Umbilical cord**
- **Amnion**
- **Germinative layer of blastocyst** forming the embryo

Chorion

The **chorionic membrane** is the outermost layer of the **blastocyst**. By producing numerous finger-like projections (**villi**) where it comes into contact with the lining of the womb (**decidua**), the chorion allows **implantation** of the fertilized egg and the formation of the **placenta**. In later pregnancy, the lower part of the chorionic layer, which has not formed the placenta, fuses with the adjacent **amnion**. In the earliest days of pregnancy it is the chorion which starts to produce the hormone **HCG (human chorionic gonadotrophic hormone)** which acts upon the **corpus luteum** in the ovary and maintains the continuing production of oestrogen and progesterone.

Placenta (complete at 3 months)

The placenta passes **nutrients**, **antibodies** and **oxygen** from mother to fetus. It also removes waste products in the form of **toxins**, **urea** and **carbon dioxide**

It acts as a barrier for some diseases and drugs from passing from mother to fetus, (although many smaller molecules of substances and micro-organisms, will pass through into the fetus).

The placenta (*see Figure 47*) continues to produce certain hormones – large amounts of oestrogen and progesterone as well as human chorionic gonadotrophic hormone (HCG) which maintain the pregnancy. This is essential for the pregnancy to continue and causes the changes to the mother's body, including the preparation of the breasts for milk production.

Umbilical cord (containing Wharton's jelly)

The umbilical cord links the fetus to the placenta. It supports two arteries and a vein which transfer blood to and from the fetus. The blood circulation of mother and fetus never actually mix, as there is a thin membrane separating the maternal and fetal parts of the placenta (*see Figure 47 and Figure 54*).

Amnion

The **amnion** is the term used to describe the **amniotic sac** (the "bag" around the fetus) and the **amniotic fluid** that surrounds the fetus.

Amniotic sac

The inner layer of cells of this sac form the **amniotic layer** which supports a bag of fluid in which the fetus develops and is cushioned. It also helps to prevent infection

Amniotic fluid

The **amniotic fluid** surrounding the fetus, consists of **water**, **salts**, **fat** and **fetal urine**. It absorbs fetal waste products and is also the medium in which the fetus swallows and learns to breathe. The fluid cushions and protects the fetus; maintains temperature and pressure around the fetus; and gives the fetus freedom of movement.

The germinative layer of the blastocyst

Following implantation, the inner layer of the blastocyst divides into three layers from which all the body organs form:

- **Ectoderm**   forming the skin (**epidermis**), **nails**, etc. and also the **brain** and **nervous system**
- **Mesoderm**   forming **dermis**, **connective tissue**, **muscle**, **blood**, **cardiovascular** and

	lymphatic tissue and most of the urogenital system
▪ **Endoderm**	forming **lining of gut**, **lining of respiratory tract**, and **glands** including the **liver** and **pancreas**

Damage

Any damage to the embryo by **drugs** (e.g. **alcohol**, prescribed drugs or **nicotine**), or **viral infection**, (e.g. rubella) at this early stage will be devastating, as so many organs will be affected. The results of the **thalidomide** disaster, are remembered as a cautionary tale of human vulnerability.

It should also be noted that all the ovum or sperm of the developing fetus, are present in a primitive form before birth, so that future generations may be affected by damage to the present yet unborn fetus.

Trimesters

The pregnancy is divided into three three-month periods:

▪ **First trimester** – the first three months

▪ **Second trimester** – the middle three to six months

▪ **Third trimester** – the last three months

The development of the embryo and fetus is shown in Figure 48.

The placenta, amnion and chorion

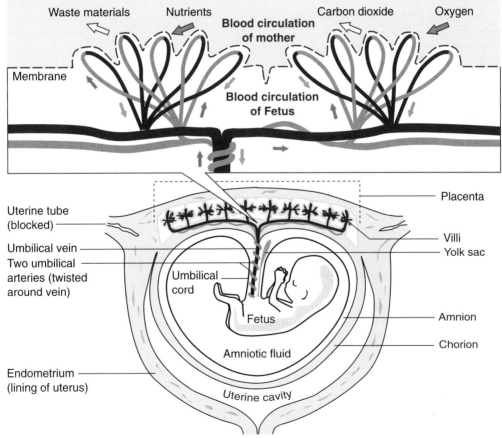

Figure 47: The placenta, amnion and chorion

Stages of embryonic and fetal development

Weeks: 4-5   Size: 4 mm long

Development:

Rudimentary organs are already forming in the **embryo** but the mother is only just aware that she might be pregnant (**gravid**)

Weeks: 6-7   Size: 8 mm long
(crown to rump)

Development:

Limb buds are forming and dimples where the ears and eyes will be

Weeks: 8-9   Size: 17 mm long

Development:

Major internal organs are developing, including the heart; the face is forming and a mouth and tongue are apparent; recognisable as a human being, it is now known as a **fetus**

Weeks: 10-14   Size: 56 mm long

Development:

All organs are formed; from now on the fetus will grown and mature; the heart beat is strong and can be detected by ultrasound; movement is occuring but is not yet felt by the mother

Figure 48: Stages of embryonic and fetal development

Weeks: 15-22   Size: 16 cm long

Development:

Hair and eyebrows begin to grow; eyelids remain closed; lines on skin are forming and nails are growing; movement is usually felt by the mother (known as **quickening**).

At 22 weeks, the fetus is covered with **lanugo**, a very fine hair which may be an aid to controlling body termperature. The fetus is termed **previable** as it is unlikely to survive if it is born at this stage

Weeks: 23-30   Size: 24 cm long

Development:

The fetus is now moving vigorously; it responds to touch and sound. Loud noise may make it kick. It is swallowing **amniotic fluid** and passing small amounts of **urine** into fluid. Hiccups occur and fetus is developing a pattern of waking and sleeping. The heart beat can be heard through a stethescope. The fetus is covered in a white, greasy substance known as **vernix**, which may be to protect the fetal skin. This usually disappears before birth.

At 24 weeks the fetus is legally **viable**, i.e. it is considered capable of survival. If pregnancy terminates at this stage, it is considered to be a **premature birth** or **still birth** (rather than a miscarriage or abortion. Registration of the birth is required.)

At 26 weeks the eyelids open and the eyes will be blue at this stage

Figure 48: Stages of embryonic and fetal development (continued)

Stages of embryonic and fetal development

Weeks: 31-40   Size: 31 cm long;
Weight: 4 kg in weight at 36 weeks

Development:

The fetus consolidates and grows plumper. Both the lanugo and vernix begin to disappear. Usually by 32 weeks the head is downwards, ready for birth. The crown of the head will move down into the pelvis some time prior to birth and is termed to be **engaged**, (**vertex presentation**). Occasionally, this does not occur until labour has commenced. If the presentation is bottom downwards, it is known as a **breech**. In the male the **testes** descend into the **scrotum** (which is necessary for the sperm to be kept at a temperature below that of the abdominal cavity, where they develop)

Figure 48: Stages of embryonic and fetal development (continued)

Height of the fundus

36 Weeks

28 Weeks

12 Weeks

As the fetus develops so the top part of the uterus (**fundus**) rises in the abdominal cavity (*see Figure 49*). Towards the last month, when it reaches the level of the rib cage, the mother finds some difficulty in breathing easily

Braxton Hicks contractions

These are episodes of light, painless, irregular tightening of the uterus during pregnancy. They commence at the end of the first trimester and increase in duration and intensity by the third trimester.

Figure 49: The height of the fundus

Multiple pregnancy

Identical twins (uniovular)

These develop when a fertilised ovum divides into two to form two fertilised eggs with exactly the same chromosomes. These grow and develop sharing one placenta (*see Figure 50*). They will be the same sex and appear alike.

Non-identical twins (binovular)

These develop from two completely separate ovum, fertilised by two different sperm. They have separate placenta (*see Figure 51*). Their chromosomes are completely different and children will have individual appearances. They may be different sexes.

Triplets and other multiple pregnancies

In triplets, they may be identical, having arisen from one fertilised egg or identical twins with a separate third non-identical fetus. With the current use of fertility drugs, several eggs may be released from the ovaries, resulting in completely separate fertilisations. Triplets, quads, quins and sextuplets are not as rare as previously, although carrying these multiple pregnancies to full term is uncommon.

Birth (parturition)

This is known as **labour** and normally commences as the result of hormone changes. The levels of oestrogen and progesterone decrease and a hormone **oxytocin** is released from the **posterior lobe** of the **pituitary gland**, causing contractions of the uterus to begin.

Stages of labour

There are three stages of labour:

Stage One
from expulsion of **mucus plug** to the dilation of the neck of the womb (cervix) until (fully dilated) approximately 10cm (**cervical effacement**)

Stage Two
the **contractions** of pushing out the fetus until **crowning** and **expulsion** (**birth**) of the baby

Stage Three
the expulsion of the placenta known as the **afterbirth**

Figure 50: Uniovular (identical) twins share one placenta

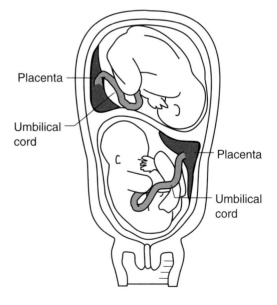

Figure 51: Binovular (non-identical) twins have separate placentas

Presentation of the fetus

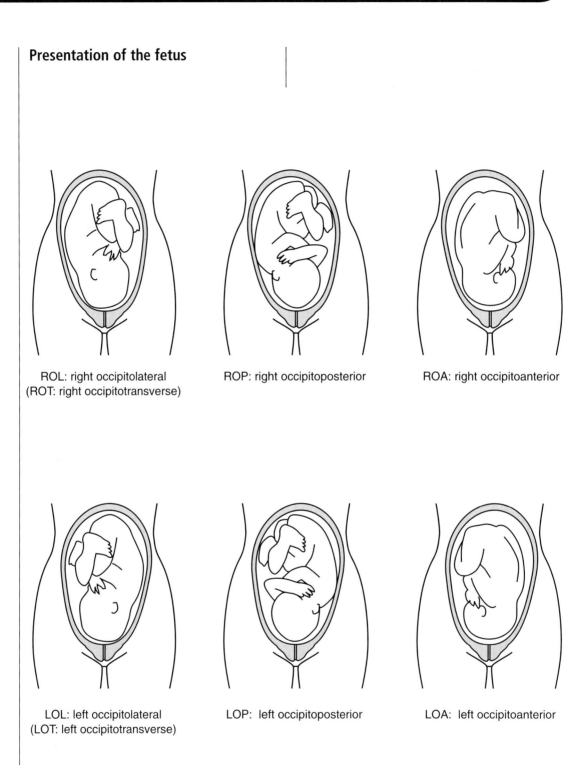

ROL: right occipitolateral
(ROT: right occipitotransverse)

ROP: right occipitoposterior

ROA: right occipitoanterior

LOL: left occipitolateral
(LOT: left occipitotransverse)

LOP: left occipitoposterior

LOA: left occipitoanterior

Figure 52: The fetus may present in different positions

Stage one

Stage one may last for up to 24 hours in a first birth. The plug of blood-stained **mucus** within the cervix is expelled and is known as a **show**. Usually the **waters (amniotic sac)** break. **Contractions** commence. They vary in length and severity and are concentrated on the cervix dilating. The last part of this stage is known as the **transitional** stage. The fetus may present (be positioned) in a number of ways *(as shown in Figure 52)*.

Stage two

Stage two is the most intense part of birth and contractions change their character, so that the mother pushes hard, and the fetus's head moves down the birth canal (**vagina**) until it **crowns** or is showing. The fetal skull bones are not fused and so they are able to move and overlap, changing the shape of the head, enabling it to adapt and squeeze through the cervix.

Contractions are frequent, usually every two or three minutes. If the area from the vagina to the anus (**perineum**) is not elastic enough or the baby is large, the skin is cut to prevent tearing (**episiotomy**). This stage usually lasts one or two hours.

As soon as the baby has cried and is breathing regularly, the umbilical cord is clamped, cut and tied off. **Apgar readings** (*see Table 4*) of the baby's condition are performed which are important indications of the baby's overall condition. These are recorded in the permanent notes for future reference. This is highly relevant, should the child develop any condition which may have been caused by deprivation of oxygen at birth etc.

The baby is given to the mother to hold as soon as possible after the birth, in order to encourage **bonding** (and breast feed if she has planned to do so). The act of breast feeding stimulates more oxytocin to be released, which causes contractions of the uterus which in turn helps to prevent bleeding.

Stage 1 Dilation of the cervix

Stage 2 Expulsion of the fetus

Stage 3 Expulsion of the placenta (afterbirth)

Figure 53: The three stages of birth

Table 4: The Apgar scores

Apgar Score	Score 0	Score 1	Score 2
1. Heart rate	Absent	Below 100	Over 100
2. Respiratory effort	Absent	Irregular, slow or weak	Lusty cry, good chest movement
3. Muscle tone (in all four limbs)	Limp	Poor tone, some movement	Active resistance, strong movement
4: Reflex irritability (response to flicking soles of feet)	No response	Slight withdrawal	Vigorous withdrawal of leg, strong cry
5. Colour (in white babies)	Blue or pale	Body pink, extremities blue	Completely pink

Total scores

Stage three

Stage three is the **expelling of the placenta** after the baby's birth. An injection of **ergometrine** is usually given, intramuscularly, which makes the uterus contract. This is intended to prevent the risk of bleeding (**post-partum haemorrhage**). The placenta is carefully examined and weighed to ensure it is intact and there is none remaining in the uterus, which would increase the risk of infection (**puerperal sepsis**). Blood loss is also measured carefully.

(Some mothers copy the action of animals in eating the placenta, following birth, although generally they ensure that it is cooked!! It is highly nutritious and also contains high levels of hormones, which probably help the mother overcome the sudden drop in hormone levels which occurs after birth).

Circulation of the fetus

The circulation (cardiovascular system) in the fetus (*see Figure 54*) is different from that post-birth. The main differences in fetal circulation are structures which bypass the blood supply to the lungs and liver. The maternal circulation carries out the main functions of those organs by supplying oxygen to the fetus and removing waste products.

There are three main differences in fetal circulation:

- **Ductus arteriosis**

- **Foramen ovale** (oval hole)

- **Ductus venosis**

Ductus arteriosis

Found between the **left pulmonary artery** (from the lung) and the **aorta** (main artery), preventing blood from going to the, as yet, non-functioning lungs.

Foraman ovale

Found in the **septum** (dividing wall) of the upper heart chambers (**atria**).

Ductus venosis

Found supplying blood from the **umbilical** to the main lower vein of the body (**inferior vena cava**), bypassing the liver.

Changes at birth

At birth (**parturition**), when the baby breathes, the **foramen ovale** and **ductus arteriosis** close, so that normal circulation is established. In the case of **'blue babies'** or some **'hole in the heart babies'**, these changes do not occur. Oxygenated blood mixes with deoxygenated blood in the heart chambers, so depriving the child of its ability to obtain sufficient oxygen from the lungs. The umbilical cord, having been cut, gradually shrivels and after approximately 7 to 10 days falls away from the fetal abdomen.

Pigmentation in pregnancy

The influence of the hormones in pregnancy, causes pigmentation of the **areola** of the breasts and also the **linea alba**, a line which is found on the abdominal wall. As pregnancy progresses, the pigmentation becomes more marked. Stretching of the skin produces stretch marks (**striae gravidarum**) on the abdomen and thighs. In dark skinned people, this can later become pigmented.

Circulation of the fetus

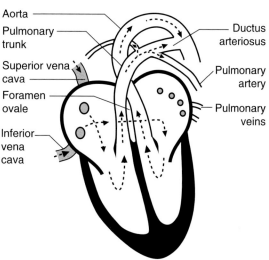

Figure 54: The circulation of the fetus

Induced labour

This is when the mother is artificially stimulated to go into labour. It may involve the rupturing of the membranes of the **amnion** and the intravenous administration of **oxytocin**.

Reasons for induction are numerous but include overdue dates and medical concerns, including **toxaemia of pregnancy** where the mother's blood pressure rises rapidly, kidneys begin to fail and the life-threatening condition known as **eclampsia**, is developing. (**Caesarian section** may be required)

The signs and symptoms of toxaemia of pregnancy (**PET)** include:

- Retention of fluid producing free fluid in the tissues especially of the face and hands (**oedema**)

- Albumin in the urine (**albuminuria**)

- Rising blood pressure (**hypertension**)

Post natal period (puerperium)

Involution

This is the period of approximately six weeks following birth, in which the mother's reproductive tract returns to normal. The uterus shrinks quickly in the first two weeks.

The vaginal discharge (**lochia**), following birth (**post-partum**), persists for several weeks, during which it changes in colour and consistency:

- **Lochia rubra**   bloody discharge first 1-4 days

- **Lochia serosa**   pinkish brown watery (serous) discharge approximately from day 5-7

- **Lochia alba**   greyish white or colourless discharge approximately 1 to 3 weeks after delivery

Neonatal period

This is the term used for the period of the first four weeks of life. The baby is known as the **neonate.**

Ectopic pregnancy

If the fertilised egg implants itself in the fallopian tube, or even into the abdominal cavity itself, it is known as an **ectopic** pregnancy, i.e. in the wrong place. This is a life-threatening condition. As the pregnancy progresses and the products of conception grow, the tube itself ruptures. This would normally occur at about 6–8 weeks of pregnancy. Loss of blood and subsequent shock can cause the death of the mother.

There have been rare ectopic pregnancies that have gone to **term**, when the implantation has

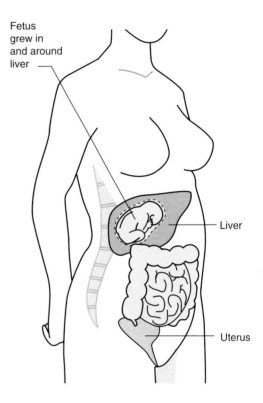

Fetus grew in and around liver

Liver

Uterus

Figure 55: A case of abdominal ectopic pregnancy. The baby was delivered successfully through surgery taken place on the mother's liver or intestine (*see Figure 55*). Usually death is inevitable for the fetus, however, in 2003 a child was born alive after a complicated surgical procedure. The fetus had developed in and around the mother's liver but was delivered successfully through abdominal surgery.

Epidural block

Some mothers are offered this procedure for the removal of pain in labour. An injection of **local anaesthesia** is injected into the **epidural space** of the **meninges** (membrane covering the brain and spinal cord). This prevents any messages of sensation travelling to the brain and gives total pain relief. There is an increased likelihood of a **forceps delivery** with this procedure as the woman does not recognise any impulse to push.

Caesarian section

This is a surgical delivery where the womb is cut into (**hysterotomy**) and the fetus removed. It is performed when:

- The presentation of the fetus would make it impossible to deliver vaginally, e.g. some **breech** or **transverse** (laying across the womb) presentations (*see Figure 56*), where it has not been possible to manually turn the fetus in the womb

- There is indication that immediate removal is necessary, e.g. **fetal distress** shows that the fetus is in danger of immediate death. (Passing of a substance known as **meconium** by the mother vaginally would indicate this, as it consists of the contents of the fetal bowel).

- Danger of infection from mother's vagina to fetus during birth is also considered.

In recent years, caesarian sections have also been performed as a convenience for social reasons. (This practice is controversial).

The name is derived from the fact that Julius Caesar, the Roman Emperor was born in this fashion. The shape of the child's head, which has not been distorted by the pressure from the vaginal delivery, is a distinctive feature.

Fetus in breech position

Figure 56: The fetus in a breech position

Weight gain during pregnancy

It is important that a woman's weight is monitored during her pregnancy to ensure that her weight gain is as expected. Excessive weight gain can lead to raised blood pressure and even eclampsia. Figure 57 shows the expected weight gain during pregnancy.

Normal weight gain during pregnancy

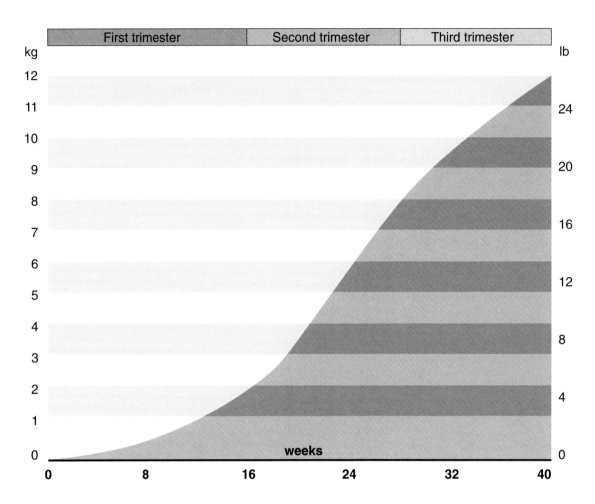

Figure 57: The normal rate of weight gain of the mother during pregnancy

Abbreviations

A&W	alive and well	**AIH**	artificial insemination by husband
ab	abortion		
AFP	alphafetoprotein (test for abnormality in fetus) in amniotic fluid or maternal blood	**AN**	antenatal
		APH	antepartum haemorrhage
		ARM	artificial rupture of membranes
AI	artificial insemination	**ART**	assisted reproductive technology
AID	artificial insemination by donor		

BBA	born before arrival
BSO	bilateral salpingo-oophorectomy (surgical removal of both fallopian tubes and both ovaries)
BW	birth weight
CIN	cervical intra-epithelial neoplasia (cervical precancer). It is graded from one to three depending on degree of abnormality
COC	combined oral contraceptive pill
COHS	controlled ovarian hormone stimulation
CVS	chorionic villus sampling (to detect fetal abnomalities)
Cx	cervix (neck of womb)
D&C	dilatation and curettage (scraping out of womb)
DCIS	ductal carcinoma in situ (a type of breast cancer)
DUB	dysfunctional uterine bleeding
EDC	expected date of confinement
EDD	expected date of delivery
EMU	early morning urine
ERPC	evacuation of retained products of conception
EUA	examination under anaesthetic
FHH	fetal heart heard
FHNH	fetal heart not heard
FMF	fetal movements felt
G&A	gas and air
GIFT	gamete intra-fallopian transplantation
HPL	human placental lactogen assay blood test (monitors health of placenta and fetus)
HPV	human papilloma virus
HRT	hormone replacement therapy
HSV	herpes simplex virus
HVS	high vaginal swab

IUCD	intra-uterine contraceptive device
IUD	intra-uterine device or intra-uterine death
IUFB	intra-uterine foreign body
IVF	in vitro fertilisation
LMP	last menstrual period
LOA	left occipitoanterior (position of fetus in uterus)
LOL	left occipitolateral (position of fetus in uterus)
LOP	left occipitoposterior (position of fetus in uterus)
LOT	left occipitotransverse – same as LOL (position of fetus in uterus)
LSCS	lower section caesarean section
NAI	non-accidental injury
ND	normal delivery
NTDs	neural tube defects (of the brain, spinal cord or meninges) e.g. spina bifida
PAP	Papanicolaou smear (cervical smear test)
PCB	post-coital bleeding
PCO	see PCOS
PCOS	polycystic ovarian syndrome
PET	pre-eclamptic toxaemia
PID	pelvic inflammatory disease (also prolapsed intervertebral disc)
PMB	postmenopausal bleeding
PMS	premenstrual syndrome
PN	postnatal
PNC	postnatal clinic
POD	pouch of Douglas (fold of peritoneum lying behind the womb)
POP	progestogen only pill (contraceptive)
PP	placenta praevia
PPH	postpartum haemorrhage
PV	per vaginam

RDS	respiratory distress syndrome
ROA	right occipitoanterior (position of fetus in uterus)
ROL	right occipitolateral (position of fetus in uterus)
ROP	right occipitoposterior (position of fetus in uterus)
ROT	right occipitotransverse – same as ROL (position of fetus in uterus)
RVS	respiratory virus syndrome
SB	still birth
SCAN	suspected child abuse or neglect
SCBU	special care baby unit
SI	sexual intercourse
SIDS	sudden infant death syndrome
STD	sexually transmitted disease
STYCAR	standard tests for young children and retardates, developed by Sheridan to assess visual development
TAH	total abdominal hysterectomy
TCRE	transcervical resection of endometrium
TOP	termination of pregnancy
TOP	termination of pregnancy
TSS	toxic shock syndrome
TUP	tubal uterine pregnancy
TV	trichomonas vaginalis (infection of vagina causing frothy yellow discharge)
TVH	total vaginal hysterectomy
USS	ultrasound scan
VI	virgo intacto (virgin)
Vx	vertex (the crown of the head of the fetus)
XX	female sex chromosomes
XY	male sex chromosomes
ZIFT	zygote intra-fallopian transfer

Terminology

Colp/o	stem for vagina
Gest/o	stem for pregnancy
Gynaec/o	stem for female
Hyster/o	stem for womb/uterus
Mamm/o (mast/o)	stem for breast
Men/o	stem for period
Metr/o	stem for womb/uterus
Nat/o, /a	stem for birth
Oophor/o (ovari/o)	stem for ovary
Salping/o	stem for fallopian tube
Uter/o	stem for womb
Vagin/o	stem for vagina
Vulv/o	stem for vulva
-gravida	suffix for pregnancy
-para, -partum	suffix for having given birth
-tocia	suffix for labour
Amniotic membrane	the innermost layer which encloses the fetus and produces amniotic fluid
Antenatal care	care given to both mother and fetus during pregnancy
Anteverted uterus	normal forward tilting of the womb
Binovular twins	derived from separate eggs (not identical – do not share genetic material
Braxton Hicks contractions	contractions felt in the womb during pregnancy from 16 weeks, which become more frequent towards full term
Breech presentation	presentation of the buttocks of the fetus during labour
Chadwick's sign	bluish coloration of vulva and vagina occurring after 6 weeks of pregnancy
Chorionic membrane	outer layer which forms the placenta

Clone	identical copy of a cell/fertilised egg (genetically identical from a SINGLE cell)
Cyesis	pregnancy
Embryo	the developing fertilised egg (first eight weeks of development while all rudimentary organs are forming)
Fetus	the developing baby after embryo stage until birth
Fundus of uterus	the area of the uterus opposite its opening into the vagina (the top part)
Gestation	duration of pregnancy
Goodell's sign	softening of the cervix as a sign of pregnancy
Grand multipara	woman who has given birth to several children from different pregnancies
Gravida	pregnant woman
Gynaecologist	specialist in diseases of the female reproductive system
Gynaecology	study of the female reproductive system
Hegar's sign	softening of lower part of uterus at approximately 7 weeks of pregnancy
in vitro	in glass (test tube)
Involution	return of the womb to its normal size following the baby's birth
Lactation	production of milk
Linea nigra	pigmented line on abdomen in pregnancy
Multigravida	pregnant woman who has been pregnant more than once
Multipara	woman who has had more than one child
Neonatal period	the four-week period following the baby's birth (pertaining to the baby)
Neonate	first four weeks of a baby's life

Nullipara	woman who has never given birth
Obstetrics	medicine concerned with pregnancy and childbirth.
Para 1	see Primipara
Parturition	giving birth
Placenta praevia	the placenta is the presenting part for birth – antepartum haemorrhage occurs – caesarean section is essential in complete placenta praevia
Presentation	the part of the fetus which presents in the birth canal (vagina)
Primigravida	woman in her first pregnancy
Primipara	woman who has given birth to a first child
Pudenda	external genital area
Puerperium	period of six weeks for mother following the birth of baby
Retroverted uterus	backward tilting of the womb
Trimester of pregnancy	a three-month period of pregnancy, e.g. first three months
Uniovular twins	derived from one egg (identical twins)
Viable	capable of independent life (i.e. the fetus from 24 weeks of pregnancy)

Diseases and disorders

Amenorrhoea	absence of menstruation
Anaplasia	highly malignant cells
Antepartum haemorrhage	abnormal bleeding from the womb before the birth
Bartholin's abscess	painful collection of pus in the Bartholin's glands of the vulva
Bicornuate uterus	abnormality where womb has two cavities

Caput succedaneum	soft swelling caused by free fluid (oedema) on the head of a newborn baby at, or shortly after, birth – disappears rapidly
Carneous mole	pregnancy ceases and products of conception are retained in the womb
Cervical erosion	erosion of the neck of the womb
Cervical polyp	a stalk-like benign tumour in the cervix
Cervicitis	inflammation of the neck of the womb
Chlamydia	an infection of the vagina
Chloasma	patchy brown pigmentation on face (like a mask) appearing in pregnancy due to hormone changes – also in women on contraceptive pill
Chorion epithelioma	malignant tumour of chorionic (embryo) cells usually after formation of hyatidiform mole complication
Conjoined twins	'siamese twins' i.e. those that share an organ (organs)
Crypto-menorrhoea	hidden menstruation – loss remains inside the womb due to an unbroken hymen
Cystic fibrosis	inherited disease in which glandular tissue abnormal and, in particular, lung tissue becomes increasingly unable to function properly
Cystocele	prolapse of the base of the bladder in women; causes bulging of the wall of the vagina
Dermoid cyst	congenital (present at birth) sac containing embryonic tissue of hair, nails, teeth, skin etc.
Down's syndrome	congenital condition in which there is often severe mental abnormality together with physical features of a mongoloid appearance, large tongue and stubby hands (abnormality of chromosome 21)
Dysfunctional uterine bleeding	heavy menstrual bleeding which does not appear to have any anatomical cause
Dysmenorrhoea	painful periods
Dyspareunia	painful intercourse
Dystocia	slow, difficult labour
Eclampsia	a condition in which fits occur as blood pressure becomes extremely high (danger to both fetus and mother, see pre-eclampsia)
Ectopic pregnancy	embedding of fertilised egg outside of the womb – usually in the fallopian tube
Endometriosis	condition where lining of womb is found in other sites, e.g. colon or pouch of Douglas
Fibroadenoma	a benign tumour composed of fibrous and glandular tissue
Fibroid	a benign tumour composed of fibrous and muscle tissue found in the womb
Fibromyoma	a fibroid (as above)
Galactocele	milk cyst
Gynaecomastia	enlargement of the male breast
Hydatidiform mole	an intrauterine neoplastic mass
Hydramnios	excessive amount of amniotic fluid
Hyperemesis gravidarum	excessive vomiting during pregnancy
Infertility	inability of woman to become pregnant or man to fertilise the ovum (does not mean sterility)
Leucorrhoea	whitish vaginal discharge

Leukoplakia vulva	chronic condition characterised by thick, hard, white patches on the vulva
Lochia	vaginal discharge following childbirth
Malpresentation	abnormal presentation of fetus for delivery
Mastitis	inflammation of the breast
Mastodynia	pain in the breast
Meconium	first fetal stools – if passed in the womb it is a clear indication of fetal distress in labour
Menorrhagia	excessive loss of blood during menstruation
Metritis	inflammation of the womb
Metrorrhagia	heavy bleeding not at the time of a period
Metrostaxis	persistent slight bleeding from the womb
Miscarriage	spontaneous abortion
Munchausen syndrome by proxy	a situation where a child or other person is deliberately made to appear ill or suffer injury so that the person responsible gains attention
Oligohydramnios	scanty amniotic fluid
Polycystic ovarian syndrome	an increasingly common condition in women in which there are multiple, enlarged follicles of the ovary, together with high levels of testosterone (male hormone). A cause of infertility and also linked with Diabetes Type II
Polymenorrhoea	frequent periods
Post-partum haemorrhage	bleeding following delivery
Pre-eclampsia	a condition during pregnancy where there is a raised blood pressure, albumin in the urine and oedema of the face and body (also known as toxaemia of pregnancy) – it precedes eclampsia

Procidentia	complete prolapse of womb into vagina through to the outside of the body
Prolapse	womb or vaginal wall protrudes into the vagina
Pseudocyesis	false pregnancy
Puerperal psychosis	severe mental illness following childbirth
Puerperal sepsis	infection of the genital tract and blood poisoning following childbirth
Pyosalpingitis	inflammation of the fallopian tube with pus formation
Pyosalpinx	presence of pus in the fallopian tube
Rectocele	prolapse of the rectum into the vaginal wall
Salpingitis	inflammation of the fallopian tubes
Striae gravidarum	silvery lines (red at first) on thighs and abdomen occurring due to pregnancy – 'stretch marks'
Supernumerary nipples	development of extra nipples (male or female)
Teratogenic	'monster producing'– a virus or factor which is capable of producing deformities in the developing fetus, e.g. drugs/rubella
Vaginismus	involuntary spasm of the vagina preventing penetration during sexual intercourse
Vaginitis	inflammation of the vagina

Procedures and equipment

Abortion	miscarriage or expulsion of the 'products of conception' from the uterus before 24 weeks:
Criminal a.	not within the legal definition;
Induced a.	intentional abortion;

Incomplete a. parts of 'products of conception' are still remaining in the womb;

Inevitable a. profuse bleeding, cervix dilated – products are bound to be expelled;

Spontaneous a. naturally occurring abortion;

Threatened a. slight bleeding (cervix closed)

Amniocentesis withdrawal of the amniotic fluid which surrounds the developing fetus for examination purposes, e.g. for Down's syndrome

Amniography procedure of x-raying the pregnant uterus after contrast medium has been injected into the amniotic sac surrounding the fetus

Apgar score/ rating an estimation of the state of the newborn baby one minute after birth and again five minutes later – respiration, colour, muscle tone, pulse and response are measured with a maximum score of 10 being awarded for a healthy condition

Ballottement passive fetal movements in response to tapping of lower uterus or cervix

Caesarian section delivery of fetus through abdominal incision

Chorionic villus sampling a sampling of cells from the chorion layer of the developing embryo for diagnostic purposes (can be done earlier than amniocentesis)

Colporrhaphy surgical repair of vaginal wall prolapse

Cone biopsy cone-shaped portion of tissue removed from cervix for microscopic examination

Cordocentesis withdrawal of fetal blood for examination directly from the umbilical vein

Cryopreservation preserving embryo, ova in cold storage

Endometrial smear/biopsy following a small amount of local anaesthetic, a thin, hollow curette is inserted through the cervical opening and a small amount of uterine lining is removed for histology

Epidural injection of anaesthesia into meninges of lumbar spine, used to remove pain of childbirth

Episiotomy cutting the perineum (area between the vaginal opening and anus) to facilitate birth

Fetoscopy direct examination and pictures recorded of the fetus 'in utero'

Fine needle aspiration aspiration of breast lump, etc. for cytological investigation

Guthrie test blood test to detect phenylketonuria performed on newborn after establishment of feeding ('heel prick test')

Hysterectomy surgical removal of the uterus which may be performed vaginally or by abdominal incision

Hysterotomy cutting into the womb

Induction causing labour to begin by artificial means

Lumpectomy (tilectomy) surgical removal of a tumour without removal of the breast itself

Mammogram (mammography) an X-ray procedure examining breast tissue

Mastectomy surgical removal of the breast

Maternal Serum Screening tests	a group of blood tests which are used to check for substances linked with birth deformities
Myomectomy	surgical removal of fibroids
Non-stress test	a non-invasive test to detect fetal heart acceleration in response to fetal movement
Nuchal translucency scan	ultrasound test to show density of neck area in diagnosis of fetal abnormality for Down's syndrome
Oestradiol – 17B	blood test for ovarian function
Oophorectomy	surgical removal of the ovary – (bilateral oophorectomy – both ovaries).
Oxytocin challenge test	a stress test to evaluate fetal ability to withstand oxytocin (hormone) induced contractions
Panhysterectomy	surgical removal of womb and surrounding reproductive organs

Pelvic ultrasound test	passes ultrasound waves through the body to diagnose pelvic disease or examine a developing fetus for abnormalities
Salpingectomy	surgical removal of the fallopian tube(s)
Salpingo-oophorectomy	surgical removal of ovary and fallopian tube
Salpingogram	X-ray of the fallopian tubes
Thermography	investigation of the breast by measuring the heat of the tissues
Tilectomy	see Lumpectomy
Version	turning of a fetus to aid delivery
Vibro-acoustic	stimulation test - non-invasive test using vibration and sound to induce fetal activity
Vulvectomy	surgical removal of the vulva.

The male reproductive system

Structure

The male reproductive system (*see Figure 58*) is composed of:

- Two **testes** ⎤
- Two **epididymides** ⎦ within the scrotum
- Two **vasa deferentia**
- Two **seminal vesicles**
- **Prostate gland**
- Two **ejaculatory ducts**
- **Bulbourethral (Cowper's) glands**
- **Penis** containing the **urethra**

Testes

These develop within the abdominal cavity in the fetus, but prior to birth they descend through a canal known as the **inguinal canal** into the **scrotum**. They produce numerous **spermatazoa** (male sex cells) (*see Figure 45 in Chapter 11*) for fertilisation of the female **ovum**. Also produced are the male hormones known as **androgens**, the main one being **testosterone**, which are responsible for secondary male characteristics (hair distribution etc).

Scrotum

The scrotum is a pouch of skin and specialised tissue lying outside the abdominal cavity and containing the **testis** and **epididymis**, together with the attached start of the **vas deferens**. It is essential that the developing spermatazoa are kept at a temperature lower than that within the abdominal cavity where the organs were first developed in fetal life. Unless this occurs the man will be infertile. The scrotum is lowered from and raised closer to the body, by special muscles dependent on the temperature of blood passing through the structure.

Epididymides

These are situated upon the testes; here the immobile **spermatazoa** become mature and are stored.

Vasa deferentia

Tubes through which the spermatazoa are released. These are cut in the operation of **vasectomy** to produce sterilisation of the male.

Seminal vesicles

These contribute their own secretion to the **seminal fluid** which keeps the spermatazoa active and alive. Some spermatazoa are stored here ready for **ejaculation**.

Ejaculatory ducts

These join the seminal vesicles to the urethra.

Bulbourethral glands

These are also known as **Cowper's glands** and produce further secretions to the seminal fluid.

Prostate gland

A gland the size of a walnut surrounding the junction of the vasa deferentia and urethra. It secretes a fluid making the spermatazoa more mobile and fertile. It commonly becomes enlarged in older men causing difficulty in passing urine due to constriction of the urethra.

Urethra

This is a common passageway for both **seminal fluid** and **urine**. A **sphincter muscle** prevents both functions occurring at the same time.

Penis

This is the male organ composed of **erectile tissue** and capable of becoming erect when distended with blood. The enlargement at its tip is known as the **glans**; the fold of skin protecting the opening of the urethra is known as the **foreskin** or **prepuce** and it is this area which is removed in the procedure of **circumcision**.

Male reproductive system

1. Vas deferens
2. Bladder
3. Prostate gland
4. Urethra
5. Penis
6. Epididymis
7. Prepuce
8. Scrotum
9. Testis
10. Cowper's gland
11. Seminal vesicle
12. Colon

Figure 58: The male reproductive system

Abbreviations

HPV	human papilloma virus
PSA	prostatic specific antigen (test for cancer of prostate)
TUR	transurethral resection (of prostate gland)
TURB	transurethral resection of bladder
TURBT	transurethral resection of bladder tumour
TURP	transurethral resection of prostate gland

Terminology

Andr/o	stem for male
Epididym/o	stem for epididymis (fine tubules)
Genit/o	stem for genital
Orchi(d)/o	stem for testis
Phall/o (pen/o)	stem for penis
Prostat/o	stem for prostate gland
Semin/o	stem for semen
Vas/o	stem for vas deferens

Diseases and disorders

Balanitis	inflammation of glans, penis and foreskin
Ectopic testes	testicles which are in the wrong place, i.e. not in the scrotum
Epididymitis	inflammation of the epididymis (tubules above the testis)
Epididymo -orchitis	inflammation of the epididymis and testis
Epispadias	opening of urethra on the upper side of penis

Haematocele — effusion of blood in area surrounding the testis

Hydrocele — collection of fluid in the tunica vaginalis (membrane surrounding the testis)

Hypospadias — opening of urethra is on the lower side of the penis

Impotence — inability to have sexual intercourse, or the inability to have or maintain an erection of the penis (may have a physical or a psychological cause)

Orchitis (orchiditis) — inflammation of a testicle

Phallitis — inflammation of the penis

Phimosis — constriction of foreskin of penis preventing retraction of skin

Prostatitis — inflammation of the prostate gland

Sterility — inability to fertilise female egg (ovum)

Urethritis — inflammation of the urethra

Varicocele — dilatation of veins around the testis and vas deferens

Procedures and equipment

Circumcision — surgical removal of part of foreskin

Ileal conduit — ureters are transplanted into the ileum (intestine) in order to discharge urine to bypass a tumour or following removal of bladder

Orchidectomy — surgical removal of a testicle

Orchidopexy — fixing of an undescended or rotating testicle into the scrotal sac

Prostatic specific antigen test — this is a screening blood test used to aid diagnosis of carcinoma of the prostate gland. Patients with prostatism (enlargement of the prostate gland) should be screened in order to eliminate the possibility of malignancy

Suprapubic cystostomy — incision above the prostate to allow drainage of the bladder

Transurethral resection of prostate (TURP) — surgical removal of the prostate through the urethra

Urethroplasty — reshaping of the urethra

Vasectomy — surgical cutting/ removal of the vasa deferentia in order to produce sterility.

Chapter **13**

The nervous system

including the terminology

of mental health

Function

This is concerned with the rapid conduction and interpretation of messages in the form of electrical impulses from one part of the body to another. It also coordinates the activities of the body.

Structure

The nervous system is made up of specialised tissue containing cells known as neurones, and is divided into three systems:

- **Central nervous system** (CNS)

- **Peripheral nervous system**

- **Autonomic nervous system** (ANS)

Nerve cells are known as **grey matter** and the fibres from them are covered in **myelin** (a fatty substance) are known as **white matter**. In the CNS, nerve cells, when damaged, are unable to regenerate themselves.

Messages can only travel in one direction along a nerve fibre.

Motor nerves (efferent)

These convey messages from the brain to parts of the body to perform an action (*see Figure 59*).

Sensory nerves (afferent)

These convey messages from the body to the brain with information about stimuli such as pain.

Central Nervous System

This consists of the **brain** and **spinal cord**.

Brain

The brain lies within the bony **cranium** of the skull. It is covered in a specialised membrane containing the blood vessels which supply oxygen and nourishment, known as the **meninges**, which also covers the spinal cord. The need for oxygen to reach every cell in the brain is critical. If deprived of oxygen for more than three to four minutes, these cells will die and death will occur.

Motor neurone

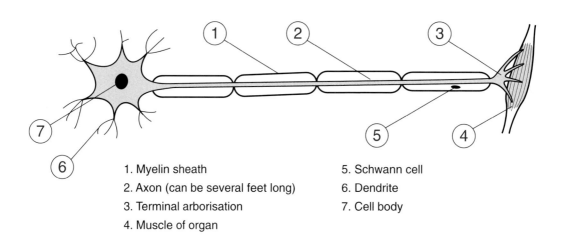

1. Myelin sheath
2. Axon (can be several feet long)
3. Terminal arborisation
4. Muscle of organ
5. Schwann cell
6. Dendrite
7. Cell body

Figure 59: A motor neurone

The brain

1. Parietal lobe of cerebrum

2. Fissure of Rolando

3. Cerebrum

4. Occipital lobe of cerebrum

5. Cerebellum

6. Midbrain (hidden)

7. Pons varolii

8. Medulla oblongata

9. Brain stem

10. Temporal lobe

11. Fissure of Sylvius

12. Frontal lobe of cerebrum

Figure 60: The brain

The brain consists of (*see Figure 60*):

- **Cerebrum**

- **Cerebellum**

- **Brain stem**

Cerebrum

This forms the larger lobes of the brain and is divided into two **hemispheres** joined together with a bridge of white matter. The cerebrum contains the **higher centres** including those of intellect, consciousness, movement, sensory perception etc.

There are many specialised centres and the **convoluted surface**, together with numerous **fissures** (giving a larger surface area), contains **grey matter**, with **white matter** within the hemispheres. There are also specialised areas of grey matter deep within the hemispheres known as the **basal ganglia**. The **hypothalamus**, which controls the ANS, is situated here.

The **cerebrum** consists of numerous **lobes** which are named from the cranial bones beneath which they lie, i.e. **frontal, parietal, temporal** and **occipital**.

Cerebellum

This also has two hemispheres joined together at the posterior portion. It is involved in the control of **muscle tone** and coordinates muscular movement as well as balance and equilibrium. Damage can cause **ataxia** (uncoordinated gait), tremor and loss of sense of balance.

Brainstem

This consists of:

- **Midbrain**

- **Pons varolii**   all interconnected

- **Medulla oblongata**

Midbrain

This joins the two cerebral hemispheres to the **cerebellum** and the **pons varolii** below. It has specialised centres deep within it. All sensory impulses pass through this area.

Pons varolii

This joins the **cerebellum** to the **midbrain** and **medulla oblongata** below.

Medulla oblongata

This is continuous with the pons above and contains the **vital centres**, including the control of respiration, heart beat and the calibre of the blood vessels etc.

Damage to these centres is very serious and often causes death, e.g. fracture of the base of the skull. This area is continuous with the spinal cord below and passes through the **foramen magnum** (large hole) of the cranium.

It is in the medulla oblongata that the white nerve fibres, travelling to the spinal cord, cross over so that the left area of the brain controls the right side of the body and vice versa.

Ventricles

Deep within the brain are spaces known as **ventricles**, which are continuous with each other and with the fine spinal canal in the spinal cord. **Cerebrospinal fluid** from the meninges circulates throughout these areas.

Meninges

This is a very specialised membrane which covers both brain and spinal cord.

It is composed of three special layers:

1. Dura mater a hard, tough outer layer.

2. Arachnoid mater a vascular layer with many blood vessels.

3. Pia mater a soft layer closely attached to brain and spinal cord

Functions

It has the following functions:

- **Supports** the delicate nervous tissue
- Acts as a **shock absorber**
- Maintains **uniform pressure** around it
- Provides **nourishment** and removes **waste products**

Cranial nerves

The 12 pairs of cranial nerves arising from the brain, are sensory and motor.

- **Motor nerves** carry messages *from* the brain *to* the body
- **Sensory nerves** carry messages *to* the brain *from* the body

List of cranial nerves

Key: (m) = motor
(s) = sensory

I	**olfactory**
	concerning sense of smell (s)
II	**optic**
	concerning sight (s)
III	**oculomotor**
	eye muscles (m)
IV	**trochlear**
	eye muscles (m)
V	**trigeminal**
	forehead and face (s)
VI	**abducens**
	eye muscles (m)
VII	**facial**
	facial expression (m)
VIII	**auditory**
	hearing and balance (s)
IX	**glossopharyngeal**
	tongue and pharynx (ms)
X	**vagus (vagal)**
	pharynx, trachea, heart, larynx, bronchi lungs, oesophagus, stomach, intestine (m & s)
XI	**spinal accessory**
	muscles of pharynx etc. (m)
XII	**hypoglossal**
	muscles of tongue (m)

Spinal Cord

Structure

This is continuous with the **medulla oblongata** above and extends to the level of the **second lumbar vertebra** below. It travels through the **neural canal** or **foramen** (hole) in the vertebrae which surround and protect it.

Unlike the brain, the grey matter of the spinal cord is found deep within it in an H-shaped pattern and the white matter distributed in the outer aspects. It is covered in **meninges** and has a small space through its centre, known as the **spinal canal**.

Arising from the spinal cord are the **peripheral nerves** of which there are 31 pairs, travelling to the various parts of the body, receiving and sending messages and interconnecting.

A group of nerve fibres (**white matter**) travelling together is known as a **plexus** and groups of cells (**grey matter**) as **ganglia**.

At the termination of the spinal cord (at the level of the second lumbar vertebra in the adult) numerous peripheral nerves give rise to the **cauda equina** (horse's tail) which supply the **lumbar-sacral** area (in the groin) and lower limbs (*see Figure 61*).

Function

Its function is to relay messages to and from the body and also at different levels of the cord itself.

Reflex action

This is the automatic reaction by the body to a stimulation. In a **reflex arc**, a message to the sensory area of the spinal cord is immediately relayed across the cord to the **motor area**, which in turn sends an impulse to a **motor organ**, e.g. a muscle. The original sensory message still travels to the appropriate part of the brain, but the resulting movement of the limb is started more quickly by the reflex action, i.e. the reaction of the body to a pin-prick of the arm is a reflex arc that moves the arm (*see Figure 62*).

Spinal cord and peripheral nerves

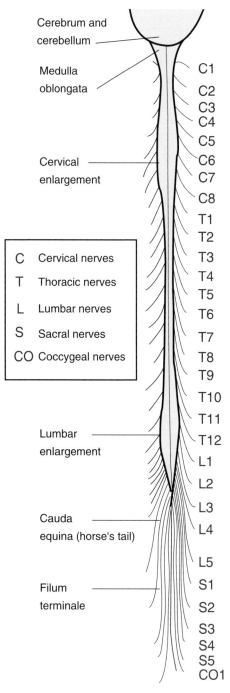

C	Cervical nerves
T	Thoracic nerves
L	Lumbar nerves
S	Sacral nerves
CO	Coccygeal nerves

Figure 61: The spinal cord and peripheral nerves

Reflex arc

Impulse from skin to spinal cord

Spinal nerve

Impulse from spinal cord to muscle

1. Posterior root ganglion
2. Sensory nerve
3. Posterior root of spinal nerve
4. Grey matter (nerve cells)
5. White matter (fibres)

6. Spinal canal
7. Association neurone
8. Synapse
9. Ganglion
10. Motor nerve

Figure 62: The reflex arc

Inhibition

This is where the resulting reflex action is over-come by the brain, e.g. picking up a very hot plate which is very expensive. The automatic dropping of the plate is overridden by the knowledge that it is expensive to replace.

Peripheral nervous system

This consists of:

- 12 pairs of **cranial nerves**

- 31 pairs of **peripheral nerves**

The cranial nerves arise from the brain itself. The peripheral nerves stem from differing lev-els of the spinal cord and supply the body. They convey sensory and motor impulses to and from the brain and spinal cord, and also to different levels of the cord itself.

Autonomic nerve supply

This is the system which controls the workings of the body organs and keeps the body in its correct state (**homeostasis**). It is not normally within the control of the will but is automatic.

It supplies all organs composed of **smooth muscle** as well as other organs, including the heart, blood vessels, respiratory system and eyes.

There are two sets of fibres to each organ which are known as the:

- **sympathetic chain**

- **parasympathetic chain**

These are controlled by a centre in the brain known as the **hypothalamus**. All systems work in conjunction with each other and the two sets of fibres work in harmony.

Sympathetic chain

This set of fibres is stimulated to prepare the body for the '**fight or flight**' response. When stimulated, it increases the heart rate and respiration, raises blood pressure, dilates the pupil of the eye and increases energy supplies as well as many other actions.

Parasympathetic chain

This set of fibres has an inhibiting or resting action and has the opposite effect upon the body to the sympathetic chain. Its action slows the heart rate, decreases the breathing rate and increases digestion and secretion of saliva.

The **vagus nerve**, as part of the parasympathetic chain, supplies the heart and many of the major organs of the body.

Abbreviations

Nervous system: abbreviations

ANS	autonomic nervous system
BSE	bovinespongiform encephalopathy ('mad cow' disease)
CA	chronological age
CAT (CT)	scan – computerised X-ray of layers of tissues
CJD	Creutzfeldt-Jacob disease
CNS	central nervous system
CSF	cerebrospinal fluid
CVA	cerebrovascular accident (stroke)
DS	disseminated sclerosis (old term for MS)
DTs	delirium tremens
EEG	electroencephalogram
EMG	electromyogram
GA	general anaesthetic
GPI	general paralysis of the insane
IQ	intelligence quotient
LA	local anaesthetic
MA	mental age

MAOI	monoamine oxidase inhibitors (antidepressants which require abstinence from certain foods, e.g. cheese - can cause bleeding in the brain)
MND	motor neurone disease
MRI	magnetic resonance imaging (see NMR)
MS	multiple sclerosis
NMR	nuclear magnetic resonance (scan)
OCD	obsessive compulsive disorder
PVS	persistant vegetative state: a continuing level of coma in head injuries where there appears to be no response. Can continue for years with patient on a life support machine
REM	rapid eye movements
RT	radiation therapy
RTA	road traffic accident
SAH	subarachnoid haemorrhage
SOL	space-occupying lesion (tumour, usually malignant, in the cranium)
TENS	transcutaneous electrical nerve stimulation
TIA	transient ischaemic attack (in the brain)
TLE	temporal lobe epilepsy (fits which originate in the temporal lobe of brain causing aura of taste, hearing, smell etc.)
vCJD	variant Creutzfeldt-Jacob disease

Mental health: abbreviations

ADD	attention deficit disorder
ADHD	attention deficit hyperactivity disorder
AIA	allergy induced autism
ANS	autonomic nervous system

AS	autistic spectrum disorder
ASD	Asperger's syndrome disorder
BP	bipolar disorder
DTs	delirium tremens
ECT	electroconvulsive therapy
GAD	general anxiety disorder
GPI	general paralysis of the insane
IQ	intelligence quotient
LD	learning disability
MA	mental age
MAOI	monoamine oxidase inhibitor - antidepressant drug which must not be taken with certain foods or drugs eg: lentils, cheese etc (can cause death)
OCD	obsessive compulsive disorder
PTSD	post traumatic stress disorder
SADS	seasonal affective disorder syndrome (depression due to lack of light in winter)
SSRI	selective serotonin reuptake inhibitor (antidepressants which affect particular enzyme actions in brain)
TCA	tricyclic antidepressant (old type of antidepressant)
TS	Tourette's syndrome

Terminology

Nervous system: terminology

Cephal/o	stem for head
Cerebell/o	stem for cerebellum (part of the brain)
Cerebr/o	stem for cerebrum (part of the brain)
Crani/o	stem for cranium
Encephal/o	stem for brain
Myel/o	stem for spinal cord
Neur/o	stem for nerve

Poli/o	stem for grey matter
Ventricul/o	stem for ventricles of brain
-kinesis	suffix meaning movement
-paresis	suffix meaning weakness
-phasia	suffix meaning speech
-plegia	suffix meaning paralysis
-somia	suffix meaning body
Cerebrospinal fluid	fluid similar to plasma found in the meninges which nourishes the brain and spinal cord
Dura mater	outermost and thickest of the three meninges surrounding brain and spinal chord.
Perception	the interpretation and response of the nervous system to sensory stimuli

Mental health: terminology

Aut/o	stem for self
Neur/o	stem for nerve
Psych/o	stem for mind/ behaviour
Schiz/o	stem for split/diaphragm
-mania	suffix meaning frenzy, wild activity
-phobia	suffix meaning irrational fear
-somia	suffix meaning body
Catharsis	an outlet of repressed emotion
Cognitive behaviour psychology	a treatment which concentrates on changing behaviour instead of treating causes of a problem
Cognitive therapy	therapy concentrated on improving person's negative thinking, perceptions and attitudes
Complex	a pattern of behaviour which demonstrates an over-reaction to a problem
Delusion	false belief, usually associated with psychological illness,

	which cannot be altered despite logic and evidence to the contrary
Perception	the interpretation and response of the nervous system to sensory stimuli
Psychiatrist	medical doctor specialising in the treatment of mental illness
Psychiatry	the medical speciality concerning mental illness
Psychoanalysis	Freudian method of exploring the mind
Psychologist	not a medical doctor; qualified in study of the mind, and behaviour; can provide therapy but not drugs etc
Psychology	scientific study of behaviour
Psychotherapy	treatment by talking etc to relieve symptoms or resolve problems

Diseases and disorders

Nervous system: diseases and disorders

Acute	rapid onset
Affective disorders	those conditions which affect mood
Akathisia	restlessness that results in an inability to sit still
Alzheimer's disease	progressive dementia – caused by destruction of the neurones (brain cells)
Amnesia	loss of memory
Anaesthesia	loss of sensitivity and feeling (local) to a part or (general) throughout the body, causing loss of consciousness
Anencephaly	partial or complete absence of the bones of the rear of the skull and of the cerebral hemispheres of the brain
Anorexia nervosa	eating disorder characterised by refusal to eat – person

	has body image of obesity (common in teenage girls)
Aphasia	inability to speak caused by brain damage
Apoplexy	a stroke
Ataxia	uncoordinated gait (limp)
Aura	warning symptoms preceding epileptic seizure or migraine attack
Autism	absorption with the self – a condition in which the person is withdrawn into their own world, showing little response to events around them; it is a development disorder arising in early years of life and is characterised by significantly impaired social and language skills – several categories classified
Babinski's sign	reflex of the toe upwards instead of down – shows damage to central nervous system
Bell's palsy	paralysis of face muscles due to injury or disease of cranial nerve supplying face muscles (usually one-sided)
Bovine spongiform encephalopathy	see Creutzfeldt–Jacob disease
Bulimia nervosa	eating disorder characterised by eating 'binges' and self-induced vomiting
Catatonia	state of stupor, strange posture, outbursts of excitement – form of autism common in schizophrenia
Causalgia	severe burning-type pain caused by nerve injury
Chorea	involuntary contraction of muscles causing writhing movements (eg: St Vitus' dance)

Chronic long-term condition or frequently recurring

Circadian rhythm chemical and psychological variations over a 24 hour period

Clonus response the production of a series of muscle contractions in response to a stimulus which are only produced in the presence of CNS (central nervous system) disease

Coma complete unconsciousness – a level where there is no response on normal stimulation

Complex a pattern of behaviour which demonstrates an over-reaction to a problem

Compression pressure on the brain tissue due to swelling, blood clot or tumour

Compulsion insistent and repetitive need to behave in unreasonable or excessive way

Concussion limited period of unconsciousness caused by injury to the head

Coning pressure on brain forcing brainstem through foramen magnum

Conversion problems expressed as physical symptoms eg abdominal pain, panic attacks, paralysis etc.

Convulsion spasmodic contraction and relaxation of muscles in a fit

Coprolalia involuntary use of vulgar/foul language as in Tourette's syndrome

Creutzfeldt-Jacob disease a disease in which the brain tissue degenerates; linked with bovine spongiform encephalopathy (mad cow disease) it is now known to be transmitted to humans

Delirium mental excitement resulting from hallucinations, e.g. in state of high fever, alcohol consumption, or mental illness

Delirium tremens mental excitement due to chronic excessive alcohol intake, known as 'DTs'

Diplopia double vision

Dysarthria difficulty in articulation of speech due to nerve damage

Dyskinesia abnormal movements associated with side-effects of major tranquillising drugs

Dyslexia word blindness – inability to decipher words by the brain producing difficulty in reading, writing etc. by an individual with the intelligence to perform these tasks

Dystonia muscle spasms occurring in the tongue, jaw, eyes, neck; side-effect of some medications

Encephalitis inflammation of the brain

Epilepsy condition of suffering seizures, convulsions – abnormal electrical activity of the brain

Familial affecting more members of family than would be chance

Fixation an arrest in psychological development at a particular stage

General paralysis of the insane paralysis caused by the terminal effects of syphilis

Glioma malignant tumour of nerve support system

Grand mal epileptic attacks which include loss of consciousness and convulsions where the disturbance in electrical activity spreads across the various areas of the brain

Hallucination	false perception without any true sensory stimuli – any sense may be involved, e.g. taste, hearing, sight etc.
Hemianaesthesia	loss of feeling of one side of the body
Hemiparaesthesia	heightened sensation of one side of the body
Hemiparesis	weakness of one side of the body
Hemiplegia	paralysis of one side of the body
Herpes zoster	shingles – painful infection along the nerve by the virus which causes chicken-pox
Hydrocephaly	'water on the brain' – excess cerebrospinal fluid present due to a blockage in its circulation – skull enlarges in the baby
Hyperkinetic	overactivity of movement
Hysteria	a neurosis arising from psychological problems producing bodily symptoms, e.g. paralysis
Idiopathic epilepsy	epilepsy of unknown cause
Jacksonian epilepsy	epilepsy having a focal area – caused by an abnormality in that area of the brain, e.g. scar tissue.
Kernig's sign	inability to straighten leg at knee joint when thigh is flexed at right angles to the body – present in meningitis
Libido	sexual energy/behaviour/drive
Limbic system	area of the brain concerned with the emotional control and memory
Meningioma	tumour of the meninges (covering of the brain and spinal cord)
Meningism	irritation of the meninges (covering of the brain and spinal cord)

Meningitis	inflammation of the meninges
Meningocele	protrusion of the meninges through the gap in the unfused vertebra of spina bifida
Microcephaly	having an abnormally small head
Migraine	headache, often one-sided, characterised by disturbance of vision, nausea, vomiting etc. caused by dilatation of the cranial arteries
Monoplegia	paralysis of one limb
Motor neurone disease	disease of the motor areas of the central nervous system causing paralysis – rapidly progressive
Multiple sclerosis	disease of central nervous system in which the myelin (fatty) sheath covering nerve fibres is destroyed and various functions are impaired, including movement. It is characterised by relapses and remissions
Myelitis	inflammation of the spinal cord
Myelo-meningocele	meningocele where the spinal cord is also protruding
Narcolepsy	compulsive sleeping (at any time)
Neuralgia	nerve pain (along the course of a nerve)
Neuritis	inflammation of a nerve
Nystagmus	involuntary rapid movements of the eyeballs
Palsy	paralysis
Panic attacks	present in anxiety states – body response produces rapid heart rate etc

Paraplegia	paralysis of both legs
Paresis	weakness
Parkinson's disease	damage to grey matter in the brain known as the basal ganglia; causes involuntary tremors of limbs etc.
Perception	the interpretation and response of the nervous system to sensory stimuli
Petit mal	type of epilepsy where the person momentarily loses concentration ('absences')
Photophobia	a fear of (or intolerance to) light
Poliomyelitis	inflammation of the grey matter of the spinal cord (infantile paralysis)
Polyneuritis	inflammation of many nerves
Post-epileptic automatism	a period following an epileptic fit when the person functions automatically and is unaware of their actions
Quadriplegia (tetraplegia)	paralysis of all four limbs
Romberg's sign	an inability to stand without swaying when the eyes are closed and the feet are together – sign of brain damage
Sciatica	pain along the sciatic nerve (down the back of the leg to the toe)
Sinus thrombosis	formation of blood clot in the brain sinuses (spaces in which the venous blood drains before entering the jugular veins)
Spastic	damage to motor area of brain producing increased muscle tone
St Vitus' dance	see Chorea
Status epilepticus	a continuous fit passing from one straight into another – very dangerous

Stupor	a level of consciousness – person not fully conscious but does respond to certain stimuli
Subarachnoid haemorrhage	bleeding between the layers of the meninges known as the pia mater and the arachnoid mater
Subdural haematoma	a blood clot between the layers of the meninges – the dura mater and the arachnoid mater
Syncope	fainting – temporary lack of blood to the brain
Syphilis	sexually transmitted disease which, in its final stages, produces damage to the central nervous system (CNS)
Tabes dorsalis	nerve damage to the (locomotor ataxia) spinal cord caused by the late stages of syphilis and giving rise to an abnormal gait
Tardive dyskinesia	side-effects of long term antipsychotic drugs; involuntary movements of face, etc.
Tetraplegia	(quadriplegia) paralysis of all four limbs
Tic	involuntary, rapid, recurrent stereotyped movement or vocalisation
Tourette's syndrome	neurological syndrome characterised by a tic disorder with mutiple muscle or vocal tics occurring in bouts. Involuntary use of foul language
Tremor	involuntary quivering of the muscles – inability to control them
Trigeminal neuralgia	inflammation of the Vth cranial nerve supplying three areas of the face; causes severe pain
Vertigo	dizziness

Mental health: diseases and disorders

Acute rapid onset

Advocate someone who speaks on behalf of the person

Affective disorder term for mood disorder

Affective psychosis major mental disorder in which there is serious disturbance of the emotions

Agoraphobia a fear of open spaces or of leaving one's home

Akathisia restlessness that results in an inability to sit still

Alzheimer's disease progressive dementia – caused by destruction of the neurones (brain cells)

Amnesia loss of memory

Androphobia a fear of men

Anhedonia incapable of experiencing pleasure from previously enjoyable activities

Anorexia nervosa eating disorder characterised by severe weight loss as result of refusing to eat. Person thinks they are fat despite obvious thinness

Anosognosia failure to recognise one's own condition or disease

Anxiety apprehension, tension

Anxiety disorder group of disorders characterised by overwhelming and persisting feelings of worry and fear which interfere with everyday life

Arachnophobia a fear of spiders

Asperger's disorder or syndrome thought to be related to autism, significantly impaired social interactions but patient is usually above average intelligence with no problems in language development

Autism development disorder arising in early years of life; significantly impaired social and language skills – several categories classified

Bipolar disorder mood disorder previously known as manic depression, characterised by extreme alternating moods of depression and mania (many different classifications by numbers)

Borderline personality disorder group of persisting maladaptive patterns of deviant and social behaviour, lifestyle etc. not caused by psychotic illness

Bulimia nervosa eating disorder characterised by recurrent bingeing and self-induced vomiting

Catatonia state of stupor, strange posture, outbursts of excitement – form of autism common in schizophrenia

Catharsis an outlet of repressed emotion

Chronic long-term condition or frequently recurring

Circadian rhythm chemical and psychological variations over 24 hr period

Claustrophobia a fear of confined spaces

Complex a pattern of behaviour which demonstrates an over-reaction to a problem

Compulsion insistent and repetitive need to behave in unreasonable or excessive way

Conversion problems expressed as physical symptoms eg abdominal pain, panic attacks, paralysis etc

Coprolalia involuntary use of vulgar/foul language as in Tourette's syndrome

Delirium mental excitement resulting from hallucinations, e.g. in state of high fever, alcohol consumption, or mental illness

Delirium tremens mental excitement due to chronic excessive alcohol intake, known as 'DTs'

Delusion	false belief that has no basis which cannot be changed despite obvious proof to the contrary
Denial	refusing to believe an unpleasant fact – a normal method of protection of the mind
Depression	mood disorder characterised by sadness, inability to experience pleasure, lack of energy, suicidal thought, guilt, indecisiveness, sleep disturbance etc
Endogenous D	caused by internal body factors, as in manic depression where there are alternating mood swings to intense euphoria
Exogenous D or *reactive D*	caused by events and environmental factors, e.g. bereavement or unemployment
Involutional D	caused by ageing process including menopause
Dissociation	disruption in integrated functions of consciousness, memory, perception etc.
Doraphobia	a fear of fur
Dyskinesia	involuntary muscle movement –side-effect of some medications
Dyslexia	word blindness learning disability
Dysphoria	unpleasant mood
Dysthymia	depression associated with imaginary illness
Dystonia	muscle spasms occurring in the tongue, jaw, eyes, neck: side-effect of some medications
Echolalia	parrot-like repetition of overheard words
Euphoria	exaggerated sense of well being
Familial	affecting more members of family than would be chance

Fixation	an arrest in psychological development at a particular stage
Fugue	period of altered awareness often associated with wandering, of which the person has no recall
Gender dysphoria	a belief that individual is the opposite gender i.e. a man a woman; a woman a man
Haemophobia	a fear of blood
Hallucination	false perception can be hearing, sight, touch, smell, taste, somatic (within the body): a psychosis
Hydrophobia	a fear of drinking
Hypochondria	an abnormality in which the person is pre-occupied with imaginary illnesses
Hypomania	mood characterised by unrealistic optimism, speech and activity
Hysteria	a neurosis arising from psychological problems producing bodily symptoms, e.g. paralysis
Libido	sexual energy/behaviour/drive
Limbic system	area of the brain concerned with the emotional control and memory
Mania	abnormal elevation of the mood and over-activity – see bipolar disorder
Manic depression	a form of depression which is characterised by alternating mood swings of overactivity (mania) and sadness (depression) – a psychosis; see Depression, endogenous
Melatonin	hormone produced by the pineal gland in response to darkness, which induces sleep and depresses mood and mental ability

Munchausen Syndrome by Proxy	someone who draws attention to themselves by causing harm to others
Mysophobia	a fear of dirt
Narcoleptic	drug used to treat psychoses, i.e. an antipsychotic
Neurosis	a form of mental illness of which the (neurotic) patient has insight (awareness that they are ill), anxiety and depression.
Nosophobia	a fear of disease
Nyctophobia	a fear of darkness
Obsession	recurrent, persistent and obtrusive ideas which is not removed by logic or reasoning
Panic attack	sudden periods of intense fear, discomfort etc. – chest pain breathlessness, dizzyness, sweating, nausea etc.
Panphobia	a fear of everything
Paranoia	condition characterised by onset of delusions often of persecution
Perception	the interpretation and response of the nervous system to sensory stimuli
Personality disorder	group of persisting maladaptive patterns of deviant and social behaviour, lifestyle, etc. – not caused by psychotic illness
Phobia	irrational fear
Phobophobia	a fear of phobias
Photophobia	a fear of (or intolerance to) light
Projection	putting our own faults or behaviour onto another person
Psychopath	a person having no social conscience
Psychosis	mental illness in which the patient has no insight

	(i.e. psychotic) – unaware that they are ill; affects the whole personality – is often characterised by delusions, hallucinations, etc.
Psychosomatic	bodily sensations produced from the mind
Rationalisation	giving a reasonable explanation for behaviour which is in fact caused by a problem which the person cannot accept
Schizoid	split personality – being more than one personality (*not* 'as in schizophrenia')
Schizophrenia	a psychosis of unknown cause in which the person suffers delusions and hallucinations – thought processes are disordered; chronic disorder which commonly arises in teens
Seasonal affective disorder syndrome (SADS)	winter mood disorder caused by lack of light
Tardive dyskinesia	side-effects of long term antipsychotic drugs; involuntary movements of face, etc.
Tic	involuntary, rapid, recurrent stereotyped movement or vocalisation
Tourette's syndrome	neurological syndrome characterised by a tic disorder with mutiple muscle or vocal tics occurring in bouts. Involuntary use of foul language
Transference	transferring strong emotions of love or hate onto another person, often the therapist or doctor
Trichophobia	a fear of hair
Xenophobia	a fear of foreigners

Procedures and equipment

Cerebral angiogram X-ray demonstration of the blood vessels of the brain using an opaque dye

Cisternal puncture same as lumbar puncture, but the needle is inserted into area at base of skull – used in investigation of cerebrospinal fluid (CSF) in children

Craniotomy cutting into the bony cranium of the skull; used to relieve pressure etc

Electro-encephalogram a tracing which records the electrical activity of the brain (used in diagnosis of epilepsy, tumours and other brain conditions)

Electromyogram a tracing which records the electrical activity of muscles to show if there is any abnormality in the pattern of activity, both at rest and on movement

Intrathecal injection directly into the meninges

Lumbar puncture insertion of a needle into the meninges of the spinal cord to withdraw CSF for investigation

Myelogram special X-ray using radio-opaque dye of the spinal cord

Transcutaneous nerve stimulation a method of relieving chronic pain by electrical stimulation of other nerve endings

Trephine instrument used for removing circular sections of tissue from skull area (trephining)

Ventriculogram X-ray demonstration of the ventricles of the brain. This procedure is being replaced by CT and MRI scans

Chapter | The sensory organs

Structure

The special senses of the body consist of sight, hearing, smell, taste, touch, temperature and pain. The receptors for these senses are found in the following sensory organs:

- **eye**   sight
- **ear**   hearing and balance
- **nose**   smell
- **tongue**   taste
- **skin**   touch, temperature and pain (dealt with in Chapter 10)

The eye

The eye is the sensory organ of sight and is situated in the bony **orbit** of the skull which protects it. It receives messages which are conveyed to the brain for interpretation.

It consists of the following structures:

- **eyeball**

appendages:

- **eyebrows**
- **eyelids**
- **lacrimal apparatus** (for producing tears)

Eyeball

The eyeball is almost spherical in shape and is embedded in fat. It is protected at the front by eyebrows, eyelids and lashes, and is composed of three layers:

- **sclera**
- **choroid**
- **retina**

It also contains the **lens** and fluids known as the **aqueous** and **vitreous humour** which **refract** (bend) the rays of light to focus upon the retinal layer and form an image very similar to that within a camera (*see Figure 63*).

Sclera

This is the tough outer fibrous coat which helps to maintain the shape of the eyeball. Muscles are attached to it and the orbit, keeping it in place and enabling movement of the eyeball. The front part is covered in **conjunctiva**, a membrane which also lines the eyelids. At the front lies the **cornea** with which it is continuous.

Choroid

This is the vascular layer attached to the sclera, forming the middle layer of the eyeball. At the front of the eyeball it is continuous with the **ciliary body**, a muscular organ from which the lens is suspended, and the **iris**.

The iris is a pigmented muscular body with a hole in its centre which forms the **pupil**, through which light rays enter to focus upon the **retina** (nervous layer).

It is capable of constricting and relaxing, so altering the size of the pupil which controls the amount of light entering the eye.

Retina

This forms the inner layer of the eyeball and is attached to the choroid. It contains nerve fibres which are the origins of the **optic nerve** and include specialised light-sensitive structures known as **rods** and **cones**, which receive light and colour information for interpretation by the brain.

Rods receive sensations of light and dark, and are more numerous towards the front of the eye. Cones are concerned with sensations of colour. They are more numerous towards the back of the eyeball; red, green and blue are the prime colours for interpretation. **Colour blindness** arises from a lack or abnormality of these receptor cells.

The optic nerve, sheathed at the back of each eye, conveys the sensations from the retina to the **occipital** area of the brain for interpretation into sight. The nerve from each eye joins at an area known as the **optic chiasma**.

The eyeball

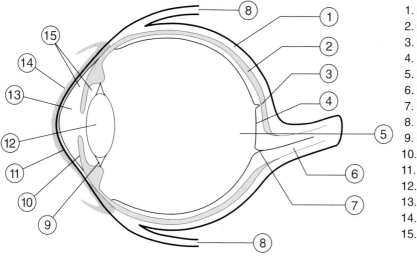

1. Sclera
2. Choroid
3. Macula (fovea)
4. Retina
5. Vitreous humour
6. Optic nerve
7. Optic disc (blind spot)
8. Rectus muscle
9. Suspensory ligaments
10. Iris
11. Cornea
12. Lens
13. Aqueous humour
14. Conjunctiva
15. Anterior/posterior chambers

Figure 63: The eyeball

Macula (fovea)

This is an area of the retina where cones are most numerous and central vision most acute. It is immediately opposite the cornea.

Optic disc

This is the area where there are no rods or cones present, and is at the back of the eye where the optic nerve leaves the eyeball. It gives rise to an area known as the 'blind spot', which is present in each field of vision. No sight is perceived from this area.

Optic fundus

This is an area including the **optic disc**, which can be examined by use of an **ophthalmoscope**. Changes to the retina and evidence of effects of high blood pressure or raised intra-cranial pressure, can be viewed in this way, enabling early diagnosis in some cases.

Muscles of the eyeball

There are three pairs attached to the sclera and the bony orbit, which enable movement of the eyeball. Normally the eyes move in unison which enables **binocular vision**. When the eyes move independently the condition produced is known as **strabismus** (squint). It is most important that any defect is diagnosed early in childhood as deficiency of sight can occur if treatment is delayed. Surgery and/or **orthoptic** exercises are used for correction.

Refraction

This is the term used for the bending of the light rays. It is necessary to ensure that images are focused upon the retina for clear vision. Images are perceived as inverted and are correctly interpreted by the brain. It is because of this that, in conditions of cerebral disturbance such as strokes and head injuries,

Visual paths

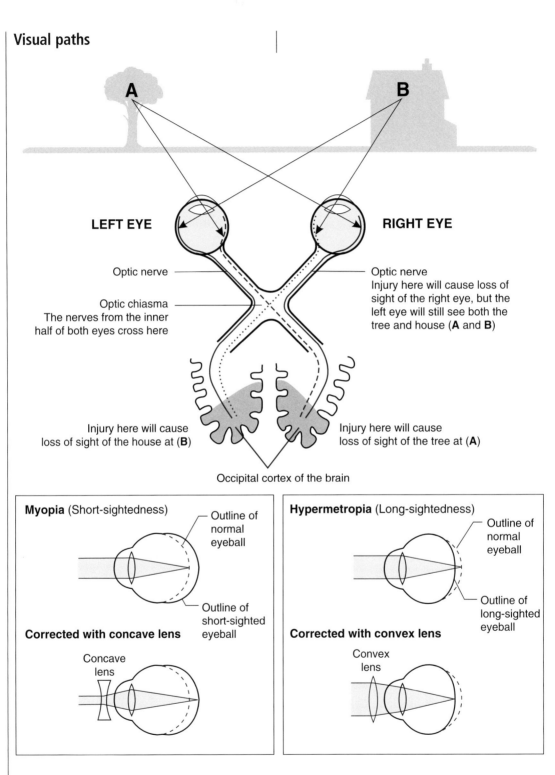

A

B

LEFT EYE

RIGHT EYE

Optic nerve

Optic nerve
Injury here will cause loss of
sight of the right eye, but the
left eye will still see both the
tree and house (**A** and **B**)

Optic chiasma
The nerves from the inner
half of both eyes cross here

Injury here will cause
loss of sight of the house at (**B**)

Injury here will cause
loss of sight of the tree at (**A**)

Occipital cortex of the brain

Myopia (Short-sightedness)

Outline of
normal
eyeball

Outline of
short-sighted
eyeball

Corrected with concave lens

Concave
lens

Hypermetropia (Long-sightedness)

Outline of
normal
eyeball

Outline of
long-sighted
eyeball

Corrected with convex lens

Convex
lens

Figure 64: Visual paths

vision is often disturbed. People who are **myopic** (short-sighted) tend to have a mis-shapen eyeball that is too long front to back, thus the images are in focus in front of the retina. The opposite of this is **hypermetropia** (long-sightedness) where a visual defect means the light rays come to focus behind the retina as a result of the eyeball being too long top to bottom (*see Figure 64*).

The structures involved in refraction are the:

- **Cornea**
- **Lens**
- **Aqueous humour**
- **Vitreous humour**

The cornea and lens, by their curvature, will bend light rays striking upon their surface.

Aqueous humour

This is a water-like fluid situated within the **anterior** and **posterior** chambers at the front of the eyeball.

Rays of light will also be bent while travelling through this substance.

Vitreous humour

This is a thick jelly-like substance which fills the posterior portion of the eyeball (situated behind the lens) ensuring it maintains its shape. Light travelling through this substance is further bent to achieve focusing of images.

Pressure in the eyeball

In conditions of **glaucoma** where the aqueous humour fails to drain effectively, **intraocular pressure** is raised and damage to the retina occurs. In acute cases, urgent treatment is required to reduce this pressure if blindness is to be prevented.

Accommodation

This is the ability of the eye to focus near objects upon the retina. This is achieved by the alteration in the shape of the lens and its

capsule by the constriction and relaxation of the **ciliary body** from which the lens is suspended. Ability to accommodate decreases with age as the elasticity of the lens and its capsule decreases.

Lacrimal apparatus

This consists of structures which produce tears:

- **Lacrimal gland**
- **Lacrimal ducts**
- **Lacrimal sac**
- **Nasolacrimal duct**

Tears consist of a slightly alkaline, salty fluid. These have a slightly antiseptic action and also keep the eyeball moist. They are involved in the expression of emotion.

The ear

This is the receptor organ of hearing and balance. Sound waves travel through the organ conveying messages to the brain for interpretation.

There are three main parts to the ear:

- **External ear**
- **Middle ear**
- **Inner ear**

External ear

This consists of the **auricle** or **pinna**, attached to the side of the head, and the **auditory canal**. The pinna acts like an ear trumpet to receive sound waves and is composed of skin and elastic cartilage.

The auditory canal within the skull carries sound waves from the pinna to the eardrum (**tympanic membrane**) which separates it from the middle ear. It is lined with skin containing hair and modified glands, which produce wax (**cerumen**) to protect the delicate membrane. If excessive wax is produced, deafness can occur because of the obstruction to the eardrum, preventing vibration. This wax may be removed by **syringing**.

The ear

1. Temporal bone
2. Ossicles of:
   Malleus
   Incus
   Stapes
3. Semi-circular canals
4. Fenestra ovalis (oval window)
5. Auditory nerve
6. Cochlea
   (concerned with hearing)
7. Fenestra rotunda (round window)
8. Naso-pharynx
9. Eustachian tube
10. Tympanic membrane (eardrum)
11. Ear lobe
12. Cerumen (wax) producing cells
13. Auditory canal
14. Pinna

External ear
(air-filled)

Middle ear
(air-filled)

Inner ear
(fluid-filled)
Endolymph and perilymph

Figure 65: The ear

Middle ear

This consists of a cavity within the temporal bone of the skull, filled with air and lined with mucous membrane. A canal known as the **eustachian tube** extends from the middle ear into the back of the nose (**naso-pharynx**) and it is through this, when swallowing occurs, that air is conducted, so ensuring an equal pressure between the external and middle ear.

Infection present in the nose or throat can easily spread to the middle ear, causing inflammation (**otitis media**), which in turn can cause **mastoiditis** (inflammation of the bone cells of the temporal bone of the skull). This can also lead to a brain abscess. It is for this reason that any infection must be treated as quickly as possible.

Ossicles

These are three tiny bony structures named from their shapes of **hammer** (**malleus**), **anvil** (**incus**) and **stirrup** (**stapes**). They are attached in a chain by ligaments, allowing them to vibrate causing the conduction of sound waves from the **tympanic membrane** into the inner ear.

The malleus is connected to the tympanic membrane and the stapes to the oval window (**fenestra ovalis**) of the inner ear. Each of these two ossicles is attached to the incus (*see Figure 65*).

Inner ear

This is situated within the bony labyrinth of the temporal bone. It consists of numerous bony canals and cavities. It is lined with a membrane known as the **membranous labyrinth** and is filled with fluid. It communicates with the middle ear with which it is continuous.

It is composed of the following parts:

- **Vestibule**
- **Semicircular canals**
- **Cochlea**

Vestibule

This forms the entrance to the inner ear and here the oval and round windows are situated, communicating with the middle ear.

Semi-circular canals

These contain specialised structures which, upon movement of the fluid within the membranes, stimulate nerve endings which convey information concerning position of the head and position in space to the brain.

Disease within these structures can cause giddiness (**vertigo**) and loss of balance.

Cochlea

This structure, within the membranous labyrinth, contains the **organ of Corti**, the true organ of hearing. It is coiled like a snail around a tiny bone.

Within it are numerous specialised nerve endings which convey the effect of sound waves received along the **auditory nerve** for interpretation by the **temporal lobe** of the brain (cerebrum).

Interpretation of sound

The round window bulges outwards as vibration is conducted through the oval window from the stapes, so maintaining the correct pressure of the fluid in the inner ear. In blast injuries these windows may perforate. Sensations of volume, pitch and harmony are perceived due to fluctuations in pressure.

The nose

The sense of smell is received by specialised nerve fibres in the mucous membrane of the nasal cavities and is conveyed to the brain via the **olfactory nerve** for interpretation *(see Figure 66)*.

The nose

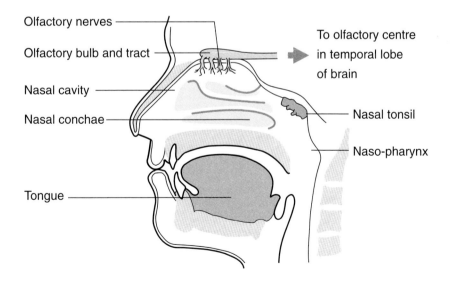

Olfactory nerves

Olfactory bulb and tract

Nasal cavity

Nasal conchae

Tongue

To olfactory centre in temporal lobe of brain

Nasal tonsil

Naso-pharynx

Figure 66: The nose

The tongue

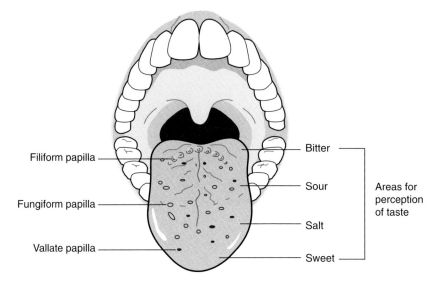

Figure 67: The tongue

The tongue

This muscular organ, attached to the **hyoid bone**, contains the **taste buds** and special **receptor cells** which convey the sense of taste (salt, bitter, sweet and sour) to the brain for interpretation. These are found within specialised structures known as **papillae** (*see Figure 67*).

Other flavours are appreciated in conjunction with the sense of smell. It is for this reason that the sense of taste is affected when the person is suffering from a cold. For the perception of these sensations, the membranes in which the special cells are situated, must be moist.

Taste buds are also present in the mucous membrane of the **palate** and **pharynx**.

Abbreviations

ABR	auditory brainstem response
Acc	accommodation
AD	right ear (auris dextra)
AMD	age-related macular degeneration
AS	left ear (auris sinister)
Ast	astigmatism
AU	both ears (aures unitas) or each ear
D	diopter (lens strength)
db	decibel (measurement of sound)
ENT	ear, nose and throat
EOM	extraocular movement
HM	hand movement
IOFB	intraocular foreign body
IOP	intraocular pressure
L&D	light and dark perceived
LASIK	laser *in situ* keratomileusia
LCS	left convergent squint (eye turns inwards)
LDS	left divergent squint (eye turns outwards)
OD	oculus dexter (right eye)
OS	oculus sinister (left eye)
OU	oculus uterque (each eye)
PERLA (PERRLA)	pupils equal (round), react to light and accommodation

PDT	photodynamic therapy
PND	post-nasal drip (catarrh dripping down the back of the throat from the nasal passages and sinuses)
PRK	photo-refractive keratotomy
RCS	right convergent squint (eye turns outwards)
RDS	right divergent squint (eye turns inwards)
REM	rapid eye movement
SC	without correction (spectacles)
Ts & As	tonsillectomy and adenoidectomy
T+	increased intraocular pressure
T−	decreased intraocular pressure
VA	visual acuity (clarity or accuracy of vision)
VF	visual field

Terminology

Blephar/o and **Tars/o**	stem for eyelid
Cor, core/o	stem for pupil
Irid/o	stem for iris (of eye)
Kerat/o	stem for cornea
Dacry/o **Lachrym/o** **Lacrim/o** **Lacrym/o**	stems for tear
Ocul/o and **Ophthalm/o**	stems for eye
Opt/o	stem for vision
Ot/o and **Aur/i**	stems for ear
Phak/o	stem for eye lens
Retin/o	stem for retina
Tars/o	stem for eyelid
Tympan/o and **Myring/o**	stems for ear drum
Uve/o	stem for uveal tract
Blind spot	area of no vision due to optic disc area where there are no sensory visual receptors
Fovea	see Macula
Fundus of eye	the whole of area at the back of the eye opposite the pupil
Macula (fovea)	area on the retina with the greatest number of receptors for sight (central vision)
Ophthalmic optician	person qualified to examine eyes, and prescribe and dispense spectacles
Ophthalmologist	specialist in the diseases of the eye
Ophthalmology	scientific study of the eye
Optician	person who makes and fits spectacles
Optometrist	person who measures/tests eyes and fits spectacles
Orthoptist	therapist who treats squints
Otologist	medical specialist in treating ear disease
Otology	study of ear disease
Otorhino-laryngologist	medical specialist in ear, nose and throat disease
Otorhino-laryngology	study of the ear, nose and throat
Refraction	bending of light rays to measure the focusing of the eye mechanisms

Diseases and disorders

6/6 vision	the normal ability to be able to read line six of the Snellen chart at six metres
Amblyopia	dimness of vision
Aphakia	condition where there is no lens present, e.g. after removal of cataract
Astigmatism	eye defect usually of shape of cornea which is irregular in curvature, causing blurring of vision
Aural polyp	pedunculated (stalk-like) tumour in the ear – not malignant

Blepharitis	inflammation of the eyelids
Cataract	an opacity of the lens or its capsule causing blurring of sight
Cauliflower ear	enlargement/deformity of the external ear due to haematoma formation after injury
Choroiditis	inflammation of the choroid layer of eyeball
Conduction deafness	loss of hearing due to the failure of the vibrations caused by sound waves to be conducted to specialised nerve cells of the inner ear
Conjunctivitis	inflammation of the conjunctiva membrane covering eyeball and lining eyelids
Corneal ulcer	open sore on cornea
Dacryo-cystectomy	surgical removal of a tear sac
Dacryocystitis	inflammation of the tear sacs
Dacryolith	stone in the tear duct
Dacryostenosis	narrowing of tear duct
Dendritic ulcer	corneal ulcer that has tree-like branches in shape (caused by the herpes simplex virus – cold sore)
Ectropion	eversion of eyelid (outward)
Entropion	inversion of the eyelid (inward)
Exophthalmos	abnormal protrusion of the eye
Glaucoma	a condition where intraocular pressure is raised, which in turn causes damage to the retina leading to blindness if not controlled
Glue ear/serous otitis media	presence of catarrh (fluid/pus) in middle ear
Hemianopia	partial blindness – ability to see only half the visual field

Hordeolum	'stye' – infection of the eyelash follicle
Hypermetropia	long-sightedness
Intraocular pressure	pressure within the eyeball
Iridocyclitis	inflammation of the iris and ciliary body (from where the lens is suspended)
Iritis	inflammation of the muscular iris of the eye
Keratitis	inflammation of the cornea
Labyrinthitis	inflammation of the inner ear
Macular degeneration	a degeneration of vision due to changes to the macular area of the eye (*see Figure 63*) which is responsible for maximum vision – at present there is little effective treatment
Mastoiditis	inflammation of the mastoid antrum (cavity containing porous sieve-like bone) of the temporal bone of the skull
Meibomian cyst	blockage of ducts of specialised sebaceous glands of the eyelid known as meibomian glands
Ménières disease	a syndrome causing vertigo (dizziness), tinnitus and deafness
Myopia	short-sightedness
Myringitis	inflammation of the eardrum
Nerve deafness	loss of hearing due to damage or disease of the nerve fibres
Optic disc	area at the back of the eyeball where there are no rods or cones, and where the optic nerve enters the eyeball – examined with an ophthalmoscope to detect swelling or abnormality to blood vessels or nervous system

Otalgia	earache
Otitis externa	inflammation of the external ear
Otitis media	inflammation of the middle ear
Otorrhoea	discharge from the ear
Otosclerosis	progressive hardening of the membranous bony labyrinth (lining of inner ear); hereditary in females – otoliths in middle ear also become fixed so cannot vibrate
Papilloedema	oedema (free fluid present) of the optic disc
Presbyopia	(old sight) long-sightedness due to failure of the lens capsule to accommodate, i.e. change shape of lens in order to focus close up objects – lens capsule becomes less elastic with the process of ageing
Proptosis	eyeballs protrude outwards/forwards
Ptosis	drooping of the eyelid
Retinal detachment	detachment of the retinal layer of eyeball from the choroid
Retinitis	inflammation of the retina (nerve layer of the eyeball)
Retinopathy	disease of the retina
Rodent ulcer	slow growing malignant tumour of the top layer of skin causing destruction of tissue
Scleritis	inflammation of the sclera (tough outer coat of eyeball)
Scotoma	normal and abnormal 'blind spots' in the visual fields
Strabismus	squint, i.e. failure of eyes to work evenly together
Uveitis	inflammation of the uveal tract (iris, choroid and ciliary body)

Procedures and equipment

Audiogram	the recorded measurement of hearing
Audiometer	instrument used to measure hearing
Audiometry	measurement of hearing
Auriscope (otoscope)	lighted instrument used to examine ear canal and eardrum
Corneal graft	grafting a donor cornea into place
Cryosurgery	cooling or freezing the area which is being operated upon
Decibels	a unit of hearing (measurement of sound)
Ear syringing	removal of excessive wax by syringing external auditory canal with warm water
Enucleation	removal of an organ from its place, e.g. eyeball from socket
Grommets	special valves fitted into eardrum to release pressure in middle ear and drain fluid
Iridectomy	surgical removal of portion of iris, forming an artificial 'hole'
Laser *in situ* keratomileusia (LASIK)	a procedure in which the cornea is moulded surgically to correct short sight
Laser surgery	surgery using a laser beam instead of scalpel or stitching
Miotics	drops which constrict the pupil of the eye
Mydriatics	drops used to dilate the pupil of the eye
Myringotomy	cutting into the eardrum
Ophthalmoscope	a lighted instrument used to examine the interior of the eyeball
Otoscope	instrument for examining the ear (see Auriscope)

Otoscopy — examination of the ear with a lighted instrument

Paracentesis tympani — drawing off of fluid within the middle ear

Perimetry — plotting of the visual fields

Photodynamic therapy (PDT) — used to treat macular degeneration. A light-sensitive substance is injected via the blood stream. It reaches the eye and a light is directed to the area, which activates the chemical causing it to stick to leaking blood vessels. This prevents formation of scar tissue on the retina

Photo-refractive keratotomy (PRK) — an older method of correcting short sight by surgery

Radical mastoidectomy — removal of large area of mastoid bone area to prevent further infection and drain area of pus (common before advent of antibiotics), a complication of otitis media

Removal of cataract — operation to remove the opaque lens

Rinne's Test — test for deafness using a tuning fork placed on the auditory opening of the ear. When the patient ceases to hear the ringing tone it is placed on the bony area below, known as the mastoid process. In normal hearing it will not be heard at this point, but in conditions of middle ear deafness a tone will still be heard by the patient

Slit lamp — special machine used to examine the eyes

Snellen chart — chart used to test visual acuity, i.e. sight

Stapedectomy — surgical removal of the stapes (stirrup bone) of the middle ear

Tarsoplasty — reshaping of the eyelid

Tonometer — an instrument used to measure intra-ocular pressure (within the eyeball)

Trephine — instrument used for cutting away a circle of tissue

Tympanoplasty — reshaping the eardrum

Visual acuity — the acuteness of sight

Visual fields — measurement or plotting of the area of vision (perimetry) to establish any damage (blind spot will be normal area)

Weber's test — test for comparison of the bone conduction of hearing in both ears. A tuning fork is struck and placed on the vertex of the skull. The patient indicates in which ear it is heard the loudest. In conditions of middle ear deafness it is louder in the affected ear.

Chapter

The endocrine system

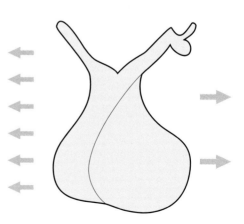

Function

This is the system concerned with the production of chemical messengers (**hormones**) which are secreted from a ductless gland (**endocrine gland**) directly into the blood stream to activate a target organ (*see Figure 68*).

Structure

The endocrine system consists of the following:

- **Pituitary gland**
- **Adrenal glands**
- **Thyroid gland**
- **Parathyroid glands**
- Pancreas
- Ovaries
- Testes
- Thymus
- Pineal body

Pituitary gland

This is situated at the base of the brain and is the size of a pea. It is known as the master gland or 'leader of the endocrine orchestra' because it controls many of the other endocrine glands. It has an **anterior** and **posterior** lobe which produce many hormones (*see Figure 69*). It is controlled by the **hypothalamus** of the brain, situated immediately above.

The endocrine system

1. Pineal gland
2. Parathyroid glands
3. Adrenal glands
   (Suprarenal)
4. Testes (male)
   Ovaries (female)
5. Pancreas
6. Thymus gland
7. Thyroid gland
8. Pituitary gland

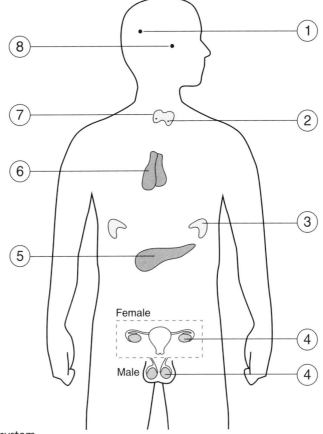

Figure 68: The endocrine system

Anterior lobe

This produces the following hormones:

Adrenocorticotrophic hormone (ACTH)
stimulates adrenal gland cortex to produce corticosteroids and sex hormones

Growth hormone (GH)
stimulates growth of bone especially long bones

Thyroid stimulating hormone (TSH)
stimulates thyroid gland to produce thyroxin

Melanin stimulating hormone (MSH)
produces pigmentation of skin but is normally inhibited by action of adrenal cortex hormones

Gonadotrophic hormones (FSH & LH)
follicle stimulating hormone (FSH) stimulates the follicles of ovaries causing egg (ovum) to ripen ready for release. In males it stimulates the testes

Prolactin or luteotrophic hormone (LTH)
stimulates production of milk

Growth hormone (GH) affects the growth of long bones. A deficiency will cause stunted growth or **dwarfism** in children. Excess will cause **gigantism**, while in adults, whose long bones can no longer grow, it will cause enlargement of flat bones of the face, hands and feet (**acromegaly**).

The other hormones mentioned act upon target organs, which are influenced in the production of their own hormones. These include the **ovaries, testes, thyroid** and **adrenal** function. The production of **milk** by the breast is stimulated by **prolactin**.

Posterior lobe

This produces:

- **Oxytocin**

- **Pitressin** or **vasopressin**

Oxytocin affects the contraction of the **smooth muscle** of the **uterus** in pregnancy and childbirth, and the ejection of milk from the breast in **suckling**.

Pitressin, also known as **antidiuretic hormone (ADH)**, stimulates the tubules of the kidney to reabsorb water and mineral salts, keeping the correct balance in the body. Absence of ADH produces a disease known as **diabetes insipidus**, where copious dilute urine is produced.

Pituitary gland

Figure 69: The pituitary gland

Adrenal glands

The adrenal glands (**suprarenal glands**), situated on the top of each **kidney**, are composed of two parts – an outside portion (**cortex**) and a middle (**medulla**) which produce different secretions and are stimulated by the pituitary gland.

Cortex

The cortex produces **steroids** which affect salt balance, protein and glucose metabolism, growth and muscle tone. Sex hormones are also produced.

In deficiency of these hormones, the patient suffers from **Addison's disease** and is administered **cortisone**. Excess produces **Cushing's syndrome**.

Medulla

The medulla produces **adrenaline**, the stress hormone concerned with preparation of the body for the **'fight or flight'** mechanism, whereby heart rate and respirations quicken, energy is released by the liver and muscles, and the body can respond to fear and excitement.

Thyroid gland

This gland is stimulated by the pituitary gland. It is situated in the neck, in front of the larynx and is concerned with the basic metabolism of the body. It produces a hormone called **thyroxine** which requires **iodine** in the diet for its production. Iodine is added to salt used for cooking purposes for this reason.

Excessive secretion causes **hyperthyroidism** or **thyrotoxicosis** with increased heart rate, excessive energy, nervousness, protruding eyeballs, etc. Treatment is usually surgical and a **partial thyroidectomy** is performed.

Under-secretion, or **hyposecretion**, causes a disease known as **myxoedema** where the patient is mentally and physically slow and all body functions are sluggish as metabolism is at a minimal rate. Treatment is with **thyroxine** and the effect can be miraculous as the patient returns to normal.

In childhood, deficiency produces **cretinism** and this is routinely tested (**screened**) for at birth.

Parathyroid glands

Deep within the thyroid gland lie the parathyroids. These produce **parathyroid hormone (PTH)**, which is involved in the control of **calcium metabolism** and the level of calcium in the bloodstream and in the bone.

Pancreas

The endocrine function of the pancreas, situated in the abdominal cavity close to the stomach, is the control of **carbohydrate** metabolism in the body.

Insulin is produced directly into the bloodstream from special cells known as the '**islets of Langerhans**'. These regulate the levels of **glucose** in the blood and allow conversion of sugars to glucose for storage in the liver and muscles, ready for release when required.

Deficiency of insulin causes a condition known as **diabetes mellitus**, which may be treated with insulin injections. Insulin cannot be taken by mouth as it is destroyed by the gastric secretions of the stomach.

Ovaries and testes

These are the **gonads** (and produce the sex cells). Their role in hormone secretion is to produce **oestrogens** and **progesterone** in the female and **androgens** in the male, the main one being **testosterone**. They are stimulated by the pituitary gland.

Thymus

This is situated in the chest (thoracic) cavity near the trachea upon the major blood vessels. It is important in childhood and puberty for growth and development. It is concerned with the production of **lymphoid tissue**, **lymphocytes** and **immunity**.

Pineal body

This is a structure within the **cerebrum** of the brain which was probably a vestigial third eye (remains from animal development). Its endocrine function is not clear, but it may have effects upon '**diurnal rhythm**' ('body clock') and production of sex hormones.

Abbreviations

ACTH	adrenocorticotrophic hormone
ADH	antidiuretic hormone (pitressin)
FBS	fasting blood sugar
FSH	follicle stimulating hormone
GH	growth hormone
IDDM	insulin-dependent diabetes mellitus
LH	luteinising hormone
LTH	luteotrophic hormone (prolactin)
MSH	melanin stimulating hormone
NIDDM	non-insulin-dependent diabetes mellitus
PBI	protein-bound iodine
PTH	parathyroid hormone
RAI	radioactive iodine
RAIU	radioactive iodine uptake
T3	triiodothyronine (thyroid hormone)
T4	thyroxine (thyroid hormone)
TSH	thyroid stimulating hormone

Terminology

Aden/o	stem for gland
Adren/o	stem for adrenal gland
Basal metabolic rate (BMR)	the rate at which the body cells work in using food substances and oxygen to create energy and waste products of carbon dioxide (CO_2) and water (H_2O) – measured at complete rest
Cortic/o	stem referring to the cortex (outer portion) of an organ
Endocrin/o	endocrine (concerning hormones)
Hypophys/o	pituitary gland
Medull/o	medulla (middle/ inside portion)
Parathyr/o	stem for parathyroid gland
Pitressin (vasopressin)	antidiuretic hormone (ADH) increases reabsorption by the kidney tubules to prevent dehydration (water loss by the body)
Thym/o	thymus gland
Thyr/o	stem for thyroid gland.

Diseases and disorders

Acromegaly	overgrowth of flat bones of face, hands and feet caused by excessive growth hormone in adults
Addison's disease	insufficient adrenal cortex hormones produced causing weakness, pigmentation of skin, wasting etc
Cretinism	under-secretion of thyroxine hormone in babies – present at birth (congenital) causing mental and physical retardation
Cushing's syndrome	excessive adrenal cortex hormones (steroids) causing abnormal distribution of hair, fat and shrinking (atrophy) of genitals
Diabetes insipidus	deficiency of pitressin hormone resulting in copious amounts of urine being produced
Diabetes mellitus	deficiency of pancreatic hormone, insulin – or development of insensitivity to insulin, leading to failure to metabolise carbohydrates
type 1 (IDDM)	early onset
type 2 (NIDDM)	late onset or very high levels of insulin leading to insensitivity to insulin
Dwarfism	insufficient growth hormone produced causing lack of growth of long bones in children

Exophthalmos abnormal protrusion of the eyeball

Gigantism excessive growth hormone in children, causes excessive growth of long bones

Goitre

Simple goitre enlargement of the thyroid gland in the neck – can cause pressure upon the trachea embarrassing breathing. Enlargement of the thyroid gland due to lack of iodine in the diet, also known as 'Derbyshire neck' as there is no iodine in Derbyshire water

Malignant goitre enlargement of thyroid gland due to hyperthyroidism causing severe toxic symptoms which are dangerous to health

Hyperpara-thyroidism excessive production of parathyroid hormone (PTH) from parathyroid glands – causes excessive calcium in the blood and can cause deposits of calcium salts (stones) in the kidneys

Hypersecretion oversecretion

Hypopara-thyroidism insufficient production of hormone PTH from parathyroid glands causing insufficient calcium in the blood

Hyposecretion undersecretion

Myxoedema undersecretion of thyroxine hormone in adults causing slowed metabolism, mental and physical dullness, loss of eyebrows and hair, oedema (free fluid) of the face, etc.

Osteitis fibrosis cystica formation of cysts in the bone due to excess parathyroid hormone production, calcium salts are removed from the bones into the blood

Tetany involuntary spasms of the muscles, particularly of the hands and feet, caused by low levels of calcium in the blood

Thyrotoxicosis hyperthyroidism – oversecretion of the hormone thyroxine, causing raised pulse, tremor, bulging eyes (exophthalmos), loss of weight, enlargement of thyroid gland etc

Procedures and equipment

Hypophysectomy surgical removal of the pituitary gland (or partial removal)

Thyroidectomy partial or complete surgical removal of the thyroid gland

Chapter **16**

Clinical imaging

The X-ray department and its services

This hospital department is primarily concerned with the diagnosis and investigation of disease using **X-rays (ionising rays)**. It is also involved with newer types of investigations such as **ultrasound**, and **magnetic resonance imaging (MRI)**.

In hospitals which do not have a separate **nuclear medicine department**, diagnostic techniques which use radioactive isotopes are performed in the X-ray department. Therapy involving the use of **radioactive isotopes**, and **radiotherapy** used in the treatment of cancer, may also form part of the work of this department.

The diagnostic **radiologist** is the medical doctor who specialises in this field, while diagnostic **radiographers** are the professional staff involved in the many procedures. Where such staff are involved in treatment of disease they are known as therapeutic radiologists and ragiographers.

X-rays

X-rays, also known as **Röentgen** rays, are short waves which are potentially very harmful, unless carefully controlled, and extreme precautions are enforced to ensure safety to both patients and staff. Scatter of the rays from the X-ray table will occur as the pictures are taken.

Careful technical design, regular testing of machines and stringent training of all staff are employed to this effect. Monitoring of **exposure to the radiation** by staff, is measured by a special type of counter (usually a **'film badge'**) attached to the person's clothing.

The wearing, by the radiographers and other personnel involved in procedures, of **lead aprons**, through which X-rays will not penetrate, is essential for their protection. Children and pregnant women are given a shield of lead material to prevent the ovaries or testes, containing immature ova and sperm, becoming affected by the radiation. X-rays of pregnant women are only performed when absolutely essential, to avoid potential damage to the fetus.

Genetic damage

While all cells are sensitive to radiation, dividing or immature cells are even more vulnerable and damage to the genetic material can occur.

Whenever possible, routine X-ray investigations are avoided during the latter part of the menstrual cycle, when a woman of childbearing age could have conceived. It is for this reason that a section for lmp (last menstrual period) is to be found on X-ray request forms.

Diagnostic radiology

This is the term used when X-rays are used for diagnosis. The term, diagnostic radiology, is also sometimes used to refer to other imaging processes which do not use X-rays but are carried out in the clinical imaging/X-ray department.

Medical imaging

X-rays are able to pass through skin and soft tissue. They can then act upon certain photographic chemicals to produce a permanent record known as a **radiograph**. They also have the property of being able to 'light up' a **fluorescent screen**, so producing a visible image of body organs on the screen, which can then be transferred to a TV monitor.

Preparation of the patient

Some X-ray investigations require special preparation of the patient by fasting, giving of laxatives or other special requirements.

Simple straight X-rays

X-rays will penetrate different types of tissue at different intensities, according to the thickness and density of the body structures through which they are passing. They are reflected by bone tissue containing calcium salts, i.e. the latter are **opaque** to X-rays. Soft tissues will appear more transparent than bone, which will appear as dense opaque structures; air present in the lungs and abdomen will give a completely transparent appearance on an X-ray film or **radiograph**. In simple straight X-rays, only a certain amount of information will be obtained from the varying degree of shadow produced. These pictures are taken on a special film and developed by the dark room technician for later reading and report by the radiologist.

Examples:
Investigations for:

- **fractured bones**

- **pneumonia**

- swallowed **foreign bodies** (e.g. safety pins).

Image enhancement

However, with the use of modern techniques, the scope of investigation of the body by X-ray has been transformed. The investigation of soft tissues requires lower radiation doses which will travel more slowly through the differing densities of tissues producing varying degrees of shadow. This differentiation of soft tissue to a higher resolution is also enhanced by implementation of techniques such as the application of the photographic process (**xeroradiography**), by use of specially sensitised film (as in the process of **mammography**) and computer-enhanced imaging techniques such as in **CAT (CT) scanning**, allowing the clear demonstration of **lesions** (abnormal changes). These techniques are now widely used in diagnostic procedures.

Fluoroscopy

This procedure is used for live visual examination of the patient by the radiologist; the image appears upon a fluorescent screen or monitor. This technique is particularly useful for examining movements such as **swallowing** and the propulsion of food along the alimentary canal by **peristalsis**. Pictures are also taken for later inspection by the radiologist. **Contrast medium** is usually used in these investigations, which include those of the urinary tract, gastrointestinal tract and blood vessels.

Contrast medium

The introduction of a **'contrast medium'** or **radio-opaque substance** (a substance which will absorbs X-rays) allows blood vessels and hollow organs to be clearly demonstrated. Substances, such as **barium sulphate** and radio-opaque **iodine dyes**, are used either by swallowing (ingestion) or via injection.

Examples:
- Investigation for gastric ulcer etc. by **barium meal, barium enema** for tumours of the bowel.

- **Intravenous pyelogram (IVP)** for introduction of radio-opaque iodine to show kidneys and bladder.

Air may also be used as a contrast medium when injected into a structure which normally absorbs X-rays. As the air will absorb considerably less X-radiation, it is said to be **radio-translucent** and will give a transparent effect on the screen or film.

Example:
- Introduction of air in a **ventriculogram** for investigation of the brain.

Examples of organ imaging

The following are examples of special procedures performed in organ imaging investigations:

Mammography

This special X-ray procedure involves the compression of the breast tissue between plastic plates which, together with low density X-rays, allows enhanced imaging of the soft tissues. Special film plate and processing are also used. It is now widely used in the detection of cancerous lesions before any clinical signs or symptoms are apparent (see Chapter 20).

Thermography

This is a method which records the emission of infrared radiation or heat rays from the body. Actively dividing cells produce more heat than other less active cells and show 'hot' spots in a picture. Inflammation of tissue will also have this effect.

Example:
- Investigation and monitoring of arthritis.

CAT or CT scan (computerised axial tomography or computerised tomography)

This is a method whereby the tissue density of any part of the head and trunk is examined by X-rays in minute layered sections (see Figure 70). The whole process is computerised to produce numerous pictures which are used to detect any abnormality. A **radio-opaque** substance may also be injected during the procedure to give further information to aid diagnosis.

Example:
- Investigation for tumours of the central nervous system etc.

MRI (magnetic resonance imaging)

This is a procedure which is mainly used to investigate the **central nervous system** (*see Figure 71*). Powerful **magnets** are used to activate the **hydrogen** component of body cells. Sensitive detectors reflect this activity, which is then translated into high resolution images by a computerised system.

As this procedure does not involve the use of X-rays, there is less risk to the patient than with CAT (CT) scanning. It will also detect smaller abnormalities. **Radioactive dye** is injected intravenously during the scanning process to give a better demonstration of any abnormality.

Example:
- Investigation of neurological conditions, e.g. multiple sclerosis.

Functional MRI scanning (FMRI)

This new type of MRI scanning, demonstrates the **functioning** of specific areas of the brain. Colourful pictures of the brain can be obtained performing complicated tasks, such as working out complicated mathematical problems. It has enabled scientists to understand differences in normal brain activity and that in those patients with certain disorders such as **schizophrenia** and **Alzheimer's disease**.

As it does not expose the patient to radioactivity, it can be used in **serial scans** which follow up

CAT scan

Figure 70: A CT scan showing an amoebic liver abscess
(Photograph courtesy of Lanarkshire Infectious Unit/Wellcome Photo Library)

the effects of treatment in psychiatric diseases and the use of newer drugs which actively change the way in which the brain works. Removal of much of the stigma of mental illness may hopefully follow, the demonstration that mental illness results from definable organic disease and not from the failure of personality.

PET – Positron emission tomography

This type of scan demonstrates the **functioning** of cells. With the use of an isotope it shows visually oxygen uptake, blood flow and glucose metabolism of specific areas of the body.

Nuclear medicine

This method of investigation uses **radio-isotopes**, i.e. unstable compounds which give off radiation. These substances are introduced into the body, usually orally or by injection.

Because different tissues absorb chemicals at different rates, specific organs can be investigated using this method. A special detector picks up

the radiation being given off from the area where it has been absorbed and converts it into a coloured picture.

Bone scan or scintigram

This is used to detect bone cancer at a very early stage; cancerous bone cells absorb more of the isotope than normal bone cells and so a brighter, or 'hotter', area is produced on the picture.

Ultrasonic scan

The ultrasound department is found within the X-ray department of many hospitals, although sometimes it is part of the obstetric department.

Ultrasound is a term used to describe high frequency vibration beyond the audible range, known as **ultrasonic waves**. 'Echoes' are reflected backwards when a beam of ultrasonic sounds is made to travel through the body tissues. Images are produced on a television-type screen which give information concerning

MRI scan

Figure 71: An MRI scan of the sagittal section of the brain
(Photograph courtesy of Wellcome Photo Library)

position, size and shape of the body structures. There are two types of scanning, type A and type B, each of which gives a different range of imaging. As ultrasound does not involve the use of X-rays, it is a safer procedure for the patient.

Examples:

- Investigation of fetal development
  (*see Figure 72*)

- Investigation of prostatic enlargement etc.

Doppler system

This is a type of ultrasonic scanning which produces audible signals and records movement within the body.

Examples:

- Investigation of blood flow in blood vessels, e.g. for diagnosis of **DVT (deep vein thrombosis)** or heart movements.

Electron beam tomography (EBT) scan

A new, non-invasive technique, which produces an improvement on conventional, CT scanning, is now available in the private sector. It produces a better quality picture with no discomfort to the patient. It is especially useful in determining those patients **at risk of developing heart disease**, who require invasive tests and possible treatments (*see Figure 73*).

The scanner works on the **gantry** principle, in that it slowly moves over the patient, who lies fully clothed on a couch. It is silent and does not require the patient to disappear into a cigar like tube, as in some scanning techniques, (a daunting and panic producing procedure for many!).

Radiation doses are at least 25% less than in CT and the speed and angle of the scanning produces clearer images. The procedure takes only 15 minutes in all. Both stills and video

Ultrasound scan

Figure 72: An ultrasound image of a normal 24 week fetus
(Photograph courtesy of Wellcome Photo Library)

recordings are made of the heart, main artery (aorta), lungs, ribs and spine.

Terahertz scanning

Research on a so far hidden spectrum of light known as 'terahertz', has been recently tested at Addenbrooke's Hospital, Cambridge and a trial on humans is commencing at St Thomas Hospital, London. Images of tumours are being produced using terahertz radiation. The light is absorbed differently by healthy and cancerous tissue. The difference is then measured, giving surgeons a clear picture of the tumour's location. This method would appear to enable cancers to be discovered earlier and with more precision than is achievable with MRI, ultrasound or X-Ray scans, which use different types of light and sound. 85% of all cancers are not visible with the conventional techniques. Terahertz scanning is said to be as big a break through as the discovery of X-Rays.

Use of X-rays as therapy

This is usually part of the department of nuclear medicine. The doctor in charge of this department is a **radiotherapist**.

Radio-isotopes, usually of **radium** or **cobalt**, are used to treat conditions such as cancerous tumours. Cancerous cells are, by their nature, immature, rapidly dividing cells and are more susceptible to exposure by radiation than normal cells. This is the principle of radiation treatment.

Normal dividing cells, such as blood cells, are also damaged by the treatment, which is why anaemia and lowered immunity can be side-effects of the treatment.

Carefully controlled dosages are given, measured for each individual patient. Great care must be taken of the skin surrounding the

EBT scan

Figure 73: An EBT scan showing calcium deposits in the coronary arteries – and indication of coronary heart disease
(Courtesy of Nathan D. Wong, PhD, Univ of California, Irvine, USA)

target area, which must be kept dry through-out and after treatment to avoid breakdown of the tissue.

X-ray requests

Special request forms for X-ray procedures are completed with the details of the patient and the type of X-ray required. *It is important that all details are correct, including the information concerning the LMP (last menstrual period).*

After the radiologist at the hospital has reported on the results of the investigation, copies are despatched to the doctor/GP who requested the procedure.

Costing for X-rays is divided into various categories, according to the complexity of the procedures.

Abbreviations

AP&L	anterior, posterior and lateral
DEXA	dual energy x-ray absorp-tometry (for osteoporosis)
EBT	electron beam tomography
ERCP	endoscopic retrograde cholangio-pancreatography
FMRI	functional magnetic reso-nance imaging
IVP	intravenous pyelogram
IVU	intravenous urogram
PET	positron emission tomography
RP	retrograde pyelogram

(See also abbreviations in other specialities)

Terminology

Angiogram (-ography)
X-ray investigation of blood vessels using an opaque medium

Aortogram (-ography)
1. recording of pulse in graph form

2. demonstration of aorta using opaque medium

Barium X-ray
X-ray using barium sulphate as contrast medium to demonstrate any abnormality in the digestive tract

Meal	the stomach and small intestine.
Swallow	the oesophagus
Enema	the large intestine
Follow through	the whole tract

Bronchogram (-ography)
X-ray examination of bronchi and bronchioles using an opaque medium

Cephalopelvimetry
measurement of fetal head in relation to maternal pelvis

Cholangiogram (-ography)
X-ray examination of the ducts of the gallbladder using an opaque medium

Cholecystogram (-ography)
X-ray examination of the gallbladder using an opaque medium given by mouth

Encephalogram (-ography)
X-ray of the brain by insertion of air

Endoscopic retrograde cholangio-pancreatography (ERCP)
special X-ray examination of the bile and pancreatic ducts by insertion of a radio-opaque dye via an endoscope

Hysterosalpingogram (-ography)
X-ray of uterus and fallopian tubes using an opaque medium to detect blockage or abnormality

Intravenous pyelogram (-ography)
X-ray of the kidney and its pelvis after injection of an opaque medium

Intravenous urogram (-ography)
X-ray of urinary tract highlighting bladder after injecting opaque medium

Mammogram (-ography)
special X-ray of the breast to detect early cancer

Micturating cystogram
X-ray of the bladder for investigation of stress incontinence etc.

Myelogram
X-ray of spinal cord using
a radio-opaque dye

Nuclear medicine
the use of radio-active isotopes in diagnosis
and treatment of disease

Radiculogram
X-ray of spinal cord using radio-opaque
dye which highlights the roots of the
lumbar-sacral spinal nerves

Radiographer
a professional person qualified in:

1. technical use of X-rays (diagnostic)

2. applying treatment with radiation
   (therapeutic)

Radiologist
medical specialist concerned with radiation
and X-rays

Radiology
scientific study of radiation and its effects

Radiotherapy
the use of radiation to treat disease

Retrograde pyelogram (-ography)
X-ray of ureters, bladder and pelvis of kidney
by insertion of an opaque dye via catheters in
the ureters from the urethra below

Sialogram (-ography)
X-ray of salivary glands using an
opaque medium

Splenangiogram
X-ray of spleen and vessels using an
opaque medium

Splenogram
X-ray of spleen using an opaque medium

Ventriculogram
X-ray of the ventricles of brain by insertion
of air

**N.B. for other types of investigations see
various specialities.**

Chapter **17** | The pathology department and its services

This hospital department is involved in special tests concerning various samples from the living body used to assist in the diagnosis and prognosis of disease. The **mortuary** is also part of the pathology department and **post-mortems** are performed by the **pathologist**, who is also the specialist doctor in charge of the whole department. Recently, private laboratories have been involved with providing services.

Organisation

As previously mentioned, apart from the chief pathologist, there will be the following personnel employed in the department:

- **Pathologists**
  (doctors) dependent on size of hospital
- **Scientific officers**
- **Trainees**
- **Laboratory assistants**
- **Phlebotomists**
  (staff who take blood from patients)
- **Administrative and clerical staff**
- **Morticians**
- **Porters**

Safety

Stringent health and safety precautions must be observed in this department as in any other hospital area. The risk is immense, as the specimens handled are hazardous due to their disease-producing potential.

Recent requirements for transport and packaging of diagnostic specimens

International agreements under the auspices of the **United Nations** have recently been introduced, in order to prevent cross-infection caused by the transporting of diagnostic specimens including those used in medicine. This involves numerous statutory regulations, which cover strict requirements for transport by road, rail, air and sea. In the UK, various legislation including the present **Carriage of**

Dangerous Goods by Road Regulations 1996 (amended 1999) is to be replaces in early **2004** with the **'ADR'** known as **'The European Agreement'**. There are also other regulations, covering transport by rail and air, in force.

All postal specimens must comply with road, rail and air regulations.

The following strict requirements for diagnostic specimens (complying with UN650) are all considered on the basis of the level of safety required:

- **Classification of risk**
- **Quality of packaging**
- **Marking of diagnostic specimens**
- **Mode of transport used**
- **Volume of specimen** (50ml maximum).

NB: there is a list of infectious substances forbidden as diagnostic specimens, as well as a stated emergency response procedure, to be followed in the event of spillage or exposure.

Sections

The following sections are part of the pathology laboratory:

- **Haematology** (including **serology**)
- **Biochemistry** or **clinical chemistry**
- **Cytology**
- **Histology** or **histopathology**
  (including oncology)
- **Microbiology**
- **Virology**
- **Epidemiology**

The Public Health Laboratory is also usually part of the pathology department, sharing facilities. This is involved in routine checking of food, milk and water samples, as well as being involved in the control of infectious diseases. Suspected carriers of infection are screened and samples from them are tested in this laboratory.

Haematology

This is one of the largest sections of the laboratory and is sometimes connected with the work of the **Regional Blood Transfusion Centre** where blood for donation is stored. Any blood ready for transfusion will be kept here in a special refrigerated unit. Dried **plasma** ready for use will also be available for emergencies.

The areas within the department will include those investigating blood cells, and the **serology section** involved with investigations on the **serum** of blood.

Tests

Various tests will be performed on cells and serum sent from the hospital and general practice in the various containers required, e.g. **haemoglobin estimation**. The department's phlebotomists also collect blood from patients attending for this purpose.

Biochemistry

This section is involved in investigation of the chemical content of the blood, urine or other body fluid.

Tests

As well as routine tests for **electrolytes**, **hormones** etc, samples from patients suffering from **drug overdose** are analysed here.

Tumour markers

The appearance or increase of certain substances in the blood, appear to indicate the likelihood of developing **cancers** and other processes occurring in the body. More is being understood about this in recent years. However, many can give **false positive results**, so care is needed in their interpretation. **Genetic markers** are also indicative of a person's tendency to develop certain diseases.

Tumour markers which indicate the likelihood of developing cancer include:

AFP (alpha-fetoprotein)	liver, ovary, testicle cancer
BRCA1 and **BRCA2**	genetic markers for breast cancer and ovarian cancer
CA 15-3	breast cancer
CA 19-9	colorectal cancer, stomach, bile duct

CA 72-4	stomach cancer
CA 125	ovarian cancer
CEA	colorectal, pancreas, lung, breast, stomach, thyroid, female genital cancers
BHCG	testicular, ovarian, liver, pancreas, stomach cancer
B2M	blood forming (haematopoietic system)
NSE	lung cancer
SCLC	pancreas, brain cancer
CYFRA 21-1	lung cancer
NSCLC	uterus, breast cancer
PSA	prostate cancer
HCG	human chorionic gonadotrophic hormone found in pregnancy but also a marker for testicular cancer

(*See Table 5 for further information*).

A number of tumour markers are already very commonly used by doctors and specialists everywhere. However the combination of improvements in biochemistry (and its 'tools' such as **computerized analysis equipment**) *and* available statistics of cases (showing which markers have actually shown up in which quantities and in what combination in actual cases), have increased the specificity and reliability of tumour marker screening dramatically.

Examples:

- **Prostate cancer:** the use of the FPSA/TPSA relationship improves our ability to distinguish between cancer and non-cancer, avoiding invasive examination procedures;

- **Lung cancer** (a very complex cancer): the use of the CYFRA 21-1/NSE associated with CEA and CA-125 allows:

  - the determination of the type of cancer we are dealing with;

  - the detection of the appearance, during the course of the treatment, of cell-clones different from the initial clone, which would bring about the immediate modification of the current treatment (having become ineffective).

Table 5: Known tumour markers – and their normal and abnormal values.

CEA

Levels	Normal: <5 ng/ml	Moderate: 5 – 10 ng/ml	High: 10 – 100,000 ng/ml

Cancers that may be indicated by high levels

Colon: colorectaladenocarcinoma
Pancreas: adenocarcinoma and endocrine
Lung: adenocarcinoma
Breast
Stomach: adenocarcinoma
Thyroid
Ovary: mucoid adenocarcinoma
Uterus: mucoid tumours
Liver: hepatocarcinoma
Oesophagus: adenocarcinoma
Thyroid: medullar

AFP

Levels	Normal: <15 ng/ml	Moderate: 15 – 200 ng/ml	High: 200 – 10,000 ng/ml

Cancers that may be indicated by high levels

Ovary: germinating
Testicle: germinating; non-seminomatous tumours
Liver: hepatocarcinoma

PSA and Free PSA (FPSA)

Levels	Normal: <4 ng/ml	Moderate: 4 – 10 ng/ml	High: 10 – 1,000 ng/ml

Cancers that may be indicated by high levels

Prostate: adenocarcinoma (The FPSA/PSA ratio improves the diagnostic differential between prostate cancer and benign prostate hypertrophy)

CA 15-3

Levels	Normal: <40 U/ml	Moderate: 40 – 60 U/ml	High: 60 – 30,000 U/ml

Cancers that may be indicated by high levels

Breast: epithelial tumours
NB: High rates of CA 15-3 *can* also apply to other cancers: colon, stomach, kidney, lung, ovary, uterus, pancreas, liver

CA 19-9

Levels	Normal: <35 U/ml	Moderate: 35 – 100 U/ml	High: 100 – 1 million U/ml

Cancers that may be indicated by high levels

Colon: colorectal adenocarcinoma
Pancreas: adenocarcinoma and endocrine
Stomach: adenocarcinoma
Bile duct
Ovary: mucoid adenocarcinoma
Uterus: mucoid tumour
Lung: adenocarcinoma

Table 5: Known tumour markers – and their normal and abnormal values (continued).

CA 125

| **Levels** | Normal: <35 U/ml | Moderate: 35 – 50 U/ml | High: 50 – 50,000 U/ml |

| Cancers that may be indicated by high levels | **Ovary:** adenocarcinoma
Uterus: adenocarcinoma (5%) and corpus adenocarcinoma (95%)
Fallopian tubes
Colon: Colorectal adenocarcinoma
Lung: adenocarcinoma and small cell carcinoma |

CA 72-4

| Levels | Normal: <5.2 U/ml | Moderate: 6 – 30 U/ml | High: 30 – 10,000 U/ml |

| Cancers that may be indicated by high levels | **Stomach:** adenocarcinoma
NB: Diagnosing gastric carcinoma is often complicated and can be extremely difficult due to presentation with vague, nonspecific symptoms which are sometimes associated with non-malignant disease. Although endoscopy, coupled with histological evaluation of biopsy specimens, is most often used to make definitive diagnosis, the search for additional non-invasive diagnostic procedures has continued: strong new clinical evidence has recently emphasized the clinical value of the CA 72-4 serum tumour marker assay in the diagnosis and monitoring of gastric cancer |

HCG and Beta HCG (BHCG)

| Levels | Normal: <5 mUl/ml | Moderate/High: 5 – 100,000 mUl/ml |

| Cancers that may be indicated by high levels | **Ovary**
Liver
Stomach
Pancreas
Lung
Testicle: seminoma and non-seminomatous tumours |

B2M

| Levels | Normal: <2 mg/l | Moderate/High: 2 – 10 mg/l |

| Cancers that may be indicated by high levels | **Haematopoietic system:**
NB: B2M, the beta2microglobulin, is used as a tumour-marker in various illnesses of the haematopoietic system, mainly where B lymphs cells are concerned |

Table 5: Known tumour markers – and their normal and abnormal values (continued).

NSE		
Levels Normal: <15 ng/ml	Moderate: 15 – 40 ng/ml	High: 40 – 4,000 ng/ml

Cancers that may be indicated by high levels	**Lung:** small cell lung carcinomas (SCLC) **Pancreas:** endocrine **Nervous system:** neuroblastomas **Thyroid:** medullar

CYFRA 21-1	
Levels Normal: <3.5 ng/ml	Moderate/High: 3.5 – 1,000 ng/ml

Cancers that may be indicated by high levels	**Lung:** non-small cell lung carcinomas (NSCLC) **Uterus** **Breast:** epithelial tumours **Oesophagus:** epidermoid

Cytology

This section of the pathology department examines cells to detect any abnormality.

Tests

These include cervical cells present in **cervical smears**, as well as cells from the respiratory tract and other areas under investigation. The aim, in many cases, is to detect early abnormalities (**precancerous conditions**) in order to prevent the development of a cancerous condition.

Histology or histopathology

This section is involved in preparing sections of tissue which have been removed from the living patient at a **biopsy**.

Tests

These tissue sections are then examined under the microscope to diagnose and classify any abnormality, such as cancer.

Oncology

This section, often part of the histology department, examines cells from tumours.

Tests

These involve microscopic examination of sections of suspected malignant tumours from any area of the body.

Microbiology

This section is involved in investigation of samples taken from wounds and other areas to detect microscopic organisms which are causing disease.

Classification of micro-organisms

The main ones are:

- **bacteria**   e.g. staphylococcus
- **viruses**   e.g. measles virus (Morbilli)
- **fungi**   e.g. thrush (Candida albicans)
- **protozoa**   e.g. amoeba

Although not a micro-organism **'Prions'**, rogue proteins, are capable of causing diseases such as **BSE (bovine spongiform encephalopathy)** and **CJD (Creudzfeldt Jacob Disease)**. The mechanism of their actions is not fully understood.

Tests

These include those on urine, sputum and blood samples etc, from which the organisms are **cultured**, i.e. put into or onto a **medium** which allows the organism to grow.

Culture

The **culture plate**, or other medium, impregnated with the specimen, is placed in an **incubator** at body temperature and left for any organisms present to multiply. The resulting culture is then removed and stained with special dye. This is taken up by the cells, which enables them to be viewed under the microscope. In this way the organism can be recognised and named.

Agar (from seaweed) is commonly used as culture medium and blood can be added as a nutrient. Not all micro-organisms will grow outside the body. Viruses require living tissue, such as blood or eggs, for culture.

Sensitivity

Bacteria respond to antibiotic treatment, but it is important that the most effective one is used to fight the infection in the patient. The culture plate used contains various areas of specific antibiotics to determine to which of them the organism is **sensitive**. The bacteria will grow around and over those antibiotics to which they have become **resistant**. A space will be left around those to which the organism is sensitive.

Virology

This section is concerned with the isolation and culture of viruses. As with all areas in the laboratory, stringent safety precautions must be taken, but here special **fume cupboards** are used to prevent the spread of any viruses present.

Tests

These are for the isolation and classification of any viruses in the specimens. Only viruses large enough to be filtered can be detected.

Epidemiology

This department, which is concerned with the study of the causes of disease (including social factors), may be attached to the pathology department or be a separate unit. Recently, some epidemiology departments have been involved in the monitoring of extra-contractual referrals of patients (patients referred to a hospital with which the health authority has no contract for services).

Collection of specimens

Types of specimen

The following are some of the common specimens sent for investigation:

Wound swabs	plain swabs usually placed in nutrient broth after collection
Nasal swabs	
Throat swabs	
Urine	
MSU	midstream specimen of urine usually for C&S (culture and sensitivity)
EMU	early morning urine usually for pregnancy test
CSU	catheter specimen of urine, if patient has an indwelling catheter; not usually a routine specimen
Blood	there are different containers for differing tests. Anti-clotting agents are included in some containers from laboratories. Tops and labels of bottles are colour-coded.
Cervical smears	on special named slides. Fixative must be added immediately after collection and allowed to dry, before placing in container (*see Figure 74*)
Faeces	for culture or content, e.g. fat, usually a series of three specimens
High vaginal swab (HVS)	charcoal swab often used for culture
Histology	tissue placed in pot with preservative (prevents drying out of cells)
Sputum	for culture or oncology, single or three specimens
Vomit	this may be sent in cases of overdose or poisoning, together with any urine passed.

In hospital, specimens of **pleural fluid**, **cerebrospinal fluid** etc. are also taken.

Cervical smear equipment

Fixative is applied immediately to prevent cells drying out

A. Ayres spatula (notched bifed end for women not having borne children)
B. Ayres spatula (broad end for women having borne children)
C. Aylesbury spatula (notched end)
D. Lerners spatula (hooked end)
E. Cytobrush
F. Cytobrush

Figure 74: Cervical smear equipment

Rules for collection and dispatch of specimens

It is most important that all rules are followed concerning pathology specimens. They are classed as a hazard within the **COSHH (Control of Substances Hazardous to Health) Regulations** in health and safety requirements. If five or more people are employed, general practices and hospitals should have written health and safety policies to protect the safety of their staff, and the handling of specimens should be included in those policies.

- Specimens must be clearly identifiable as to the patient and the source; laboratory personnel will not accept specimens which do not comply.
- Gloves should be worn when handling specimens – if a rigid container is kept in the reception area, patients can be requested to place their specimens in it themselves when bringing them to the surgery. In this way the box can be collected by the practice nurse and the receptionist does not normally need to handle the specimen.

- All forms and labels must be correctly completed and legible; clinical details **must** be included.
- All tops **must** be firmly fixed.
- Specimens (except smears) should remain upright.
- The request form must be placed in the plastic envelope provided and **must not** be in contact with the specimen itself.
- **High-risk specimens** must be labelled with the warning label as well as the form.

Royal Mail Safebox

Card to prevent accidental closure

Self seal bag

Absorbent material

Transparent inner chamber

Compartment for accompanying documents

Hard outer case

Figure 75: The Royal Mail Safebox for safe transportation or posting specimens
(Courtesy of The Royal Mail)

- Special care must be taken with common names, e.g. John Smith, and any middle names included.

- Posted specimens **must** comply with **United Nations requirements** (see above). The Royal Mail provides special specimen containers, known as **'Royal Mail Safebox'**, (*see Figure 75*) which comply with all transport requirements.

- These specimens should be sent by **first class post** (or similar such as 'Special Delivery' or 'Recorded Delivery'), in order to avoid delay which would increase the risk factor. If sent by 'Royal Mail Safebox' this may be simply placed in the post box in the usual way. ('Safeboxes' are prepaid at time of purchase).

- **High-risk specimens must not be posted**.

Patients should be given the following instructions:

- How to collect their own specimen (a leaflet is preferable);

- Where it must be taken and the opening times of the laboratory;

- How to obtain the results and that an appointment should be made accordingly.

- All specimens should be stored in a cool place and not left on window ledges in the sun or near radiators etc.

Delay

If there is any delay in the dispatch of specimens to the laboratory (apart from cervical smears and histology specimens) they should be placed in the ordinary part of the refrigerator. A separate refrigerator should be provided for this purpose and must not be the one used for food. **Never place specimens of blood etc. on a radiator**. Stale specimens can give false results.

Prevention of cross-infection

It is important that hands are washed after handling any specimen. Waterproof plasters should always be placed on any broken skin surfaces when working at the surgery.

Blood and body fluids may contain the viruses of **hepatitis B**, **HIV** or other **pathogens**. **Needles** and other **sharps**, such as scalpel blades, must be placed in the **sharp** boxes provided, together with used syringes. These are collected and effectively disposed of by incineration to prevent spread of disease. They should never be more than two-thirds full.

There have been incidents of **'needle-stick injuries'** occurring where needles have been placed in the ordinary waste bin and unsuspecting staff have been injured in this way when handling the bag involved. This can only occur with bad practice by other members of staff.

Needle-stick injuries

In the event of a 'needle-stick' injury, there are certain rules which must be followed. The wound should be immediately washed under cold water and encouraged to bleed as a first measure. These events must be **reported immediately** to the named person in the health and safety policy and to the doctor responsible. Details of the relevant patient whose used needle has caused the injury (if possible), should be traced together with their relevant history. Blood should be taken as a precaution from the person injured and kept as a control specimen.

Clinical waste

This is also a hazard and includes dressings and linen soiled with body fluid. Special colour-coded bags are used to prevent ordinary disposal or accidental mishandling.

Immunisation

It is recommended that those staff exposed to the risk of hepatitis B infection are offered protection with immunisation. This is given to practice nurses and personnel regularly coming into contact with blood and body fluids. Some GPs offer it to all surgery staff.

Reports

Results of tests will be returned to the doctor requesting the investigation. Urgent results may be sent by telephone from the laboratory, but would only usually be given to the doctor directly. The growing use of modems on computers will probably result in direct transmission of results, but the important requirement of **confidentiality** must be ensured. Similarly, this must be maintained in the use of fax machines, where mistakes can so easily be made.

Abbreviations

NB: Many of the terms relating to pathology have already been included in the terminology of the blood (Chapter 4), but a further explanation is included here for some of the common tests performed in the laboratory.

AHF	antihaemophilic factor VIII
APTT	activated partial thromboplastin time
AST*	aspartate transaminase (cardiac enzyme)
BUN	blood urea nitrogen
C&S	culture and sensitivity
CPK*	creatinine phosphokinase (cardiac enzyme)
CRP	C-reactive protein indicates the presence of inflammation within the body. It may be a truer indication of those at risk of an acute heart attack (coronary thrombosis, myocardial infarction) as inflammation of the fatty plaques in the lining of the

	arteries cause them to break away and block blood vessels
ESR	erythrocyte sedimentation rate (rate at which red cells drop to the bottom of the tube) – it is read after one hour, raised in cases of tuberculosis, rheumatic fever and other inflammatory diseases – shows the progress of a disease
FBC	full blood count – gives the total numbers of all the different blood cells for a comparison with the normal ranges. White cells increase in the presence of infection:
Erythrocytes	red cells
Leucocytes	white cells:
	polymorphonuclear leucocytes: neutrophils basophils eosinophils **non-granular leucocytes:** lymphocytes mononocytes
Platelets or thrombocytes	clotting cells
FBS	fasting blood sugar to determine diabetes mellitus or low blood sugars, performed in early morning before any intake of food
GOT*	glutamicoxalo-acetic transaminase (cardiac enzyme)
GTT	glucose tolerance test to diagnose diabetes mellitus
HAI	hospital acquired infection
Hb	haemoglobin is the iron compound carrying oxygen Normal levels are: **women -** 12.5 - 16.0 g/dl (grams per decilitre). **men -** 14.0 - 18.0 g/dl. *The variation in the female is caused by blood loss at menstruation.*

HbA1c	blood test for diabetes which shows the amount of glucose that has bound to the haemoglobin of the red cell
HDL	high-density lipoprotein
HUS	haemolytic uraemic syndrome
LBC	liquid based cytology
LD*	lactate dehydrogenase (cardiac enzyme)
LDL	low-density lipoprotein
LFT	liver function test, to diagnose liver disease
MC&S	microscopy culture and sensitivity
MCV	mean corpuscular volume (size of cell)
MRSA	multiple resistant staphylococcus aureus, a resistant strain of bacteria
RBC	red blood cells
T_4	serum thyroxine test for thyroid disease
TPHA	treponema pallidum haemagglutination assay (blood test for syphilis)
U&Es	urea and electrolytes; urea is the part of protein broken down by the liver for excretion by the kidneys – raised in kidney damage and dehydration; electrolytes in body fluid include sodium, potassium, calcium, magnesium, bicarbonates, chlorides and phosphates
VDRL	veneral disease research laboratory (for syphilis)
WBC	white blood count – this is raised in infection, inflammation and leukaemia, different types according to the type of cause

* These enzymes also show changes in metabolism of other tissues

Units used in biochemistry

IU or U	international unit
mmol	millimole
mmol/l	millimole per litre
nmol	nanomole
μmol	micromole

Common abbreviations used in laboratory results

d, deci	10^{-1} (divided by 10)
f, femto	10^{-15} (divided by 1 000 000 000 000 000)
g/dl	grams per decilitre
g/l	grams per litre
IU/l	international units per litre
m, milli	10^{-3} (divided by 1 000)
mg/ml	milligrams per millilitre
mm3	cubic millimetre
mU/l	milliunits per litre
ng/ml	nannograms per millilitre
n, nano	10^{-9} (divided by 1 000 000 000)
p, pico	10^{-12} (divided by 1 000 000 000 000)
μ, micro	10^{-6} (divided by 1 000 000)

Terminology

Abscess	collection of pus in a cavity
Acid-fast bacteria	takes up the acid stain
Adenovirus	virus which affects the glands, e.g. mumps
Aerobic bacteria	type of bacteria which requires O_2 to maintain its life
Airborne or droplet infection	transmission of infection via the air as tiny droplets
Anaerobic bacteria	type of bacteria that thrives in the absence of O_2
Anaplasia	abnormal cell formation (malignant)
Animal vectors	infection transmitted from animals, e.g. rabies from cats, foxes etc.

Arbovirus	virus that is transmitted from types of insect vectors such as mosquitos, e.g. Yellow fever/Colarado Fever
Bacillus	rod-shaped bacteria
Campylobacter	type of bacteria which causes food poisoning
Carbuncle	a boil discharging through many openings
Communicable	transmissible from one person to another by either direct or indirect contact
Contact	direct or indirect (see Contagious and Fomites)
Contagious	transmitted by direct contact with a person or fomites
Coombs' test	test for Rhesus incompatibility
Coronavirus	virus which appears to have a crown-like halo around it, e.g. SARS
Diplococcus	bacteria which are like berries and are found in pairs
Dysplasia	formation of abnormal cells
Endemic	a disease always present in an area
Enterovirus	virus which affects the gut (intestine), e.g. Norwalk virus, polio virus
Epidemic	a disease attacking a large number of people at one time in an area
Escherichia coli	type of bacillus bacteria responsible for some types of food poisoning, normally found in the bowel; can cause illness when present elsewhere in the body. Type E0157:H7 is responsible for virulent illness
Exudation	oozing of fluid into, and out of, capillaries
Fibrosis	excessive formation of fibrous tissue

Fomites	objects which are contaminated with organisms of disease, e.g. a toy from a child with chicken-pox
Fulminating	sudden onset of an infection which is rapid in its course
Gangrene	death of a piece of body tissue
Dry	tissue is dry and shrivelled/mummified
Wet	bacterial infection is present causing cellulitis of the affected area
Gram-negative bacteria	do not take up Gram stain
Gram-positive bacteria	take the Gram stain into their cell
Granulation	healing of a wound where capillaries and other tissues renew from the surface
Haemolytic streptococcus	type of bacteria which causes sore throats and wound infections
Healing by first intention	edges of clean wound heal together side by side - little scarring
by second intention	edges of a wound not held together; gap between forms granular tissue before upper skin can grow across the wound
Herpes zoster	shingles
Immunoglobulins	antibodies of various types, i.e. Igm, IgG, IgA, IgD and IgE
Infection	the successful invasion, establishment and growth of micro-organisms in the body
Infectious	disease transmissible from one host to another
Infectious parotitis	mumps
Infestation	the presence of animal parasites in, or on, a living body

Inflammation	reaction of living tissues to injury, infection or irritation (a body defence)
Insect vectors	transmission of infection via insects, e.g. flies, lice
Keloid scar	overgrowth of scar tissue forming an elevated ridge
Koplik's spots	small white spots found on the mucous membranes of the mouth – indicative of measles (morbilli)
Legionella	organism which causes legionnaire's disease
Liquid-based cytology (LBC)	a relatively new cervical cytology test now approved by NICE as routine testing
Lymphadenitis	inflamed lymph gland
Lymphangitis	inflammation of lymph vessel as infection spreads
Metaplasia	a type of cell that grows beyond where it is usually found
Morbilli	measles
Necrosis	death of tissue
Neurotropic virus	virus with an affinity for nerve tissue, e.g. rabies
Nosocomial	hospital acquired infection, e.g. MRSA
Oncovirus	virus which can cause cancer, e.g. herpes virus
Pandemic	as epidemic, but worldwide
Parotitis (infectious)	mumps
Paul-Bunnell test	serology test for glandular fever
Pertussis	whooping cough
Phagocytosis	the action of the white blood cells which engulf foreign particles of bacteria etc
Pus	yellowish liquid composed of bacteria and dead leucocytes – the result of infection.
Putrefaction	breaking down of tissue by bacteria accompanied

	by offensive odour, due to gases produced
Pyaemia	pus in the blood stream
Resolution	subsidence of an infection (recovery)
Rose-Waaler or **Waaler-Rose test**	blood test for rheumatoid arthritis
Retrovirus	virus which has the ability to alter genetic material; often slow-growing, e.g. leukaemia, HIV. (Retroviruses are also used in gene transfer therapy)
Rubella	German measles
Salmonella	type of bacillus bacteria which causes food poisoning, including typhoid fever
Septicaemia	bacteria multiply in the blood stream
Slough	dead tissue which separates from healthy tissue in a wound
Sporadic	disease occurring in isolated cases
Staphylococcus	bacteria which are shaped like berries and are found in clusters
Staphylococcus aureus	type of bacteria which causes food poisoning, skin and wound infections and sore throats
Streptococcus	bacteria which are shaped like berries and are found in chains
Suppuration	formation of pus
Toxaemia	generalised spread of toxins (poisons) in the body – products from

	bacteria or other invasive micro-organisms
Varicella	chicken-pox
Viraemia	viruses circulating and multiplying in the blood stream
Waterborne or **faecal infection**	transmission of infection via contaminated water usually taken in by eating or drinking
WR and **Kahn tests**	blood tests for syphilis

Classification of bacteria

-bacillus	bacteria which are rod-shaped
-coccus	types of bacteria which are round-shaped (like berries)
Spirochaete	shaped like a corkscrew
Vibrio	bacterium shaped like a comma

Bacteria are also classified by the stains which they absorb and which show under the microscope, e.g:

Acid fast bacillus	takes up the acid stain
Gram-negative (-ve) bacteria	does not take the gram stain
Gram-positive (+ve) bacteria	takes the gram stain

Some bacteria causing gastro-enteritis:

- *Campylobacter*
- *E. Coli* (and haemolytic uraemic syndrome)
- *Giardiasis*
- *Salmonella*
- *Shigella* (bacillary dysentery)

Chapter

Drugs and prescribing

A drug is any substance which, when taken into the body or onto its surface, alters the body's structure or function.

Drugs or medicines are powerful chemicals and the greatest care must be taken to avoid **abuse** or **misuse** of these substances. Dependency or addiction may be physical or psychological. Prevention of abuse is an important responsibility of the doctor and his/her staff.

Misuse or abuse of drugs within medicine refers to any drug that is used in any other way than that for which it is intended.

Legal responsibility

Drugs used in medicine are subject to legislation, introduced to prevent harmful or illegal use of these substances. Various regulations have been drawn up and **must** be followed. The doctor is legally responsible for that which he or she prescribes, and also for the storage and disposal of any drugs within his/her control. In the case of a hospital consultant advising a GP which drugs to prescribe for a patient, it is the doctor signing the prescription who is held responsible.

The main legislation involved is:

- The *Medicines Act* 1968
- The *Misuse of Drugs Act* 1971 and its subsequent MODA regulations.

The Medicines Act 1968

This includes **all** drugs used in medicine and is concerned with their manufacture, supply, use and storage. It divides medicines into three categories:

1. **General Sales List (GSL)** – those which can be sold over the counter at retail stores, no pharmacist needed. Small quantities only and must be in childproof containers (foil packs accepted), e.g. up to 16 aspirin or paracetamol. There is a list of drugs.

2. **Pharmacy Only Drugs (P)** – all other medicinal products which are not on the GSL and are marked with a P. Pharmacist must be present for sale (on premises). Includes small quantities (up to 32 tablets

of aspirin 300 mg and paracetamol), some antihistamines etc. **NB:** Tablets aspirin 75 mg are exempt from these quantity restrictions.

3. **Prescription Only Medicines (POM)** – lists products which may only be supplied with a prescription and are marked POM. Includes antidepressants, antibiotics, ampoules etc. Large quantities of paracetamol and aspirin are now included in this category. Controlled drugs are also included, but these have added requirements under MODA.

The Misuse of Drugs Act (MODA) 1971 (and subsequent regulations)

This Act controls the manufacture, supply, storage and prescribing of so-called controlled drugs, i.e. drugs of addiction. They are classified into various schedules according to their potential for addiction. There are five schedules, the most important in medicine being schedules two and three.

Schedule one (S1)	is concerned with drugs not used in medicine, e.g. LSD, marijuana etc. **It is an offence to possess them without a special licence from the Home Office**.
Schedule two (S2)	includes derivatives of opium, such as morphine and heroin (diamorphine), as well as cocaine and amphetamines.
Schedule three (S3)	includes most barbiturates, minor stimulants, and the tranquilliser Temazepam.

Drugs in schedules two and three are known as **controlled drugs**.

Stringent rules must be observed for these prescriptions and for **storage** of the drugs within Schedule two and for some in three. **No 'repeat' prescribing of these drugs is allowed**.

Schedule four (S4)	includes anabolic steroids and tranquillisers, e.g. diazepam. There are no special prescribing requirements at present for these drugs (other than POM requirements).

Schedule five (S5) contains drugs which have a very small amount of schedule two or three in their formula, e.g. codeine compound tablets. There are no special requirements at present for these drugs within these regulations, although a pharmacist must be present for their sale.

Controlled drugs

Controlled drugs are those referred to in schedules 2 and 3 of the *Misuse of Drugs Act (MODA), 1971* (see page 184).

The abbreviations **CD** or **cd** or the symbol CD refer to controlled drugs.

Controlled drugs also have very strict requirements concerning both supply and disposal. A special **register** is required for supply of schedule 2 drugs. Invoices for controlled drugs (S2 & S3) and S5 should be kept for 2 years. It is unwise for staff to accept any return of controlled drugs from a patient and they should be referred to the dispensing pharmacist or GP.

Prescriptions for controlled drugs

Controlled drugs for schedule 2 and schedule 3 (see The *Misuse of Drugs Act 1971*, Section 18) have very stringent requirements for prescriptions. These must be prepared by the doctor who is prescribing.

The following requirements are in addition to those for ordinary prescriptions (see later):

- It must be written throughout in the **doctor's own handwriting**.

- **Name and address** of patient.

- The **form and strength** of preparation.

- **Total quantity** of preparation or number of dose units in words and figures.

- The date on the script must be the **date that the prescription is signed**. A date stamp may be used but not a computer generated date.

The prescribing doctor must be known to the dispensing pharmacist so that his/her writing and signature are recognised. **It is an offence for a doctor to issue an incomplete prescription** for these drugs and the pharmacist must not dispense it. No repeats are allowed on the same prescription.

There are other rules concerning **instalments** of the drug being issued, and the issuing of quantities to travellers going abroad is limited to 14 days' supply.

A prescription for a controlled drug is valid for only 13 weeks, whereas an ordinary prescription is valid for six months.

> **Phenobarbitone**
>
> *Although barbiturates are controlled drugs, phenobarbitone is **exempt** from the strict rules of handwriting by the doctor. It can be placed on a computer and printed, **but** the date must be handwritten at the time of signing. This drug is extensively used to control epilepsy.*

N.B. Any prescription for a controlled drug should be placed in a sealed envelope and locked in a drawer or other safe place while awaiting collection.

> **Temazepam**
>
> ***Temazepam** is exempt from **all** special writing requirements for prescription **but** special storage requirements are applicable.*

Rules for prescriptions

The following details must be included on all prescription forms (FP10) which must be written in ink or be otherwise indelible:

- Full name and address of patient (to include surname, one forename and initials).

- **Age and date of birth** of the patient should preferably be stated. It is a **legal requirement**, in the case of prescription only medicines (POM), to **state the age for children under 12 years**. It is also recommended to print the age of adults over 60 years, and to incluse years and months for children under 5 years.

- **Name of drug**.

- **Form of drug**.

- **Strength of drug**.

- **Dosage of drug** with instructions to patient on administration.

- **Quantity of drug** to be dispensed or number of days' treatment in box provided.

- **Signature** in ink by the prescriber.

- **Date** of signing.

The directions to the patient **should never** say simply 'as directed' as this can lead to mistakes being made e.g. it is not acceptable to say 'one as directed'. Similarly prn should also state the time interval, e.g. 4 hourly prn.

The name, address and telephone number of the doctor prescribing, together with his PCT

number, will be printed or stamped on the prescriptions supplied by the PCT. **Private prescriptions**, often written on the doctor's headed notepaper, **must always** contain the doctor's name, qualifications, address and telephone number.

Supply of NHS prescription pads FP10

These are supplied to GPs directly by the Prescribing and Pricing Authority (PPA) paid for by PCTs. Each prescription (*see Figure 76*) is already printed with the name, address and

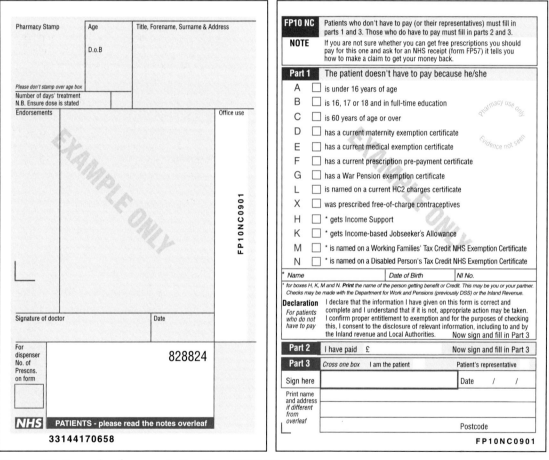

Figure 76: Example of a prescription Form FP10 NC

Form FP 57:   a receipt of prescription charge, issued to patient to claim a refund

Form FP 95:   Prepayment Certificate for patients requiring multiple items each month – available from GP practices, Post Offices and Benefit Agencies – completed form is sent to the PCT

Form HCII: explains eligibility for free prescriptions and information on prepayment certificates and refunds. This should be displayed prominently at the surgery.

telephone number of the doctor. Also included is the doctor's PCT number. All now carry a serial number and have a coloured background to deter photocopying. A message, which is visible under ultraviolet light, also aids in the detection of forged prescriptions by addicts.

Repeat prescriptions

Patients on long-term medication form a large part of the GP's prescribing requirement. It is essential that certain rules are followed to prevent dependency occurring and also to monitor compliance by the patient, i.e. taking the required amount of medication at the correct intervals.

Regular review of prescribing and examination of the patient by the doctor will also highlight any side-effects produced by the treatment being given. Requests to see the patient before the next prescription is supplied may be placed on the computerised slip accompanying the prescription.

Procedures for repeat prescriptions

In many general practices the receptionist will be involved in the process of the provision of 'repeat prescriptions'. Prescriptions must **never** be signed by the doctor before all details have been entered.

It is essential that a recognised procedure for repeat prescriptions is adopted by every GP and that the staff involved are aware of the part they must play in its implementation.

The procedures for repeat prescriptions may be divided into the following stages:

- **Requests**
- **Preparation**
- **Storage and collection.**

Requests for repeat prescriptions

Minimum period of notice

Most surgeries require a minimum period of notice for these prescriptions but it must always be flexible. There are always circumstances where it is imperative that a patient does not miss dosages of their prescribed drugs, e.g. conditions of epilepsy, asthma etc.

Methods of request

These may be by the provision of a computerised 'tear-off' sheet from the prescription or a special card provided to the patient by the doctor, listing all repeat medications to be provided. The patient may bring it in person or post it, stating which drugs are required. A stamped addressed envelope may also be provided for return of the new prescription.

Alternatively, patients may telephone a request. This should then be written in a special book or in the general message book according to the practice policy. Writing messages on scraps of paper should be avoided. If telephones are involved, a special number should be used especially for this purpose. This should never be listed in the telephone book, as addicts can easily use this method to try to obtain illegal supplies.

Telephone requests are prone to errors and for this reason many GPs do not encourage this method. Although nowadays most prescriptions are computer-generated, handwritten ones are required if the computer fails, or in emergencies.

Preparation of repeat prescriptions

Methods of preparing repeat prescriptions (manual) on FP10 NC green

The following procedures should be followed:

- Check the **notes are correct** for the patient requesting repeat prescription.

- Check that the drug requested **is to be repeated** by checking the patient's request card and notes for the 'rep' instruction.

- Check the **date of the last prescription** and the **amount of drug** given. **Any discrepancy must be reported to the doctor before any script is written**.

- Check if the **review date is due**. If so a note must be attached to the prescription requesting the patient to make an appointment to see the doctor **before** requesting the next prescription.

- Write the prescription following the entry on the **notes and request card** – ensure spelling of drug, dosages and total quantity are all correct; **nothing that the doctor has written on the card or notes should be altered in any way**.

- **Quantity** to be supplied may be stated indicating the number of days of treatment required in the box provided. In most cases the exact amount will be supplied. This does **not** apply to items directed to be used 'as required' – if the dose and frequency are **not** given, the quantity to be supplied needs to be stated.

- Ideally, instructions should not be abbreviated, but should be **written in full**, e.g. twice a day. Care should be taken with decimal points, e.g. '.5' should be written as '0.5' but only when the dosage cannot be expressed as milligrams or micrograms (e.g. '0.5 g' will become '500 mg').

- The use of a capital 'L' in mL is a printing convention throughout the BNF: both 'mL' and 'ml' are recognised standard abbreviations in medicine and pharmacy. The terms cc or cubic centimetre must not be used.

- Directions should preferably be **in English without abbreviation**; it is recognised that some Latin abbreviations are used (details are given in the British National Formulary. See also page 195 of this book.)

- The strengths microgram and nanogram, **should never be abbreviated** (death of patients has resulted with errors made because these have been mistaken for milligram). Similarly, the word 'units' must **not** be abbreviated.

- A maximum of **three items** is recommended to be placed on one prescription form. Any space underneath the written instructions should be cancelled with a **diagonal line or Z pattern** to fill the space. This prevents unauthorised addition at a later date

- The request card and the notes should all have entries made with the **date, drug** and **amount** as a record of prescribing

- A prescription for a preparation that has been withdrawn or needs to be specially imported for a named patient should be handwritten. The name of the preparation should be endorsed with the prescriber's signature and the letters **'WD'** (withdrawn or specially imported drug). There may be considerable delay in obtaining the drug.

- It is permissible to issue carbon copies of NHS prescriptions as long as they are individually signed in ink (**apart** from for controlled drugs).

- Computer-generated facsimile signatures **do not** meet the legal requirement.

If there are any queries or discrepancies, the doctor must be informed before any prescription is issued.

The prepared prescription should now be placed, together with the patient's notes, ready for signing by the appropriate doctor.

Preparing computerised repeat prescriptions (on FP10 C green)

The drugs required by individual patients will have already been entered into the particular system used by the practice, usually by the doctor. A procedure for these computerised prescriptions should have been agreed with the doctor, and it should ensure safety and prevention of drug abuse similar to the process for manual repeat prescriptions.

- **Care must be taken to ensure that it is the correct patient's computer file that is accessed.**

- It is also important that a routine check is made each time a prescription is processed to ensure that the drug is **authorised** and that it is **due** by date etc.

- The number of items on the script can be entered on the prescription at the bottom of the completed items section, or the space can be cancelled by other printed signs, so preventing **unauthorised additions**.

- The number of items per form need be limited only by the ability of the printer to produce **clear and well demarkated instructions** with sufficient space for each item. A space line **must** be placed before each fresh item.

- Entries should also be made in the **patient's notes** (or other permanent record) stating dates and quantities of the drug concerned for recording purposes.

- The accompanying sheet with the computerised prescription may be used for many purposes and can be given to the patient as a future request slip. However, no code must appear on this sheet although the name of the patient is allowed but the word 'CONFIDENTIAL' should be inserted before it.

- Alterations are best avoided and only made in exceptional circumstances. **It is preferable to print out a new prescription**. However, if any alterations are made, they should be clear and unambiguous; strike through incorrect items and **add prescriber's initials against altered items. Any alteration must be made in the doctor's own writing**.

- Names of medicines **must come from a dictionary held in the computer's memory**, to provide a check on spelling and to ensure that the name is written in full. Programming of the computer, to recognise the generic and proprietary names and to print out the preferred choice is recommended. It must **not print out BOTH names**.

- For **medicines NOT in the dictionary, separate checks are required** and the user should be warned that no dictionary check was possible.

- **Names of controlled drugs must not be printed from computers in any form (see exceptions for phenobarbitone and Temazepam on page 185)**.

The requirements for the doctor's own name, address etc. are the same as with ordinary prescriptions:

Reference books

The main reference books used in prescribing are the *British National Formulary*, the recognised authoritive publication on prescribing (now also available for use with computers) and *MIMS (Monthly Index of Medical Specialities)* a book of proprietary preparations published on behalf of drug companies.

The *BPC* or *British Pharmaceutical Codex* is the official publication on drugs. The *ABPI Compendium of Data Sheets and Summaries of Product Characteristics*, supplied by the pharmaceutical companies in the UK, contains information on storage, legal requirements, drug categories and overdose etc.

The Drug Tariff from the Prescription Pricing Authority for the Department of Health, contains information on the costing of drugs and appliances on the NHS and information on the 'blacklist', i.e. drugs not available on the NHS, 'endorsement' requirements, prescribable appliances and prescription charges, and is updated each month and supplied free to GPs.

Food substances – borderline substances

Prescriptions for these substances, which are foods and not drugs, e.g. soya milk, must have **'ACBS'** (Advisory Committee on Borderline Substances) marked on the prescription or they will not be dispensed.

Dressings and appliances

Prescriptions for these must be precise and include substances such as **oxygen cylinders, surgical hosiery** and **urine testing equipment**. They must always be written on a separate FP10 from drugs.

SLS prescribing for specific conditions

There is a list of specific conditions for which individual patients may receive NHS prescriptions (further information is found in the Drug Tariff list). These prescriptions must be endorsed with SLS (**i.e. selected list scheme**), e.g. "Viagra".

Generic names

This is the official name for the drug, e.g. salbutamol, and the one that doctors are requested to use in prescribing. Many manufacturers produce the substance and so costs are lower. However, the base of the preparation may not be the same as the proprietary brand and it may have different effects on some individuals.

Proprietary names

This is the individual brand or 'trade name' of the drug, e.g. Ventolin, and is usually more expensive than the generic name drugs. However, in a proprietary drug, a standard preparation will be produced to acceptable standards, with which the prescribing doctor will be familiar.

EU directives on information

Bubble packs in containers with written information and warnings have been introduced for all tablets and capsules. This will ensure compliance with the EU directive which requires information to be provided for the person being dispensed or purchasing medicines.

Pharmacists can provide the bubble pack quantity nearest to the amount stated on the prescription. In order to ensure accuracy, care will have to be taken to adjust the patient's repeat prescription records.

Oral syringes

When liquid medicines for the oral route, (i.e. by mouth) are prescribed in doses other than multiples of 5 ml, an oral syringe (marked in divisions of 0.5 ml from 1 to 5 ml) is provided. This helps to ensure that doses of less than 5 ml are accurately measured. It is provided with an adaptor and instruction leaflet. The 5 ml spoon is used for doses of 5 ml or multiples of 5 ml.

Limited list NHS

Since 1985, regulations have been introduced which name a list of preparations which are not allowed to be prescribed on the NHS as they were considered too expensive and many had cheaper generic equivalents. It is known as the limited list and also as the **blacklist**. This includes preparations such as proprietary pain-killers (analgesics), e.g. Disprin, as well as other types of drugs. Should these be accidentally prescribed, the doctor will be charged for the preparation him/herself.

PACT (prescribing analysis and cost) and PPA

Information is issued to each general practice at regular intervals from the Prescription Pricing Authority (PPA), comparing the prescribing habits of the doctor with the average for the area.

Practice formulary

Many practices will have a practice formulary. This is a standard list of drugs in different categories, produced by the practice. The list will be the first choice of drugs to be prescribed by the doctors for various conditions from which patients may be suffering. Partners will all have agreed to the choice of drugs within it. All practices will have a practice formulary as part of their budgeting process.

National Institute for Clinical Excellence (NICE)

This is an agency, which examines clinical treatments and drugs for their efficacy and cost benefit, advising which new drugs may be prescribed on the NHS

Storage and collection of repeat prescriptions

The following rules apply:

- The signed prescriptions should be placed in an appropriate box away from the reach of anyone coming to the reception desk. They must **never** be left for patients to help themselves.

- The identity of the person collecting the prescription must be **verified**, e.g. request for a date of birth or a middle name etc. of the patient for whom it is written.

- Ensure two pages are **not** stuck together.

- Take care that it is the **correct** prescription for the correct patient – verify address, spelling etc.

- Repeat prescriptions should **not** be handed to children unless the doctor or parent has made special provision.

- All uncollected prescriptions should be **locked away at night** and when the desk is unattended.

Prescriptions directed to outside pharmacies

Some general practices have arrangements with local pharmacists for prescriptions to be sent directly to the pharmacist ready for dispensing. If this procedure is in force it is essential that individual patients have signed that they consent to this arrangement.

Exemptions from prescription charges

Certain categories of patients are exempt from prescription charges, these include those aged under-16, students aged 17 and 18 years in full-time education, the over-60s, pregnant women and those patients suffering from some named chronic conditions:

- **Colostomy, tracheostomy** or **ileostomy** patients.

- **Epilepsy**, on continuous anticonvulsant treatment.

- **Diabetes mellitus**, unless the treatment is by diet alone.

- Patients requiring supplemental **thyroxine**.

- **Hypoparathyroidism**.

- **Diabetes insipidus** or **hypopituitarism**.

- **Hypoadrenalism** including **Addison's disease**.

- **Myasthenia gravis**.

The details of other exemptions are to be found on the back of an FP10 form. Many patients may require assistance from the receptionist with the completion of this form.

Measures taken to recognise drug addicts

The previous requirement for GPs to report the name of anyone whom they suspect of being a drug addict to the Home Office has been removed, except for in Northern Ireland.

There is a new special centre, **'The National Drugs Treatment Monitoring System'** whom GPs should notify when commencing treatment of a patient for drug addiction. This is an anonymised, database system. There are various regional offices in England, Scotland and Wales which may be contacted by telephone.

NB: Only doctors with a special licence issued by the Home Secretary, are allowed to treat drug addiction to diamorphine, dipipanone or cocaine; other practitioners must refer any addict requiring these drugs, to a special treatment centre.

Special FP10 (MDA) prescription forms are used by GPs for prescribing controlled drugs to addicts in installments. There are 10 light blue double-sided, numbered forms in each pad.

However, a GP or other doctor may prescribe these drugs in the usual way, for any patient requiring them for the relief of pain, due to organic disease or injury.

Letters are sent from each PCT, warning GPs of suspicious people in the area. This is in order that the doctor may be aware of a particular ruse used to obtain drugs by that person. If the receptionist has any suspicions about someone visiting the premises, s/he should immediately inform the practice manager or doctor.

The regular review of repeat prescribing for all patients plus the alertness of the receptionist involved in writing repeat prescriptions, helps in the prevention and awareness of any abuse of drugs.

Security of the premises

A good burglar alarm system is vital and the surgery window curtains are usually drawn back at night and lights left on so that policemen are able to inspect premises more easily.

Further requirements to prevent drug abuse

FP10 prescription pads are now designed to prevent unauthorised alteration and photocopying. Special print and coloured paper are used for various categories of prescription. Special inscriptions, visible only in UV light, also aid detection of forgeries. All prescriptions now include serial numbers.

Batches of prescription pads, delivered to the surgery from the PCT, should be checked to ensure that all are present. Any discrepancy must be reported to the PCT and the police. All unused prescription pads must be stored in a safe place and should be locked away at night and when the doctor's room is unattended. Should any prescriptions be stolen there is a procedure for writing all future prescriptions in red. This is for a stated period of time. It alerts the pharmacist to the possibility of an illegal script.

Drugs should not be stored in cupboards where patients have access, e.g. in the waiting room. Clear directions must be given to patients concerning the dosage and mode of administration. Drug storage cupboards should be locked and should not be marked. The controlled drugs (CD) cupboard keys should be kept on the person of a suitable member of staff, usually the doctor and the practice nurse.

If the doctor's bag contains drugs (as is usual) it must be kept locked and in a safe place. If controlled drugs are contained in the bag, a locked car is not recognised as being a sufficiently secure place. **It must be locked in the case in the locked boot of the car**. Prescription pads should **never** be left in a car where the public may see them.

Any drugs left in the doctor's room, e.g. by drug firm representatives, should be collected and locked away in the appropriate place (usually by the practice nurse).

Disposal of drugs

Drugs are sometimes returned to the surgery by patients. These should be returned to the pharmacist or placed in the special collection service provided by some PCTs. This complies with the requirements of the *Environmental Protection Act*. Controlled drugs have stringent requirements and should only be handled by appropriate designated staff. Returned drugs must never be reused. **Expired drugs should be disposed of in the same way. Expired drugs must never be mixed with other batches of drugs already in the surgery, for re-use**.

Supply and disposal of controlled drugs in general practice

There are stringent requirements under The *Misuse of Drugs Act*, covering Schedules 2 and 3 (drugs of addiction used in medicine).

The requirements cover:
- Supply
- Prescription writing (see previous section)
- Safe custody
- **The Controlled Drugs Register**
- Destruction/disposal.

The Controlled Drugs Register

Supply of and dispensing of Schedule 2 controlled drugs is required to be recorded and signed for in the Controlled Drugs Register.

Entries must include:
- **Drugs received**
- **Date received**
- **Name and address of GP authorised to hold and supply the drugs or the supplying person/firm**
- **Amount received**
- **Form in which supplied**, e.g. ampoule/tablet.

The Register itself must:
- Be **bound** with ruled and headed columns
- Entries written in **ink** or indelible form
- Have separate sections for **each class** and **form** of drug
- Have transactions entered **on the day of occurrence** or, at latest, the following day
- Have **no cancellations or alterations** (any corrections **must** be made in the margin provided **or** as a footnote and must be signed and dated)
- Be **kept on the premises** to which the register relates
- Be **kept for two years** from the date of the last entry
- Be **available for inspection** at any time (by

medical officer or a Home Office drugs inspector).

The following are also recommended:

- A separate column to record **the balance of stock** remaining (this allows the actual stock to be checked easily, enabling any stock discrepancies to be immediately reported and investigated)

- A separate Controlled Drug Register for *each* **GP's bag**.

Disposal/destruction of controlled drugs

Normally, controlled drugs in Schedule 2, must be destroyed, only, in the presence of **an authorised person**, such as a police officer or Home Office drugs inspector. The name of the drug, the amount and date of destruction is entered in the Controlled Drugs Register and signed by the person in whose presence the drugs were destroyed.

There is an **audit trail** (from importation) at every stage, ending at the supply to the patient. However, there is no requirement within The *Misuse of Drugs Act*, of any recording to be made of any drugs returned to the GP by the patient or patient's relatives, or of their destruction.

Following the terrible revelations of the **Shipman murders**, interim proposals by Professor Richard Baker are being considered for implementation.

Professor Richard Baker's report

The main proposals of Professor Richard Baker's report are:

- Systems for **monitoring GPs** should be reviewed and include routine monitoring of **death rates** and improved methods for overseeing the prescribing of controlled drugs and quality of medical records.

- A system for collecting information about the number of deaths of GPs' patients, and **death certificates** issued by them, should be investigated and a practical system introduced as soon as possible.

- Information about the circumstances of death and the patient's clinical history should be recorded both in the case of **cremations** and **burials**.

- The procedure for **revalidating GPs** should include an assessment of appropriate samples of a GP's records.

- The policy of offering to return **records** to GPs after the expiry of the period of storage by PCTs should be reviewed. If GPs are allowed to retain records, arrangements for their **secure storage** should be established.

- An effective system for the **inspection of GPs' Controlled Drugs Registers** should be introduced.

- GPs should record **batch numbers** in clinical records when they personally administer controlled drugs, and batch numbers should be included in the Controlled Drugs Registers of GPs and pharmacists.

The need to ensure that there are more effective controls on controlled drugs is abundantly clear. The loop-hole of returned Schedule 2 drugs, such as heroin, (diamorphine), and morphine, to doctors from the relatives of deceased patients, who have received palliative (terminal care), has illustrated enormous potential for their misuse. The lack of any requirement for GPs to record possession or destruction of these controlled drugs, enabled the means for Dr Shipman to enact his evil crimes with relative ease.

PCT controls

Primary Care Trusts are trying to ensure that steps are being taken to ensure that all controlled drugs are witnessed as they are being destroyed. The list of persons to be present as witnesses, has been extended to include :

- Primary Care Trust Chief Pharmacists

- Registered medical practitioner appointed with responsibility for Clinical Governance or Risk Management

- Medical Director of a Primary Care Trust.

Further information

CSM reporting of adverse reactions

Reporting on the 'yellow card' to the CSM (Committee on the Safety of Medicines) via the

Medicines and Health Care Products Regulatory Agency (MHRA) is an important part of research in general practice and can help to avoid another thalidomide disaster, i.e. the deformities produced in children born to mothers who had been prescribed this drug during pregnancy in the late 1950s and early 60s. reporting may also be made at the website: www.medicines.mhra.gov.uk

New drugs are always monitored in this way and are marked with a *black triangle* **for at least the first** *two years* **following the release to the public on prescription, in order to alert the doctor to the necessity of reporting any untoward side-effects.**

Prescription event monitoring

In addition to the CSM's Yellow Card scheme, an independent scheme monitors the safety of new medicines using a different approach. The **Drug Safety Unit** identifies patients who have been prescribed selected new medicines and collects data on clinical events in these patients. This is a voluntary scheme and the data is submitted by general practitioners using green forms.

Adverse Reactions to Medical Devices

Suspected adverse reactions to medical devices, including dental or surgical materials, intra-uterine devices and contact lens fluid, should also be reported to the MHRA.

Nurse practitioners and community nurses

Some of these personnel have been given the legal right to prescribe certain drugs directly to patients. The nurse's NMC (Nurses and Midwives' Council) PIN number must be included on the prescription as well as the practice identification number and address.

Practice nurses qualified as District Nurses or Health Visitors who have attended an approved nurse prescribers' course may prescribe from a limited list of drugs (see BNF, NPF [Nurses' Prescribing Formulary] or Drug Tariff). The FP10 PN used is coloured lilac. Community Nurses and Health Visitors who have also attended the required course may prescribe from the same list on FP10 CN which is coloured grey.

There is also an extended list for those first level nurses and registered midwives nurses who have completed the, 'Extended Formulary Nurse Prescriber' Course, which allows approximately 140 prescription only medicines, (POMs), to be prescribed for therapeutic areas of:

- **Minor illness**
- **Minor injury**
- **Health promotion**
- **Palliative care**

Private prescriptions

These may be required when substances are not available on the NHS. All requirements for prescriptions are as for the Medicines Act. Private headed notepaper is normally used and the name and qualifications are required, as well as all other details as already stated for other medicines. Charges are suggested in the BMA list.

Complimentary medicine

It is important to remember that a number of herbal medicine have been found to interfere with conventional therapy, e.g. St John's Wort. Information on this subject can be found at www.mhra.gov.uk

Abbreviations

BNF	British National Formulary
CD or **cd** or CD	controlled drug (schedule 2 or 3 of MODA, 1971)
HRT	hormone replacement therapy
NHS	not available on the NHS
NIDDM	non-insulin dependent diabetes mellitus
IDDM	insulin dependent diabetes mellitus
NSAID	nonsteroidal anti-inflammatory drug
OP	original pack (manufacturer's own pack)

P or [P] pharmacy only drugs

PGD patient group direction/directive – a written direction on the supply and/or administration of medicines by a healthcare professional (not a doctor) for a stated type of patient, e.g. "morning after pill"

POM or [POM] prescription only medicine

PPI proton pump inhibitor (reduces amount of acid stomach produces)

SLS selected list scheme

SSRI selective serotonin reuptake inhibitor (antidepressant)

TTA to take away

▲ special reporting requirements

Prescriptions

Abbreviation	Meaning [Latin]
a.a.	of each – equal amount [ana]
a.c.	before food [ante cibum]
alt die	alternate days [alt die]
alt noct.	alternate nights [alt nocte]
b.d.	twice daily [bis die]
c.	with [cum]
ex. aq.	water [ex aquain]
h.n.	tonight [hac nocte]
mane	in the morning [mane]
nocte	at night [nocte]
NP	proper name [nomen proprium]

o.m.	every morning [omni mane]
o.n.	every night [omni nocte]
p.a.	to the affected part [parti affectae]
p.c.	after food [post cibum]
p.r.n.	whenever necessary [pro re nata]
q.d.s.	four times daily [quater die sumendum]
q.i.d.	four times daily [quater in die]
q.q.h.	every four hours [quarta quaque hora]
R	take [recipe]
rep.	let it be repeated [repetitur]
s.o.s.	if necessary (one dose only) [si opus sit]
stat.	at once [statim]
t.d.s.	three times daily [ter die sumendum]
t.i.d.	three times daily [ter in die]

BNF approved abbreviations for directions

The following are **approved** for use by the BNF:

a.c.	before food
b.d.	twice daily
o.m.	every morning
o.n.	every night
p.c.	after food
p.r.n.	whenever necessary
q.d.s.	four times daily
q.q.h.	every four hours
stat.	at once
t.d.s.	three times daily

Preparations

Abbreviation	Meaning [Latin]
caps.	capsules
neb.	nebulizer
occ. or oc.	for the eyes [occulentae]
p.o.c.	for the eyes
p.r.	via the rectum [per rectum]
p.v.	via the vagina [per vaginam]
pessary	for the vagina
suppos.	suppository
tabs.	tablets

Abbreviation	Meaning [Latin]
tinct.	tincture [tincture]
troch.	lozenge [trochisci]
ung.	ointment [unguentum]
vap.	vapour [vapore]

Measurements

g	gram
mcg	microgram
mg	milligram
ml	millilitre
ng*	nanogram
S.I.	International System
µg*	microgram

must not be used on prescriptions according to British National Formulary recommendations

Terminology

Classification of drugs etc.

Continuous subcutaneous infusion	drugs given into the layer under the dermis via a syringe driver or 'pump'
Intradermal (ID)	into the skin
Intramuscular (IM)	into the muscle
Intravenous (IV)	via the vein
Materia medica	drugs used in medicine
Oral	by mouth
Parenteral	drugs administered, other than by the oral route
Pharmacologist	specialist in drugs
Pharmacology	study of drugs
Systemic	by injection – affects whole body.

Types of preparation

Elixir	a sweetened aromatic substance containing alcohol
Enema	a liquid substance inserted into the rectum
Lavage	a washout – fluid inserted through a tube usually into the stomach to remove contents
Linctus	sweet syrupy liquid for coughs
Pessary	solid form of drug inserted in the vagina (pv)
Suppository	solid form of drug inserted in the rectum (pr)
Tincture	solution of a drug in alcohol

Drug types (classification)

ACE inhibitor — (ACE: angiotensin-converting enzyme) drug which is used for treatment of hypertension or heart failure

Anaesthetic — drug for removal of feeling

General — to the whole body – produces unconsciousness.

Local — to a part – produces numbness

Angiotensin-II receptor antagonists — drug used to treat hypertension

Analgesic — drug for relief of pain

Antacid — a substance which neutralises stomach acid

Anti-arrhythmic — drug which controls abnormal rhythm of the heart

Antibiotic — drug which kills bacteria

Anticoagulant — drug which reduces clotting

Antidepressant — drug which lifts the patient's mood

Anti-emetic — drug which reduces nausea

Antifungal — drug which kills fungi

Antihistamine — drug which reduces production of histamine – for allergies

Antihypertensive — drug which reduces blood pressure

Anti-inflammatory — drug which reduces inflammation

Anti-obesity — drug which helps reduce weight

Antipyretic — drug which reduces fever

Antipsychotic — also known as 'neuroleptics', drug which quietens disturbed patients suffering from mania, hallucinations etc. used as a short term measure

Antispasmodic — drug which reduces spasms of muscle, e.g. colic

Antitussic — drug which reduces coughing

Anxiolytic — drug which reduces anxiety

Beta-blocker — drug which lowers blood pressure etc. – by affecting specific beta-nerve receptors

Bronchodilator — drug which dilates the bronchial tubes as in treatment for asthma

Calcium channel blockers — drugs which depress cardiac function

Carminative — drug which reduces flatulence (wind)

Chemotherapy — toxic drugs which are given to kill malignant cells

Contraceptive — drug which prevents conception

Cox 2 inhibitor — drug to reduce inflammation in arthritis better tolerated by the gastro-intestinal system than NSAIDs

Cytotoxic — drugs which kill cells – used to treat malignant disease by killing cancerous cells

Decongestant — drug which relieves congestion of mucous membranes

Depressant — a drug which depresses function of the central nervous system

Diuretic — drug which increases the production of urine

Expectorant — liquid form of drug which encourages coughing up of secretions from the respiratory tract

Hypnotic — drug which induces sleep

Miotic — for the eyes – to constrict the pupil

Mydriatic	for the eyes – to dilate the pupil
Narcotic	drug derived from opium which will induce deep sleep
Prophylactic	a substance used to prevent disease
Proton pump inhibitor	drugs which inhibit the production of hydrochloric acid in the stomach
Sedative	a drug which lowers function
Statins	drug which lowers cholesterol blood levels
Steroids	drugs containing hormones – usually of the adrenal cortex
Corticosteroids	drugs from the cortex of the adrenal glands or synthetic preparations, which reduce inflammation etc., e.g. prednisolone
Stimulant	a drug which increases function of the central nervous system
Tranquilliser	a drug which reduces anxiety
Vaccine	a substance prepared specially to stimulate the body to produce its own antibodies or antitoxins

Chapter 19

Preventive medicine

Health

The World Health Organisation's definition of health states:

"Health is a state of complete physical, mental and social well-being and not merely the absence of disease or infirmity . . . Good Health is held to be fundamental to all peace and security."

This is the ideal state and is very difficult to achieve.

Each one of the three factors (**physical, mental,** or **social**) will affect the other two, e.g. problems with physical health will cause mental and social problems for the patient; similarly, problems with social factors will affect mental and physical well-being.

Preventive medicine is concerned with the prevention of disease in all forms. It is aimed at all people worldwide of all age ranges, *not just* the developing countries. Based on the concept 'prevention is better than cure', it is intended to provide a better span and quality of life for human beings wherever possible. It is also considered cheaper to prevent disease than cure it.

Prevention can be divided into three main categories:

1. Primary prevention

2. Secondary prevention

3. Tertiary prevention.

Primary prevention

This is the complete **avoidance** of the disease, e.g. by **immunisation** and **lifestyle modifications**.

Secondary prevention

This is concerned with the **early detection** of disease in patients who have **no symptoms**, e.g. **screening of babies, cervical cytology**, routine **mammography**. All screening processes are secondary prevention.

Tertiary prevention

This is concerned with the **limitation of chronic disease** by the discovery and management of the disease before complications have produced disability or handicap; e.g. **careful management** of diabetes mellitus, hypertension and asthma, as well as care of those with the effects of diagnosed coronary heart disease

Data

The setting up of **age-sex registers** and use of **Read Codes** on computers are essential tools for the implementation of preventive medicine in general practice. The New GP Contract 2003 requirements for setting up of specific disease registers will provide a useful tool in complying with clinical governance.

Read codes provide a clinical coding system on the data of patients, concerning disease, drugs, etc. These systems enable easy recall of information which can be used for research, statistics and regular recall of patients.

Primary Health Care Team (PHCT)

The Primary Health Care Team is a group of professional health care workers within the community, each contributing their own special skills to the benefit of patients' well-being (*see Figure 77*). They are normally the first professionals involved in the care of the patient.

In general practice, it is the PHCT who is at the front line of preventive medicine. This aspect was given a definite emphasis in the 1990 GP Contract and continues to be regarded as of vital importance in the **2003 GP Contract** as a part of the quality requirements.

The PHCT requires:

- Clear **goals**

- Clear **roles** and **responsibilities** ensuring best use of different expertise

- Good **relationships**

- Good **communication.**

Goals

It is important that the PHCT work together as a team towards a common goal. Each member should be aware of the specialist skills provided by each of the other members, thus providing support to each other and the best care for the patient. It is always important to remember what the overall achievement should be, i.e. the best care of the patient.

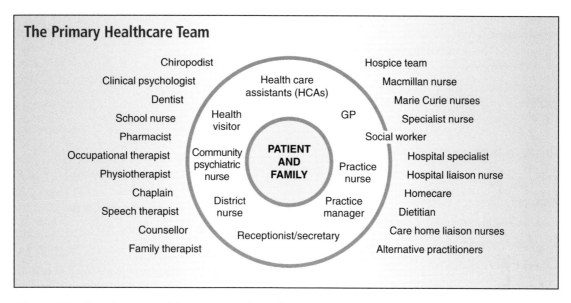

Figure 77: The Primary Health Care Team (PHCT) *(Reproduced from The Primary Care Nurses' Companion, edited by Sue Hinchliff. In press: Magister Consulting)*

Among the common goals is that of preventive medicine. The new **'Primary Care Organisations' (PCOs)**, include all disciplines and (together with the **National Plan** and the continuing expansion and implementation of the **National Service Framework**) should help to achieve the overall targets for 2010, of the 1999 White Paper, *'Saving Lives: Our Healthier Nation'*.

Members

The basic PHCT is composed of:

- **GP**
- **Health visitor**
- **Community nurse/midwife**
- **Nurse practitioner**
- **Practice nurse**
- **Health care assistants**
- **District nurse**
- **Social worker**
- **Practice manager**
- **Receptionist/secretary**
- **Community psychiatric nurse**

The administrative support from the practice manager, receptionists and secretaries is absolutely vital and ensures the smooth running of the team. Good communication is vital and it is here that the receptionist can bring invaluable support by ensuring accuracy in conveying messages.

The other specialist members of the primary team include (*see Figure 77*):

- **Counsellors**
- **Clinical Nurse Specialist in Palliative Care (CNS) – Macmillan nurse**
- **School nurses**
- **Continence advisors**
- **Chiropodists**
- **Dietitians**
- **Domiciliary physiotherapists**
- **Occupational therapists**
- **Speech therapists**
- **Orthoptists**
- **Pharmacists**
- **Dental officers.**

Nurses at **'NHS Direct'** and **'Walk in Centres'** can be described as part of the PHCT as they are often the first contact the patient has with a health professional.

The patient and his/her carer (voluntary or a Home Care Assistant), are the basis of the team, allowing the patient to remain in the community.

Areas of primary preventive medicine

These include:

- **Immunisation**
- **Public health and housing controls**
- **Health education**
- **Dental fluoridation.**

Immunisation

This is one of the main areas of prevention (*see Chapter 22*). Before the advent of immunisation of children against infectious diseases (such as **diphtheria**), many children died before reaching puberty.

Public health and housing controls

Without the sweeping changes in these areas, which came about in the late 19th century ensuring better **housing**, clean **water** supplies and **disposal of sewage**, the general standard of health would be very poor. These controls should never be under-estimated as control of the **environment** is paramount in the battle for health. Increasing **pollution** of the atmosphere is producing health hazards for many of the population at the present time.

Health education/promotion

Health education and promotion is aimed at persuading people to live **healthy lifestyles** and adopt a positive view towards taking responsibility for their own, and their children's, health.

The greatest problem is the 'it won't happen to me' attitude. Anti-smoking, anti-drugs and AIDS campaigns, together with all the other areas in which the **Health Development Agency** is involved, play a major part in these fields.

The provision of the many available health education leaflets is of great help to the GP practice and to the health visitor in their relationship with the patient. Leaflets can be obtained from the **'Health Promotion and Resources'** department within Primary Care Organisations.

Health education begins with **preconceptual advice** and continues through to, and includes, old age. Parents and teachers play a major role in childhood: **'example'** is the greatest teacher of all.

Important areas of preventive medicine

There are many different areas of health promotion in different sectors of the community. Some examples of the wide range of preventive medicine are described below:

Maternal care (antenatal and postnatal)

- Screening for defects in the **fetus**
- Screening for diseases in the **mother**
- Early detection or prevention of **toxaemia** of pregnancy.

Child care

- Detection of abnormalities by **screening** tests – physical, mental and social
- **Developmental surveillance** – hearing, speech and visual defects etc
- **Immunisation**
- **Prevention of accidents** – avoidance of poisoning, burns etc
- **Prevention of child abuse – non-accidental injury** and **sexual abuse**
- **Prevention of dental caries**
- **Prevention of drug abuse.**

Adolescents

- **Smoking** prevention/cessation
- **Contraception** and dealing with unwanted pregnancy

- **Accident prevention** at work and home.
- **Alcohol** and **drug abuse**
- **Sexually transmitted disease** including AIDS
- **Suicide/self-harm.**

Adults: 16 to 64 years

- Complications of **pregnancy**
- **Smoking**
- **Chronic Obstructive Airway/ Pulmonary Disease (COAD** or **COPD)**
- **Sexually transmitted disease** including HIV and AIDS
- **Rubella** (German measles)
- **Motor accidents**
- **Alcohol and drug abuse**
- **Cancer of the breast and cervix**
- **Testicular and prostate cancer**
- **Hypertension**
- **Coronary heart disease**
- **Suicide/self-harm**
- **Cancer of the oesophagus and colon.**

Elderly: 65 years and over

- **Hypertension**
- **Loss of autonomy**
- **Dementia**
- **Hearing defects**
- **Feet problems**
- **Visual defects**
- **Influenza,** with emphasis on those at risk due to other diseases
- **Hypothermia**
- **Accidents** and loss of **balance**
- **'Granny bashing'** – abuse of the elderly by carer/relative.

All age ranges

- **Diet** and **obesity**
- **Asthma**
- **Diabetes mellitus type 2**
- **Exercise.**

The range of preventive medicine is a vast one and these are only examples of the many areas where the individual may benefit from the prevention of disease, health education or screening processes.

Opportunistic screening

Instead of special health promotion clinics, it is now accepted and recognised that **opportunistic screening** is more effective in primary and secondary preventive medicine.

The GP and his/her staff have always been involved in the routine testing of **urine** and recording of **blood pressure**, and hidden cases of **diabetes mellitus** and **hypertension** have been regularly detected. Hypertension is a 'silent killer' as no symptoms occur until there has already been extensive damage to the body.

The role of the receptionist in preventive medicine

The receptionist in general practice will be involved in the collection and programming of **statistics** and also the maintenance of the **age/sex register** or **morbidity register**. Various letters and questionnaires will need to be given or sent to patients. Efficient recording and filing of notes are essential.

Ensuring there is always a good supply of **health education leaflets** available for patients, is a valuable contribution to the work of the PHCT. Local Health Promotion Departments will readily supply these on request as well as assist in the setting up of specialist displays on many aspects of preventive medicine.

Immunisation and **cervical smear** targets will also be a priority. An understanding of the reasons for these important requirements will enable the receptionist to assist the PHCT with an even greater motivation.

Saving Lives: Our Healthier Nation

A white paper issued by the government in 1999 entitled *'Saving Lives: Our Healthier Nation'* stated their intentions for the planned improvement of the nation's health up to the year **2010**.

The paper states that good health is a top priority for the government. The aim is to prevent people falling ill in the first place by **'tackling the root causes of the avoidable illnesses'**. In recent years emphasis has been placed on the individual's responsibility to live healthy lives via **lifestyle** changes. This has been beneficial but has also led to an attitude which blames the individual for his/her poor health. The plan now is for more attention and government action to be placed on controlling those factors which damage health and are beyond the individual's control.

Inequality

Poor health has complex causes, some of which are fixed, such as **genetic factors** and **ageing**. However, many other factors which may cause bad health can be changed, e.g. lifestyle, diet, physical exercise, sexual behaviour, smoking, alcohol and drugs.

Social and economic factors also play a part, for instance **poverty, unemployment** and **social exclusion**. Our environment, including air and water quality, housing, as well as access to good services such as education, transport, social services provision and the NHS, all affect our health. It is a fact that poor people are ill more often and die sooner.

There is now an emphasis on fundamental inequalities and attention and resources are being given to the areas most affected by: air pollution, low wages, unemployment, poor housing, and crime and disorder, all of which can make people both mentally and physically ill.

Linked programmes

A series of programmes linked to improving factors affecting health are to be implemented by the government, including measures on:

- **'Welfare to work'** (tackling unemployment)
- **Crime**
- **Housing**
- **Education**
- **Health.**

Key aims

There are two key aims for improving the health of the population:

1. **'To improve the health of the population as a whole by increasing the length of people's lives and the number of years people spend free from illness.'**

2. **'To improve the health of the worst off in society and to narrow the health gap.'**

The government has set out a new way to achieve this goal 'between the old extremes of individual victim blaming' and 'nanny state social engineering on the other' by introducing the **National Contract for Better Health**.

Partnerships

To achieve the main aims, the following groups work together:

- **Government**
- **Health care trusts**
- **Local authorities**
- **Businesses**
- **Voluntary bodies.**

Individuals also play a part in taking decisions about their own health

Targets of
Saving Lives: Our Healthier Nation

Based on health statistics from 1996, four priority areas are targeted for 2010. The new goals are as follows:

1. Cancer

to reduce the death rate in people under 75 by at least a fifth (20%)

2. Coronary heart disease and stroke

to reduce the death rate in people under 75 by at least two fifths (40%)

3. Accidents

to reduce the death rate by at least a fifth (20%) and to reduce the incidence of serious injury by at least a tenth (10%)

4. Mental Illness

to reduce the death rate from suicide and undetermined injury by at least a fifth (20%)

Additionally wider action has been taken on the following:

- **Smoking**

- **Sexual health**

- **Drugs**

- **Alcohol**

- **Food** safety (Food Standards Agency established)

- **Fluoride** and **oral health**

- **Communicable diseases**

- **Genetic factors** (Genetics Task Force)

- The health of **black and minority ethnic groups.**

Local targets

Other health problems, particular to each locality in the country, are also targeted, according to the local needs – e.g. problems of the elderly in localities with high levels of retired residents and their associated health problems. The relevant areas targeted, will be decided by the Local Primary Care Trusts and Local Authorities. Auditing and monitoring will be performed by the **Strategic Health Authority (SHA)**

The Department of Health issued the following advice:

Ten Tips – your guide to better health

1. Don't smoke. If you can, stop. If you can't, cut down.

2. Follow a balanced diet with plenty of fruit and vegetables.

3. Keep physically active.

4. Manage stress by, for example, talking things through and making time to relax.

5. If you drink alcohol, do so in moderation.

6. Cover up in the sun, and protect children from sunburn.

7. Practise safer sex.

8. Take up cancer screening opportunities.

9. Be safe on the roads: follow the Highway Code.

10. Learn the First Aid ABC - airways, breathing and circulation.

issued by Liam Donaldson, Chief Medical Officer

National Service Framework (NSF)

Following the white paper 'A First Class Service: quality in the new NHS' (Department of Health, 1998), the National Institute for Clinical Excellence (**NICE**) has established the 'National Service Framework' for specific named conditions. This has been introduced with the aim of ensuring all patients are treated in the same clinical way, regardless of their post code, so that health is not a lottery according to the area in which you live. Each framework lays down the ways in which risk assessment is made as well as the recommended treatment which should be given to the patient.

Each National Service Framework covers:

- **Prevention**
- **Diagnosis**
- **Management**
- **Rehabilitation**

for each specific condition.

These frameworks are intended for use in:

- **Public health**
- **Primary care**
- **Secondary care**

Their aim is to ensure that the main targets of *'Saving Lives: Our Healthier Nation'*, will be achieved by 2010.

To date there are **National Service Frameworks** established for:

- **Coronary heart disease**
- **Diabetes mellitus**
- **Mental health**
- **Older people**
- **Renal health**
- **Children**

and

- a National Health Service Plan has also been introduced for **cancer.**

(A summary of the current NSFs and the NHS Cancer Plan are given below).

They are delivered by means of clinical governance, underpinned by professional self-regulation and lifelong personal development plans

They are monitored by the:

- **Commission for Health Improvement (CHI)**
- **NHS Performance Assessment Framework**
- **National Survey of NHS Patients.**

Strategic Health Authorities are responsible for the auditing of compliance with these standards and the new **2003 GP Contract** is heavily orientated to the provision of these quality requirements. GPs' remuneration will reflect their performance in these fields.

Summary of NSF standards and the NHS Cancer Plan

Coronary Heart Disease (CHD)

- Reducing heart disease in the population
- Preventing CHD in high risk patients
- Heart attack and other acute coronary syndromes
- Stable angina
- Revascularisation
- Heart failure
- Cardiac rehabilitation.

Diabetes mellitus

- Prevention of type 2 diabetes
- Identification of people with diabetes
- Empowering people with diabetes
- Clinical care of adults with diabetes
- Clinical care of children and young people with diabetes
- Management of diabetic emergencies
- Care of people with diabetes during admission to hospital
- Diabetes and pregnancy
- Detection and management of long-term complications.

Mental Health Services for Working Age Adults

- Promoting Social Inclusion
- Service User and Carer Empowerment
- Promotion of opportunities for fulfilling and socially inclusive patterns of daily life
- Equitable, accessible services
- Commissioning effective, comprehensive and responsive services
- Delivering effective, comprehensive and responsive services
- Effective client assessment and core pathways
- Ensuring a well-staffed, skilled and supportive workforce.

Older People

- Rooting out age discrimination
- Person centred care
- Intermediate care
- General hospital care
- Stroke
- Falls
- Mental health in older people
- Promoting an active healthy life in older age.

Renal

- Primary prevention, pre-dialysis and acute renal failure
- Effective delivery of dialysis
- Transplantation
- Alternative models of care.

Children, young people and maternity services

This framework is still being developed as a partnership between health and social care with links to education, housing, leisure, the voluntary sector and other stakeholders including parents/ carers, children and young people. The aim of the Children's NSF is that *"all children and young people achieve optimum health and well being and are supported in achieving their potential"*. The scope of the Children's NSF includes all children and young people from pre-conception to 18th birthday (and beyond for young people with special needs).

The standards for children, young people and maternity services will cover nine specific groups:

- Children and young people with acute and chronic illness or injury
- Disabled children and young people
- Improving health and well-being of all children and young people
- Children and young people in special circumstances
- Mental health and psychological well-being of children and young people

- Maternity
- Medicines
- Workforce development
- Performance development.

NHS Cancer Plan

More than one in three people in England will develop cancer at some stage in their lives. One in four will die of cancer. This means that, every year, over 200,000 people are diagnosed with cancer, and around 120,000 people die from cancer. So better prevention of cancer, better detection of cancer, and better treatment and care, matter to us all.

The Cancer Plan has four aims:

- to save more lives
- to ensure people with cancer get the right professional support and care as well as the best treatments
- to tackle the inequalities in health that mean unskilled workers are twice as likely to die from cancer as professionals
- to build for the future through investment in the cancer workforce, through strong research and through preparation for the genetics revolution, so that the NHS never falls behind in cancer care again.

For the first time this plan provides a comprehensive strategy for bringing together prevention, screening, diagnosis, treatment and care for cancer and the investment needed to deliver these services in terms of improved staffing, equipment, drugs, treatments and information systems.

At the heart of the Plan are **three new commitments**. These will be:

- In addition to the existing *Smoking Kills* target of reducing smoking in adults from 28% to 24% by 2010, new national and local targets to address the gap between socio-economic groups in smoking rates and the resulting risks of cancer and heart disease
- New goals and targets to reduce waiting times for diagnosis and treatment

■ Additional NHS investment in hospices and specialist palliative care, to improve access to these services across the country.

General lifestyle advice

Opportunistic screening for lifestyle risks is probably most effective as the patient is more receptive to advice when attending the surgery for a visit for some other condition, or prescription review, than actually having to make a separate appointment to attend a well-person clinic.

Opportunistic screening includes assessment of:

- **Smoking**
- **Diet**
- **Alcohol consumption**
- **Exercise**
- **Stress** levels with a view to increasing an awareness of the concept of good mental health
- Awareness of the benefits of regular **breast self-examination** for women or **testicular self-examination** for men (*see Chapter 20: Screening tests*).

Health risks of cigarette smoking

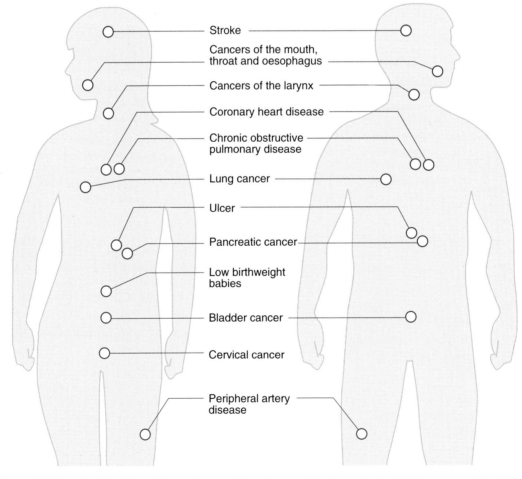

Figure 78: The health risks of cigarette smoking *(based on "Smoke-free for Health" [Department of Health, 1994] and the US Office on Smoking and Health, Centres for Disease Control and Prevention Report [1990])*

Smoking

Complete cessation should be the overall aim. Smoking is a very large factor in both the development of cancers and coronary heart disease (*see Figure 78*). Helpful advice, as well as medication, in the form of patches and oral tablets (on NHS prescription), are available.

Benefits of stopping smoking

The benefits of cessation of smoking are:

- A decrease in the ease of blood clotting within two weeks, **lowering the risk of thrombosis**
- A **lowering of blood cholesterol** to normal for the individual within one month
- A **reduction in the complications associated with chronic heart disease** within one year
- A restoration of the **risk of stroke to 'normal' range** within five years
- A **reduction** of the chances of **atheroma** (furring up of arteries with fatty deposits).

Passive smoking

The damage suffered through passive smoking is now an accepted fact and parents should be advised on the effect it has on their children.

Diet

The following is recommended:

- Regular intake of five portions of **fruit** or **vegetables** per day (80g each)
- Eat *less* **fat, salt** and **sugar**
- Eat *more* **fibre**
- Drink at least **3 litres of fluid** per day

The British Heart Foundation produced a newsletter for children and adolescents called *"Intake"*. It provides advice on diet and, while it is aimed at children, the advice is sound for people of all ages (*see Figure 79*).

The **Food Standards Agency** monitors food and farming methods, acting as a watch dog following the **BSE (bovine spongiform encephalopathy)** disaster. Recently it has prevented a chocolate manufacturer's planned competition in schools, which would have encouraged large amounts of chocolate consumption by children.

Alcohol

The government's recommended sensible drinking advice is **2 to 3 units of alcohol maximum per day for women** and **3 to 4 units maximum per day for men** (*see Figure 80*).

However, overall and as the guidelines from the British Hypertension Society state, people should be advised to limit their **weekly** alcohol intake to < 21 units (men) <14 units (women).

It is not intended that these daily unit totals are to be drunk **every** day, 7 days a week! There should be days of abstinance or lesser consumption. A maximum daily total has been advised in order to prevent "binge drinking", because it has been found that individuals have drunk a whole week's recommended total intake in one session!

For **pregnant women**: when planning conception or when pregnant, women are advised to consume fewer units (or abstain from alcohol completely). The potential damage to the fetus from alcohol – especially in the first weeks of pregnancy– can be devastating.

Damage to health

Alcohol travels to every cell in the body, every tissue, and every organ. It is a **poison** and has to be broken down by the **liver**. Over time, using too much alcohol can damage the heart, raise the blood pressure, and cause cancer, liver disease, and brain damage; it can cause ulcers, weaken the muscles, and even lead to death. In pregnancy it can severely damage the fetus causing a condition of deformities, known as **'fetal alcohol syndrome'** in which there is extensive damage to the brain and major organs.

Physical exercise

The Health Development Agency (2001) recommended that individuals should take 30 minutes exercise of moderate intensity on five days a week. Brisk walking, swimming, dancing and gardening are all recommended. Two 15-minute sessions is acceptable, providing they are both performed on the same day. The aim of increasing the rate of breathing is an important factor (i.e. **aerobic exercise**). As well

Food "rools!"

How we look and feel has a lot to do with what we eat.
If you want less spots, great hair and bags of energy just follow these simple tips:

We're only human!

Don't make drastic changes to your diet. The "naughty" things
we like (cakes, chocolate, chips, fizzy drinks, crisps) are okay every
now and then – but just not everyday!

Variety is the spice of life!

Eat a variety of foods everyday so that you don't get bored
with eating the same things all the time.

Don't skip breakfast!

Breakfast gives your body the energy you need to kick-start the day.
Try high fibre cereals instead of sugary ones; or baked beans on
wholemeal toast; or fresh fruit and low fat yoghurt – and if you're
running really late, grab a couple of pieces of fresh fruit.

Be wary of adverts!

Don't just believe what they say in the adverts. Work out for
yourself which foods are the healthiest to eat – and which
advertisers are trying to get you to eat unhealthy stuff.

Be radiant!

Eat five portions of fruit or veg every day. Not only are they good
for your insides but it makes your hair and skin healthier too
– a difference that shows on the outside!

Drink lots of water!

Water is good for your looks and it's important for your health.
Our bodies are about two-thirds water. We need plenty of water
– especially after exercise and in hot weather.

Figure 79: Dietary advice for children and young people but applicable to all age groups
(adapted from the British Heart Foundation newsletter "Intake")

Sensible drinking

If you drink 3 or more units a day there is an increased risk to your health!

 Women

2 or 3 units per day

- Most women can drink up to 2 or 3 units of alcohol a day without significant risks to their health

- Women who are trying to conceive or who are pregnant should avoid getting drunk and are advised to consume no more than 1 or 2 units of alcohol once or twice a week

- After the menopause there is evidence that drinking one to two units a day, **but no more**, can result in positive health benefits

 Men

3 or 4 units per day

- Most men can drink up to 3 or 4 units of alcohol a day without significant risks to their health

- For men aged 40 and over there is evidence that drinking 1 or 2 units a day, **but no more**, can result in positive health benefits

NB. These 'benchmarks' are not targets to drink up to. There are times and circumstances when it makes sense not to drink at all

✗ Don't

- Drink and drive

- Operate machinery, use electrical equipment or work at heights after drinking

- Drink before playing sport or swimming

- Drink while on certain medications – check labels and ask a doctor if unsure

- Drink when it would affect the quality of your work

- Drink if your doctor advised you not to

- Binge drink – it can lead to health and other problems

 Remember

- Drinks poured at home are often more generous than pub measures

- If you drink heavily in the evening you may still be over the drink/drive limit the following morning

✔ Do

- Abstain for 48 hours, if you have an episode of heavy drinking, to let your body recover

- Remember drinks poured at home are often bigger than pub measures

- Work out how much you drink and try to stick to the guidelines – which are daily benchmarks not weekly targets

- Get help from a doctor or a specialist agency if worried about your drinking

- Remember that drinking responsibly can be enjoyable and is compatible with a healthy lifestyle

Figure 80: Government guidelines on sensible drinking *(adapted from "It all adds up: the sensible drinking guidelines explained" published by The Portman Group: www.portmangroup.org.uk and "Think about drink" a leaflet published by the Health Education Authority)*

What is 1 unit of alcohol?

1 unit of alcohol =
- about half a pint (284ml) of ordinary strength lager, beer or cider, typically 3.5% alcohol by volume (ABV)
- a 25ml pub measure of spirit, typically 40% ABV
- a small glass of 9% ABV wine.

What does this mean in terms of drinks?

Beer, lager and cider
- 330ml bottle at 4% or 5% ABV = 1.5 units
- 440ml can at 4% or 5% ABV = 2 units
- 440ml can at 8% or 9% ABV = 3.5 to 4 units
- 500ml can at 8% or 9% ABV = 4 to 4.5 units

Low alcohol beer and lager
- 440ml can at 1.2% ABV = 0.5 units

Wine
- 125 ml glass of wine at 11% or 12% ABV = 1.5 units
- 175ml glass of wine at 11% or 12% ABV = 2 units

Spirits
- 25ml measure of spirit at 40% ABV = 1 unit

Sherry, port, madeira and vermouth
- 50ml measure at 20% ABV = 1 unit

Alcopops
- 330ml bottle at 4% to 6% ABV = between 1.3 and 2 units
- 200ml bottle at 13.5% ABV = 2.7 units

A word of caution
Some drinks are stronger than others. For example, a pint of premium lager has more units of alcohol in it than a standard strength beer. Most bottles of wine at 11% or 12% ABV. You can work out the number of units in a drink by multiplying the volume in ml by the percentage ABV and dividing the total by 1000. The figures listed here are rounded to the nearest half unit.

If you drink heavily you have an increased risk of:

- **Hepatitis** (inflammation of the liver)
- **Cirrhosis** (scarring of the liver) – up to 3 in every 10 long-term heavy drinkers develop cirrhosis
- **Stomach disorders**
- **Pancreatitis** (severe inflammation of the pancreas)
- **Mental health problems** including **depression, anxiety** and various other problems
- **Sexual difficulties**, such as **impotence**
- **Muscle** and **heart muscle disease**
- **Hypertension** (high blood pressure)
- **Damage to nervous tissue**

- **Accidents** – drinking alcohol is associated with a much increased risk of accidents, in particular injury and death from fire and car crashes (about 1 in 7 road deaths are caused by drinking alcohol)
- **Some cancers** – mouth, gullet, liver, colon and breast
- **Obesity** – alcohol has many calories
- **Damage to an unborn baby** in pregnant women
- **Alcohol dependence (addiction)**.

In the UK about 33,000 deaths a year are related to drinking alcohol – about one quarter of these are due to accidents.

as other benefits, exercise brings a feeling of 'well-being', because the body produces chemicals known as **'endorphins'**. (These are similar to the effects of morphine which produces a feeling of euphoria.)

Obesity

According to the National Audit Office (NAO, 2001), obesity predisposes the individual to a higher risk of associated diseases. The increase in incidence of obesity is a worrying factor for the overall health of the population at the present time. A useful tool for measuring this is to calculate the **Body Mass Index (BMI)** of people.

Body Mass Index (BMI) recordings

The body mass index (BMI) of an individual can be used to calculate the obesity risk to health of that individual (*see Tables 6, 7 and 8*).

The BMI is calculated with the following formula:

$$\frac{\textbf{Weight (kg)}}{\textbf{Height (m) squared}} = \textbf{BMI}$$

Classification for adults is as follows:

Underweight	**BMI <18.5**
Normal	**BMI 18.5 – 25**
Overweight	**BMI 25 – 30**
Obese	**BMI 30 – 40**
Extreme obesity	**BMI > 40**

Girth

Waist circumference is another useful measure for 'at risk patients', as it may indicate **intra-abdominal fat mass**, which is linked to various diseases such as **coronary heart disease (CHD), insulin resistance, type 2 diabetes mellitus, hyperlipidaemia** (raised blood fats) and **hypertension** (high blood pressure).

The typical **'apple shaped'** figure, where extra weight is carried on the waist area is a warning sign as opposed to the **'pear shaped'** figure

Table 6: Body mass Index as an indicator of health weight

weight in kilograms

height	124	122	120	118	116	114	112	110	108	106	104	102	100	98	96	94	92	90	88	86	84
2.00 m	31	30	30	29	29	28	28	27	27	26	26	25	25	24	24	23	23	22	22	21	21
	32	32	31	31	30	30	29	29	28	28	27	27	26	26	25	24	24	23	23	22	22
1.92 m	34	33	33	32	31	31	30	30	29	29	28	28	27	27	26	25	25	24	24	23	23
	35	35	34	33	33	32	32	31	31	30	29	29	28	28	27	27	26	25	25	24	24
1.84 m	37	36	35	35	34	34	33	32	32	31	31	30	30	29	28	28	27	27	26	25	25
	38	38	37	36	36	35	35	34	33	33	32	31	31	30	30	29	28	28	27	27	26
1.76 m	40	39	39	38	37	37	36	36	35	34	34	33	32	32	31	30	30	29	28	28	27
	42	41	41	40	39	39	38	37	37	36	35	34	34	33	32	32	31	30	30	29	28
1.68 m	44	43	43	42	41	40	40	39	38	38	37	36	35	35	34	33	33	32	31	30	30
	46	45	45	44	43	42	42	41	40	39	39	38	37	36	36	35	34	33	33	32	31
1.60 m	48	48	47	46	45	45	44	43	42	41	41	40	39	38	37	37	36	35	34	34	33
	51	50	49	48	48	47	46	45	44	44	43	42	41	40	39	39	38	37	36	35	35
1.52 m	54	53	52	51	50	49	48	48	47	46	45	44	43	42	42	41	40	39	38	37	36
	57	56	55	54	53	52	51	50	49	48	47	47	46	45	44	43	42	41	40	39	38
1.44 m	60	59	58	57	56	55	54	53	52	51	50	49	48	47	46	45	44	43	42	41	41
	63	62	61	60	59	58	57	56	55	54	53	52	51	50	49	48	47	46	45	44	43
1.36 m	67	66	65	64	63	62	61	59	58	57	56	55	54	53	52	51	49	49	48	46	45

| 19 st | | 18 st | | 17 st | | 16 st | | 15 st | | 14 st |

Extreme obesity > 40   Obese 30 – 40   Overweight 25 – 30

where the excess weight is carried on the hips and thighs. Present recommendations are that waists should be less than 40 inches (preferably 37 inches) for men and less than 35 inches, (preferably under 32 inches) for women.

Sexual health/diversity and mental well-being

More recent developments in treatments for impotence (**erectile dysfunction**) and **frigidity**, as well as the addressing of such areas as **'gender identity'**, **sexual orientation** and other areas, together with changing attitudes to diversity of lifestyle, will hopefully assist in more fulfilled lives for the individual. In this context, this should help in the prevention of mental illness such as depression with its ultimate risk of suicide.

School bullying and child health

More recognition and prevention of this distressing problem in our society will hopefully continue and cases of subsequent suicide, be reduced.

Environment

Government efforts to reduce **pollution**, reduce **speed limits**, cut crime, improve **social attitudes** and opportunities for all members of society etc. are all geared to produce better health in its widest sense.

Skin cancer and sun

Skin cancer is increasing and warnings of risk exposure are now included in weather weight in kilograms

82	80	78	76	74	72	70	68	66	64	62	60	58	56	54	52	50	48	46	44	42	height
20	20	19	19	18	18	17	17	16	16	15	15	14	14	13	13	12	12	11	11	10	
21	21	20	20	19	19	18	18	17	17	16	16	15	15	14	14	13	12	12	11	11	6 ft 6 in
22	22	21	21	20	20	19	18	18	17	17	16	16	15	15	14	14	13	12	12	11	
23	23	22	22	21	20	20	19	19	18	18	17	16	16	15	15	14	14	13	12	12	6 ft 3 in
24	24	23	22	22	21	21	20	19	19	18	18	17	17	16	15	15	14	14	13	12	
25	25	24	23	23	23	22	21	20	20	19	19	18	17	17	16	15	15	14	14	13	6 ft 0 in
26	26	25	25	24	23	23	22	21	21	20	19	19	18	17	17	16	15	15	14	14	5 ft 9 in
28	27	26	26	25	24	24	23	22	22	21	20	20	19	18	18	17	16	16	15	14	
29	28	28	27	26	26	25	24	23	23	22	21	21	20	19	18	18	17	16	16	15	5 ft 6 in
30	30	29	28	28	27	26	25	25	24	23	22	22	21	20	19	19	18	17	16	16	
32	31	30	30	29	28	27	27	26	25	24	23	23	22	21	20	20	19	18	17	16	5 ft 3 in
34	33	32	31	30	30	29	28	27	26	25	25	24	23	22	21	21	20	19	18	17	
35	35	34	33	32	31	30	29	29	28	27	26	25	24	23	23	22	21	20	19	18	5 ft 0 in
37	37	36	35	34	33	32	31	30	29	28	27	26	26	25	24	23	22	21	20	19	4 ft 9in
40	39	38	37	36	35	34	33	32	31	30	29	28	27	26	25	24	23	22	21	20	
42	41	40	39	38	37	36	35	34	33	32	31	30	29	28	27	26	24	23	22	21	4 ft 6 in
44	43	42	41	40	39	38	37	36	35	34	32	31	30	29	28	27	26	25	24	23	

13 st | 12 st | 11 st | 10 st | 9 st | 8 st | 7 st |

Normal 18.5 – 25 ☐   Underweight < 18.5 ☐

forecasts. A high **barrier cream** should always be applied, especially to children. The less time spent in direct sunshine, especially during peak times the better. **Malignant melanoma** is the most serious type of skin cancer and is the most frequently occurring although incidents of squamous cell carcinoma are increasing and can be equally invasive if not treated at an early stage.

Warning signs of skin cancer:

- An existing mole becomes larger
- A new mole is growing
- A mole has a ragged, irregular outline
- A mole has a mixture of different shades of brown or black
- A new growth or sore does not heal within 4 weeks

- A spot or sore continues to itch, hurt, scab or bleed
- Skin ulcers persist which are not explained by other causes.

Stress

Teaching people the nature of stress, its benefits and dangers and how to recognise and cope with it, plays an important part in prevention of wider ill health. Recent research indicates that prolonged stress lowers the body's immunity, thus allowing many medical problems to arise

Signs of stress include:

- Feeling guilty when relaxing – uneasy if not always busy
- Lying awake at night worrying about tomorrow

Table 7: Interpretation of height/weight ratios for adults

	Mean weight for medium build (kg)				**Mean weight for medium build (st lb)**				
	Height (cm)	**Mean -10%**	**Mean**	**Mean +10%**	**Mean +20%**	**Height (ft in)**	**Mean -10%**	**Mean**	**Mean +10%**	**Mean +20%**
MEN	155	49	54	59	64	5. 1	7. 9	8. 7	9. 4	10. 2
	157	50	55	61	66	5. 2	7.12	8.10	9. 8	10. 6
	160	51	57	63	68	5. 3	8. 1	8.13	9.11	10.10
	162	52	58	64	69	5. 4	8. 3	9. 2	10. 1	10.13
	165	54	60	66	71	5. 5	8. 7	9. 6	10. 4	11. 3
	167	55	62	68	74	5. 6	8.10	9. 10	10. 9	11. 8
	170	57	64	70	76	5. 7	9. 0	10. 0	11. 0	12. 0
	172	59	65	72	78	5. 8	9. 4	10. 4	11. 4	12. 4
	175	60	67	74	80	5. 9	9. 7	10. 8	11. 9	12. 9
	177	63	69	76	83	5.10	9.11	10.13	12. 0	13. 1
	180	64	71	79	85	5.11	10. 2	11. 3	12. 5	13. 6
	183	66	74	80	88	6. 0	10. 6	11. 8	12. 9	13.11
	186	68	75	83	90	6. 1	10.10	11.12	13. 0	14. 3
	188	70	78	85	93	6. 2	10.14	12. 3	13. 6	14. 9
	191	72	80	88	96	6. 3	11. 5	12. 8	13.11	15. 0
WOMEN	142	40	45	49	54	4. 8	6. 5	7. 0	7.10	8. 6
	145	41	46	51	55	4. 9	6. 7	7. 3	7.13	8. 9
	147	43	47	52	56	4. 10	6.10	7. 6	8. 2	8.12
	150	44	49	54	58	4. 11	6.12	7. 9	8. 6	9. 2
	152	45	50	55	60	5. 0	7. 1	7.12	8. 9	9. 6
	155	46	51	56	61	5. 1	7. 4	8. 1	8.12	9. 9
	157	48	53	58	63	5. 2	7. 7	8. 5	9. 2	9.13
	160	49	55	60	65	5. 3	7.10	8. 8	9. 6	10. 4
	162	51	57	63	68	5. 4	8. 0	8.13	9.11	10. 9
	165	52	59	64	70	5. 5	8. 4	9. 3	10. 1	11. 0
	167	54	61	66	72	5. 6	8. 7	9. 7	10. 6	11. 5
	170	57	63	68	74	5. 7	8.11	9.11	10. 10	11. 9
	172	58	64	70	76	5. 8	9. 1	10. 1	11. 0	12. 0
	175	59	66	72	79	5. 9	9. 4	10. 5	11. 5	12. 5
	177	61	68	74	81	5.10	9. 8	10. 9	11. 9	12. 10

- Feeling tense – neck feels 'knotted up'
- Being impatient or irritable – interrupting others when they are talking
- Feeling you have a lot on your mind – finding it difficult to concentrate
- Smoking more and/or drinking more alcohol – eating in a hurry

- Life seems full of crises – and a tendency to have more rows
- Difficulty in make decisions
- Feeling frustrated when people do not do what you want
- Frequently experiencing 'butterflies in the stomach', a dry mouth, sweaty palms or a 'thumping heart'.

Table 8: The increased relative risk of obesity (BMI > 30) causing disease in men and women
(National Audit Office, 2001)

Disease	Relative increase in risk for: women (BMI > 30)	men (BMI > 30)
Type 2 diabetes	12.7	5.2
Hypertension	4.2	2.6
Myocardial infarction	3.2	1.5
Colon cancer	2.7	3.0
Angina	1.8	1.8
Cholecystitis	1.8	1.8
Ovarian cancer	1.7	*Not applicable*
Osteoarthritis	1.4	1.9
Stroke	1.3	1.3

NB: Relative risk BMI < 25 = 1

Individual national campaigns

These play their part in health promotion, e.g. **'No Smoking Day'** and **'Walk to School Day'**. The collective initiative of everyone trying to change lifestyle has a positive effect. However, the long-term effect may not be so beneficial. Evidence suggests that in the longer term, reinforcement of the message is needed in an acceptable form. The problem of 'it doesn't happen to me' prevails!

Contraception and teenage pregnancy

Advice is available from the GP surgery on contraception generally.

There has also been a recent campaign by practice nurses and school nurses to alert teenagers to the decision to allow **'the morning after pill'** (e.g. levonorgestrel), to be available without prescription at pharmacies, as well as available on prescription, issued, (under the **Patient Group Directives** scheme). The preparation requires two doses, twelve hours apart. The first should be taken within 72 hours of unprotected intercourse but earlier

administration increases its efficacy. The risk of **STDs** must always be considered.

These measures demonstrate the attempts to reduce the (still rapidly rising) number of teenage, single mothers.

Sexually transmitted diseases (STD)

These include:

- **HIV** and **AIDS**
- **Gonorrhoea**
- **Syphilis**
- **Chlamydia** (a common cause of infertility in the female)

Advice leaflets and campaigns on these areas are well covered. Despite this, infections are increasing at an alarming rate. The recent decision to enable drug addicts to have clean needles and syringes, is a step to prevent spread of the viruses of HIV and **hepatitis B, C, D and E.**

With recent research indicating that new medications have a significant effect on delaying the onset of AIDS, in HIV positive patients, it is hoped that individuals will come forward for screening at an early stage, which may help to slow the transmission of HIV.

Communicable disease control

The recent impact of **SARS (Severe Respiratory Disease Syndrome),** demonstrated the essential influence of the **World Health Organisation**, together with the various international disease surveillance centres, in controlling and preventing the world-wide spread of diseases (**pandemics**). Incidentally, publicity given to the importance of frequent hand-washing, was beneficial in an educational context.

Conventional and complementary medicine

Individuals are looking at a wider concept of health and taking initiative for themselves about the choices available.

Complementary medicine includes:

- **Yoga**
- **Osteopathy**
- **Chiropractic**
- **Homeopathy**
- **Acu-puncture**
- **Acu-pressure**
- **Reflexology**
- **Medical herbalism**
- **Aromatherapy**
- **Indian head massage**
- **Chinese medicine.**

These, together with the vast amount of readily, available information on the Internet, empower people to a degree, never seen before. Indeed, doctors have been alerted to available, authentic treatments, of which they were not aware, by their patients. Whilst it is accepted that vulnerable people need some protection, wise doctors *listen* to their patients!

Chronic disease management clinics within the GP surgery

Coronary heart disease (ischaemic heart disease)

This is a condition in which fatty deposits (**atheroma**) are laid down in the lining of arteries as plaques, causing narrowing of arteries (**arteriostenosis**). If walls are also hardened it is known as **atherosclerosis**. Those particularly affected are the coronary arteries supplying the heart muscle, itself with blood. These plaques can become inflamed and break away, completely blocking an artery, causing an acute heart attack (**myocardial infarction**). The sudden formation of a blood clot (**thrombus**), which blocks the artery is known as a **thrombosis** (or **coronary thrombosis** when it affects the coronary arteries).

Stroke

Similarly, these changes can occur in the brain where blockage of an artery (**occlusion**) is known as a **stroke** (sometimes also referred to by the outdated term of cerebrovascular accident). Strokes can also occur due to bleeding from a blood vessel in the brain due to a weakness in the wall (**aneurysm**) or as the result of high blood pressure.

Risk factors for heart disease, stroke and other cardiovascular disorders

The number of risk factors for the patient must be assessed (*see Figure 81*) and drugs which lower cholesterol (**statins**) are considered if indicated as well as the obvious treatment to lower blood pressure where required.

Risk factors include:

- **Family history**
- **High cholesterol** and **lipid levels**
    - A high cholesterol level is known as **hypercholesterolaemia**
    - High levels of certain fats (lipids) is known as **hyperlipidaemia**
    - High levels of **triglycerides** (also a type of lipid) is another risk factor.

Risk factors for coronary heart disease

Figure 81: Risk factors for coronary heart disease

NB: **High density lipids (HDLs)** *are considered protective, whereas* **low density lipids (LDLs)** *are considered harmful. When measured together they are together known as* **total cholesterol (TC).**

- **High blood homocysteine** levels (a protein substance)
- **Smoking**
- **Obesity**
- **Lack of exercise**
- **High blood pressure (hypertension)**
- **Diabetes mellitus**
- **Asian origin**
- **Stress.**

Cholesterol

At present it is thought that the use of **'statins'** to lower cholesterol levels, considerably extends life expectancy for those with cardio-vascular disease and especially for those who have already suffered a first, acute heart attack. As well as reducing cholesterol levels, it appears to reduce areas of inflammation in the fatty plaques of the artery linings, stopping them from breaking away and blocking the artery space (**lumen**).

Lifestyle changes are advised. Regular follow-up checks and blood tests are performed (as stated in the National Service Framework standards). Regular daily oral aspirin 75mg, is usually recommended, if appropriate for the patient, as a prevention of clot formation.

The effects of asthma

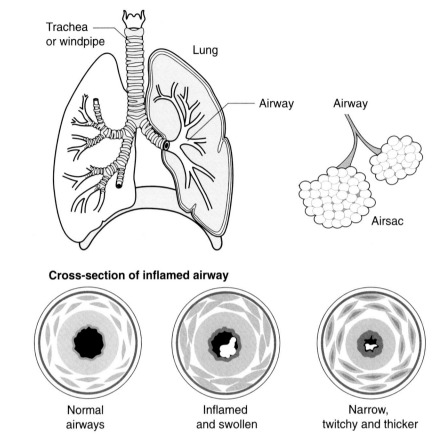

Figure 82: The effects of asthma

Asthma

Asthma (*see Figure 82*) is a long-term, common condition in which:

- The lining of the **airways** in the lungs becomes inflamed and swollen with an increased **mucous secretion**

- Airways become narrower (**constriction**)

- Airway walls become thicker and 'twitchy'.

Triggers (including pollen, cold air, cigarette smoke and perfume), cause the asthma response.

Signs and symptoms:

- Shortness of breath (**dyspnoea**)

- A feeling of **tightness** in the chest

- **Cough** usually episodic

- **Wheezing**

- **Being woken at night with increased shortness of breath**

- **Increased shortness of breath on waking** in the morning

- **Shortness of breath on exertion**

- **Inability to breathe out easily – decreased Peak Expiry Flow Rate (PEFR)**

Not all these may be present and a cough may be the only symptom presented. Some patients are encouraged to use an asthma symptom chart to monitor their condition (*see Figure 83*).

Goals of treatment:

- Be free from symptoms

- Normal or best Peak Flow reading to be restored and maintained (*see Figure 84*)

- Reduce the risk of severe attacks

- Minimise absence from school or work

- Restore normal living.

Areas to be assessed:

- The patient's understanding of the disease and the importance of prevention

- Compliance with drugs and recognition of effects of different inhaled medications

  - **Preventer** (brown) – e.g. beclometasone dipropionate (**corticosteroid**)

  - **Reliever** (blue) – e.g. salbutomol (**bronchodilator**)

  - **Protector** (green) – e.g . sodium cromoglycate

- Inhaler technique

- Measurement of Peak Flow reading and interpretation

- Recognition of worsening situation and response, e.g. need to increase inhaler use

- Number of days lost from school or work

- Asthma episodes disturbing sleep

- Any emergency situation requiring hospitalisation.

ASTHMA IS A COMMON CAUSE OF SUDDEN DEATH and must never be treated as trivial!

Asthma symptom chart

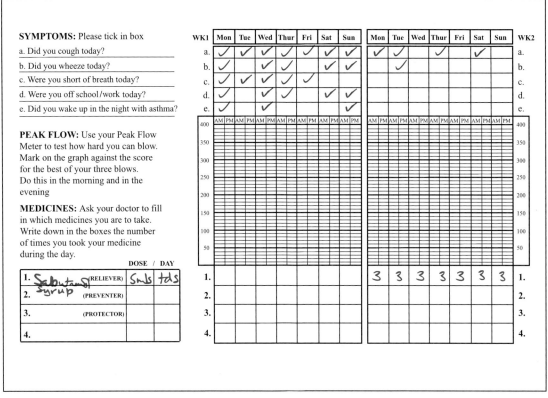

Figure 83: An asthma symptom chart for use by the patient

Normal peak expiry flow (PEF)

Figure 84: Normal peak expiry flow (PEF) values for men and women of different ages and heights

Chronic obstructive pulmonary disease (COPD)

This chronic, slowly progressive disorder, is usually a result of **chronic smoking**, although chronic asthma may produce similar deformities.

The permanently **constricted airway** (caused by loss of elasticity in the tissues), does not completely respond to **bronchodilators** although symptoms are relieved on their administration.

Deformity of the chest and the so-called '**barrel chest**' develop due to the inability to breathe out properly (**expiration**). These patients are usually in the >45 age range. They may eventually require **oxygen** administration. The conditions of air in the pleural cavity, (**emphysema**) and dilatation of the bronchioles, (**bronchiectasis**) are usually present, resulting in foul smelling **sputum** being coughed up from the lungs. **Spirometry** testing usually confirms the diagnosis.

Diabetes mellitus

A condition in which the body is **unable to metabolise glucose** (i.e. convert it to energy or store it in the body). In people with diabetes, the pancreas (*see Figure 85*) does not produce enough of the hormone **insulin**, or the insulin it produces does not work properly. (In healthy people, insulin is produced by small organs in the pancreas which are called the **Islets of Langerhan.**) In people who have diabetes, sugar builds up in the tissues of the body and is excreted in the urine (**glycosuria**).

There are two types of diabetes:

Type 1 previously known as **IDDM** (insulin dependent diabetes mellitus) or '**Early Onset**' diabetes

Type 2 previously known as **NIDDM** (non-insulin dependent diabetes mellitus) or '**Maturity Onset**' diabetes.

Type 1

Also known as **'Early Onset Diabetes'**. It affects children and young people. This disease is thought to be caused by the affects of a virus on the cells of the pancreas (**Islets of Langerhan**) which produce the hormone insulin or to the body's reaction to the secretion of insulin. There appears to be an hereditary factor.

As insulin is destroyed by the gastric secretions in the stomach it cannot be taken by mouth. Insulin replacement **injections** are required throughout life usually from two to four times a day. (The transplantation of pancreatic cells is being researched as a potential future treatment).

Signs and symptoms:

- **Loss of weight**

- **Thirst**

- Increased passing of urine (**polyuria**) especially at night (**nocturia**)

- **Tiredness**

- Itching/soreness of external genitalia (**pruritis vulva**), **thrush** infections

- **Recurring skin infections**

If not diagnosed, Type 1 diabetes can result in:

- **Ketones** building up in the blood as fats are unable to be burnt efficiently into carbon dioxide and water by the body, without the presence of glucose.

- **Unconsciousness, coma** and **death** due to high levels of sugar in the blood and tissues (**hyperglycaemia**).

Type 2

Associated with obesity, lack of exercise and middle age, although there is great concern as young people are beginning to develop this disease through bad lifestyle.

Also, although not normally required, it has been necessary to treat some of these categories of patient with insulin injections in order to control blood sugar.

The pancreas

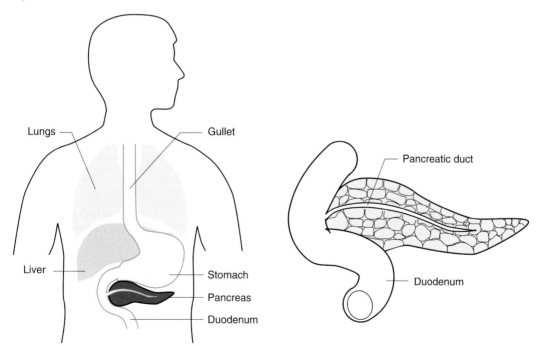

Figure 85: The pancreas

The main causes are that the body no longer responds normally to its own insulin and/or that the body does not produce enough insulin. There appears to be a family connection and also genetic: It tends to be more common in Asian and African-Caribbean communities.

Signs and symptoms:

Similar to Type 1 but Type 2 develops slowly and symptoms are generally less severe. Some people may not notice any symptoms and it is then only diagnosed at a routine medical check up. Many put their symptoms down to 'getting older' or 'overwork'.

In both types of diabetes early treatment reduces the chances of developing serious health problems such as **coronary heart disease, stroke, hypertension, circulation problems,** nerve damage (**neuropathy**), kidney (**nephropathy**) and eye damage (**retinopathy** and **cataract**) leading to blindness.

Treatment

- **Control of blood glucose levels,** if necessary by various types of medication for Type 2 and regular insulin injections for Type 1 (for life)

- **Control blood pressure** levels

- **Diet** – eating healthily

- **Control of weight**

- **Regular physical exercise**

- **No smoking**

- **Regular medical check ups** – to detect health problems early – at least annually

Acute medical emergency – hypoglycaemia

It is important to remember that any inbalance of insulin and glucose in the body resulting in too much insulin and too little glucose causing very low blood sugar (**hypoglycaemia**) can result in **unconsciousness** and **death**.

This is an acute medical emergency and should be treated with the immediate administration of **sugar by mouth** (orally) in any form, *before* the patient loses consciousness. (Unconscious patients must *never* be given anything by mouth as this could block their airway and cause death).

Patients on insulin are made aware of the symptoms and signs of a hypoglycaemic attack before they are discharged from hospital at their initial stabilisation treatment. They are also advised to carry sugar lumps in their pockets as well as wearing **'medic alert'** diabetic identity bracelet or necklace. It should be noted that antibiotics may temporally affect the level (**threshold**) at which sugar is found in the urine. Pregnancy can also cause similar effect, (**gestational glycosuria**).

New GP Contracts 2003 and 2004

The **new GP Contract**, which was accepted by GPs in June 2003 (and renegotiated by GPs in 2004), is the most radical change to general practice since 1948, and applies to those GPs still working under the **General Medical Services scheme**.

At the heart of the contract is:

- A new categorisation of services will help GPs to manage their workload by enabling practices to transfer responsibility for providing some services e.g. out-of-hours care, contraceptive care and chronic disease management, to other practices or their PCO

- Individual GP patient lists will be replaced by a combined list for the whole practice

- Payment will be provided for an identified population, rather than for items of service

- Each practice will be given an allocation to cover their staffing and running costs, based on a formula reflecting the needs of local patients

- Greater and fairer remuneration for GPs, who will be rewarded according to the quality of care they provide rather than the number of patients they treat

- A new quality framework, setting standards of care based on evidence, with two thirds of the increased investment for practices linked to a new system of quality payments

- A guarantee that all patients will receive the full range of existing services, with greater choice for some services and faster access

- Set services provided will still include essential services for ill patients, but different levels of payment will be available for individual practices across the PCO that supply enhanced services or extend the range of services provided

- Enhanced services include; ENT, trauma and orthopaedics, dermatology, ophthalmology, chronic disorders, including diabetes or CHD, anticoagulant therapy, advanced minor surgery etc., where treatment in primary care can offer a more convenient service to patients and reduce demands on hospitals

- Supporting practices where extended evening, weekend or open access surgeries are offered in response to patient preferences, allowing fast and convenient patient access to PHC with GP appointments available within 48 hours

- A recruitment and retention package to tackle GP shortages

- The new contract will be accompanied by an unprecedented increase in investment to revitalise general practice and transform services for patients, and investment in GP premises and IT.

(Sources NHS Confederation 2002 and 2003)

Not all practices with GMS contracts will provide services other than those classified as **'essential'**.

Essential services (ES)

These cover:

- Management of patients who are ill or believe themselves to be ill, with conditions from which recovery is generally expected, for the duration of that condition, including relevant health promotion advice and referral as appropriate, reflecting the patient choice wherever practicable

- General management of patients who are terminally ill

- Management of chronic disease in the manner determined by the practice in discussion with the patient.

'Enhanced Services' include:

- Ear, nose and throat (ENT)
- Trauma and orthopaedics
- Dermatology
- Ophthalmology
- Extended minor surgery
- Chronic disorders, including:
    - Diabetes mellitus
    - CHD (coronary heart disease)
    - Anticoagulant therapy.

Directed Enhanced Services (DES)

Enhanced services which are under national direction with national specification and benchmarked pricing which all PCOs must commission to cover their relevant population. These cover:

- Support services to staff and the public in respect of care and treatment of patients who are violent

- Improved access

- Childhood vaccinations and immunisations

- Influenza immunisations

- Quality information preparation

- Advanced minor surgery.

National Enhanced Services (NES)

These have national specifications and benchmark pricing, but are NOT directed. They include:

- Intrapartum care
- Anticoagulant monitoring
- Intra-uterine contraceptive device fitting, more specialised drug and alcohol misuse services
- More specialised sexual health services
- More specialised depression services
- Multiple sclerosis
- Enhanced care of terminally ill
- Enhanced care of the homeless
- Enhanced services for people with learning disabilities
- Immediate care and first response care and minor injury services.

Local Enhanced Services (LES)

These are services developed locally according to the special needs of the area. Terms and conditions will be discussed and agreed locally between the PCO and the practice with, if wished, the involvement of the LMC.

There are other specialties, e.g. Holistic Services, Expert Patient Initiatives etc. which can be provide and attract extra income for the practice.

Practices will choose which services they wish to provide. PCOs will be responsible for ensuring all services are supplied in the area and SHAs will audit and monitor services.

PMS contracts allow GPs to transfer their contracts for patient care to PCOs and become employed instead of being self-employed (independent contractors).

Finally, the government, through its many agencies and the **Commission for Health Improvement**, monitors and audits services, establishing the cost-benefit analysis of all these treatments and methods of care.

However, the value to the individual and the family is incalculable, a loved one's life being irreplaceable, beyond any costing system produced by authorities or statisticians!

Abbreviations
(New GP Contracts 2003/2004)

AP	Aspiration Payments
CHI	Commission for Health Improvement
CPPIH	Commission for Patient and Public Involvement in Health
DES	Directed Enhanced Services
EPI	Expert Patient Initiatives
ES	Essential Services
HCP	Holistic Care Payments
HDA	Health Development Agency
HPE	Health Promotion England
LES	Local Enhanced Services
NCAA	National Clinical Assessment Authority
NES	National Enhanced Services
NICE	National Institute for Clinical Excellence
NSF	National Service Framework
OSC	Overview and Scrutiny Committee
PCO	Primary Care Organisation
PALS	Patient Advisory and Liaison Service
PCT	Primary Care Trust
PF	Patient's Forum
SHA	Strategic Health Authority
SSDP	Strategic Service Development Plan

(Other abbreviations and terms appear in the previous chapters).

Chapter 20

Screening tests

Screening

Screening is the detection of disease before the presence of symptoms.

It is a form of secondary preventive medicine, aiming to detect the presence or absence of a disease or condition. It may be done on an individual (**opportunistic screening** at the practice) or through **mass screening** of the whole population.

The purpose of screening is to prevent early death, reduce disease, and improve the quality of life. The principle is based on the fact that certain diseases and conditions can be recognised by a simple test well before any serious disease has developed or symptoms occurred.

There are certain ethical requirements before screening is approved:

- The disease being searched for should always be a **serious** one

- The screening test itself should always be **simple** to perform and **not give false results**

- As far as possible the test should be an **objective rather than a subjective** test; i.e. the results must be clear and not left to individual opinion

- The test should be **safe** and **not induce undue fear** in people tested; counselling of participants is important, they must understand its nature

- **Effective treatment** must be available for the disease or condition for which the screening is being performed.

Antenatal screening

Tests performed on pregnant women are important in detecting abnormalities of both mother and fetus at an early stage. One of the main aims is to ensure that a healthy baby is born to a healthy mother.

The following screening tests are performed:

- **Urine testing** to detect any abnormal content e.g. albumin may suggest a urine infection or kidney disease. Its occurrence later in pregnancy may indicate developing **toxaemia** of pregnancy. Sugar can indicate **diabetes mellitus**.

- **Blood pressure** to detect its state at the start of pregnancy and watch for any sign of **hypertension** developing – indicative of developing **toxaemia** of pregnancy (see terminology of the female reproductive system, Chapter 11). All measurements should be done with the pregnant patient either **sitting or lying on their left side** as lying on their back (**supine**) may produce a large drop in blood pressure.

Blood tests

Antenatal blood tests are carried out to:

- determine **blood group** and **Rhesus factor**

- detect **anaemia**

- determine random **blood glucose**

- detect immunity to **rubella** (German measles)

- detect **syphilis** if present in order to treat and prevent fetal deformities

- detect **hepatitis B** antibodies

- detect **HIV** antibodies

- detect **sickle-cell anaemia** and **thalassaemia** (test offered to women of West Indian, African and Mediterranean origin).

An examination **per vaginam** may be performed at first visit to detect any abnormality of the reproductive system and the size of the uterus.

Later visits

Urine, blood pressure, weight, height of fundus of uterus and any fluid retention (**oedema**) will be checked at each visit. The main aim of detecting the early onset of **toxaemia of pregnancy (PET)** in order to avoid **eclampsia** where fits occur and death of baby and mother can result, is paramount in antenatal care. Rapid weight gain, fluid retention, albumin in the urine and hypertension are all signs of the developing condition.

Blood tests at 28 weeks
- Full **blood count**
- **Antibody screening**
- Random **blood glucose**.

Ultrasound scan

Ultrasound waves build up a picture of the fetus in the uterus (*see Figure 72, in Chapter 17, page 164*). This is used to:

- check fetus' **measurements**, size for dates, growth etc.
- check for **multiple pregnancy**
- detect **abnormalities**, particularly of head or spine (**spina bifida**)
- check position of placenta (**placenta praevia**).

Procedure

The woman is asked to drink plenty of fluid as a full bladder produces a better picture of the uterus by pushing it up into the abdominal cavity. Jelly is then placed on the abdomen with the patient lying on her back.

An instrument is passed backwards and forwards over the skin and high frequency sound is beamed through the abdomen. This is reflected back and creates a picture on the screen.

Nuchal translucency scan:

This ultrasound scan measures the thickest tissue of the nape of the neck to detect **Down's syndrome** and **neural tube (brain and spinal chord) defects**. It is carried out at between 11 and 13 weeks.

Amniocentesis

Ultrasound transducer

Amniotic fluid is drawn off

Amniotic fluid

Fetus

Figure 86: Amniocentesis

Alpha-fetoprotein test

This is a blood test performed at about 16-18 weeks of pregnancy; used to determine the level of **alpha-fetoprotein (AF)** in the blood which, if raised, may indicate a **neural tube defect**, such as **spina bifida** or **ancencephaly** (undeveloped brain). low levels may suggest other abnormalities such as **Down's syndrome**.

'Triple screening' or 'triple plus' test

This is a blood test for **Down's syndrome**. It combines the levels of AFP with levels of two hormones present in the mother's blood and predicts the likelihood of Down's syndrome.

Amniocentesis

The test (*see Figure 86*) may be offered at 12-18 weeks of pregnancy to older women (over 35 years) where the risk of Down's syndrome is higher, or where there is a family history of the condition. Positive testing for spina bifida or Down's syndrome with the AFP test will usually be followed by **amniocentesis**. It produces a very small increase in the risk of **spontaneous abortion** (miscarriage).

Procedure

An ultrasound test will first determine the position of the fetus and placenta. After a local anaesthetic, a needle is passed through the wall of the abdomen to withdraw amniotic fluid which surrounds the fetus. This fluid is sent to the laboratory for testing for chemical content and also the genetic content of cells. In Down's syndrome the chromosomes are abnormal – a splitting of number 21 or the presence of an extra chromosome. Other abnormalities will also be investigated.

Chorionic villus sampling

This test, available in some hospitals, can be carried out earlier than amniocentesis at eight to 11 weeks of pregnancy. It has a higher risk of abortion than amniocentesis. It is used to detect:

- **Down's syndrome**
- inherited diseases, such as **sickle-cell anaemia** or **thalassaemia**
- some sex-linked diseases, for example **haemophilia**.

It will not detect spina bifida. The full effects of this test upon the developing fetus are not yet known.

Procedure

Using ultrasound as a guide, a fine tube is passed through the vagina and cervix, or sometimes through the abdomen, and a small piece of the developing placenta, called **chorionic tissue**, is withdrawn. This is sent to the laboratory for testing.

Fetoscopy

This is a direct inspection of the fetus via a tube in the uterus or a camera attached to the needle piercing into the amniotic fluid. Performed at 15 – 18 weeks. It increases the risk of miscarriage and infection.

Cordocentesis

This is the direct sampling of fetal blood through the **umbilical cord** or **intra-hepatic vein** of the fetus, to detect genetic abnormalities, infection or well-being of the fetus (performed from 12 weeks onwards).

Tests on the newborn

A baby is completely examined soon after birth, to detect any **congenital abnormalities** so that measures can be introduced to minimise resulting problems. Conditions such as **club foot** or **cleft palate** are an obvious handicap. The screening for **undescended testicles** in males and other conditions is continued throughout infancy and childhood.

Apgar rating (see also Chapter 11, page 108)

This is a test performed on all newborn and involves awarding of a rating for the following:

- **heart rate**
- **respiratory effort**
- **muscle tone**
- **reflex state**
- **colour.**

A baby in the perfect state at birth will score two points for each category giving a total score of 10.

This test is repeated at certain intervals following birth. It gives good indication of the probability of developmental problems and/or epilepsy, due to lack of oxygen at birth.

Blood tests

These include blood tests for the detection of:

- **Phenylketonuria (Guthrie test)**

- **Hypothyroidism** or cretinism.

The Guthrie test, also known as **'the heel-prick test'** as the blood is taken from the newborn's heel, is performed after feeding has been established (usually at five days). It is used to detect a chemical known as **phenylketone** which is an abnormality present in babies unable to properly break down certain proteins. If not detected at birth and special diet implemented, it causes damage to mental development.

Hypothyroidism, if detected, can be treated by the administration of **thyroxine** and the abnormal mental development will be prevented.

Otalani's test

Otalani's test for **congenital dislocation of hip** is done following birth. It is also known as the 'click test'. When the baby's hips are rotated a click is heard if a dislocation is present.

Children

Screening tests for children are done routinely by the health visitor, medical officer or GP in **child health surveillance**.

These tests are done at different ages, the main concentration being in the infant and preschool periods.

Five main areas are involved for developmental screening:

- **locomotion** and **posture**

- **muscle control** and **function**

- **speech** and **language**

- **growth**

- **social development**.

Hearing testing is an important area of screening, and **routine testing** is an important tool for preventing loss of language development due to unidentified problems. **Squints** are usually minimised if early detection is made.

Adult screening

Tests for recognising **precancerous conditions** are now recommended and include those for **carcinoma of the cervix, breast cancer, large bowel cancer** and **testicular and prostate cancer**.

Screening for coronary **heart disease, hypertension** and **obesity** are also very important. These are discussed in Chapter 19.

Cervical smears

The **'Pap' test**, named after the man who introduced it – Papanicolaou – is one of the foremost screening tests at present. In England and Wales a programme of screening for women aged from 25 years to 64 years is available on the NHS (20 to 60 years in Scotland), although women may request the test after this age. Targets are at present set at 80% for the higher level and 50% for the lower. This will exclude those women who have had a hysterectomy with the removal of the cervix. An automatic three-year **recall scheme** is in operation, although some PCOs still only recall five-yearly. It is planned that the age ranges will be extended by 2004 to 70 years of age.

The smear must not be taken during **menstruation**. Cells are removed with a special spatula (**Aylesbury**) or **cytobrush** from the area of the cervical canal. It is important that they are removed from the correct area. These are then placed on a glass slide and immediately **'fixed'** with fixing solution. This prevents the cells from drying out so that the laboratory can read the smear. The 'fixed' smear should be placed in a cool area and allowed to dry for 20 minutes (*see page 176*).

The patient's details are written on the slide and the **cervical cytology form** must be completed. The slide is dispatched to the cytology section of the pathology department for examination and reporting.

It is of vital importance that the patient is informed how she will obtain the results of the test. Patients should be informed in writing of any abnormal result or request for repeat of the test if an inadequate smear has been sent. Deaths have occurred due to failure to follow this procedure.

The following are some factors predisposing to cervical cancer:

- **Early age at first intercourse**

- **Many sexual partners**

- **Genital warts** (including those on partners)

- **Genital herpes**

- **Smoking** – 20 cigarettes per day increases the risk by seven times.

Promiscuity is considered to be a factor as the more partners involved the more likely the causative factor (the wart virus is a strong suspect) may be encountered.

Positive results state findings such as:

- **dysplasia**   abnormal form

- **dyskaryosis**   abnormal nucleus

- **koilocytosis**   having a spoon-shaped appearance, warty changes.

Depending on the degree of abnormality of the cervical smear, the patient may be checked in six months or referred to the gynaecologist for a colposcopy and treatment.

Liquid-based cytology (LBC)

NICE (National Institute for Clinical Excellence) has recently approved the use of this test for cervical cytology on the grounds of cost and efficiency. At present, many cervical smears (Pap test) are classed as 'inadequate', requiring further smear tests. Reading of these is often marred by mistakes.

In this new test (known about for several years but only recently available on the NHS), a brush-like device collects cells from the neck of the womb (**cervix**). This is then rinsed in a preservative, making the test reading by technicians, easier to analyse. It is estimated that more lives will be saved by this new method.

Breast examination

Self-examination (*see Figure 87*) is still recommended for detection of this condition, but unfortunately if the lump can be felt the cancer is usually already well established. In the UK one in 12 women suffer from breast cancer at some time in their lives.

It is important that women are "breast aware", i.e. they should be familiar with the look and feel of their breasts and be able to recognise any changes.

Figure 87 shows the recommended procedure for self-examination of the breast. Women who find any changes in their breasts should immediately go to their GP, practice nurse of well-woman clinic. Most breast changes are **not** cancer – but it is important that any change is investigated quickly.

Mammography

This X-ray examination is recommended for women of **50 years to 64 years** although patients are able to request their inclusion beyond this age. It is presently proposed to extend the recommended age from 64 years to 70 years by 2004. Breast tissue in women younger than 50 is not considered to provide an accurate reading due to its density, prior to the effects of the **menopause**.

It should be remembered that, although rare, men (as well as women) are susceptible to breast cancer. A high fat diet is thought to increase the risk of its development in both sexes.

The following are danger signs and should be reported immediately to the doctor:

- **Change in the shape or size of the breast**

- **An inversion, change in position or in colour, of the nipple**

- **Nipple discharge, dimpling, denting or discolouration of the skin**

- **A lump or swelling in the breast, in the armpit, or in the arm near the collar bone (clavicle)**

- **Pain in the breast or the armpit.**

Examining your own breasts

During each of the following stages, you should turn from side to side whilst carefully looking at your breasts in a mirror:

A Place your hands by your sides

B Raise your arms above your head

C Place your hands on your hips with your elbows pushed forward

How to feel for changes:

D Feel each breast in turn. Keeping your fingers together and flat, firmly move over the whole breast, including the nipple and armpit

E You may prefer to do this lying down

Figure 87: Self-examination of the breasts *(adapted from North West Thames Breast Programme leaflet)*

Health Care Trusts have introduced mass screening for women of the appropriate ages and a three-year **recall scheme** is in operation.

Testicular screening

Testicular screening is recommended for men, and routine **manual examination** of the scrotum is advised for detecting any abnormal development. Advances have been made in the treatment of this rapidly growing cancer.

Prostate cancer

For men with **prostatism** (enlargement of the prostate gland) a blood test for **PSA (prostatic-specific antigen)** will detect an increase in levels of this substance which may indicate the presence of carcinoma. There is growing pressure to increase the use of this test in men as is done in the USA.

Cancer code

There is a 10-point European **cancer code** which aims to encourage people to live a healthy lifestyle to help avoid development of cancer. It includes:

- Stop smoking

- Go easy on the alcohol – 21 units for men and 14 for women are the recommended weekly maximums

- Avoid being overweight

- Take care in the sun

- Observe the Health and Safety at Work Regulations

- Cut down on fatty foods

- Eat plenty of fresh fruit and vegetables and other foods containing fibre

- See your doctor if there is an unexplained change in your normal health which lasts for more than two weeks.

Cholesterol levels

A blood test for cholesterol levels is included in routine screening of at-risk adults. This is one of the fat components of the blood and is thought to be a factor in disease. A **cholesterol level** above 5.0 mmol/l is considered an unnecessary risk . The aim should be to reduce it by 20% - 25%. **LDL** levels should be <3.0 and, if greater, the aim should be to reduce them by 30%.

Levels should be checked in those with a family history of premature coronary disease and hypercholesterolaemia (high levels of cholesterol in the blood).

Diet is the first action to be taken in trying to reduce cholesterol/lipid levels. The **'statin'** group of drugs is now being widely prescribed for those with **CHD risk**. Research indicates that **high density lipids, (HDLs)** are beneficial. They also reduce inflammation found at the site of fatty plaque deposits in the lining of arteries. This reduces the risk of these detaching and causing blockage (**occlusion**) of coronary arteries. (The **low density lipids, LDLs** are considered harmful).

Other tests

There are many other conditions where screening would benefit the patient, including:

- **glaucoma**

- **tuberculosis**

- **large bowel cancer**

- **diabetes mellitus**

- **hypertension.**

Many of relevant tests are covered in Chapter 21.

HIV screening

The screening to detect antibodies to **human immunodeficiency virus (HIV)** is very carefully controlled. As there is no cure and the financial and social problems resulting are so devastating for the patient, counselling must be given before any test is undertaken. Anonymous testing is being performed on blood taken from patients for other reasons. This is never associated back to the source and is purely to gain some knowledge of the spread of the disease.

New patient screening

This is a form of screening which is required under the 1990 Contract and continues with the **2003 GP Contract**. Routine testing of urine and taking of **blood pressure** will often identify undetected health problems. Information on **lifestyle** and **family history** should identify at-risk individuals.

Screening of elderly people

Routine yearly screening of patients of **75 years and over** is also a requirement for GPs and various factors are assessed (*Figure 88*), including:

- **sensory function**
- **mobility**
- **mental condition**
- **physical condition including continence**
- **social environment**
- **use of medicines.**

Elderly people are often suffering from the **side-effects of medication**, as with a reduced liver and kidney function due to the ageing process, smaller dosages may be required.

Screening of the elderly card

Figure 88: Screening of the elderly card

Abbreviations

AFP — Alpha-fetoprotein

AIDS — Acquired immuno-deficiency syndrome

CHD — Coronary heart disease

CIN I-IV — Cervical intra-epithelial neoplasia (classified according to the invasiveness of the neoplasm. CIN I denotes non-invasive)

CVS — Chorionic villus sampling

HDL — High density lipids

HIV — Human immunodeficiency virus

LDL — Low density lipids

LBC — Liquid-based cytology

NICE — National Institute for Clinical Excellence

PET — Pre-eclamptic toxaemia (of pregnancy)

PSA — Prostatic-specific antigen

TC — Total cholesterol

Terminology

Dyskaryosis — Abnormal nucleus

Dysplasia — Abnormal form

Koilocytosis — Having a spoon-shaped appearance, warty changes

Metaplasia — Type of cells found to be growing outside their normal area, e.g. cells that are normally only found in the lining of the stomach are found to have spread to the oesophagus

Chapter **21**

Miscellaneous tests

Blood pressure measurement

This is a common test used in general practice to measure **arterial blood pressure**. Arterial blood pressure is the tension/pressure exerted in the walls of the arteries.

It is affected by the following factors (all of which can alter with age or illness (see Chapter 5):

- Beating of the heart (**cardiac output**)

- Amount (**volume**) and thickness (**viscosity**) of the **circulating blood**

- Resistance of the **peripheral arterioles** (diameter of the small arteries)

- The **elasticity** of the walls of the **main arteries**.

The blood pressure is measured in **millimeters of mercury - mmHg.**

The **systolic pressure** is the pressure exerted against the walls of the arteries when the ventricles are contracting. The **diastolic pressure** is the pressure exerted on the walls of the arteries when the heart is relaxed. The condition of **hypertension** is diagnosed when the readings are abnormally high on three separate occasions.

Blood pressure fluctuates throughout the day and night and is usually lower in the evening than in the morning.

Procedure

Blood pressure can be measured using a **sphygmomanometer** (*see Figure 89*) a special cuff is applied to the arm of the patient, who should be lying or sitting and be relaxed. With patients who are on **antihypertensive** drugs, it should also be recorded with the patient standing.

The **pulse** should be felt (**palpated**) by hand, at the **brachial artery** (*see Figure 90*) after the cuff has been attached to the patient's arm and connected to the sphygmomanometer. The cuff should now be inflated until the brachial pulse can no longer be felt. The measurement should be noted. The cuff should be released and the patient allowed to rest for 1 to 2 minutes. The cuff is now reflated and pumped up to 30 mmHg **above** the reading where the pulse disappeared previously.

A **stethoscope** is applied to the pulse of the brachial artery at the inner aspect of the **elbow** flexure. The cuff is inflated to obliterate the pulse and then the air in the cuff is slowly released. The pulse will return as a tapping sound. This will be the reading of the systolic pressure. These sounds will continue but will then become fainter and rapidly diminish until they disappear. It will be at this point that the diastolic pressure will be interpreted. Readings should be measured to the nearest 2mmHg.

Sphygmomanometers containing mercury are being phased out (in favour of new electronic meters), although they have *not* been banned by the **Medical Devices Agency** at the present time. Most health professionals consider that sphygmomanometers give more accurate readings.

There are many causes for false readings, including:

- Temperature

- Smoking

- Recent consumption of caffeine or alcohol

- Taking of vigorous exercise, within the last 30 minutes

- Incorrect stance

- Incorrect application

- Incorrect size and height of the cuff

- Incorrect gauge at the incorrect level

- Recording on the relevant arm of those who have had a mastectomy.

In very low blood pressure (e.g. in severe shock) the systolic pressure may be obtained by palpation of the radial pulse. There will be no obtainable diastolic reading.

Ambulatory monitoring of blood pressure (ABPM)

In some people the blood pressure is higher when measured by a health professional (so called **'white coat hypertension'**). Normal readings are likely to be lower when taken at home (by **ABPM**). A device to measure blood pressure is worn by the patient while they

Korotkoff sounds

(the sounds heard when measuring blood pressure with a sphygmomanometer).

Five Phases of Blood Pressure

Phase	Sounds
I	Faint tapping sounds heard as the cuff deflates (systolic reading)
II	Soft swishing sounds
III	Rhythmic, sharp, distinct tapping sounds
IV	Soft tapping sounds that become faint
V	No sound (diastolic reading)

Equipment used to measure blood pressure

Figure 89: Equipment used to measure blood pressure

Veins and arteries of the elbow

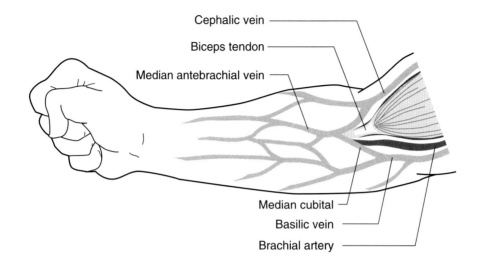

Figure 90: The veins and arteries of the elbow

continue with their normal activities. Blood pressure is usually recorded over a 24-hour period and normal activity should continue, excepting when the automatic recordings are being made. During these periods, the arm should be kept still and driving should not take place. A diary of activities of the patient, during the recording period can be most helpful. Recordings by day are usually taken every 20-30 minutes, whilst by night they are usually every 1 – 2 hours.

Electrocardiography (ECG)

An electrocardiogram (ECG) is a recording of the electrical impulses of the heart muscle as it beats. The apparatus transfers the impulses into a graph tracing so that they can be read and interpreted (*see Figure 91*). It is used to detect possible irregular rhythm and damage caused by myocardial infarct (coronary thrombosis). Most general practices have their own portable apparatus.

Tracings

The normal tracing of the heart is shown as the following:

The P-wave	illustrates the **contraction of the atria**
The QRS complex	illustrates the conduction of the nerve impulse through the **bundle of His** in the **ventricular septum** of the heart into the ventricles
The T-wave	illustrates the recovery of the ventricles.

Procedure

The leads, which are labelled for arms, legs and chest are placed on the patient, who must be at rest and lying on his/her back (*see Figure 92*). Special conducting jelly is applied to the plates attached and any excessive hair is removed with the patient's permission, by shaving.

Electrocardiography

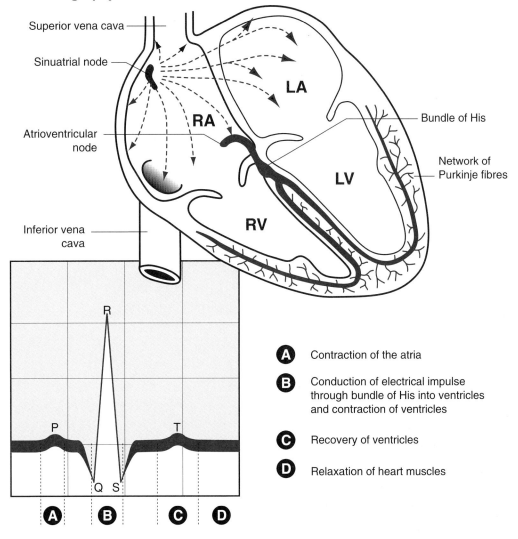

Figure 91: The conducting system in the heart

The following labels appear in the figure:

- Superior vena cava
- Sinuatrial node
- Atrioventricular node
- Inferior vena cava
- LA
- RA
- Bundle of His
- Network of Purkinje fibres
- LV
- RV

ECG trace labels: P, Q, R, S, T

- **A** Contraction of the atria
- **B** Conduction of electrical impulse through bundle of His into ventricles and contraction of ventricles
- **C** Recovery of ventricles
- **D** Relaxation of heart muscles

Any electrical interference must be eliminated; this may be from:

- wrist watch
- other electrical apparatus,
- shivering of the patient if cold or apprehensive
- main lead passing too close to the limb leads
- nearby electric radiator.

Angiography

This shows the state of the blood vessels, when a **radio-opaque medium** (a dye that shows up under X-rays) is inserted intravenously into the patient's arm. Pictures are taken, which enable the physician to see any blockage or narrowing indicating lack of blood supply (**ischaemia**) to an area, especially to the heart

Electrocardiography: position of the chest leads

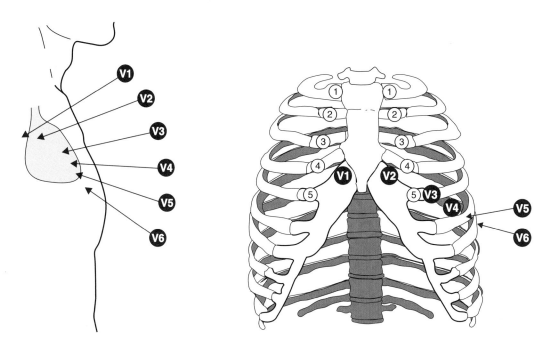

Figure 92: Electrocardiography: position of the chest leads

muscle itself. It is performed prior to making a decision to perform a **coronary bypass graft** operation or the insertion of a **'stent'**.

Exercise stress test

The patient is wired up for an **ECG** and tracings recorded, as increasing **exercise** is performed. This may demonstrate a hidden problem with the functioning of the heart, which may only show under pressure.

Thallium scanning (radionuclide)

This procedure is used to demonstrate the width of the blood vessels of the heart (**patency of the lumen**), which has not been demonstrated on other tests. Radioactive thallium is injected, intravenously and pictures of the heart taken. The thallium is shown in the vessels, which would otherwise be seen merely as shadows. It is used to demonstrate hidden deficiency in the blood supply to the heart

muscle itself (**ischaemic heart disease**), in some family members, where siblings have suffered sudden death from unsuspected heart disease at an early age. A special type of camera is used. It should be noted that women who are breast feeding must not do so, for at least 48 hours following this test, as the milk will remain radioactive.

Insertion of stent

Narrowing of a coronary artery, due to fatty plaques and loss of its elasticity, can be temporarily treated with the insertion of a **'stent'** which hold open the artery **stricture**, so that a better blood supply is delivered to the heart muscle. This is a quicker measure provided, when a coronary bypass is unattainable but immediate treatment is required, as is shown by the prior performance of an angiogram. (See Chapter 16, page 51 for an angiograph of a stent).

Electroencephalography (EEG)

An electroencephalogram (EEG) is used to detect **abnormal electrical activity of the brain** in the diagnosis of **epilepsy** and other **lesions** (abnormalities) such as **tumours** of the brain. The electrical activity is converted by the apparatus into a graph which can be read and interpreted.

Special **conducting jelly** is applied to the scalp and the leads attached. Differing areas are read and at one point lights are flashed to detect any abnormal response. Readings are taken with the patient's eyes closed and then open. The effect of **hyperventilation** (over-breathing) is also recorded.

Types of waves

These include **alpha, beta** and **theta** waves, the names given to the various types of electrical discharge from the brain.

Early morning urine specimen (EMU)

This is a test for **pregnancy**. It is usually performed in the laboratory and the specimen collected must be a concentrated one, i.e. the first urine passed in the morning before drinking, and it must be uncontaminated by blood (in cases of threatened abortion etc.). If necessary a tampon must be inserted before the urine is passed.

The chemical test is based on the presence of **HCG (human chorionic gonadotrophic hormone)** present in the urine in pregnancy and verifies the presence of this chemical which is produced by the developing chorionic layer of the embryo.

A negative test does not necessarily signify that the patient is not pregnant. The test should be repeated. It is necessary for sufficient of the HCG to be present to give a positive result.

Midstream specimen of urine (MSU)

This test is performed to detect the presence of **protein** and **micro-organisms** in urine.

It is essential that the specimen is free from

contamination by body fluids which may be present on the external genitalia and it is for this reason that it is the middle part, or 'mid-stream', is used. The patient is requested to wash the external genitalia before passing the specimen.

The first urine is passed in the normal way into the toilet, thus washing away any mucus present in the urethra. The next urine passed is received into the receptacle provided for the specimen, while the surplus urine is again passed into the toilet.

It is important that all specimens are immediately and correctly labelled to avoid any mistakes occurring. *Children or other vulnerable patients should never be left alone or given a glass receptacle for this test.* A suitable sterile jug or receiver should be used.

If the patient is to collect the specimen at home, a handout with full instructions on how to collect it is invaluable.

The specimen will usually be sent to the laboratory for culture and sensitivity (see Chapter 17).

Routine urine testing

This consists of testing for a variety of abnormalities.

Normal fresh urine is a sterile aromatic amber liquid with a specific gravity of 1.005 to 1.030 and a pH of five to seven (slightly acid).

The specific gravity will depend on the concentration of the urine. It can indicate disease of the kidney and other conditions, e.g. diabetes insipidus.

Abnormal pH may indicate renal or other disease, but fever and diarrhoea will also affect this reading as well as the specific gravity.

Abnormal constituents tested for are:

Bile salts	present in certain types of jaundice
Bilirubin	present in certain types of jaundice
Blood	present in tumours of the bladder, cystitis, urethritis and kidney stones

Glucose	present in diabetes mellitus and when taking certain drugs
Ketones also known as **acetone**	present when fats are inadequately burnt by body; present in diabetes mellitus imbalance acidosis and starvation states
Nitrites	present in bacterial infection of the urine
Phenylketones	present when the patient is unable to metabolise properly the nutrient phenylalanine. Accumulation of this in blood stream can cause mental retardation.
Protein	usually albumin and blood – present in infection, hypertension etc.
Urobilinogen	present in certain types of jaundice.

There are numerous **reagent test strips** on the market and it is vital that the urine is fresh and that the 'in-date' reagent strips are read at the correct time limits. *Instructions must be carefully followed, both for testing and storage of the components.*

Blood tests performed at practice premises

Many practices offer onsite blood testing as a fast service to patients, although these have decreased since concern of cross-infection from body fluids has been highlighted.

Glucose estimation

This determines the current levels present in blood. It is used for assisting in diagnosis of diabetes mellitus, routine monitoring of glucose levels and screening of patients where appropriate. Further laboratory tests are used to ensure accuracy. Reagent strips are used as in urine testing. There are also meters which measure content. Capillary blood is used, gathered from finger/heel prick as appropriate.

Cholesterol estimation

This is often offered as part of the 'well-person' check and can be used to back up dietary advice and assess patients' response to diet or medication (See also Chapter 20, page 234 for information on cholesterol testing).

Other tests

Some surgeries offer the following tests:

Haemoglobin	measure of the oxygen-carrying capacity of the blood
Erythrocyte sedimentation rate (ESR)	rate at which red blood cells separate from plasma.

Lumbar puncture (LP)

This is a common **neurological invasive test**, performed to detect abnormality of pressure of the **cerebrospinal fluid** (as in a **tumour**) or **infection** (**meningitis**).

Cerebrospinal fluid (**CSF**) is drawn off from the spinal canal space of the **meninges** at the level, of the **3rd and 4th lumbar vertebra** in an adult. (In adults, the spinal cord terminates above the 2nd lumbar vertebra, so there is no danger of hitting the cord itself).

The patient is usually curled into the fetal position and must remain very still. The fluid is placed into a sterile specimen pot for laboratory investigation, (chemical content, culture and sensitivity), after a meter has been attached to measure pressure within the meninges. It is observed whether the fluid is cloudy or clear or under pressure. A cloudy fluid would indicate infection is present.

This procedure is also used to insert drugs such as **antibiotics** in the treatment of infections or **cytotoxic drugs** (able to kill primitive dividing cells) to treat **leukaemia**.

It is important to ensure that the area does not leak any fluid, after the test has been completed and that the dressing remains dry. Lying flat, following the test, will help prevent the patient from having a severe headache.

Monitoring blood glucose at home

The patient pricks their finger (usually with a special "pen" designed for this purpose) and collects a drop of blood on a reagent strip. The strip is then put into an electronic monitoring device that provides an accurate reading of the blood glucose level. The patient records the reading in a log book.

Figure 93: Monitoring blood glucose at home

Temperature, pulse and respirations (TPR)

The common tests performed to indicate whether there is any indication of abnormality such as fever, infection, bleeding etc. It is the vital centres in the brain stem which control these body functions.

Temperature

There are many types of **thermometer** (*see Figures 94 and 95*). The thermometer used mostly at the GP's surgery is the **electronic ear thermometer**. New disposable covers must be used for each patient for all types of thermometers to prevent cross-infection.

Normal temperature measurements	
Oral	37˚C
Rectal	37.6˚C
Axillary (armpit)	36.4˚C
Tympanic (ear)	37˚C
35˚C and below is called **hypothermia**	
40˚C and above is called **hyperpyrexia**	

Electronic thermometers

The **electronic ear thermometer** (*see Figure 95*) must be inserted far enough into the canal and left in place, until a bleep is heard. Mercury thermometers have generally been replaced by digital or electronic ones. They should never be placed in the mouth of anyone under 5 years or anyone who has fits or other similar conditions. Rectal measurement must only be used by professionals trained to understand the process and its dangers.

Types of thermometer

Mercury thermometer

Thermodot thermometer

LCD thermometer

Electronic ear thermometer

Figure 94: Types of thermometers

Hypothermia

Hypothermia in the very young, the elderly and those exposed to freezing conditions, is usually measured with a special low reading thermometer. This condition occurs when the core temperature drops to 35 °C and below. Once the temperature falls to < 30 °C, it is usually fatal as very little can be done to reverse the process.

Hyperpyrexia

Hyperpyrexia is a condition in which the body temperature rises to 40 °C and above. At this temperature, the body cells start to 'cook' and the 'thermostat' in the brain no longer works. Causes are fever from **infection**, prolonged **exposure to heat** and the use of drugs such as **'ecstasy'**. The pulse is full (strong) and bounding. **'Heat-stroke'** is the lay term for this condition.

With these two extremes, the temperature control centre in the brain is no longer capable of maintaining mechanisms for achieving correction of heat.

Pulse

The pulse can be felt where an artery crosses a bone, near the surface of the body. It reflects the pumping of the heart and the rebound in the artery wall. It is felt using 2 or 3 fingers (not the thumb, which has its own pulse) placed upon the pulse area – usually at the wrist (radial) on the thumb side and gently pressed.

Measurement will indicate any deviation from the normal range. If the temperature is elevated, the pulse will normally increase accordingly. However, **emotion, fever** and **exercise** will all affect it.

The rate, **volume** (strength) and rhythm should be recorded over one minute. In **shock**, the volume will be very weak and the pulse easily compressed, but also very rapid (120 plus). Panic attacks will also produce a rapid pulse.

The act of breathing may cause an irregular pulse. Asking the patient to hold their breath for a few seconds will quickly result in return to a normal rhythm (**sinus rhythm**), if this is the cause of the irregularity.

Using an electronic ear thermometer

A For children under one year, pull the ear straight back

B For children over one year and for adults, pull the ear up and back

C Place the probe gently into the ear canal ensuring a snug fit

Eardrum

D Press the start button. Some models may 'beep' when the temperature has been recorded

Eardrum

Figure 95: Using an electronic ear thermometer

Normal pulse range
(number of beats per minute)

In the newborn	**140**
Infants	**120**
Children at 10 years	**80 - 90**
Adults	**60 - 80**
	(average 72)

Emotion, exercise, age and health will all affect the pulse rate.

Respirations

Respiration reflects the **metabolism** of the body and will vary according to the activity being performed. Measurement of this will indicate any increase or decrease from the normal range.

The number of times the chest rises and falls is counted per minute (**inspirations** and **expirations**). The breathing in and out, counts as one respiration.

There are many reasons for changes in respiration rates, and other factors will be taken into consideration when interpreting the results. If a person is aware that their respiration is being counted, the normal breathing pattern will alter. It is therefore often recorded at the same time as their pulse so that the patient is unaware that their respirations are being observed. In cases of **severe haemorrhage** (bleeding), the respirations will eventually become gasping, and are known as **'air-hunger'**. This indicates the lack of oxygen available to the tissues caused by insufficient red blood cells to transport it.

Chest infections and **heart failure** are also among conditions which will cause rapid breathing.

Note: if a patient has recently had a hot or cold drink, been smoking or had any alcohol or other drug, e.g. caffeine, the TPRs will be affected.

Dual energy X-ray absorptometry (DEXA)

This **bone density screening test** may be performed to determine the loss of normal density of bone (**osteoporosis**) and those who may be at risk of this condition. The bone becomes spongy in this condition as the normal **calcium salts** and the **protein** and **collagen**, are unable to be deposited. This leads to an increase in the risk of breaking bones (**fractures**) in every normal day to day activity. Loss of **oestrogen** in the female after **menopause** is an important factor but men also develop this condition.

Those recommended for DEXA screening by the National Osteoporosis Foundation are:

- Postmenopausal women below 65 who have risk factors for osteoporosis

- Women aged 65 years and older

- Postmenopausal women with fractures

- Women whose decision to use medication to stop bone loss will depend on the result of the screening.

If bone density screening is done, it is recommended it should only be performed on those willing to be treated.

Abbreviations

ABMP	ambulatory blood pressure monitoring
BP	blood pressure
BS	blood sugar
C°	celsius
DEXA	dual energy x-ray absorptometry (for the diagnosis of osteoporosis)
ECG	electrocardiograph
EEG	electro-encephalograph
EMU	early morning urine
ESR	erythrocyte sedimentation rate
FBS	fasting blood sugar
HCG	human chorionic gonadotrophic hormone
LP	lumbar puncture
mmHg	millimetres of mercury
MSU	midstream urine/ specimen of urine
TPR	temperature, pulse and respirations

Terminology

Diastole	phase when the heart is relaxing
Systole	phase when the heart is contracting
Urinalysis	testing of urine

Immunisation

Introduction

This is one of the most important areas of preventive medicine. It is concerned with the protection of the individual from specific diseases. The first instance of immunisation in the modern world, in the late 18th century, was carried out by **Jenner** who vaccinated people with the cowpox virus to produce immunity against the killer virus of **smallpox**.

Immunity

Immunity is the ability of the body to fight disease. It may be **natural** or **artificial**.

Natural immunity

Natural immunity is either an **inbuilt resistance** to a disease, (e.g. human beings do not suffer from distemper found in dogs), or one that is **'acquired'** by coming into contact with the actual disease and overcoming it.

Active immunity

This is a state in which the body has produced antibodies to a disease. It may be **natural** (by suffering an attack of the disease) or **artificial**, i.e. by introducing the weakened disease, or its poisons, into the body to allow the body to produce antibodies to the disease without suffering the harmful effects of the disease itself. This is the principle of immunisation.

Live viruses, such as the measles virus, are **attenuated** (weakened) so that they do not cause damage to the body but are still able to stimulate the body's immune system to produce antibodies against the virus.

Dead viruses, or bacteria, are also used in some vaccines as well as **weakened toxins**, e.g. **diphtheria, tetanus** and **pertussis** (whooping cough) **vaccines**.

Several doses at differing intervals usually have to be given to produce a sufficiently high level of **antibodies** to achieve immunity. This immunity will be **long-lasting** as the body has learnt how to produce the specific antibodies to the disease. It will immediately recognise the foreign protein of the disease should the person subsequently come into contact with it.

Passive immunity

This is achieved when **antibodies**, or **antitoxins**, produced by **another person or animal** are introduced into a person's body to fight disease. This immunity only lasts as long as the anti-bodies are present in the body, as the individual does *not* produce his/her own antibodies. Therefore this is only a **temporary immunity**, e.g. occurring naturally in **breast feeding** and artificially when **immunoglobulin**, containing **hepatitis A** antibodies, is given to travellers, or susceptible people are given immunoglobulin against an attack of chicken-pox.

Reasons for immunisation

Immunisation is carried out to:

- **Protect** the individual

- **Limit the spread** of a disease

- Produce a **'herd' immunity**

- Assist in **eradication** of a disease.

Recommended schedules

The Department of Health, through its Chief Medical Officer, recommends a schedule for children and travellers (see the **'Green Book'** – *Immunisation against infectious disease*, HMSO).

Advice should always be sought from the Community Physician/Medical Officer when there is any query regarding suitablility and dosage for the individual patient.

Table 9 shows the present recommendations for children and young persons:

- **Live vaccines** (BCG, oral poliomyelitis, measles, mumps, rubella) are either given together or separated by 3 weeks.

- **DTwP** contains whole cell pertussis vaccine

- **DTaP** contains acellular pertusis vaccine

- **DTwP** is more likely to cause reactions. The acellular version **DTaP** is less likely to cause a reaction and is now given instead

Table 9: Recommended schedules for immunisation

Age	Diseases	Type of immunisation
At 2 months (8 weeks) & 3 months (12 weeks) & 4 months (16 weeks)	**HIB, DTaP** diphtheria, tetanus and acellular pertussis (whooping cough), Inactivated Poliomyelitis IPV	1 injection: combined vaccine
	Meningitis C	1 injection
6 months - 4 years	**HIB** "catch-up" programme (commenced in 2003)	1 injection
12 - 18 months	**1st MMR** vaccine (measles, mumps, rubella)	1 combined injection
4 - 5 years (usually prior to school entry)	**DTaP** (diphtheria, tetanus and acellular pertussis), Inactivated Poliomyelitis IPV	1 booster combined injection
	2nd MMR dose (measles, mumps, rubella)	1 combined injection
Usually 10 – 14 years (but sometimes shortly after birth)	**BCG** (live attentuated) anti-tuberculosis	1 injection after skin testing (e.g. with Heaf or Mantoux tests)
Girls aged 13 years	**MMR/rubella** (if they have not already had 2 doses when younger or have immunity already)	1 booster injection
School leavers 15 – 18 years	**Td** (tetanus and low-dose diphtheria), Inactivated Poliomyelitis Td/IPV	1 booster combined injection

---

The above schedule is due to commence from 27 September 2004

The DTwP vaccine has been replaced with an acellular Pertussis combined vaccine (**DTaP**: see above). It is thought that this will cause less side-effects although it is stated to be just as effective.

The Oral Poliomyelitis Vaccine (OPV), a live type of vaccine, is replaced by the less effective Inactivated Poliomyelitis (IPV), administered by injection. Global control of this disease is said to allow this change.

These new vaccines are thiomersal free (a mercury compound). This will meet the internationally agreed aim of reducing the exposure of children to mercury if it can be avoided. Further information can be found on the website: http:/www.immunisation.nhs.uk

- Requirements for children up to 4 years old to have a further booster injection for **HIB** is the result of the use in recent years of the acellular, vaccine for diphtheria, tetanus and pertussis, combined with **HIB**, being used routinely. Unfortunately, it has been found that levels of immunity to **HIB** have been lowered - hence the requirement.

Relevant childhood diseases

Diphtheria

This **acute upper respiratory disease**, caused by bacteria, is unfortunately increasing in its occurrence after having been relatively well-controlled through the routine immunisation of children. The toxins produced by the causative organism *Corynebacteria diphtheriae* can cause damage to the heart and nervous system. It can also cause an acute and rapid onset in difficulty in breathing as a result of the production of a greyish membrane in the airway, causing death in severe cases. It is an **airborne** disease usually spread by droplet infection and contact with **fomites** (objects contaminated by an infected person).

The vaccine is composed of **weakened toxins**.

Tetanus

Tetanus is caused by **contact** with the bacteria *Tetanus bacillus* which is commonly found in soil. The organism is capable of producing **protective spores** which enable it to survive in **anaerobic** (without air) conditions. Entrance to the body may be through cuts, burns or scratches (e.g. from roses). In developing countries such as Africa and Asia, the newborn baby's umbilical stump sometimes becomes infected.

Tetanus is not transmitted from person to person. The toxins produced by the bacteria may cause spasms and paralysis, and the inability to breath can cause death if treatment is delayed; emergency **tracheostomy** (artificial opening into the windpipe) is used to treat this complication.

The vaccine is composed of **weakened toxins**.

Pertussis (whooping cough)

Pertussis is a killer disease and in unimmunised children produces prolonged coughing spasms and a characteristic 'whoop' as air rushes into the airway as a spasm ceases. The toxins produced by the bacteria cause vomiting and periods of **apnoea** (absence of breathing), and death from choking (and other complications e.g. **bronchopneumonia**) is common in children under 6 months of age. This highly infectious **airborne disease**, caused by the bacteria *Bordetella pertussis*, is spread by droplet infection.

The vaccine is composed of **dead bacteria**.

HIB (Haemophilus influenzae type B) and meningitis

HIB causes serious illnesses, such as **meningitis, pneumonia, epiglottitis** and other problems in young children. The vaccine is mainly given to prevent meningitis, but is only active against the specific infection caused by HIB and **does not prevent meningitis caused by other organisms,** e.g. meningococcal meningitis and viral meningitis.

The HIB bacteria are airborne, spread by droplet infection. Incidence of the disease, usually found in children under 1 year, has dropped dramatically since the introduction of the HIB vaccine schedule. The vaccine does not consist of live organisms.

The early signs and symptoms of meningitis are headache, fever, irritability, restlessness, vomiting and refusal of feeds (common with the symptoms of other illnesses such as colds and influenza). Babies can become seriously ill within hours; the presence of a high-pitched, moaning cry together with drowsiness are both signs. In older children, dislike of light and neck rigidity are warning signs. The presence of a red or purple skin rash, which does not fade under pressure, indicates **septicaemia**.

Advice can be obtained from the leaflet *A Guide to Childhood Immunisations* produced by the Health Education Authority, which also provides specific advice on what to look for in babies and children and how to act accordingly.

Meningitis: what to look for

in babies:

- A high-pitched, moaning cry

- The child being difficult to wake

- Refusing to feed

- Pale or blotchy skin

- Red or purple spots that do not fade under pressure – do the 'Glass Test' (see below)

in older children:

- Red or purple spots that do not fade under pressure

- Stiffness in the neck – can the child kiss his/her knee, or touch his/her forehead to the knee?

- Drowsiness or confusion

- A severe headache

- A dislike of bright light

The 'Glass Test':

Press the side of a glass firmly against the rash – you will be able to see it if it fades and loses colour under the pressure. If it doesn't change colour, contact your doctor immediately.

- If your child becomes ill with one or more of these symptoms and signs, contact your doctor urgently. You may be asked to go straight to the surgery.

- If your child has a rash of red or purple spots or bruises, get medical help immediately.

Source: Health Education Authority (1997): A Guide to Childhood Immunisation.

Poliomyelitis

Polio is caused by a viral infection which, following invasion of the gastrointestinal tract, attacks the grey matter in the **central nervous system**. Spread via **water** and **faeces**, it can cause paralysis and death from the inability to breath.

The faeces passed by the recently immunised child or person can cause the illness to develop in an unprotected person. Baby carers who change the immunised child's nappies should ensure that they are properly protected and immunised (oral vaccine only). The recommended new programme removes the risk by using an inactivated polio vaccine by injection.

Poliomyelitis remains **endemic** in many developing countries. In industrialised countries, such as the UK, there are sporadic outbreaks, usually associated with unimmunised individuals.

The **oral vaccine** consists of a **live attenuated** (weakened) virus.

Measles

Measles is highly infectious and can kill, so it is important that routine immunisation is given. General **malaise, coryza** (runny nose) and **headache** herald the beginning of the infection. On approximately the fourth day of the disease a distinctive skin rash appears consisting of **macules. Koplik spots** in the mouth may be apparent prior to the skin rash and will determine a differential diagnosis of this condition. Measles occurs due to an **airborne virus** which can cause high fever, **otitis media** (inflammation of the middle ear), **conjunctivitis, convulsions**, respiratory infection such as **bronchopneumonia**, and **brain damage**.

The vaccine given is a **live attenuated** preparation.

Mumps

Mumps is an **airborne, viral** infection and causes inflammation and swelling of the **salivary glands**, especially the **parotid glands**. Complications can cause **deafness, pancreatitis** (inflammation of the pancreas) and swelling of the **testicles** and **ovaries**, which may result in sterility. Spread by **droplet infection**, mumps may also inflame the brain, causing **meningitis** and **encephalitis**.

The vaccine contains a **live attenuated** virus.

Rubella

Rubella (commonly known as German measles) is caused by an **airborne virus** spread by **droplet infection**. It usually produces a mild illness characterised by a fleeting rash similar to measles and a fever. **Serological** investigation, where indicated, is required for proof of the infection as many diseases produce a similar skin rash. However, if a woman catches the disease in **early pregnancy**, **deformity** of the developing fetus is common. Damage may also be done if the woman is not aware that she is pregnant. The routine immunisation of girls in their early teens has now been replaced with the routine **MMR immunisation** of all children at an earlier age.

The vaccine is a **live attenuated** one.

Tuberculosis

Tuberculosis is caused by an infection with bacteria (e.g. *Myobacterium tuberculosis*). It is an **airborne** infection which is easily spread by **droplet infection**. Infection of the lungs is the most common form of the disease, but other organs can become infected as a result of drinking milk from infected animals, particularly in developing countries. Unfortunately, drug-resistant strains have emerged and are increasing worldwide. Despite the increase in reported cases, the disease is relatively rare in the UK.

BCG (*Bacillus Calmette-Guérin*) vaccine

BCG is a **live attenuated** vaccine given to protect against tuberculosis. A routine skin test (**Heaf** or **Mantoux** test) is performed on the arm by introducing dead tuberculin bacilli intradermally in order to determine the person's antibody levels to tuberculosis. If the person has been exposed to the disease, the results of the skin test will show a **positive** reaction. The vaccine will not be given if the skin test is positive. Cases of positive reaction will be screened for active tuberculosis.

Varicella (chickenpox)

Varicella is a highly infectious disease caused by a virus. **Papules, vesicles** and subsequently **pustules** appear on the face and scalp, spreading to the trunk, abdomen and limbs. The major distribution is towards the centre of the body surface, and lesions also occur on the **mucous membranes** of the respiratory tract.

The three stages of skin eruption will be present as successive crops of papules arise throughout the course of the disease. Eventually all lesions will dry up and the scabs will be shed. The disease is spread by **droplet infection, personal contact** and **fomites**.

Shingles (*herpes zoster*) is a condition in which the varicella virus is reactivated in the body of an individual who has previously recovered from a case of chickenpox.

At present there is **no active vaccine** available in this country, but a **live attenuated** one is licenced in other countries such as the USA.

Some other childhood diseases

Slapped cheek syndrome (*Erythema infectosum*)

Caused by a virus, this causes a 'slapped cheek' appearance with a measles-type rash appearing on the face but spreading to give a 'lacy' appearance over the trunk and limbs. A mild fever is usually present. No treatment is required.

Hand, foot and mouth disease (*Coxsackie virus*)

A relatively mild infection causing blistering of the hands, feet and mouth. Fever and a feeling of being unwell (malaise) are usually present. No treatment is necessary but parents require reassurance.

Roseola (*Roseola infantum*)

A viral disease which produces a pink measles type rash on the third or fourth day after infection. Commonly affects children at around the age of 2 years.

Impetigo

Caused by a bacteria (*staphylococcus*) and is extremely contagious, spread through direct contact. The commonest site is the face but can occur anywhere on the body. It produces yellow crusty areas (**lesions**), which spread rapidly. Treatment is by antibiotics either topical or by mouth (oral). Strict hygiene is required and children should be isolated from school or play areas until scabs fall off.

Adult immunisation

It is recommended that adults receive **booster immunisations** for **tetanus** and **poliomyelitis**. It is advisable to check the immunisation status of all new patients. The continued coverage of protection against **diphtheria** is also vital to stop the disease recurring in this country.

Tetanus

At present a booster dose is recommended **every 10** years (previously five years). Checking of current status is important for all new patients.

Poliomyelitis

Adults under the age of 40 years should receive boosters every 10 years if travelling outside the UK, and parents should receive boosters at the same time as their baby commences immunisation (oral vaccine only).

Diphtheria

A low-dose vaccine is available for those individuals over the age of 10 years. Primary immunisation is indicated for all adults not previously protected. (The old **Schick test** for susceptibility to the disease is now no longer used.)

Contraindications to immunisation

Each case must be looked at individually by the physician responsible for administering the vaccine.

The following should be considered as **contraindications** (reasons not to proceed) to immunisation in children:

- If the child is **unwell** or has a **fever**

- If the child has had a **reaction** to previous immunisations

- If the child has had previous **severe allergic** reaction to eating **eggs**.

- If the child is **taking medicines** for other conditions (especially **steroids**), is **immunodeficient**, or has recently received **passive immunisation** of immunoglobulin

- If the child suffers from **fits** or there is a close family history, the doctor will discuss and review any likely problem with the parent. Stable neurological conditions may not indicate contraindication.

Contraindications for **adults** are similar, but **pregnancy** is also included as any immunisation may damage the fetus.

When **live vaccines** are to be given, special consideration of risks must be made in order to ensure the patient's immune response is not impaired because of any already existing condition or disease. Certain live vaccines must not be given within a fixed period of each other.

Consent

Consent from the parent for **children under 16 years** is normally essential and there should be a protocol to be followed for children accompanied by someone other than the parent. *This is extremely important from a legal aspect.* Written consent is not essential but provides permanent **proof** of agreement should future problems arise. Consent is required for each immunisation given.

Any likely side-effect etc., must be discussed by the doctor with the parent before consent is given. **It should be noted** that **a young person under 16 years of age** may give or refuse consent for immunisation or treatment provided that he/she understands fully the benefits and risks involved. Whether giving or refusing consent, the child should always be encouraged to involve the parent or guardian in the decision. **Immunisation should not be given against the young person's wishes**.

Vaccine damage payments

Unfortunately, a few children suffer damage as a result of immunisation. There is now a single tax-free payment for people who have suffered **severe mental and/or physical disablement** of 80% or more as a result of immunisation against one or more of the following diseases:

- Diphtheria

- Tetanus

- Pertussis

- Poliomyelitis

- Rubella

- Measles

- Tuberculosis

- Mumps

- Smallpox

- *Haemophilus influenzae* type B (HIB)

There is a time and age limitation to this compensation award.

Reporting of adverse reactions

Any adverse reaction to immunisation should be reported on the 'yellow card' system and sent to the Medicines and Health Care Products Regulatory Agency (MHRA). Information should include vaccine and batch numbers, which will alert the authority to any general problems arising and so prevent further damage (as seen in the 'thalidomide' disaster when a drug was prescribed to women in the first trimester of pregnancy which resulted in children being born with varying degrees of deformity, especially the presence of only rudimentary limbs).

Evidence is considered by the Joint Committee on Vaccination and Immunisation (JCVI), an independent body providing expert advice on policy, safety and efficacy of vaccines.

Reporting is voluntary for doctors, but is a statutory requirement for drug companies and vaccine manufacturers.

Targets

Prior to the introduction of new requirements, the Primary Care Trusts are expected to immunise 90% of children under five years against diphtheria, tetanus, pertussis, poliomyelitis and HIB to achieve the higher target payment and 70% to receive the lower payment.

Role of the receptionist

The receptionist will be involved in recall of children for immunisation and in keeping records. It is important that all data are properly recorded and notes are properly filed (*see Figure 96*).

The immediate reporting to the doctor or nurse, of any information that may have been told to the receptionist by the parent, concerning a baby's reaction to a previous immunisation or fears concerning a particular injection, such as pertussis, is most important. This can avoid problems as often these fears are not repeated to the person administering the vaccine.

The provision of current health education leaflets and posters is also an important requirement.

It is also important that the receptionist is aware of the need to be alert to patients who visit the doctor following recent return from abroad. If illness occurs within three weeks, it is necessary to isolate the patient from other patients in the waiting room in order to avoid cross-infection. *Until the patient has been diagnosed s/he must be considered a health risk to others.*

Batch numbers and expiry dates

These are recorded on the special forms by the person giving the injection and records must be kept in case of any reaction.

Storage

Vaccines must be kept at the correct temperature as stated on the bottle and in the literature. *A refrigerator, other than the one used for food and milk etc., must be kept for this purpose and temperature levels must be carefully checked*; a temperature of between 2 and 8 °C is the usual requirement, although some polio vaccines require storage at 0 – 4 °C. The contents and strength of the vaccine will be adversely affected if it is incorrectly stored.

The temperature should never be allowed to sink below 0 °C, as freezing can damage the efficacy of the vaccine and also break the container.

Immunisation record card

1. YOUR TRAVEL VACCINE RECORD

✓ Visit your surgery well in advance as some vaccines need to be given a month or more before you go.

✓ Remember that for some vaccines, to ensure long-term protection, you will need to come back for a booster vaccination.

Vaccine		Date received	Booster due date
Hepatitis A	Primary		
	First Booster		
Typhoid			
Meningococcal A+C			
Yellow Fever			
Diphtheria/Tetanus			
Tetanus			
Polio			

Continued on inside back cover

1. YOUR TRAVEL VACCINE RECORD (cont.)

Vaccine		Date received	Booster due date
Japanese Enc	Dose 1		
	Dose 2		
	(Dose 3)		
Tick-borne encephalitis			
Rabies	Dose 1		
	Dose 2		
	Dose 3		
Hepatitis B	Dose 1		
	Dose 2		
	Dose 3		
	(Dose 4)		
Other			
Malaria	Remember to ask your doctor/nurse/pharmacist for advice where appropriate		

Figure 96: Immunisation record card *(Reproduced with kind permission from Pasteur Mérieux MSD Ltd.)*

Position in the refrigerator is also important; shelves or compartments in the **door must never be used**. Specialist refrigerators designed for medicine and vaccines are obtainable.

Maximum and minimum temperatures should be recorded regularly, preferably daily. Written procedures should be provided and, if the temperature requirements are breached, necessary reporting to the appropriate person. There should be clear designated responsibility for both monitoring and reporting.

Arrangements for cold storage must be made to allow regular defrosting of refrigerators if an alternative one is not available.

Transportation of vaccines

Transportation of vaccines must be carefully monitored to ensure damage to their content does not occur. **Temperature control** must be maintained and monitored throughout the period of transportation.

If vaccines have been sent by post, they **should not be accepted if more than 48 hours have elapsed** since the time of dispatch.

First-class post must be used and all necessary instructions regarding the materials and hazards should be followed.

Disposal

Great care must be taken to ensure **safe disposal** of empty or unused, expired vials by **incineration** or **heat inactivation**. The requirements of the **Environmental Protection Act 1990** and regulations governing the disposal of clinical waste must be strictly followed and written procedures should be provided. Disposal in the **'sharps'** bin followed by incineration is usually the required procedure in general practice. Information and advice may be obtained from the local consultant in Communicable Disease Control.

Travellers

Travellers require special protection according to the area in which they are to be travelling. Information and advice is available to doctors from the **Communicable Disease Surveillance Centre**. The newspaper *Pulse* issues **monthly bulletins** on these requirements. This is based on recommendations issued from the **World Health Organisation**.

Recommended schedule for travellers

As well as the following schedule for travellers, a recent special health education card produced by the Health Education Authority with advice on preventing HIV risk is shown in Figure 97.

Travellers to remote areas or developing countries are also advised to carry a **sterile set of basic dental and surgical requirements**, including an intravenous 'giving set'. The reuse of injection needles is a common occurrence in these areas, and travellers have been **cross-infected** with **Hepatitis B** and **HIV**. **Hepatitis C** is also a hazard and at present there is no vaccine available. Hepatitis B is far more virulent than HIV; it is not killed by boiling the equipment and requires strict **autoclaving procedures** for its elimination.

All travellers are recommended for immunisation against **diphtheria**, **poliomyelitis** and **tetanus** if not previously immunised.

The current immunisation schedules are:

All areas except North and West Europe, North America, Australia and New Zealand	**poliomyelitis**
All areas with poor standards of hygiene and sanitation	**typhoid and hepatitis A**
Infected areas as advised	**anti-malaria tablets, precautions against mosquitoes, yellow fever, tuberculosis**
In some circumstances	**diphtheria, hepatitis B, rabies, Japanese encephalitis, tick encephalitis, meningococcal meningitis**

International certificates

These are internationally recognised certificates verifying that the named person has received immunisation against a particular disease. They are available for **yellow fever**, but **not for cholera** as people do not require immunisation against it. **At present, a signed medical statement to this effect can be issued to those travelling to an epidemic area**.

International certificates are signed by the doctor responsible for administering the vaccine. It is compulsory to have an international certificate for entry to some countries.

The Travel*Safe* Code

HIV, the virus that causes AIDS, is worldwide. When abroad you can reduce your risk if you follow the Travel Safe Code:

- **Avoid unnecessary medical or dental treatment and situations which may make this necessary.**

- **If you have sex with someone new, always use a condom.**

- **Don't inject drugs or share needles and syringes.**

- **Remember alcohol and drugs affect your judgement.**

- **Avoid having a tattoo, acupuncture or your ears pierced unless sterile equipment is used.**

Have a good journey.

Travel*Safe*

Travel the world HIV*Safe*

Figure 97: The "TravelSafe" Code card
(Source: Health Education Authority).

The special vaccines available for travellers are:

Yellow fever

This is a **live vaccine** and is only available from **special centres**. Special storage is required. An initial immunisation is followed by booster injection every 10 years.

Cholera

Currently, there is **no vaccine** available in this country. However, an oral vaccine is being developed which will hopefully prove more efficient than previous ones.

Typhoid

There are **three vaccines** available at present; two for **injection** and one **live attenuated oral** preparation. Requirements of dosage and boosters vary according to the preparation used. The current recommended final boosters are required at **3-year intervals**, however manufacturer's suggestions should be followed. **Immunity to paratyphoid infection is not provided.**

Smallpox

This is now no longer required as the disease has been eradicated.

Hepatitis A

This is advised for visitors to developing countries or areas where sanitation is poor. **Until recently** this has been a **passive form** of immunisation provided by the administration of human immunoglobulin containing antibodies to the disease. However, there is now an **active immunisation** available, which has replaced the need for passive immunisation.

The single protection vaccines for hepatitis A active immunity advise booster doses **every 10 years** following the initial schedule. Manufacturer's recommendations vary according to the product.

Hepatitis A and B

There is now a **combined vaccine** available for both hepatitis A and B which, following the administration of the initial recommended schedule, gives protection for 5 years. Antibody levels must be measured to ensure protection.

Three injections are required; two within a month and a third injection 6 months later. Antibody levels must be checked to ensure successful immunisation. Booster doses are required at **3- to 5-yearly intervals** according to levels of **antibody titre**.

Poliomyelitis

This immunisation should be given to travellers to developing countries where **hygiene** is primitive. A booster dose is required **every 10 years**.

Tetanus

This is recommended for **all travellers** if their present immunisation against tetanus is not up to date. A **10-yearly booster** is recommended.

Diphtheria

Those previously covered by routine immunisations should be offered **low-dose** immunisation **every 10–20 years**. Travellers to **Russia** and certain **eastern European countries** where the disease is **endemic** should be offered boosters. (**Primary** immunisation is indicated for individuals who have never received immunisation for this disease.)

Meningococcal meningitis

This is a vaccine available to protect travellers against certain strains of this bacterial infection. Travellers to **sub-Saharan** areas of **Africa** are advised to be immunised with this vaccine.

Meningococcal ACWY

A certificate is required for pilgrims to the **Hajj** in **Saudi Arabia**.

Malaria

Travellers to declared areas of **known malarial risk** should be advised to take precautions to avoid this disease. The **mosquito** is the carrier for this disease and it is prevalent in tropical and subtropical areas over a wide area, e.g. **India** and **Africa**.

Unfortunately, due to mosquitoes entering **aeroplanes**, it is also possible to contract malaria from airports en route, where the disease of malaria would not be expected. There have even been cases thought to have been contracted in this way close to **Gatwick Airport** in England.

The sharing of **infected needles** is also a means of infection.

Advice concerning prevention of mosquito bites must be given. **Special tablets must be started at least a week before departure and continued for a period of one month following return.** However, manufacturers' recommendations should always be followed and those using **'mefloquine'** are advised to commence the treatment at least two to three weeks prior to departure.

Unfortunately, **resistance** is increasing to many forms of treatments and the drug given will depend upon the area to be visited.

Japanese B encephalitis

This vaccine may be offered to those travellers residing in **south-east Asia** for 1 month or more. It is a viral infection and the vaccine is composed of a **killed virus**.

White Nile Fever

This is related to Japanese Encephalitis and is prevalent in the **USA** as well as present in **Canada, Central America** and the **Caribbean**. There is **no licenced vaccine** available and prevention is by vector control. The USA has a comprehensive spraying policy. **Bite prevention** measures are vital during outbreaks. It is spread by the **Culex mosquito** and is caused by a virus.

Other immunisations available

Other immunisations available include those against **influenza, pneumococcal disease** and **hepatitis B**. Vaccines are also available against **anthrax** for those workers at risk and **rabies** (hydrophobia) for those persons who may have been bitten by a rabid animal.

Influenza

This is commonly given to patients 'at risk', i.e. **elderly people**, patients with **asthma** and those with other **chronic respiratory** or **cardiovascular disease**. It is usual to have campaigns alerting patients to protect themselves against the yearly epidemics which occur. Booster doses are given **yearly** and the vaccine is developed wherever possible to combat the particular strain of the virus. Special fees are payable at present.

Pneumococcal infections

This vaccine is offered routinely to those at risk from **bacterial respiratory infections**. Patients recommended for this vaccine include those with **immunodeficiency, diabetes mellitus, chronic liver, lung** and **heart disease**, and individuals who have had their **spleen removed**. One dose is given and booster doses are not normally administered.

Hepatitis B

This **active immunisation** is available for those at risk, whether due to their **lifestyle** or **occupation**.

Practice staff who are likely to come into contact with body fluids from infected persons need to be protected (a requirement under regulations of the Health and Safety at Work).

It is not always known who is infected with this virus as the incubation period can be up to 6 months and carriers have no symptoms.

Three injections are required; two within a month and a third injection 6 months later. Antibody levels must be checked to ensure successful immunisation. Booster doses are required at **3- to 5-yearly intervals**, according to levels of antibody titre. There are different varieties of vaccine and the manufacturer's recommendations must be followed.

A **passive immunisation** of a specific immunoglobulin (**Hepatitis B immune globulin**) is also available for immediate temporary protection in cases of **accidental inoculation**, **'needle-stick'** injuries, or contamination with **antigen-positive blood**. This specific passive immunity does not affect the development of active immunity, so combined passive/active immunisation is recommended in certain cases of post-exposure treatment.

NB: It should be noted that immunisation schedules are subject to change and immunisation information should be checked regularly.

Anaphylactic shock

There is always the risk of a patient being administered a vaccine and developing **anaphylactic shock**. This potentially fatal condition, occurring in response to the administration of a foreign protein, can happen rapidly without any warning, producing a variety of clinical features, ranging from **respiratory difficulties** to immediate **cardiovascular collapse** and **death**.

Signs may include **skin rash**, noisy breathing due to **bronchospasm** and **oedema**, and **loss of consciousness**. Immediate resuscitation techniques must be available and life-support drugs such as adrenaline must always be available whenever immunisation is being performed. Guidelines are available from the Department of Health and the local community physician/medical officer.

Abbreviations

DTaP   Diphtheria, Tetanus, acellular Pertussis

IPV   Inactivated Poliomyelitis vaccine

Instructions to parents/carers following immunisation of a child

If your child has a fever there are several things you can do to control it. You should consult your GP if your child appears unusually ill or if the fever persists. The following measures will help to lower your child's temperature:

Skin exposure

A child loses heat through his skin. If your child feels hot, take off most of his clothes. *Do not* wrap up the child because this will raise his/her temperature.

Fluids

Give plenty of fluids. Frequently a child with a temperature does not feel hungry – plenty of fluids will prevent dehydration, may reduce the temperature and will make the child more comfortable.

Medication

A slight temperature is not dangerous and does not always require paracetamol.

Paracetamol is only given to babies under 12 weeks for fever following vaccination.

- **For babies age 8 weeks** the dose is 60mg (2.5ml paediatric paracetamol solution e.g. Calpol)

- **For children 3 months -1 year** the dose is 60-120 mg (2.5ml - 5ml)

- **For children 1 - 5 years** the dose is 120-250mg (5ml - 10ml).

This dose may be repeated every 6 hours, but for no longer than 24 hours.

Always follow the instructions on the bottle. Paracetamol taken in excess can be dangerous so return the bottle to a safe place after every dose.

Tepid Sponging

If you are unable to control the temperature with the above measures, sponge the child with *lukewarm* water. Do not use cold water as this will take the blood away from the skin and therefore delay cooling. Rub the skin briskly so that the blood will come to the skin surface where it can be cooled. Sponge no more frequently than every 2 hours and no longer than half an hour at a time. If an electric fan is available, this will help with the cooling.

Convulsions

Convulsions are fits - which commonly occur in children up to the age of about 4 years if their temperature rises unduly highly and rapidly. If a child has a fit, lie them on their side so that any moisture in the throat will drain out. *Do not attempt to put anything between the teeth and gums* and contact your GP immediately.

Polio

If you or anyone who will be changing the baby's nappies has not been immunised against polio, there is a risk of infection. Please discuss this with the nurse or doctor. **NB:** The new inactivated polio injection does *not* carry this risk as it is not a live vaccine.

Chapter 23

Miscellaneous terminology

R$_x$

+ve

−ve

↑/↓

Terminology of medical specialties

Anaesthesia (anaesthetist)
concerning the administration of anaesthetics

Cardiology (cardiologist)
concerning the heart and blood vessels

Dermatology (dermatologist)
concerning skin

Endocrinology (endocrinologist)
concerning the endocrine system

Gastroenterology (gastroenterologist)
concerning the digestive system

Genitourinary (genitourinary physician)
concerning the urinary system and male
reproductive system

Geriatrics (geriatrician)
concerning disorders of elderly people

Gynaecology (gynaecologist)
concerning the female reproductive system

Haematology (haematologist)
concerning the blood

Immunology (immunologist)
concerning immunity (defence of the body)

Nephrology (nephrologist)
concerning the urinary system
(particularly the kidneys)

Neurology (neurologist)
concerning the nervous system

Obstetrics (obstetrician)
concerning pregnancy and childbirth

Ophthalmology (ophthalmologist)
concerning eye disease

Orthopaedics (orthopaedic surgeon)
concerning disorders of the locomotor system

Otorhinolaryngology (ENT physician/surgeon)
concerning ear, nose and throat disorders

Paediatrics (paediatrician)
concerning children's diseases

Pathology (pathologist)
concerning diagnosis of disease and examination of patient samples and dead bodies by
post-mortem
  Forensic pathology: criminal investigation

Physician
concerning medical conditions
(as opposed to surgical)

Psychiatry (psychiatrist)
concerning mental illness

Radiology (radiologist)
concerning use of X-rays in diagnosis
and treatment

Rheumatology (rheumatologist)
concerning disease and conditions
of connective tissue

Surgery (surgeon)
concerning surgery
(as opposed to medical treatment)

Urology (urologist)
concerning the urinary system

Venereology (venereologist)
concerning sexually transmitted diseases.

Non-medical specialties

Audiometry (audiometrist)
concerned with the measurement of hearing

Gerontology (geriatrician)
the study of old age

Optometry (optician)
concerning the measurement of refraction
(ability to focus) of the eye and dispensing
spectacles

Orthodontistry (orthodontist)
concerning correction of teeth (dentition)

Orthoptics (orthoptist)
treatment and diagnosis of squints etc.

Physiotherapy (physiotherapist)
concerning treatment by physical exercise etc.

Psychology (psychologist)
concerning behaviour including the normal

Radiography (radiographer)
concerning the taking of X-rays
and delivery of treatment.

Classification of diseases and associated terms

Acquired	occurring after birth
Acute	of sudden onset
Aetiology	the scientific study of the cause of disease
Allergic	hypersensitivity to foreign protein
Atrophy	wastage or shrinking of an organ

Benign	not malignant – has a good prognosis
Chronic	of long, slow duration
Congenital	present at birth
Diagnosis	deciding what is wrong with the patient by considering signs and symptoms
Differential diagnosis	One of a list of possible diagnoses, given the signs and symptoms presented, e.g. differential diagnoses of chest pains include indigestion, myocardial infarction etc.
Dystrophy	abnormal nourishment or function of an organ
Empirical	treatment that is given because it works although there is no known scientific reason why it does
Epidemiology	study of the cause of disease including social factors
Exacerbate	make worse
Functional	effects the body function
Hypertrophy	excessive growth or development of an organ with its own tissue
Iatrogenic	condition caused by the doctor, usually by side-effects of medication
Idiopathic	of unknown origin
Infective(ious)	a disease capable of being spread from one person to others
Malignant	harmful, damaging, e.g. cancer
Metabolic	concerning the basic working or metabolism of the body
Morbid	abnormal
Neoplastic	producing new growths, i.e. cancerous
Organic	effects the structure of the body
Prognosis	the forecast of the probable course and outcome of a disease

Sub-clinical	not producing any obvious signs or symptoms
Syndrome	a collection of three or more signs and symptoms which together form a disease, e.g. Down's syndrome
Systemic	widespread/throughout the body
Toxic	caused by poisons – poisonous
Traumatic	caused by injury/damage.

Miscellaneous abbreviations

A&E	accident and emergency
AET or **aet**	aged
ARC	AIDS-related complex
BID	brought in dead
BP	blood pressure
BS	breath sounds
Ca	carcinoma (or calcium)
C/O or **CO**	complains of (or carbon monoxide)
Cx	cervix
Dec	deceased
DNA	did not attend (or deoxyribonucleic acid)
DNR	do not resuscitate
DOA	dead on arrival
DOB/dob	date of birth
Dxr	deep X-ray
ENT	ear, nose and throat
ESN	educationally sub-normal
FH	family history (or fetal heart)
FNA	fine needle aspiration (for cytology investigation)
GOK	god only knows
HAI	hospital acquired infection
HDU	high dependency unit
HI or **hi**	hyperdermic injection
H/O	history of
Hx	history

IA, i.a.	intra-articular
ICU	intensive care unit
IgA	immunoglobulin (gamma) A
IgBF	immunoglobulin (gamma) binding factor
IgD	immunoglobulin (gamma) D
IgE	immunoglobulin (gamma) E
IgG	immunoglobulin (gamma) G
IgM	immunoglobulin (gamma) M
IM, i.m.	intramuscular
IP	inpatient
IQ	intelligence quotient
ISQ	in status quo (no change)
IT	intrathecal
ITU	intensive therapy unit
IV, i.v.	intravenous
K	potassium
NAD	no abnormality detected/demonstrated
NG	new growth (neoplasm)
NOAD	no other abnormality detected
NOS	no other symptoms/signs
OA	on arrival/osteoarthritis
OE	on examination
OP	outpatient
OPD	outpatient department
PCO	patient complains of
PH	past history
PMH	past medical history
POP	plaster of Paris
PP	private patient
PR	per rectum (rectal examination)
PUO	pyrexia of unknown origin
PV	per vaginam
RSI	repetitive strain injury
RTA	road traffic accident
SMI	school medical inspection
SOB	shortness of breath
Sx	surgery (or suction, or symptoms and signs)
TATT	tired all the time

TCA	to come again
TCI	to come in
TLC	tender loving care
TPR	temperature, pulse and respirations
TTA	to take away
UPLD	upper limb disorder
WRULD	work related upper limb disorder
YOB	year of birth

Signs and symbols

Δ	diagnosis
$\Delta\,\Delta$	differential diagnoses
$>$	greater than
$<$	less than
+ve	positive
−ve	negative
$\uparrow / \downarrow$	increase/decrease
R_x	recipe/take (prescription)
c.	with
s.	without
3/7	three days
1/52	one week
1/12	one month
°**jaundice**	no jaundice
°**oedema**	no oedema
#	fracture
μ**g**	microgram
$\leftrightarrow$ or **N**	normal
Ψ	psychiatric
♀	female
♂	male
†	deceased
*	birth
⚢	female homosexual
⚣	male homosexual

Chapter **24**

Notifiable and infectious diseases

Acute encephalitis

Cholera

Diphtheria

Erysipelas

Food poisoning

Infectious diseases

An infectious disease is one that is easily transmitted. It may be passed from person to person or from animals or insects to humans.

Transmission may be:

- **Airborne** (**droplet** infection) – from sneezing, coughing, talking and dust

- **Waterborne** (contaminated water, food etc)

- Through **contact** – **direct transmission** including from touching an infected person, body fluids etc or **indirect contact** by transfer from inanimate objects (fomites) such as door handles, pens etc

- By **vectors** – from animals (known as 'zoonosis') or insects.

Entry to the body may be by:

- **Ingestion** (via the mouth)

- **Inhalation** (via the lungs)

- **Inoculation** (via the skin or mucous membranes; or through animal/insect bites or 'needle-stick' injury).

Carriers of disease may include persons incubating or suffering from the disease.

Silent carriers are those persons who display no signs or symptoms of disease but remain able to transmit organisms to infect others. They may have recovered from the disease itself (e.g. hepatitis B) but also, may not actually know that they have been infected.

Certain infectious illnesses and food poisoning are reportable (*see Table 10*).

In England and Wales this is governed by:

- **The Public Health (Control of Diseases) Act 1984**

- **The Public Health (Infectious Diseases) Regulations 1968 and 1985 (concerning AIDS) and various other regulations.**

In Scotland the following legislation applies:

- **Infectious Diseases (Notification Act 1889)**

- **Public Health (Scotland) Act 1897**

- **Food and Drugs (Scotland) Act 1957.**

If the medical practitioner considers or suspects that a patient is suffering from a notifiable disease, it is a legal requirement to immediately inform the **'proper officer'**. The proper officer is usually, but not always, the Medical Officer of the Environmental Health Department of the Local Authority. Similarly, in Scotland it may be the Chief Administrative Medical Officer to the Health Board.

Doctors are **paid a nominal fee** for the notification, and special forms are provided by the Public Health Department for this purpose. The certificate (completed by the attending physician) is normally the means of notification and requires information on the patient's:

- **Name**
- **Address**
- **Sex and age**
- **Name of the disease**
- **Date of the onset of the illness.**

If the patient is in hospital, then further details are required, including:

- The **address** from which the patient was admitted
- **Date** of admission
- An opinion as to whether the disease or poisoning from which the patient is, or is suspected to be, suffering from **was contracted in hospital.**

The purpose of this requirement is to:

- Identify the responsible **organism**
- Identify the **source** and **mode** of spread of the infection
- Identify **carriers**
- Identify **contacts**
- **Control** the spread of the disease by appropriate means.

According to the seriousness of the threat to the community, certain diseases are required to be notified immediately by telephone to the 'proper officer', e.g. suspicion of typhoid fever. Further powers under the regulations provide compulsory examination of those suspected of suffering from, or being 'carriers' of, the notifiable disease. The Health Protection

Table 10: Notifiable Diseases *(Source: The Medical Protection Society, 1988)*

Notifiable diseases

England and Wales	Northern Ireland	Scotland
Acute encephalitis	Acute encephalitis/	Anthrax
Acute poliomyelitis	meningitis: bacterial	Chickenpox
Anthrax	Acute encephalitis/	Cholera
Cholera	meningitis: viral	Diphtheria
Diphtheria	Anthrax	Dysentery (bacillary)
Dysentery (amoebic	Chickenpox	Erysipelas
or bacillary)	Cholera	Food poisoning
Food poisoning (all sources)	Diphtheria	Legionellosis
Leprosy	Dysentery	Lyme disease
Leptospirosis	Food poisoning	Measles
Malaria	Gastroenteritis (persons	Membranous croup
Measles	under two years of age only)	Meningococcal infectiom
Meningitis	Hepatitis	Mumps
Meningococcal septicaemia	A Hepatitis	Paratyphoid fever
(without meningitis)	B Hepatitis	Plague
Mumps	unspecified: viral	Poliomyelitis
Opthalmia neonatorum	Legionnaire's disease	Puerperal fever
Paratyphoid fever	Leptospirosis	Rabies
Plague	Malaria	Relapsing fever
Rabies	Measles	Rubella
Relapsing fever	Meningococcal septicaemia	Scarlet fever
Rubella	Mumps	Smallpox
Scarlet fever	Paratyphoid fever	Tetanus
Smallpox	Plague	Toxoplasmosis
Tetanus	Poliomyelitis: acute	Tuberculosis
Tuberculosis	Rabies	Typhoid fever
Typhoid fever	Relapsing fever	Typhus
Typhus	Rubella	Viral haemorrhagic fevers
Viral haemorrhagic fevers	Scarlet fever	Viral hepatitis
Viral hepatitis	Smallpox	Whooping cough
Whooping cough	Tetanus	
Yellow fever	Tuberculosis: pulmonary	
	and non-pulmonary	
	Typhoid fever	
	Typhus	
	Viral haemorrhagic fevers	
	Whooping cough	
	Yellow fever	

NB: Although smallpox disease has been eliminated, it remains a notifiable disease.

Agency is also involved in the reporting process and certain diseases are reported directly to their staff.

It is an offence in Scotland to send a child to school with a notifiable infectious disease.

Environmental Health Officers are widely involved with disease prevention and control. The Medical Officer is responsible for ensuring necessary procedures are carried out and that all authorities liaise with and take advice from the Chief Medical Officer of Health at the Department of Health together with liaison with the Health Protection Agency. There are Health Protection Units set up locally who work closely with each Primary Care Trust and Local Authority. Further liaison with the various International Centres for Communicable Disease Control and the World Health Organisation helps to ensure the pattern of disease is monitored and pandemics (world-wide epidemics) are anticipated, prevented, controlled and monitored.

Communicable Disease Surveillance Centre (CDSC)

The CDSC in Colindale, London, coordinates information and response acting on behalf of the Health Protection Agency for those **national** duties concerning control, surveillance and provision of expert advice on control of infectious diseases.

The tasks of the CDSC include:

- Leading at a national level on the surveillance, alerting and response functions for infectious disease

- Responding to, and coordinating control measures in an infectious disease outbreak, incident or issue that is national (or of national significance) or involves a number of regions

- Providing a comprehensive authoritative public health information and news service for infectious diseases, including publishing the Communicable Disease Report and the relevant portions of the HPA web-site

- Providing authoritative, expert public health advice for those responsible for controlling infectious disease

- Participating in training programmes for those involved in the surveillance and control of infectious diseases

- Supporting national policy development by the Department of Health and other Government bodies, for example on vaccines and vaccine preventable diseases

- Undertaking research and development to support the above public health responsibilities

- Working with other national bodies to deliver UK wide protection against infectious diseases and provides the public health point of contact in the UK for those working to control infection across Europe (the European Commission and WHO-Europe) and the rest of the World (WHO-CSR)

All this is undertaken in collaboration with laboratory, clinical, and public health colleagues within the Agency and elsewhere.

Health Protection Agency (HPA)

Following publication of the White paper *Getting Ahead of the Curve* in 2002, the Chief Medical Officer for Health, announced the need for an agency (the Health Protection Agency) which would ensure that skills and expertise in a number of organisations would work in a more coordinated way. This was intended to reduce the burden and consequences of various health protection threats or disease. The examples of the problems of BSE and newer terrorist threats, of anthrax contamination etc had highlighted a need for fast tracking and response by government.

Specialists in the HPA*

- **Specialists in communicable disease control** – who tackle outbreaks of infectious diseases and prevent the spread of disease through vaccination and other measures

- **Public health specialists**

- **Infection control nurses**

- **Emergency planning advisers**

- **Microbiologists** – who study the organisms that cause infectious diseases

- **Epidemiologists** – who monitor the spread of disease

- **Toxicologists** – who study the effects of chemicals and poisons on the body

- **Laboratory scientists and technicians**

- **Information specialists**

- **Scientists**

- **Information technologists.**

Many of these staff have national and international reputations for their work.

(*Source: The HPA website:* www.hpa.org.uk)

The role of the HPA*

- **Advising government** on public health protection policies and programmes

- **Delivering services** and supporting the NHS and other agencies to protect people from infectious diseases, poisons, chemical and radiological hazards

- Providing an impartial and authoritative source of **information and advice** to professionals and the public

- **Responding to new threats** to public health

- Providing a **rapid response** to health protection emergencies, including the deliberate release of biological, chemical, poison or radioactive substances

- **Improving knowledge** of health protection, through research, development, education and training.

(*Source: The HPA website:* www.hpa.org.uk)

Recently the HPA has been directly involved in the drawing up of contingency plans for reaction to the incidence of possible cases of **Sudden Acute Respiratory Syndrome (SARS)** and **White Nile Fever** (a viral disease similar to Japanese Encephalitis carried by the mosquito), arising in the country. At present these are *not* notifiable diseases. Whilst risks are low, there is a need to prepare for the possibility of a UK acquired case. Plans include the definition of roles and responsibilities of parties involved in tackling the diseases should the need arise and presents a strategy for limiting the impact of the viruses.

Sexually transmitted diseases (STD)

It should be noted that sexually-transmitted diseases, e.g. HIV, AIDS and gonorrhoea, are not normally reportable. This is because it is feared that people would be inhibited from seeking treatment. However, there are various measures which can be taken if there is **imminent danger** to the public.

It is essential that necessary **reporting** is carried out; practice staff may be involved in ensuring that certificates are dispatched to the appropriate person in the area. There is also a special 'spotter' scheme of reporting, via the Royal College of General Practitioners. Those persons attending surgery who have **recently returned from abroad** and are complaining of illness should be **isolated** in order to ensure other patients are not **exposed** to infectious illness. Similarly, patients who appear to have skin rashes due to infectious disease should be **separated** from others in the waiting room until they are seen by the doctor and a **diagnosis** is made.

Abbreviations

BCG	bacillus Camille-Guérin – vaccine against tuberculosis
DT	diphtheria, tetanus – vaccine
DtaP	vaccine of diphtheria, tetanus and acellular pertussis (whooping cough) – not so effective as DTwP but causes less reaction (better tolerated)
DTP	diphtheria, tetanus, pertussis (whooping cough) – vaccine against the three diseases
DTwP	vaccine of diphtheria, tetanus and whole cell pertussis (whooping cough)
Hep A	hepatitis A viral infection (water-borne)
Hep B	hepatitis B viral infection (body fluids), also known as serum hepatitis
Hep C	hepatitis C viral infection

Hep non A	hepatitis caused by virus other than A, B or C. These are now recognised as D and E
Hep non B	
Hep non C	
HIB*	Haemophilus influenzae bacillus – immunisation for babies against meningitis caused by bacteria
IPV	inactivated polio vaccine
MMR	measles, mumps, rubella – vaccine against the three diseases
SARS	sudden acute respiratory syndrome
STD	sexually transmitted diseases
Td	low-dose diphtheria vaccine

*N.B. Hib vaccine is now usually combined with DTP vaccine or DT.

Appendices

I - VII

Appendix I: Prefixes

Prefix	Meaning
a-	absence of
ab-	away from
acou-	hearing
acro-	extremities
ad-	towards
aero-	air
af-	towards/near
agora-	open space
ambi-	both
amblyo-	dim/dull
an-	absence of
ana-	up/excessive
aniso-	unequal
ankylo-	crooked/bent
ante-	before
anti-	against
apo-	away from
audio-	hearing
auto-	self
baso-	basic
bi-	two
bin-	double/two
bio-	life
blasto-	immature/germ cell
brady-	slow
cata-	down
centi-	a hundredth
chemo-	chemical
chromo-/ chromato-	colour
circum-	around
co-/con-	together/joined
contra-	against
cryo-	cold
crypto-	hidden
cyano	blue
de-	away, from/removing
deca-	ten
deci-	tenth

Prefix	Meaning
demi-	half
dextra-	to the right
di-	two
dia-	through
diplo-	double
dis-	against/separation
disto-	far
dorso-	dorsal (back)
dys-	difficult/abnormal/painful
ec-	out of/away from
ecto-	external/outside/without
em-	in
en-/endo-	within/in/into
ent-	within
epi-	upon/above/on
ery-/erythro	red
eu-	well/good/normal
ex-/exo-	out of/away from
extra-	outside
flav-	yellow
fore-	before/in front of
gen-	birth or producing
hecta-	one hundred
hemi-	half
hetero-	unlike/dissimilar
hexa-	six
homeo-/homo	like, similar, same
hyper-	above/high/in excess of normal
hypo-	low/below/under/ less than normal
ichthyo-	dry/scaly
idio-	peculiar to individual/own
in-	not/into/within
infra-	below
inter-	between
intra-	within/inside
intro-	inward
iso-	equal
juxta-	next to
kilo-	one thousand

Prefix	Meaning
koilo-	spoon
kypho-	crooked/humped/rounded
latero-	side
leavo-	left
lepto-	thin/soft
leuco-/leuko-	white
lordo-	bent forward
macro-	large
mal-	poor/abnormal
mano-	pressure
medi-	middle
mega-/megalo-	big/enlarged
melano-	black/dark/pigment
meso-	middle
meta-	after/beyond
micro-	small/one-millionth
milli-	thousandth
mio-	smaller
mono-	one/single
multi-	many
narco-	stupor
neo-	new
nocto-/nycto-	night
nulli-	none
oct-	eight
oligo-	scanty/deficiency
opistho-	backwards
ortho-	straight
os-	opening or bone
pachy-	thick
pan-	all
para-	alongside
ped-	foot or child
penta-	five
per-	through/by
peri-	around
photo-	light
pluri-	many
polio-	grey
poly-	many

Prefix	Meaning
post-	after
pre-/pro-	before
presbyo-	old age
proto-	first
proximo-	near
pseudo-	false
quadri-	four
quinqu-	five
re-	again/back
retro-	backwards/behind
sapro-	dead/decayed
sarco-	flesh
sclero-	hard
scolio-	crooked
scota-	darkness
semi-	half
sex-	six
sono-	sound
squamo-	scaly
staphylo-	grapes/cluster
steno-	narrow
strepto-	chain
sub-	below
super-/supra-	above
syn-	with/together/union
tachy-	rapid/fast
tact-	touching
ter-	three
tetra-	four
trans-	across/through
tri-	three
ultra-	beyond
uni-	one
ventro-	front/anterior
xantho-	yellow
xero-	dry

Appendix II: Word roots

Word root	Meaning
abdomino-	abdomen
acetabulo-	acetabulum (part of the hip)
actino-	ray/sun
adeno-	gland (any)
adipo-	fat
adreno-	adrenal gland
albumen-/ albumin-	albumin
alveolo-	air sac
amylo-	starch
ano-	anus
andro-	man
angio-	vessel
antro-	antrum
aorto-	aorta
appendico-	appendix
aqua-	water
arterio-	artery
athero-	plaque lining blood vessels/porridge
arthro-	joint
articulo-	joint
atrio-	atrium (upper chamber of heart)
auri	ear
axillo-	axilla (armpit)
balano-	penis
bili-	bile
blenno-	mucus
blepharo-	eyelid
brachio-	arm
broncho-	bronchus
bronchiolo-	bronchiole
bucco-	cheek
caeco-	caecum
cardio-	heart
carpo-	wrist, part of hand
cephalo-	head

Word root	Meaning
cerebello-	part of brain (cerebellum)
cerebro-	brain
cervico-	cervix/neck
cheil-	lip
cheiro-	hand
cholangio-	bile/biliary vessels
chole-	bile
choroido-	choroid (layer of eye)
cholecysto-	gallbladder
choledocho-	common bile duct
chondro-	cartilage
claviculo-	clavicle (collar bone)
colo-/colono-	colon (large intestine)
cor-/coreo-	pupil
coro-	pupil/dermis
corono-	heart
corporo-	body
costo-	rib
coxygo-	coccyx
cranio-	part of skull containing brain
culdo-	recto-uterine sac (Pouch of Douglas)
cyclo-	ciliary body (of eye)
cysto-	bladder
cyto-	cell
dacryo-	tear/tear duct
dactyl-	finger
dento-	tooth
derm-/dermato-	skin
digit-	finger/toe
disc-	disc between vertebrae
duodeno-	duodenum (part of intestine)
electro-	electricity
embolo-	plug
encephalo-	brain
endocardio-	lining of heart
endometrio-	endometrium (lining of uterus)
entero-	intestine
epiglotto-	epiglottis

Word root	Meaning
ery-/erythro-	red
ethmoid-	part of the cranium
faci-	face/surface
femoro-	femur (thigh bone)
ferri-/ferro-	iron
feto-/foeto-	fetus
fibulo-	fibula (lower leg bone)
fronto-	front part of cranium
galacto-	milk
gastro-	stomach
genito-	genital
gingivo-	gums
glomerulo-	glomerulus (part of nephron)
glosso-	tongue
glyco-	sugar
gnatho-	jaw
gyno-/gynaeco-	woman
haemo-/ haemato-	blood
hallux-	great toe
hep-/hepato-	liver
hernio-	hernia, rupture, protrusion
hidro-	perspiration
histo-	tissue
humero-	humerus (upper arm)
hydro-	water
hygro-	moisture
hystero-	womb
iatro-	physician
ileo-	ileum (part of intestine)
ilio-	ilium (bone of the pelvis)
immuno-	immunity
irido-	iris (of eye)
ischio-	ischium (part of hip bone)
jejuno-	jejunum (part of intestine)
kalo-	potassium
karyo-	nucleus
kerato-	cornea/skin
labyrintho-	labyrinth (part of ear)

Word root	Meaning
lacrimo-/ lachrymo-/ lacrymo-	tear
lacto-	milk
lamino-	lamina (part of vertebra)
laparo-	abdomen/abdominal wall
laryngo-	larynx
leuco-	white
linguo-	tongue
lipo-	fat
lobo-	lobe
lympho-	lymphatic, lymph
lymphadeno-	lymph gland
lymphangio-	lymph vessel
malo-/malar	cheek bone
mammo-/masto-	breast
mandibulo-	lower jaw
mastoido-	mastoid (part of ear)
maxillo-	upper jaw
meningo-	meninges
menisco-	meniscus (knee cartilage)
metacarpo-	hand bones
metatarso-	foot bones
metro-	womb
morpho-	form/dream
myc-/myco-/ myceto-	fungus
myelo-	marrow/spinal cord
myo-/myos-	muscle
myocardio-	myocardium (heart muscle)
myometrio-	myometrium (muscle of uterus)
myringo-	ear drum
myxo-	mucous membrane
narco-	deep sleep/stupor
natro-	sodium
naso-	nose
necro-	death
nephro-	kidney
neuro-	nerve
nocto-	night

Word root	Meaning
nucleo-	nucleus
nycto-	night
occipito-	part of the cranium (occipital bone)
oculo-	eye
odonto-	tooth
olecrano-	part of the elbow
onycho-	nail
oesophago-	oesophagus (gullet)
oestro-	oestrogen
onco-	tumour
oo-	egg/ovum
oophoro-	ovary
ophthalmo-	eye
opto-	sight
orbito-	part of the eye socket
orchio-/orchido-	testis
oro-	mouth
os-	bone/mouth
ossic-/ossiculo-	ossicles (bones)
osteo-	bone
oto-	ear
ovari-	ovary
paedo-	child
palato-	roof of the mouth
pancreato-	pancreas
parieto-	part of the cranium (parietal bone)
paroto-	parotid gland
patello-	knee cap
patho-	disease
ped-	foot
pericardio-	outer layer of heart (covering of heart)
perineo-	perineum
peritoneo-	peritoneum
phago-	swallow, eat
phako-	lens
phalangio-	fingers, toes
phallo-	penis
pharmaco-	drug

Word root	Meaning
pharyngo-	pharynx (throat)
phlebo-	vein
phono-	voice
phreno-	diaphragm/mind
pilo-	hair
pleuro-	lung
pneumo-/ pneumono-	air/gas/lung
podo-	foot
pollex-	thumb
procto-	anus/rectum
psycho-	mind
ptyalo-	saliva
pubo-	pubis
pyelo-	pelvis of the kidney
pyloro-	pylorus of the stomach
pyo-	pus
pyro-	fever
prostato-	prostate gland
rachio-	spine
radiculo-	nerve root
radio-	radiation/main bone of lower arm
recto-	rectum
ren-	kidney
retino-	retina
rhabdomyo-	striated muscle
rhino-	nose
saccharo-	sugar
sacro-	sacrum
salpingo-	fallopian/uterine/ eustachian tube
sanguino-	blood
sarco-	flesh
scapulo-	shoulder blade
sero-	serum
sialo-	salivary gland
sigmoido-	sigmoid colon
sino-	space/sinus
socio-	sociology
somato-	body

Word root	Meaning
splancho-	viscera/organs
spermato-	spermatazoa/semen
sphenoido-	part of the cranium
sphygmo-	pulse
spiro-	breath
spleno-	spleen
spondylo-	vertebra
steato-	fat
sterno-	breast bone (sternum)
stetho-	chest
stoma-/stomato-	mouth
synovo-	synovial
syringo-	cavity/tube
tabo-	tabes
tarso-	foot/eyelid
temporo-	part of the cranium (temporal bone)
tendino-/teno-	tendon
thelo-	nipples
thermo-	heat
thoraco-/ thoracico-	chest/thorax
thrombo-	blood clot
thymo-	thymus gland
thyro-	thyroid
tibio-	tibia (main lower leg bone)
tilo-	breast
tonsillo-	tonsils
tox-/toxico-	poison
tracheo-	windpipe/trachea
tricho-	hair
tropho-	nourishment
turbino-	bone in the nose (turbinate)
tympano-	ear drum
ulno-	lower arm bone (ulna)
uretero-	ureter
urethro-	urethra
urino-	urine
uro-	urine/urinary organs
utero-	womb

Word root	Meaning
uveo-	uveal tract (part of eye)
uvulo-	uvula
valvo-/valvulo-	valve
varico-	varicose veins
vasculo-	blood vessel
vaso-	vessel
veno-	vein
ventrico-/ ventriculo	ventricle (lower chamber of heart)
vertibro-	vertibra
vesico-	vesicle/bladder/ fluid-filled blister
vestibulo-	vestibule of inner ear
volo-	palm
zoo-	animal
zygo-/zygomato-	cheek bone (zygomatic)

Appendix III: Suffixes

Suffix	Meaning
-a	condition of
-aemia	blood
-ac	concerning/pertaining
-aesthesia	feeling/sensibility
-al	concerning/pertaining to
-algia	pain
-an	concerning/pertaining to
-ase	enzyme
-ate	a salt
-blast	immature cell
-cele	swelling/protrusion
-centesis	to puncture/tapping
-cide	kill/destroy
-cision	cutting
-clasis	destruction of/breaking
-clysis	injection/infusion
-coccus	round cell, type of bacteria
-crine	secrete
-cyte	cell
-derm	skin
-desis	binding together
-dipsia	thirst
-drome	running together
-dynia	pain
-ectasis	dilatation
-ectomy	surgical removal of
-form	having the formation or shape of
-fuge	expelling
-gen	
-genesis	producing/forming/origin
-genic	
-gogue	increasing flow
-gram	picture/tracing
-graph	machine that records/tracing
-graphy	procedure of recording/tracing
-gravid/-gravida	pregnancy

Suffix	Meaning
-ia/-iasis	condition of/state of
-iac	pertaining to
-iatric	pertaining to medicine/physician
-ic	concerning/pertaining to
-iosis/-ism	condition of/state of
-itis	inflammation of
-kinesis	movement/activity
-lalia	speech
-lith	stone
-lithesis	slipping
-lithiasis	condition/presence of stones
-lysis	destruction/splitting/breaking down
-malacia	softening
-megaly	enlargement of
-meter	measure
-oedema	swelling caused by excess fluid
-oid	likeness/resemblance
-ology	study of/science of
-oma	tumour
-opia	condition of the eye/vision
-opsia	vision
-opsy	looking at
-orrhaphy	sewing or repair
-oscopy	examination with a lighted instrument
-ose	sugar
-osis	condition of
-ostomy	artificial opening into
-otomy	cutting into/dividing/incision
-ous	like/similar to
-para	given birth
-paresis	weakness
-pathy	disease
-penia	lack of/decreased
-pexy	fixation of
-phage/-phagia	eating/ingesting/swallowing

Suffix	Meaning
-phakia	lens (of the eye)
-phasia	speech
-philia	liking/loving/affinity for
-phobia	irrational fear
-phylaxis	protection/prevention
-plasia	formation
-plasty	form/mould/reconstruct
-plegia	paralysis
-pnoea	breathing
-poiesis	making/production
-ptosis	drooping/falling
-ptysis	cough
-rrhage	burst forth/bleeding
-rrhagia	condition of heavy bleeding
-rrhaphy	sew/repair/suture
-rrhexis	rupture/break
-rrhoea	flow/discharge
-rrhythmia	rhythm
-sclerosis	hardening
-scope	lighted instrument used to examine
-scopy	examination with a lighted instrument
-scotoma	blind spot
-somatic	pertaining to the body
-sonic	sound
-spadia	to draw out
-stasis	cessation of movement/flow
-stat	an agent to prevent moving or change
-staxis	dripping (blood)/continuous slight loss
-stenosis	narrowing
-sthenia/ -stheania	strength
-taxia	co-ordination/order
-tocia	labour/birth
-tome	cutting instrument
-tripsy	crushing

Suffix	Meaning
-triptor	instrument used to crush
-trophy	nourishment/food
-tropic/-trophic	affinity/turning toward
-tussis	cough
-uria	condition of urine

Appendix IV:
Abbreviations of degrees, qualifications, titles and awards

Abbreviation	Meaning
BA	Bachelor of Arts
BAO	Bachelor of the Art of Obstetrics
BC or BCh or BChir	Bachelor of Surgery
BM	Bachelor of Medicine
BS	Bachelor of Surgery
BSc	Bachelor of Science
CCDC	Consultant in Communicable Disease Control
ChB or CCHir	Bachelor of Surgery
CM or ChM	Master of Surgery
CPH	Certificate in Public Health
CPN	Community Psychiatric Nurse
DA	Diploma in Anaesthetics
DCH	Diploma in Child Health
DCh	Doctor of Surgery
DCP	Diploma in Clinical Pathology
DDS	Doctor of Dental Surgery
DHyg	Doctor of Hygiene
DIH	Diploma in Industrial Health
DLO	Diploma in Laryngology and Otology
DN	District Nurse
Dip Med Rehab	Diploma in Medical Rehabilitation
DM	Doctor of Medicine
DMR	Diploma in Medical Radiology
DO	Diploma in Ophthalmology
DObstRCOG	Diploma in Obstetrics of the Royal College of Obstetricians and Gynaecologists
DOMS	Diploma in Ophthalmological Medicine and Surgery

Abbreviation	Meaning
DPH	Diploma in Public Health
DPM	Diploma in Psychological Medicine
DR	Diploma in Radiology
DSc	Doctor of Science
DTH	Diploma in Tropical Hygiene
DTM	Diploma in Tropical Medicine
FAMS	Fellow of the Association of Managers, Medical Secretaries, Practice Administrators and Receptionists
FDS	Fellow of Dental Surgery
FFARCS	Fellow of Faculty of Anaesthetists, Royal College of Surgeons
FFHom	Fellow of Faculty of Homeopathy
FFR	Fellow of the Faculty of Radiologists
FRCGP	Fellow of the Royal College of General Practitioners
FRCOG	Fellow of the Royal College of Obstetricians and Gynaecologists
FRCP	Fellow of the Royal College of Physicians (London)
FRCPE or FRCPEd* or FRCPEdin*	Fellow of the Royal College of Physicians of Edinburgh
FRCPS	Fellow of the Royal College of Physicians and Surgeons
FRCPath	Fellow of the Royal College of Pathologists
FRCPsych	Fellow of the Royal College of Psychiatrists
FRCS	Fellow of the Royal College of Surgeons (England)
FRCSE*	Fellow of the Royal College of Surgeons of Edinburgh
FRIPHH	Fellow of the Royal Institute of Public Health and Hygiene

Abbreviation	Meaning
FRS	Fellow of the Royal Society
HVCert	Health Visitors Certificate
LAH	Licentiate of Apothecaries Hall (Dublin)
LDS	Licentiate in Dental Surgery
LM	Licentiate in Midwifery
LRCP	Licentiate of Royal College of Physicians
LSA	Licentiate of Society of Apothecaries
MA	Master of Arts
MAO	Master of the Art of Obstetrics
MAMS	Member of the Association of Medical Secretaries, Managers, Practice Administrators and Receptionists
MB	Bachelor of Medicine
MCh	Master of Surgery
MChD	Master of Dental Surgery
MChir	Master of Surgery
MChOrth	Master of Orthopaedic Surgery
MCPath	Member of College of Pathology
MCPS	Member of College of Physicians and Surgeons
MD	Doctor of Medicine
MDS	Master of Dental Surgery
MFCP	Member of the Faculty of Community Physicians
MFHom	Member of the Faculty of Homeopathy
MHyg	Master of Hygiene
MMSA	Master of Midwifery of Society of Apothecaries
MPH	Master of Public Health
MRCGP	Member of the Royal College of General Practitioners
MRCOG	Member of the Royal College of Obstetricians and Gynaecologists

Abbreviation	Meaning
MRCP	Member of the Royal College of Physicians (London)
MRCPath	Member of the Royal College of Pathologists
MRCPsych	Member of the Royal College of Psychiatrists
MRCS	Member of the Royal College of Surgeons (England)
MS	Master of Surgery
MSc	Master of Science
MSW	Medical Social Worker
OT	Occupational Therapist
PhD	Doctor of Philosophy
RGN	Registered General Nurse
RN	Registered Nurse
SEN	State Enrolled Nurse (old title)
SCM	State Certified Midwife
SRN	State Registered Nurse (old title)
SRP	State Registered Physiotherapist

* It is correct to put the initial of the appropriate college after MRCS or FRCS, or LRCP and FRCP for the Royal Colleges of Scotland

Appendix IV continued: Abbreviations of organisations and institutions associated with medical practice

Abbreviation	Meaning
AMSPAR	Association of Medical Secretaries, Practice Managers, Administrators and Receptionists
AP	Aspiration Payemts
BMA	British Medical Association
BMJ	British Medical Journal
BRCS	British Red Cross Society
CDSC	Communicable Disease Surveillance Centre

Abbreviation	Meaning
CHI	Commision for Health Improvement
CPPIH	Commision for Patient and Public Involvement in Health
DES	Directed Enhanced Services
DoH	Department of Health
DSS	Department of Social Security
EHO	Environmental Health Officer
EPI	Expert Patient Initiatives
ES	Essential Services
FPA	Family Planning Association
GMC	General Medical Council
GMSC	General Medical Services Committee
HA	Health Authority
HCHS	Hospital and Community Health Services
HCP	Holistic Care Payments
HDA	Health Development Agency
HPA	Health Protection Agency
HPE	Health Promotion England
HPU	Health Protection Unit
IHSM	Institute of Health Service Managers
LES	Local Enhanced Services
LMC	Local Medical Committee
LMG	Local Medical Group
MAAG	Medical Audit Advisory Group
MASTA	Medical Advisory Service for Travellers Abroad
MDU	Medical Defence Union
MHRA	Medicines and Health Care Products Regulatory Agency
MPS	Medical Protection Society
MRC	Medical Research Council
NAHAT	National Association of Health Authorities and Trusts

Abbreviation	Meaning
NBTS	National Blood Transfusion Service
NCAA	National Clinical Assessment Authority
NES	National Enhanced Services
NHS	National Health Service
NICE	National Institute for Clinical Excellence
NMC	Nurses and Midwives Council
NPSA	National Patient Safety Agency
NSF	National Service Framework
OSC	Overview and Scrutiny Committee
PALS	Patient Advisory and Liaison Service
PCG	Primary Care Groups
PCO	Primary Care Organisation
PCT	Primary Care Trust
PF	Patient's Forum
RCGP	Royal College of General Practitioners
RCN	Royal College of Nursing
RHE	Regional Health Executive
SSDP	Strategic Service Development Plan
SHA	Strategic Health Authority
WHO	World Health Organisation

Appendix IV continued: General medical abbreviations

Abbreviation	Meaning
μmol	micromole
A&E	accident and emergency
A&W	alive and well
ab	abortion
ABC	aspiration, biopsy, cytology
abd	abdomen/abdominal
abdo	abdomen/abdominal

Abbreviation	Meaning
ABMP	ambulatory blood pressure monitoring
ABR	auditory brain stem response
Acc	accommodation
ACTH	adrenocorticotropic hormone
AD	right ear (auris dextra)
ad	auris dextra (right ear)
ADD	attention deficit disorder
ADH	antidiuretic hormone
ADHD	attention deficit hyperactivity disorder
AET/aet	aged
AFP	alpha-fetoprotein
AGN	acute glomerulonephritis
AHF	antihaemophilic factor
AI	artificial insemination
AIA	allergy induced autism
AID	artificial insemination by donor
AIDS	acquired immunodeficiency syndrome
AIH	artificial insemination by husband
ALL	acute lymphocytic leukaemia
ALS	amyotrophic lateral sclerosis
AMD	age-related macular degeneration
AML	acute myeloid leukaemia
AN	antenatal
ANS	autonomic nervous system
AP	artificial pneumothorax
AP&L	anterior, posterior and lateral
APH	antepartum haemorrhage
APT	activated prothrombin time
APTT	activated partial thromboplastin time
ARC	AIDS-related complex
ARM	artificial rupture of membranes

Abbreviation	Meaning
ART	assisted reproductive technology
AS	autistic spectrum disorder or left ear (auris sinister) or aortic stenosis
ASD	Asperger's syndrome disorder
asD	atrial septal defect
ASHD	arteriosclerotic heart disease
Ast	astigmatism
AST	aspartate transaminase (cardiac enzyme)
AU	both ears (aures unitas) or each ear
au	aures unitas (both ears) or auris uterque (each ear)
BaE	barium enema
BaM	barium meal
BBA	born before arrival
BCG	bacillus Camille-Guérin – vaccine against tuberculosis
BI	bone injury
BID	brought in dead
BM	bowel movement
BNO	bladder neck obstruction
BO	bowels open
BP	bipolar disorder or blood pressure
BS	breath sounds
BS	blood sugar
BSE	bovine spongiform encephalopathy ('mad cow' disease)
BSO	bilateral salpingo-oophorectomy (surgical removal fallopian tubes and ovaries)
BUN	blood urea nitrogen
BW	birth weight
Bx	biopsy
C&S	culture and sensitivity
C/O	complains of

Abbreviation	Meaning
C1, C2, etc	cervical vertebrae
Ca	carcinoma/calcium
CA	chronological age
CABG	coronary artery bypass graft
CABS	coronary artery bypass surgery
CAD	coronary artery disease
CAPD	continuous ambulatory peritoneal dialysis
CAT (CT)	scan – computerised X-ray of layers of tissues (computerised axial tomography)
CCF	congestive cardiac failure
CCU	coronary care unit
CD, cd or CD	controlled drugs
CDH	congenital dislocation of the hip
CHD	coronary heart disease
CHF	congestive heart failure
CIN I-IV	cervical intra-epithelial neoplasia
CIN	cervical intra-epithelial neoplasia
CJD	Creutzfeldt-Jacob disease
CLL	chronic lymphocytic leukaemia
CML	chronic myeloid leukaemia
CNS	central nervous system
CNS	central nervous system
CO	carbon monoxide
C°	Celsius
CO, C/O	complains of (or carbon monoxide)
CO₂	carbon dioxide
COAD	chronic obstructive airway disease
COC	combined oral contraceptive pill
COHS	controlled ovarian hormone stimulation

Abbreviation	Meaning
COLD	chronic obstructive lung disease
COPD	chronic obstructive pulmonary disease
CPK	creatine phosphokinase (cardiac enzyme)
CPR	cardiopulmonary resuscitation
CPT	carpal tunnel syndrome
CRP	C-reactive protein indicates the presence of inflammation within the body
CSF	cerebrospinal fluid
CSU	catheter specimen of urine
CVA	cerebrovascular accident (stroke)
CVP	central venous pressure
CVS	chorionic villus sampling (to detect fetal abnormalities) or cardiovascular system
Cx	cervix (neck of womb)
D	diopter (lens strength)
D&C	dilatation and curettage (scraping out of womb)
D&V	diarrhoea and vomiting
db	decibel (measurement of hearing)
DCIS	ductal carcinoma in situ (a type of breast cancer)
Dec	deceased
DEXA	dual energy x-ray absorptometry (for the diagnosis of osteoporosis)
DLE	disseminated lupus erythematosus
DNA	did not attend or deoxyribonucleic acid
DNR	do not resuscitate
DOA	dead on arrival
DOB/dob	date of birth
DS	disseminated sclerosis (old term for MS)

Abbreviation	Meaning
DT	delirium tremens or diphtheria, tetanus – vaccine
DtaP	vaccine of diphtheria, tetanus and acellular pertussis
DTP	diphtheria, tetanus, pertussis (whooping cough) – vaccine
DTs	delirium tremens
DTaP	vaccine of diphtheria, tetanus and acellular pertussis
DTwP	vaccine of diphtheria, tetanus and whole cell pertussis
DU	duodenal ulcer
DUB	dysfunctional uterine bleeding
DVT	deep vein thrombosis
Dx	diagnosis
Dxr	deep X-ray
EBT	electron beam tomography
ECG	electrocardiogram
ECT	electroconvulsive therapy
EDC	expected date of confinement
EDD	expected date of delivery
EEG	electroencephalogram
EMG	electromyogram
EMU	early morning urine
ENT	ear, nose and throat
EOF	end organ failure
EOM	extraocular movement
ERCP	endoscopic retrograde cholangiopancreatography
ERPC	evacuation of retained products of conception
ESL	extracorporeal shock-wave lithotripsy
ESN	educationally subnormal
ESR	erythrocyte sedimentation rate
EUA	examination under anaesthetic

Abbreviation	Meaning
FB	foreign body
FBC	full blood count
FBS	fasting blood sugar to determine diabetes mellitus or low blood sugars
Fe	iron
FEV_1	forced expiration volume (subscript shows timed interval in seconds)
FH	family history or fetal heart
FHH	fetal heart heard
FHNH	fetal heart not heard
FMF	fetal movement felt
FMRI	functional magnetic resonance imaging
FNA	fine needle aspiration
FSH	follicle-stimulating hormone
G&A	gas and air
GA	general anaesthetic
GAD	general anxiety disorder
GH	growth hormone
GI	gastrointestinal
GIFT	gamete intra-fallopian transplantation
GOK	God only knows
GOT	glutamicoxalo-acetic transaminase (cardiac enzyme)
GPI	general paralysis of the insane
GTT	glucose tolerance test (to diagnose diabetes mellitus)
GU	genitourinary or gastric ulcer
GVHD	graft versus host disease (in transplants)
H/O	history of
H_2O	water
HAI	hospital acquired infection
Hb	haemoglobin (pigmented protein which carries oxygen)
HbA_1 or HBA_1	blood test for diabetes

Abbreviation	Meaning
HbA1c	blood test for diabetes
HCG	human chorionic gonadotrophic hormone
HCl	hydrochloric acid
HCM	see HoCM
HCT	Haematocrit
HDL	high-density lipoprotein
HDU	high dependency unit
Hep A	hepatitis A viral infection (water-borne)
Hep B	hepatitis B viral infection (body fluids), also known as serum hepatitis
Hep C	hepatitis C viral infection
Hg	mercury
HI	hypodermic injection
HIB	Haemophilus influenzae bacillus – immunisation for babies
HIV	human immunodeficiency virus
HM	hand movement
HNPU	has not passed urine
HoCM	hypertrophic (obstructive) cardiomyopathy
Hp	helicobacter pylori
HPL	human placental lactogen
HPU	has passed urine
HPV	human papilloma virus
HRT	hormone replacement therapy
HS	heart sounds
HSV	herpes simplex virus
HUS	haemolytic uraemic syndrome
HVGD	host versus graft disease
HVS	high vaginal swab
Hx	history
i.a.	intra-articular (into a joint)
IBS	irritable bowel syndrome/disease
ICU	intensive care unit

Abbreviation	Meaning
IDDM	insulin-dependent diabetes mellitus
Ig	immunoglobulin
IgA	immunoglogulin (gamma) A
IgBF	immunoglobulin (gamma) binding factor
IgD	immunoglobulin (gamma) D
IgE	immunoglobulin (gamma) E
IgG	immunoglobulin (gamma) G
IgM	immunoglobulin (gamma) M
IM or im	intramuscular
INR	international normalised ratio (prothrombin time)
IOFB	intraocular foreign body
IOP	intraocular pressure
IP	inpatient
IPPB	intermittent positive pressure breathing
IPV	inactivated polio virus/ vaccine
IQ	intelligence quotient
ISQ	in status quo (no change)
IT	intrathecal
ITU	intensive therapy unit
IU or U	international unit
IUC	idiopathic ulcerative colitis
IUCD	intra-uterine contraceptive device
IUD	intra-uterine device or intra-uterine death
IUFB	intra-uterine foreign body
IV, i.v.	intravenous
IVC	intravenous cholangiography
IVF	in vitro fertilisation
IVP	intravenous pyelogram
IVU	intravenous urogram
K	potassium
KUB	kidney, ureter, and bladder (X-ray)
L&D	light and dark (perceived)
L1, L2, etc	lumbar vertebrae

Abbreviation	Meaning
LA	local anaesthetic/ left atrium
LASIK	laser *in situ* keratomileusia
LBC	liquid-based cytology
LCS	left convergent squint (eye turns inwards)
LD	learning disability or lactate dehydrogenase (cardiac enzyme)
LDL	low-density lipoprotein
LDS	left divergent squint (eye turns outwards)
LFT	liver function test (to diagnose liver disease)
LH	luteinising hormone
LIF	left iliac fossa
LIH	left inguinal hernia
LLQ	left lower quadrant
LMP	last menstrual period
LOA	left occipitoanterior
LOL	left occipitolateral
LOP	left occipitoposterior
LOT	left occipitotransverse – same as LOL (position of fetus in uterus)
LP	lumbar puncture
LRTI	lower respiratory tract infection
LSCS	lower segment caesarean section
LTH	luteotropic hormone (prolactin)
LUQ	left upper quadrant
LV	left ventricle
MA	mental age
MAOI	monoamine oxidase inhibitor (antidepressant)
MC&S	microscopy, culture and sensitivity
MCH	mean corpuscular haemoglobin
MCHC	mean corpuscular haemoglobin concentration

Abbreviation	Meaning
MCV	mean corpuscular volume (size of cell)
Mg	Magnesium
mg	milligram
ml	millilitre
mmHg	millimetres of mercury
mmol	millimole
MMR	measles, mumps, rubella – vaccine against the three diseases
MND	motor neurone disease
MOF	multiple organ failure
MRI	magnetic resonance imaging
MRSA	multiple-/methicillin-resistant Staphylococcus aureus
MS	multiple sclerosis
MSH	melanocyte-stimulating hormone
MSU	midstream specimen of urine
N&V	nausea and vomiting
Na	sodium
NAD	no abnormality detected/demonstrated
NAI	non-accidental injury
NBI	no bone injury
ND	normal delivery
NFR	not for resuscitation
NG	new growth or nasogastric (tube)
NIDDM	non-insulin-dependent diabetes mellitus
nmol	nanomole
NMR	nuclear magnetic resonance (scan – see MRI)
NOAD	no other abnormality detected
NSAID	non-steroidal anti-inflammatory drug
NSCLC	non-small cell lung carcinoma

Abbreviation	Meaning
NTDs	neural tube defects (of the brain, spinal cord or meninges) e.g. spina bifida
NT-proBNB	blood test for heart failure
O_2	oxygen
OA	on arrival or osteoarthritis
OCD	obsessive compulsive disorder
OD	oculus dexter (right eye)
OE	on examination
OGD	oesophagogastroduodenoscopy
OP	outpatient or original pack (manufacturer's own pack)
OPD	outpatient department
ORD	oesophageal reflux disease
OS/os	oculus sinister (left eye)
OU/ou	oculus uterque (each eye)
P or P	pharmacy only medicine
PAP	Papanicolaou smear (cervical smear test)
PAT	paroxysmal atrial tachycardia
PBI	protein-bound iodine
PCB	post-coital bleeding
PCO	patient complains of
PCO	see PCOS
PCOS	polycystic ovarian syndrome
PCP	Pneumocystis carinii pneumonia
PCV	packed cell volume
PDT	photodynamic therapy
PE	pulmonary embolism
PEFR	peak expiratory flow rate
PERLA/PERRLA	pupils equal (round), react to light and accommodation
PET	pre-eclamptic toxaemia or positron emission tomography
PGD	patient group direction
PH	past history

Abbreviation	Meaning
pH	acid/alkaline balance
PID	pelvic inflammatory disease or prolapsed intervertebral disc
PMB	postmenopausal bleeding
PMH	past medical history
PMS	premenstrual syndrome
PN	postnatal
PNC	postnatal clinic
PND	paroxysmal nocturnal dyspnoea or post-nasal drip
POD	pouch of Douglas (retro-uterine fold of peritoneum lying behind the womb)
POM or POM	prescription only medicine
POP	plaster of Paris or progestogen only pill (contraceptive)
PP	placenta praevia or private patient
PPH	postpartum haemorrhage
PPH	postpartum haemorrhage
PPI	proton pump Inhibitor
PR	per rectum (rectal examination)
PRK	photo-refractive keratotomy
PSA	prostatic-specific antigen (test for cancer of prostate)
PTCA	percutaneous transluminal coronary angioplasty
PTH	parathyroid hormone
PTSD	post traumatic stress disorder
PU	peptic ulcer
PUO	pyrexia of unknown origin
PV	per vaginam
PVC	premature ventricular contraction
PVS	persistant vegetative state
RA	rheumatoid arthritis/right atrium
RAI	radioactive iodine

Abbreviation	Meaning
RAIU	radioactive iodine uptake
RBC	red blood cell
RCS	right convergent squint (eye turns outwards)
RCS	right convergent squint (eye turns inwards)
RD	respiratory disease
RDS	respiratory distress syndrome or right divergent squint (eye turns outwards)
REM	rapid eye movement
RGP/RP	retrograde pyelogram
RIF	right iliac fossa
RIH	right inguinal hernia
RLQ	right lower quadrant
ROA	right occipitoanterior
ROL	right occipitolateral (position of fetus in uterus)
ROP	right occipitoposterior (position of fetus in uterus)
ROT	right occipitotransverse – same as ROL (position of fetus in uterus)
RP	retrograde pyelogram
RSI	repetitive strain injury
RT	radiation therapy
RTA	road traffic accident
RUQ	right upper quadrant
RV	right ventricle
RVS	respiratory virus syndrome
SA	sarcoma
SADS	seasonal affective disorder syndrome
SAH	subarachnoid haemorrhage
SARS	sudden acute respiratory syndrome
SB	still birth
SC	sine correctione (without correction-spectacles)
SCAN	suspected child abuse or neglect
SCBU	special care baby unit

Abbreviation	Meaning
SCLC	small cell lung cancer
SGOT	serum glutamic oxaloacetic transaminase (liver enzyme)
SGPT	serum glutamic pyruvic transaminase (liver enzyme)
SI	sexual intercourse or international system of units
SIDS	sudden infant death syndrome
SLE	systemic lupus erythematosus
SMI	school medical inspection
SMR	submucous resection
SOB	shortness of breath
SOL	space-occupying lesion
SSRI	selective serotonin reuptake inhibitor
STD	sexually transmitted disease
STYCAR	standard visual tests for young children and retards
Sx	surgery (or suction, or symptoms and signs)
T−	decreased intra-ocular pressure
T	tumour
T&A	tonsillectomy and adenoidectomy
T+	increased intra-ocular pressure
T1, T2, etc	thoracic vertebrae or tumour sizes
T_3	triiodothyronine (thyroid hormone)
T_4	serum thyroxine test for thyroid disease
TAH	total abdominal hysterectomy
TATT	tired all the time
TB	tuberculosis
TC	total cholesterol

Abbreviation	Meaning
TCA	to come again or tricyclic antidepressant (old type of antidepressant)
TCI	to come in
TCRE	transcervical resection of the endometrium
Td	low-dose diphtheria vaccine
TENS	transcutaneous electrical nerve stimulation
THR	total hip replacement
TIA	transient ischaemic attack (in the brain)
TIBC	total iron-binding capacity
TKR	total knee replacement
TLC	tender loving care
TLE	temporal lobe epilepsy
TMR	transmyocardial revascularisation
TNM	tumour nodes metastases
TOE	trans-oesophageal echocardiography
tomo	tomogram
TOP	termination of pregnancy
TPHA	Treponema pallidum haemagglutination assay (blood test for syphilis)
TPR	temperature, pulse and respiration
TS	Tourette's syndrome
TSH	thyroid-stimulating hormone
TSS	toxic shock syndrome
TTA	to take away
TUP	tubal uterine pregnancy
TUR	transurethral resection (of prostate gland)
TURB	transurethral resection of bladder
TURBT	transurethral resection of bladder tumour
TURP	transurethral resection of prostate gland

Abbreviation	Meaning
TV	*Trichomonas vaginalis* (infection of vagina causing frothy yellow discharge)
TVH	total vaginal hysterectomy
U&E	urea and electrolytes
UA	urinalysis
UC	ulcerative colitis
UGI	upper gastrointestinal
UPLD	upper limb disorder
URI	upper respiratory infection
URTI	upper respiratory tract infection
USS	ultrasound scan
UTI	urinary tract infection
VA	visual acuity (clarity or accuracy of vision)
VC	vital capacity of lungs
vCJD	variant Creutzfeldt-Jacob disease
VCU, VCUG	voiding cystourethrogram
VDRL	veneral disease research laboratory (for syphilis)
VF	visual field
VI	*virgo intacto* (virgin)
VSD	ventricular septal defect
Vx	vertex (the crown of the head of the fetus)
WBC	white blood count
WBC&diff.	white blood count and different percentages present
WRULD	work-related upper limb disorder
XX	female sex chromosomes
XY	male sex chromosomes
YOB	year of birth
ZIFT	zygote intra-fallopian transfer

Appendix V: Eponyms

The following are a list of eponyms: diseases, syndromes, procedures and tests named after the person or area associated with it.

Addisonian anaemia
pernicious anaemia

Addison's disease
destruction of the adrenal cortex causing deficiency of hormone production

Albee's bone graft
operation of spinal fixation

Albee's operation
producing fixation of hip

Albers-Schonberg
a type of osteoporosis disease ('marble bones')

Allen-Master's sign
pelvic pain resulting from old laceration of broad ligament during childbirth

Alzheimer's disease
early dementia

Argyll Robertson pupils
reacting to accommodation but not to light

Aschoff's nodules
nodules in heart muscle (myocardium) in rheumatism

Asperger's syndrome
a type of autism

Babinski's reflex
stroking of the sole of foot causing downward flexion (dorsiflexion)

Bacillus Calmette–Guérin
vaccine for immunisation against tuberculosis

Bankart's operation
treatment of recurrent dislocation of shoulder joint

Banti's syndrome
enlarged spleen in children due to backpressure of veins, anaemia, jaundice, etc.

Bannwarth's syndrome
neurological manifestation of Lyme disease

Barbados leg
elephant leg

Barlow's disease
infantile scurvy (vitamin C deficiency)

Barrett's oesophagus
chronic ulceration of lower oesophagus due to chronic inflammation and epithelial changes

Bartholin's abscess
an abscess of the glands of the vulva

Bell's palsy
one-sided facial paralysis due to pressure on VIIth cranial (facial) nerve

Billroth's operation
partial gastrectomy

Binet's test
IQ intelligence test

Blalock's operation
for correction of Fallot's tetralogy (congenital deformity of the heart)

Boeck's disease
sarcoidosis

Bornholm disease
pain in pleura

Brandt–Andrew's technique
method of delivering the placenta

Braxton Hicks contractions
irregular contractions of uterus occurring after third month of pregnancy

Bright's disease
nephritis

Brodie's abscess
chronic inflammation of the bone marrow (osteomyelitis)

Brudzinski's sign
knee and hip flexion when raising head from pillow

Burkitt's tumour
a form of malignant lymphoma found in African children caused by a virus

Burow's operation
technique for repairing defect of lip

Chadwell-Luc operation
technique for drainage of maxillary antrum (facial sinus)

Charcot's joints
effects of third stages of syphilis or other neurological defect

Charcot's triad
staccato speech, nystagmus (oscillation of eyeballs) and intention tremor in multiple sclerosis

Christmas disease
congenital bleeding disorder due to lack of clotting factor

Chvostek's sign
excessive facial twitching on stimulating facial nerve found in cases of tetanus

Colles' fracture
dinner fork deformity of wrist caused by fracture of lower end of radius

Coombs' test
blood test for antibodies

Creutzfeldt–Jacob disease
degenerative brain disease associated with BSE

Cushing's syndrome
effects of excessive corticosteroid hormones

Da Costa's syndrome
cardiac neurosis (psychological origin of heart symptoms)

Delhi boil
tropical sore

Dengue fever
a viral disease transmitted by mosquitos, occurring in epidemics in tropical and subtropical areas

Derbyshire neck
goitre (enlargement of thyroid gland caused by insufficient iodine in diet)

Dick test
for susceptibility to scarlet fever

Down's syndrome
deformity of chromosome 21 causing mental impairment, enlarged tongue, oval tilted eyes, squint, etc. (formerly known as mongolism)

Duchenne's syndrome
spinal paralysis with polyneuritis

Dupuytren's contraction
painless deformity causing contraction of fingers towards palm

Ebola fever
a haemorrhagic disease

Erb's palsy
deformity of hand causing finger flexion, known as 'waiter's tip paralysis'

Ewing's tumour
sarcoma of shaft of long bone in under 20-year-olds

Fallot's tetralogy
comprising of four congenital heart defects

Felty's syndrome
chronic arthritis associated with leukopenia (deficient number of white blood cells) and enlarged spleen (splenomegaly)

Fothergill's operation
surgical repair of uterine prolapse

Freidreich's ataxia
progressive disease of nervous system resulting in weakness of muscles and staggering

Frölich's syndrome
deficiency of pituitary hormones

Graves' disease
oversecretion of thyroid hormones

Guillain–Barré syndrome
a type of polyneuritis characterised by an ascending paralysis

Gulf War syndrome
a condition associated with participants in the Gulf War

Hanta virus
a virus causing haemorrhagic disease transmitted by rodents; first identified in USA

Hashimoto's disease
chronic auto-immune disease of the thyroid gland

Haygarth's nodules
swelling of finger joints in arthritis

Henoch's purpura
purple patches caused by bleeding into and from the tissues of the intestinal wall

Hirschsprung's disease
enlarged colon present at birth

Hodgkin's disease
tumour of the lymph glands caused by a virus

Hunter's syndrome
similar to Hurler's syndrome, but less severe

Hurler's syndrome
mental retardation, abnormal development of skeleton, dwarfism, and gargoyle-like facial development due to a metabolic disorder

Huntington's chorea
degenerative genetic disease of the nervous system

Hutchinson's teeth
abnormally notched teeth; part of the signs of congenital syphilis

Jacksonian epilepsy
epilepsy caused by injury or tumour of brain

Kaposi's tumour
pigmented tumour of the skin (common in AIDS)

Kernig's sign
inability to straighten leg at knee joint when thigh is bent at right angles; indicates irritation of meninges

Klinefelter's syndrome
abnormal chromosome content (47) with XXY chromosomes, causing aggression and sterility

Koch's disease
tuberculosis

Koplik's spots
white spots found in mouth in measles prior to the skin rash occurring; only present in measles

Küntscher nail
used for fixation of fractures of long bones

Kveim test
test for sarcoidosis; intradermal injection followed by later biopsy

Lassa fever
a haemorrhagic disease transmitted by rodents

Legionnaires' disease
acute infection; pneumonia/influenza-type illness caused by legionella pneumophilia

Little's disease
spastic paralysis; form of palsy

Ludwig's angina
inflammation of subcutaneous layer of skin of the neck (cellulitis)

Lyme disease
infectious disease caused by ticks, causing widespread neurological and arthritic symptoms

McBurney's point
area on abdomen where pain is felt when testing for appendicitis

Malta fever
undulant fever caused by drinking infected milk (also called brucellosis and Mediterranean fever)

Mantoux test
intradermal test for tuberculosis reaction

Mendel's law
a theory of hereditary

Ménière's disease
disease of inner ear affecting hearing and balance; causes ringing in ears (tinnitus)

Osler's nodules
small painful areas on fingertips in cases of bacterial inflammation of the lining of the heart (endocarditis)

Paget's disease
disease causing brittle bones and cancer of the nipple

Parkinson's disease
progressive disease of the brain producing 'shaking palsy'; treated with L-dopa

Paul–Bunnell test
blood test for glandular fever

Pel–Ebstein fever
recurring fever in Hodgkin's disease

Pott's disease
spinal lesions

Pott's fracture
fracture/dislocation of the ankle

Queckenstedt's test
test performed during lumbar puncture to determine obstruction to flow of cerebrospinal fluid

Ramstedt's operation
surgery to release tight constriction of pyloric sphincter muscle between stomach and duodenum in babies; the condition is congenital

Raynaud's disease
intermittent spasms of arteries supplying extremities

Reiter's syndrome
recurrent urethritis, arthritis, inflammation of the iris, lesions of the mucous membranes, diarrhoea

Rett's syndrome
progressive autism, dementia, etc. associated with metabolic abnormality, principally found in girls

Reye's syndrome
acute disease of brain in young children following a febrile illness (avoid aspirin medication)

Richter's syndrome
a type of lymphoma occurring in the course of chronic leukaemia

Rinne's test
test for deafness

Romberg's sign
inability to stand without swaying when eyes are closed and feet placed together

Rose's test/Rose Waaler
blood test for rheumatoid arthritis

Rovsing's sign
pressure applied to left iliac fossa which causes pain in right iliac fossa (aspirin advised)

Sabin vaccine
live, attenuated (weakened) oral vaccine for poliomyelitis

Salk vaccine
first vaccine developed using dead organisms (given by injection)

Schick test
determines susceptibility to diphtheria

Schilling test
special test using radioactive isotopes to determine the levels of vitamin B12 in urine (pernicious anaemia)

Shirodkar's operation
purse string suture applied to incompetent cervix during pregnancy to prevent miscarriage

Simmonds' disease
anterior pituitary hormone deficiency, usually developed following childbirth when low blood pressure (hypotension) due to haemorrhage has deprived the pituitary gland of its blood supply

Smith-Peterson nail
used to fix fractures of neck of femur (hip)

Spitz-Holter valve
inserted in the brain in hydrocephalus (CNS unable to circulate, causing pressure on brain)

Still's disease
a type of arthritis in children

Stoke–Adam's syndrome
attacks where the heart stops momentarily and loss of consciousness occurs

Tay–Sach's disease
progressive metabolic disease, occurring especially in the Jewish population, causing weakness in muscles and blindness in infancy

Tourette's syndrome
obsessive–compulsive disorder involving motor and vocal tics

Turner's syndrome
a congenital disorder in which there are only 45 chromosomes; the missing X chromosome causes dwarfism, etc.

Wasserman test
blood test for syphylis

Weil's disease
infection caught from the urine of rats; this is the most serious form of leptospirosis

Widal's test
blood test for typhoid

Wilms' tumour
malignant tumour of kidney found in young children

Wilson's syndrome
disorder causing cirrhosis of liver and widespread jaundice, abnormal metabolism of copper, brain disease, green deposits of pigment in cornea, etc.

Zollinger–Ellison tumour
tumour of the non-insulin-producing cells of the pancreas

Appendix VI: Infection control and universal precautions

Infection Control Policy and Universal Precautions should address the following issues:

- Basic hygiene, for example **handwashing** which is the most important single action to prevent cross-infection (*see Figures 98 and 99*)

- **Pre-cleaning of instruments**

- Chemical **disinfectants** including advice on handling and storing

- When **protective clothing** should be worn, e.g. gloves, aprons, eye shields and protective footware. Recommended use of single use non-sterile latex or PVC gloves should be used to handle body fluids.

- **Body fluids*** should be handled with the same precautions as blood.

- **Gloves changed** between patients – not washed.

- How to dispose of or clean **contaminated articles**

- **Prohibition of eating, drinking and smoking**, except in designated areas

- The use and maintenance of **decontamination equipment**, e.g. how to load and unload operate autoclaves, including guidance on changing water, switching on machines and frequency of servicing as well as recording of temperature and pressure readings on a regular basis.

- **Handling toxic materials**

- What constitutes **clinical waste**, its safe disposal, where to store it prior to collection (with particular reference to 'sharps')

- **Sharps** procedure to prevent 'needle-stick' injuries

- **Procedure for accidents**, in particular follow up required in the event of a 'sharps' or 'needle-stick' injury' and to whom it should be reported.

*As well as blood, body fluids include:

- **Amniotic fluid**

- **Cerebrospinal fluid**

- **Peritoneal fluid**

- **Pleural fluid**

- **Pericardial fluid**

- **Synovial fluid**

- **Semen**

- **Vaginal secretions**

- **Saliva**

- **Urine and faeces.**

REMEMBER, assess the risk of the task – NOT the patient!!!!!

The Infection Control Nurse of your PCO should provide all guidance on this area

---

Hand washing

☐ Most frequently missed

▨ Less frequently missed

■ Not missed

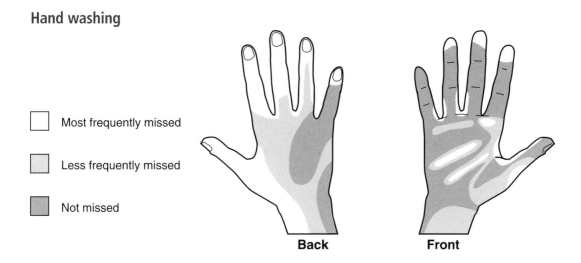

Back **Front**

Figure 98: The areas of the hands that are frequently missed in hand washing

1 Massage palm to palm

2 Rub right palm over back of left hand and vice versa

3 Rub palm to palm with fingers interlaced

4 Massage backs of fingers in opposing palm

5 Rotate right thumb clasped in left palm and vice versa

6 Rotate fingers of left hand in right palm and vice versa

7 Rinse hands with water

Figure 99: The correct procedure for effective hand washing

Appendix VII: The Caldicott Principles

Data Protection Act 1998

The Data Protection Act 1998 came into force in 2000. It legislates for the control and protection personal data generally. The more stringent requirements of the Act do not apply to some kinds of healthcare research (e.g. research using anonymised unlinked data and some epidemiological research) because of an 'exemption' clause research in the Act. Adherence to this law and advice on compliance in the UK is monitored by the Information Commissioner.

> NB: The Act covers all identifiable, manual and computerised personal data and replaces the Access to Health Records Act 1990 for **living** persons. The Access to Health Records Act 1990 remains in force **only** for deceased patients' personal data.

Main provisions of the Data Protection Act 1998

Personal data, in written or electronic form must be:

- Fairly and lawfully processed
- Processed for limited purposes
- Adequate, relevant and not excessive for the purpose
- Accurate
- Kept no longer than necessary
- Processed in accordance with the data subject's rights
- Secure
- Only transferred to countries with adequate data protection systems.

The Caldicott Committee and the Caldicott Guardian

The Caldicott Principles go further than the 1998 Data Protection Act and were the result of the "Report on the Review of Patient-Identifiable Information' by the Caldicott Committee, Department of Health 1997 (http://www.doh.gov.uk/ipu/confiden/report/caldrep.pdf). The Caldicott Guardian in each Healthcare Trust is the person who is responsible for ensuring that these principles are respected and acted upon.

The Caldicott Principles

The Caldicott Principles apply in addition to the requirements of the Data Protection Act 1998. They are:

Principle 1 – Justify the purpose(s)
Every proposed use or transfer of patient-identifiable information within or from an organisation should be clearly defined and scrutinised, with continuing uses regularly reviewed by an appropriate guardian.

Principle 2 – Don't use patient-identifiable information unless it is absolutely necessary
Patient-identifiable information items should not be used unless there is no alternative

Principle 3 – Use the minimum necessary patient-identifiable information
Where use of patient-identifiable information is considered to he essential, each individual item of information should be justified with the aim of reducing identifiability.

Principle 4 – Access to patient-identifiable information should be on a strict need to know basis
Only those individuals who need access to patient-identifiable information should have access to it, and they should only have access to the information items that they need to see.

Principle 5 – Everyone should be aware of their responsibilities
Action should be taken to ensure that those handling patient-identifiable information – both clinical and non-clinical staff – are aware of their responsibilities and obligations to respect patient confidentiality.

Principle 6 – Understand and comply with the law
Every use of patient-identifiable information must be lawful. Someone in each organisation should be responsible for ensuring that the organisation complies with legal requirements.

Informed consent

Informed consent for the use of personal data should be sought wherever this is practically possible and will not cause more harm in terms of distress to the patient or their family. This should be balanced against the possibility of contributing to the advancement of medical knowledge. People are usually happy to allow access to their data: it is often the omission to ask which causes offence. There is a need for more research and public debate about the levels of access to personal data the public will allow without consent. Where consent is not sought this should be justified to the Research Ethics Committee.

Practical tips

- Where informed consent is not possible, justify this in detail to the Research Ethics Committee.

- Identify the local Data Protection Officer for the Directorate in which you work.

- Store all non-electronic research data in locked filing cabinets (including cassette tapes, CD and video recordings).

- Make sure that sponsors (who have access to the data) do not remove it to a country outside the EU without adequate data protection systems.

- Remember that the Funders have no right to check patient records on which research is based unless they have taken on formal responsibility as 'sponsors' of research.

- Any researcher from outside the NHS must have an honorary contract with the Trust before they are allowed access to data, samples or patients.

- The principal or lead investigator is responsible for ensuring the appropriate archiving of data when the research has finished.

- Ensure data is stored securely for a minimum of 15 years.

Index

Malpresentation: 117
Mammary glands: 95
Mammogram
  (mammography): 118, 161, 166,
      200, 232
Mandible: 22
Mania: 138
Manic depression: 138
Mantoux test: 65, 251, 254, 295
Manubrium: 25
Mass screening: 228, 234
Mastectomy: 118, 238
Mastitis: 117
Mastodynia: 117
Mastoiditis: 146, 150
Maternal care: 202
Maternal Serum
  Screening tests: 119
Maxilla: 21, 22
McBurney's point: 73, 295
Measles: 174, 250, 251, 253,
      254, 256, 268
Meatus: 80, 94
Meconium: 111, 117
Medial: 15
Mediastinal space: 44
Medical herbalism: 218
Medical imaging: 160
Medicines Act, the
  1968: 184, 194
Medicines and Health Care Products
  Regulatory Agency: 194, 256
Medulla: 15, 16, 78, 156
Medulla oblongata: 127, 128, 129
Meiosis: 14, 98
Melanin: 86
Melanin stimulating hormone: 155
Melanoma: 89, 215
Melatonin: 138
Membranous labyrinth: 146, 147
Menarche: 92, 96
Ménières disease: 150
Meninges: 111, 126, 128,
      129, 244
Meningioma: 135
Meningism: 135
Meningitis: 135, 244, 251, 252,
      253, 258, 260, 268
Meningitis C: 251
Meningocele: 135
Meningococcal ACWY: 260
Meningococcal

meningitis: 252, 260, 258
Meniscectomy: 33
Menopause: 92, 96, 211,
      232, 248
Menorrhagia: 37, 117
Menses: 96
Menstruation: 92, 94, 95, 231
Mesoderm: 100
Metabolism: 14, 80, 81, 156, 247
Metaplasia: 16, 73, 181, 236
Metastases: 12, 54, 55
Metastasis: 55
Metritis: 117
Microbiology: 170, 174
Micro-organisms: 100, 174,
      175, 243
Micturition: 80, 81, 83
Midbrain: 127, 128
Midstream specimen
  of urine: 243
Migraine: 135
Milk: 95, 96, 100, 155, 242
Mineral salts: 14, 34, 36, 70, 155
Miscarriage: 103, 117, 230
Misuse of Drugs Act, the
  (MODA) 1971: 184, 185,
      192, 193
Mitosis: 14
Mitral valve: 44
MMR vaccine: 251, 254, 270
Monocytes: 39, 54
Mononuclear leucocytes: 37, 39
Mons veneris: 94
Morbidity register: 203
Morbilliform: 89
Morticians: 170
Morula: 98, 99
Motor nerves: 126, 128
Motor neurone: 126, 135
Mouth: 68, 70, 102, 148,
      253, 254
MRSA: 179
Mucous membranes: 14, 86, 254
Mucus: 14, 68, 96, 105, 107, 243
Multigravida: 115
Multipara: 115
Multiple organ failure: 56
Multiple pregnancy: 105, 229
Multiple sclerosis: 135, 162,
      225, 293
Mumps: 250, 251, 253, 256, 269
Munchausen syndrome

by proxy: 117, 139
Murmurs: 45
Muscles: 20, 26, 30, 31, 59, 60,
      68, 87, 122, 128, 142,
      143, 156, 209
Myalgia: 18
Myasthenia gravis: 18, 191
Myelin: 126
Myelitis: 135
Myelogram: 140, 166
Myelomeningocele: 135
Myocardial
  infarction: 50, 178, 217,
      218, 240
Myocarditis: 50
Myocardium: 44, 293
Myogenic muscle: 30
Myoma: 18
Myomectomy: 119
Myometrium: 94
Myopia: 144, 150
Myopic:145
Mysophobia: 139
Naevus: 89
Nails: 86, 87, 100, 103
Narcolepsy: 135
Narcoleptic: 139
Nasal: 22, 62, 147, 175
National Contract for
  Better Health: 204
National Institute for Clinical
  Excellence (NICE): 190, 205, 232
National Plan: 201
National Service
  Framework: 201, 205, 206, 219
Natural immunity: 250
Necrosis: 18, 181
Necrotising fasciitis: 18
Needle-stick injuries: 178, 261, 298
Neonatal: 110, 115
Neonate: 110, 115
Neoplasm: 18
Neoplastic: 18, 265
Nephrectomy: 83
Nephritis: 82, 293
Nephron: 78, 79
Nephropathy: 82, 224
Nephrosis: 82
Nerve: 12, 23, 27, 30, 44,
      86, 125 - 140, 142,
      143, 147, 150,
      224, 240

Notes

Notes